BOOSTERS,
HUSTLERS,
AND SPECULATORS

*Entrepreneurial Culture and the Rise of
Minneapolis and St. Paul, 1849–1883*

JOCELYN WILLS

BOOSTERS, HUSTLERS, AND SPECULATORS

 MINNESOTA HISTORICAL SOCIETY PRESS

C.W. HALE. DRY GOODS.

BILLIARD HALL

TEA · C

www.mnhs.org/mhspress

The Minnesota Historical Society Press is a member of the Association of American University Presses.

Manufactured in the United States of America

10 9 8 7 6 5 4 3 2 1

∞ The paper used in this publication meets the minimum requirements of the American National Standard for Information Sciences—Permanence for Printed Library Materials, ANSI Z39.48–1984.

International Standard Book Number 0–87351–510–2 (cloth)

Maps on pages 12 and 18 by CartoGraphics, Inc. All other images from MHS Collections.

Library of Congress Cataloging-in-Publication Data

Wills, Jocelyn, 1960–
    Boosters, hustlers, and speculators : entrepreneurial culture and the rise of Minneapolis and St. Paul, 1849–1883 / Jocelyn Wills.
        p. cm.
Includes bibliographical references and index.
ISBN 0-87351-510-2 (cloth : alk. paper)
    1. Industrialization—Minnesota—
        Minneapolis—History—19th century.
    2. Industrialization—Minnesota—Saint
        Paul—History—19th century.
    3. Urbanization—Minnesota—
        Minneapolis—History—19th century
    4. Urbanization—Minnesota—Saint Paul—
        History—19th century.
    5. Businesspeople—Minnesota—
        Minneapolis—History—19th century.
    6. Businesspeople—Minnesota—
        Saint Paul—History—19th century.
    7. Minneapolis (Minn.)—History—
        19th century.
    8. Saint Paul (Minn.)—History—
        19th century.
    9. Minneapolis (Minn.)—Economic
        conditions—19th century.
    10. Saint Paul (Minn.)—Economic
        conditions—19th century.
    I. Title.
    HC108.M7W55 2005
    338.09776'579'09034—dc22
                                    2004013114

For Beth

BOOSTERS, HUSTLERS, AND SPECULATORS

Acknowledgments

NO BOOK WRITES ITSELF, and few authors have no one to thank but themselves. *Boosters, Hustlers, and Speculators* began nearly ten years ago, as a dissertation idea. I could not have turned my research interests into a book without the foundations that sustained me financially, the archival staff who made my investigations rewarding, the scholars and colleagues who supported my work, and, most importantly, the family members and friends who nurtured me and continue to enrich my life. Although I cannot thank each and every one of them, some deserve special mention.

For the generous funding I received to research and write this book, I gratefully acknowledge the Social Sciences and Humanities Research Council of Canada, the Texas A&M University History Department and International Student Services, the Texas Higher Education Coordinating Board, the Minnesota Historical Society, the James J. Hill Reference Library, Brooklyn College, City University of New York, the PSC-CUNY Research Foundation, and the Mrs. Giles Whiting Foundation.

I have profited enormously from my decade-long association with the Minnesota Historical Society (MHS) and the James J. Hill Reference Library (JJHRL). On my first trip to St. Paul in 1994, I had no intention of writing about the Twin Cities. I planned to use the MHS's Great Northern collections as a springboard into a topic on the Pacific Northwest. Thanks to the MHS's indefatigable research champion, Deborah Miller, I soon learned that the Twin Cities had a great deal to tell about the global economy-in-the-making, urban-industrialization, nineteenth-century American history, and the synergies between urban and rural spaces. I therefore packed up my belongings and moved to St. Paul. During my fifteen-month tenure there, Deb introduced me to Minnesota history, made my stay at the MHS a memorable and rewarding one, and gave me an office in the research suite where I had access to several scholars and friends who paved the way for my own work. The latter include Rhoda Gilman and Lucile Kane. Together with Deb, these amazing women created a stimulating and nurturing environment in which to work. The MHS's archival staff, particularly Ruth Bauer Anderson and Hampton Smith, also enhanced my stay in St. Paul, not only walking me through large collections but also sharing the hidden treasures they had uncovered over the years. My research also steered me toward Thomas White, curator of the Hill papers at the JJHRL. From our first meeting, Tom encouraged my work, shared his expertise, and made sure the Hill collections never disappointed. He also read and commented upon portions of the manuscript. I trust he will recognize his suggestions.

Throughout the decade, I have continued to receive dividends from MHS/JJHRL investments in my work. As the most recent example, I neither can imagine nor would want to know what I would have faced in the final stretch without Shannon Pennefeather, the patient, skillful, and good-humored editor I have worked with at the MHS Press. At every step along the way, she prodded me to make things clearer, to abandon tired ideas. At the same time, she managed to make editing pleasant and the final push toward publication less painful. In the wake of her meticulous work, any remaining errors can only belong to me.

Because this book began as a dissertation, I have many academic debts. When I arrived in Texas during 1989, I had no intention of undertaking graduate work, never mind remaining in the state for long. But as luck would have it, I met there my dissertation advisor, mentor, and friend—Harold C. Livesay. By 1993, I had but one choice: I applied for grants and loans and turned my attention to full-time graduate work. For more than a decade, Harold has provided encouragement, constructive criticism, editorial and professional advice, and friendship beyond any duty described in the mentor's handbook. Mere words fail to describe how much I appreciate all he has done. My other dissertation committee members—Cynthia Bouton, Tom Dunlap, and Jonathan Smith—only served to enhance my journey into the profession. Cyndy opened windows into worlds I had not yet seen, including those of the friend I value more than I can say. Tom pushed me through doors I had never dared to open. And Jonathan persuaded me to think both historically and geographically. Again, I trust they recognize their collective influence in the pages that follow.

Both before and after I moved to Brooklyn in 1999, numerous colleagues and friends offered either to read and comment upon my work or to support me in other less tangible but no less significant ways. In addition to those already mentioned, I am particularly grateful to Chris Diehl-Taylor, Angel Kwolek-Folland, Philip Scranton, Susan Yohn, and the MHS Press's anonymous reviewers for their careful readings and scrupulous critiques of some or all of the manuscript. In addition, although many colleagues at Brooklyn College deserve special notice, I have just enough space to highlight a few. While chair of the history department, Phil Gallagher worked assiduously to ensure that I received sufficient release time to complete the book, while provost Roberta Matthews sanctioned such requests. K. C. Johnson offered to read the dissertation while still hot-off-the-printer and quickly produced a critique with assorted useful comments. And Ted Burrows not only read a near-final version but also, by sharing the depth and breadth of his knowledge about American and urban history, helped me to frame several important arguments. A hearty thanks must also reach others who have provided sagacious advice, valuable support, and good fellowship over the past few years: Bonnie Anderson, Adina Back, Christopher Barnes, Charles Fears, Verna Gillis, Doris and Larry Hill, Chris Hosgood, Carmela Landes, Carla Lother, Heidi MacDonald, Larry Malone, John McGettrick, Sheila McManus, Susan Miller, Jennifer Mittelstadt, Arline Neftleberg, Carol Noblitt, Doug Parker, Charlene Sawatsky, Bambi Schieffelin, Gunja SenGupta, Jim Tagg, and George Weber. Once again, after all this generosity, I alone own any mistakes that remain.

Of course, none of the above would have mattered without the support of my family. Five years ago, Tom Predhome walked into my life. Since then, he has enhanced my life in every way, daily reminding me that life's too short to waste time on irrelevant people or things, that regular and faraway vacations matter, and that taking one's self too seriously is a snare and a delusion. Thanks to him, I am the luckiest person I know. Of course, if any doubts remain about my good fortune, my family provides further evidence. I grew up with three creative, smart, and witty siblings—Don, Rhonda, and Rich—whose adventures and graceful moves under pressure never fail to inspire me. I feel blessed to have them as friends. I won the in-law lottery as well, and gratefully acknowledge the members of that club: on my side, Alana, Marisol, and Rory; and on Tom's, Ruth, Bob, and Deb. In addition, my nieces and nephews—Laura, Patrick, Eva, Noah, and now baby Delia—always let me join in their fun and simply make most things much more worthwhile. Last, but definitely not least, the influence of my mother, Beth McMurchie, looms large over my life and work. Her lifelong quest for knowledge, thirst for travel, and enthusiasm for daring feats all rubbed off. For these, and so many other gifts she has bestowed upon me and others, Beth deserves a peerage within the realm. Alas, since I do not move in royal circles, I cannot arrange such a decoration. Happily, however, I can dedicate this book to her. Thanks, Mom.

BOOSTERS,
HUSTLERS,
AND SPECULATORS

Introduction

THIS BOOK EXPLORES the expansion of American entrepreneurial culture in the nineteenth century and the urban boosters, political hustlers, and western speculators who constructed St. Paul and Minneapolis, Minnesota, between 1849 and 1883. Before 1849, the few people living in what is now Minnesota erected villages along major river arteries and inhabited an isolated world on the fringe of American society. Thirty-five years later, Minnesota's Twin Cities had emerged as the metropolitan center of a region stretching north and west for thousands of miles. By 1883, railroads extended from St. Paul and Minneapolis to the Pacific Coast, and the territory's expanding population occupied a landscape linked to the institutions of the larger American nation and integrated into the international market economy. At the center of these transitions stood neither kings and noblemen, nor priests and scholars, but rather a host of entrepreneurial self-starters and nation builders searching for moneymaking opportunities, political advancement, and social mobility in a region that seemed to offer Euro-Americans a limitless plenty.

With larger competitive forces driving entrepreneurship westward, these Atlantic world migrants hoped to profit by creating the next in a series of commercial-industrial emporiums for the expanding American nation. Most arrived with limited means, and many failed to realize their dreams. But from the ranks of their early cohort—among them fur traders, merchants, lumbermen, millers, mechanics, and laborers—a few ascended into prosperous and powerful positions in the cities of St. Paul and Minneapolis. Their enterprises remapped the future of the New Northwest, including the American-Canadian borderlands from Minnesota and Manitoba to the Washington–British Columbia divide. As the region's new elite, they thus bolstered the continental expansion of the "business civilization" first envisioned by the United States' founding fathers.[1]

St. Paul and Minneapolis provide windows into entrepreneurship as practiced in the nineteenth-century United States, into the important role government intervention played in the market during the period, and into the federal government's critical function in promoting and regulating economic expansion through contracts, land grants, and other legal and extralegal inducements. Never totally immersed in a "free market" environment, entrepreneurs in St. Paul and Minneapolis knew they needed more than business acumen to succeed in the rapidly expanding industrial economy. The best among them also possessed the political savvy necessary to broker with local and then regional, national, and international businessmen and politicians and to navigate economic regulations, government contracting and patronage networks, and Indian removal and land-grant policies.[2]

Minnesota's Twin Cities also emerged as part of a larger process of urban-industrial expansion that followed local, regional, national, and then international patterns of integration, first embracing parts of Britain and then linking Europe, the United States, and Canada with a wider international economy. The process involved the global divisions of capital, people, and natural resources the market set in motion as well as the immigration, production, and distribution patterns industrialization engendered. Urban boosters and builders in St. Paul and Minneapolis recognized these trends, including both the important synergy between urban and rural developments and the competitive forces shaping the global economy-in-the-making and American-Canadian relations.[3]

In many ways, Minnesota's "urban pioneers" repeated patterns of earlier North American settlements. Eager to benefit from American expansion but finding barriers in more established regions, early inhabitants of St. Paul and Minneapolis embraced the market economy and the innovations in transportation that promised to attach them to it. At first, Minnesota's urban residents—both American- and foreign-born—tried to imitate successful cities to the east by building upon their strategic locations along a major body of water and by exploiting their competitive advantages in regional resources such as furs, timber, and wheat. As time passed, they also hoped to pull immigrants, capital, raw materials, and additional resources away from other aspiring urban centers and into their own production and distribution networks. St. Paulites modeled their town after other commercial waterway ports such as Cincinnati, St. Louis, and especially Chicago. Situated along the St. Anthony waterfall, Minneapolitans emulated water-powered manufacturing cities like the famed textile center at Lowell, Massachusetts, and the flour-milling hubs of Buffalo and Rochester, New York.[4]

In other ways, St. Paul and Minneapolis enjoyed distinctive opportunities and confronted unique problems. Urban enthusiasts preceded rural developers, and these commercial and manufacturing go-getters dreamed of exploiting the region's resources for their own city-based successes. While they had no intention of cultivating the soil themselves, urban boosters and builders knew that success depended upon their abilities to attract capital, railroads, and commercial farmers to the wheat-growing hinterland they hoped to control. Aware of the power emanating from Chicago once railroads reached the Great Lakes entrepôt in 1848, Minnesota's empire builders also had to develop strategies to pull the untapped resources of the American-Canadian borderlands into their own realm before entrepreneurs in Chicago and other established centers beat them to it. But Minnesotans never hoped to dethrone eastern cities; instead, they sought to emerge as the next prominent urban center west of Chicago. Achieving this goal meant ousting nearby rivals—other developing towns along major waterways in western Wisconsin and Illinois and in Iowa and Nebraska. Strivers in St. Paul and Minneapolis also competed with each other throughout the period, generating rivalries that influenced each city's development and inspiring building booms that led to redundant expansion, glutted markets, and economic busts.[5]

The Twin Cities also offer an opportunity to explore regional and international rivalries as they unfolded during a critical period in American and Canadian history. Minnesota's urban entrepreneurs not only sought to dominate the American hinterland stretching to the Pacific; over time they also coveted the rich potential of the Canadian prairies west of Winnipeg. Those visions became increasingly problematic after Canadians received political (though not necessarily cultural) independence from Great Britain in 1867. From that moment forward, the once-fluid border zone became more rigid as newly independent Canadians embarked upon industrial expansion of their own. Because Twin Cities entrepreneurs enjoyed reciprocal influence over industrial and agricultural developments on both sides of the border, the history of St. Paul and Minneapolis also reveals how the dynamics of American and Canadian expansion influenced cross-border negotiations, tariff and other government policies, and competitive posturing between the two countries.[6]

U.S.–Canadian rivalries and cultural divisions became visible as both nations expanded railroad lines from east to west. Seeking to explain these differences in *Continental Divide,* Seymour Martin Lipset argued that Canadians tended to look to the government for settlement patterns, infrastructure, and economic-social-political networks, whereas Americans, predisposed to individual undertakings, believed that they had the right to settle where they pleased, to create infrastructures appropriate to their wants, and to form voluntary associations to solve their social-political problems. Over the past decade, scholars have debated Lipset's assertions, particularly those that define the United States as a less regulated society. Regardless, the following pages reveal that subtle differences existed long before industrialization and, further, that railroads exacerbated Canadians' desire for freedom from the entrepreneurial and governmental control of their southern neighbors.

Finally, this volume seeks to correct the long-held view that James J. Hill—architect of the Great Northern Railway empire—not only built the Twin Cities single-handedly but also emerged as one of the few righteous industrial statesmen in a sea of robber barons. Fueled by the legend that his railroad construction to the Pacific uniquely involved neither government assistance nor corruption, many histories of the Great Northern Railroad reinforce the myth that Hill rose to prominence on the power of his laissez-faire philosophy and on the strength of his character. *Boosters, Hustlers, and Speculators* exposes a different James J. Hill, and another side of nineteenth-century entrepreneurship. Hill accomplished much, but he neither built the Twin Cities unaided nor assembled the Great Northern based solely on his market perceptions and moral virtue. Rather, he scratched and clawed his way to wealth and glory on the backs of the overlapping generations of entrepreneurs, politicians, producers, and consumers who had built St. Paul and Minneapolis. Canadian by birth, American by choice, and empire builder by design, Hill ascended from obscurity to notoriety not by eschewing government assistance but rather by acquiring most of Minnesota's federal land grants. Further, he secured the backing of political friends and patrons and mastered the brokering skills and deal-making techniques required to capture lucrative opportunities and coveted railroad lines. Indeed, he distinguished himself from the multitude by keeping himself *au courant* in the business of private enterprise as practiced in the United States and Canada and by scrutinizing the political environments of the expanding nations.[7]

As it unfolds, this story is, in part, Hill's, but first and foremost it is a history of market competition, business-government collaboration, urban rivalries, and the many entrepreneurial dreamers and political schemers who made his ascent possible. Neither heroes nor villains, the majority of Minnesota's urban builders simply hoped to participate in—and profit from—American westward expansion. Many failed to acquire the kind of wealth Hill later enjoyed, but they remain no less important to our understanding of nineteenth-century American culture, entrepreneurship, and industrialization. Then as now, luck, timing, cunning, ambition, and connections mattered as much as insight or talent in achieving entrepreneurial success. Moreover, whether successes or failures, Minnesota's urban boosters and builders did not jettison the larger nation's cultural aspirations. They exemplified them.

* * *

Minnesota's successful cities in the race for nineteenth-century regional supremacy—St. Paul on the east and Minneapolis on the west—stand on promontories overlooking the Mississippi River, 700 feet above sea level and 2,000 miles northwest of the river's mouth at the Gulf of Mexico. From its wellhead at Minnesota's Lake Itasca, the legendary Mississippi flows for 2,200 serpentine miles to the Louisiana delta. Adding the 2,100 miles of its tributary rivers, lakes, and streams makes the Mississippi the longest river in the world. Minneapolis sits alongside the river's only significant waterfall, a fifty-foot drop known as the Falls of St. Anthony. At one time impassable, the falls made St. Paul's bluffs, ten southeasterly miles downriver, the head of navigation for nineteenth-century steamboats plying their way north from New Orleans and St. Louis. Bending at its confluence with the Minnesota River, the Mississippi divides and defines the two cities and reminds their inhabitants of nature's enduring power. The river punctuates their long winter sentences. No innovations save the cities from its freeze. Nothing stems the tide of regional devastation when its banks overflow. And neither people and vehicles nor skyscrapers and factories can intimidate the mighty Mississippi, at least not for long.[8]

In the vernacular of modern-day commuters, most call these riverine places either Minneapolis–St. Paul or the Twin Cities. Throughout the states and provinces of the American Northwest—Iowa, Minnesota, the Dakotas, eastern Montana, Manitoba, and Saskatchewan—however, people simply know them as *the Cities*, for, along with their suburbs, they remain the primary urban center for this sparsely populated, still largely rural region. For northwestern prairie dwellers, the Cities earned their distinction during the second half of the nineteenth century, after John O'Sullivan proclaimed it the United States' "manifest destiny to overspread and to possess the whole of the continent which Providence has given us" for American expansion. After eastern railroads met western wheat during the 1860s, prairie farmers increasingly associated St. Paul–Minneapolis with the empire builders who seemed to swallow up their agricultural profits. Nineteenth-century urban dwellers saw things differently, perceiving themselves as the benevolent leaders of an often ungrateful region.[9]

Although at a glance from the air St. Paul and Minneapolis seem to flow into one another, present-day residents regard their cities as separate and distinctive. St. Paul is the older city and the seat of state government. It became the adopted home of nineteenth-century railroad magnate James J. Hill and now declares itself blue-collar, unobtrusive, and custodian to the state's past. When automobiles replaced railroads, St. Paul went into a period of decline, but its Victorian mansions and assorted museums attest to its former importance and abiding wealth. Its younger twin, Minneapolis, is the upstart. Home to the state university and headquarters for the Cargill conglomerate, Minneapolis succored flour-milling families like the Pillsburys and Washburns, their modern legacy the behemoth General Mills. Minneapolis now proclaims itself white-collar, a northern jewel of the trans-Mississippi West, forward-looking, and detached from the past. After the automobile transformed the region, Minneapolitans remade their city with all the glitz of the New West, but a trip through older wards reveals the railroad tracks and manufacturing sector that first gave the waterfall city its strength.

In spite of their proximity and shared moniker, the Cities emerged from the river separately, as St. Paul and Minneapolis, the Mississippi setting the stage for the roles each would play in the unfolding drama of the young United States. The Northwest Ordinance of 1787 marked the bluffs of present-day St. Paul as the northwestern limit of the new American nation. When Thomas Jefferson purchased the Louisiana Territory in 1803, American territorial rights crossed the Mississippi, claiming the waterfall and the grassland plateau that became Minneapolis. For several decades, both sides of the river remained in the hands of the region's established residents, the Dakota and the Ojibwe, who shared the land with an assortment of French, British, and American fur traders and squatters. With the introduction of steamboats in the 1810s, however, Americans quickly "discovered" the possibilities of the two locations.[10]

As the practical head of steamboat navigation along the Mississippi when American "highways of progress" zigzagged north and south, St. Paul claimed two strategic riverboat landings, complete with embankments that promised to protect business and residential districts from floods. The Lower Levee accommodated steamboats arriving from St. Louis while the Upper Levee provided a place to service boats wending their way northwest toward the Minnesota River and beyond. Upstream, where St. Anthony Falls offered an enormous power source for manufacturing, inhabitants of two towns on either side of the river—later united as Minneapolis—hoped to harness that power and prosper from it. With these natural advantages at their disposal, Mississippi River migrants transformed these modest encampments into American towns during the second half of the nineteenth century.[11]

*　*　*

As Minnesotans joined the larger nation in entrepreneurial experimentation, three discrete periods delineated St. Paul's and Minneapolis's odysseys from isolated outposts to fully integrated national cities. The riparian start-up, from 1849 to 1861, marks the first period, when Congress, Minnesota's founding entrepreneurs, and like-minded migrants sanctioned St. Paul–Minneapolis's local position as the Mississippi gateway for regional expansion. The second phase, stamped by intrastate railroad building and commercial, manufacturing, and agricultural networking between 1861 and 1872, reveals the ways in which government contracts, land grants, and lawmakers helped entrepreneurs confirm the Cities' dominance over urban and rural developments in Minnesota, the Dakotas, and Manitoba. Consolidation between 1873 and 1883 defines the final stage, when overlapping generations of entrepreneurs and politicians realized the ambitions of St. Paul–Minneapolis's founders. Together, they transformed the Cities into the seat of transportation, commerce, and manufacturing for an agricultural empire extending west to the Pacific Ocean, north into Canada, south into Iowa and parts of Nebraska, and east into western Wisconsin.

At each stage along the way, Minnesota's urban entrepreneurs faced enormous risks, particularly when rapid expansion threatened to undermine the very successes they had achieved. Despite numerous failures and setbacks, a number managed to survive. Those who prospered took their place as the region's elite. The composition of this group changed over time, and success in one realm never guaranteed it in another. The following chapters reflect this reality, as "entrepreneurial shake-outs" push some actors from center stage while unlocking opportunities for others. As each group worked its way through various crises, Minnesota's urban entrepreneurs, government agents, western speculators, and regional boosters transformed St. Paul and Minneapolis from fur-trading outposts containing fewer than 800 people in 1849 into a metropolitan complex with over 240,000 inhabitants in 1883. From river-dependent (and thus seasonably vulnerable) isolation the Twin Cities matured into the region's focal point, complete with eight thousand miles of railroad track radiating outward in every direction. As entrepreneurs lavished their new wealth on the Cities' business, political, educational, charitable, and social networks, they increased the region's attractions. Some even enjoyed the patronage and glory they had sought for their roles in the rise of St. Paul–Minneapolis.

These stages in the Twin Cities' development influence the actors selected for examination in this volume. Although some arrive and depart quickly, their entrepreneurial spirit remains. Many characters represent success or failure "types" rather than important individuals in their own right. Some make cameo appearances in one or several chapters because they illustrate the kinds of people who descended upon St. Paul–Minneapolis and other of the nation's nineteenth-century urban enclaves. A few, such as St. Paul's empire builder, James J. Hill, and Minneapolis's waterfall baron, William D. Washburn, surface in the 1850s as early settlers and continue to

work the region with an unequaled singleness of purpose. Finding themselves in the right place at precisely the right time, with visions of expansion guiding their every move, Hill and Washburn exemplify the zenith of
the entrepreneurial culture. But they shared the stage with others striving
to create wealth-generating opportunities, and wider developments mattered as much, if not more, than their particular, individual ascents. The often chaotic comings and goings of minor characters are relevant to the
larger story, for their arrivals and departures, more than the linear rise of
one or two individuals, accurately reflect the nature of American entrepreneurship and urban-industrial expansion.

By examining the actors who trod the stages of St. Paul–Minneapolis
between 1849 and 1883, this book seeks to portray the symbiosis between
urban-rural developments as well as the evolution of the American business environment, the creation of regional networks, and the United States'
larger bourgeois aspirations. In St. Paul–Minneapolis, that process began
well before Minnesota's territorial announcement, when entrepreneurial
Americans designed a framework for market and industrial expansion into
the New Northwest.

1787–1849

Market Expansion and
Minnesota's Territorial Vanguard

WHEN THE U.S. CONGRESS APPROVED the March 3, 1849, "Act to Establish the Territorial Government of Minnesota," the Presbyterian Church of Pennsylvania decided to erect a place of worship at the territorial capital so that members of its flock could join Minnesota's founders in the "conversion" of the northwestern "wilderness." They sent young Edward Duffield Neill as their representative. Neill reached St. Louis by mid-March 1849. From there, he took the first available steamboat headed north for St. Paul, the trading village designated as the government seat for the newly acquired domain. Traveling up the Mississippi River some eight hundred miles, Neill landed at St. Paul in April, when the river's northern reaches finally thawed.[1]

His spiritual training had little prepared the young reverend for what he encountered when he reached St. Paul on April 9. Upon debarking at the landing, Neill found "no Lord Baltimore as the presiding spirit—no graduate of the University of Paris, like the founder of Philadelphia—no men of faith and principle, like the settlers at Plymouth Rock." Instead, descending an embankment to meet him was a rather "ignoble" crowd, including a motley assortment of profit-oriented men of big dreams and slim means, the unfettered practitioners of the North American fur trade. This rambunctious "aristocracy of the wilderness" soon told Neill what others had already observed. They had arrived in this place during the 1830s and 1840s, neither to convert the Indians nor to cultivate the land. Instead, they claimed it their "business to barter with the Indians for their furs, as the agents of some established fur company, [with] the glittering dollar the star of [their] ambition." On this "extreme verge of the civilized world," near the

11

confluence of the Mississippi and Minnesota Rivers, they had settled along the head of steamboat navigation at St. Paul, upriver at the Falls of St. Anthony, and on the Fort Snelling Military Reserve.[2]

On the Mississippi River's eastern shores in St. Paul, fur traders, merchants, and steamboat captains had created a rendezvous for commerce and for those who hoped to take part in U.S. expansion toward Oregon Territory and the Pacific. Upstream at the Falls of St. Anthony, a ragtag set of lumbermen and former military personnel had established sawmills on the Mississippi's eastern shoreline. Another cluster across the river included several agricultural squatters who had started to grind grain for the families gathered at Fort Snelling. In these small places, all-purpose outlets housed the isolated region's scarce goods, along with several hundred Euro-Americans who possessed abundant ambitions for Minnesota.

Among those Neill encountered, several fur traders and millers introduced themselves as the vanguard of Minnesota's entrance into the larger United States. Over the course of months, as Neill tended to his flock he heard about the ways in which the market economy, the federal govern-

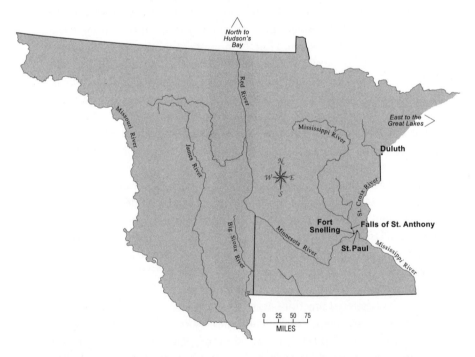

Minnesota Territory's earliest Euro-American settlers chose a promising location at the confluence of the Minnesota and Mississippi Rivers, home to the military installation at Fort Snelling and the region's principal trading hub at St. Paul. Soon enough, agricultural squatters and aspiring millers would develop the waterpower potential at the Falls of St. Anthony.

ment, and the transportation revolution had nurtured their dreams. These inducements had inspired hundreds of thousands of Euro-Americans like themselves to wend their way west from the Atlantic seaboard during the first half of the nineteenth century in search of the possibilities. Indeed, preparations for their arrival had begun in 1787, when national leaders framed the rules for American business and territorial expansion. Thereafter, transportation improvements lured more merchants, millers, and then families into the region.[3]

The Federal Government and American Entrepreneurial Expectations

Long before Minnesota took its legal place as an American territory, the federal government had laid foundations for extending entrepreneurial undertakings into the region west of the Appalachian Mountains. There, as elsewhere in the United States, the future hinged upon developing a viable and orderly economic system in order to profit from the region's principal asset: the vast expanse of cheap land that Americans had coveted since independence. In establishing that order, the federal government became a relatively silent though powerful partner in the business of private enterprise. It sought to sustain and expand Euro-American entrepreneurship wherever white men settled by creating a blueprint that promoted bourgeois values, protected middle-class drives for expansion, and provided incentives to those who promised to "mold the 'plastic elements' [of business enterprise] for the good" of the nation.[4]

Business for personal gain had played a long and distinguished role in Britain's North American colonies, and by the nineteenth century the young United States had emerged as the Atlantic world's most flamboyant symbol of the entrepreneurial impulse. The Continental Congress had laid the foundations for the future expansion of consumption, speculation, and investment through the Land Ordinances of 1784, 1785, and 1787. The first two settled issues of land surveying, sale, and settlement, while the Northwest Ordinance of 1787 established a legal framework for permanent governance over the northwestern empire, in grids eventually reaching west to the Pacific Ocean and north beyond Canada to Alaska. When the nation's architects drafted the Constitution and common-law statutes during 1787, the reorganized United States supplemented the land ordinances by laying the legal foundations for individual undertakings and guaranteed freedoms. The new federal government then extended the young nation's real estate holdings south and west of the Northwest Ordinance. Striving to "release" entrepreneurial energies, American legislators also created an environment that forgave those who failed, protected infant manufacturing enterprises, and rewarded risk takers through Indian treaties and various other subsidies and grants.[5]

The land ordinances of 1784 and 1785 set the stage for private real estate transactions and entrepreneurial undertakings for those who ventured to Minnesota during the 1830s and 1840s. Traveling from near and far in the Americas and Europe before arriving in the remote but promising region, many new Minnesotans had established themselves along the confluence of the Mississippi and Minnesota Rivers to seek opportunities that had eluded them in more settled regions. They selected choice pieces of land, erected rough "claim shanties" along the Mississippi's eastern shores, and then traveled by foot, horseback, dog sled, and canoe some twenty-five miles northeast of St. Paul to St. Croix Falls, Wisconsin. There, at the nearest federal land office, they declared their intention to settle, claiming that their "crude houses [show] that the place has already an owner." This land claim system, first developed in the 1780s, foreshadowed passage of the 1841 Preemption Act that allowed squatters—settlers on public lands not yet surveyed and put on the market at public auction—to purchase up to 160 acres of land at the minimum government price of $1.25, provided they made "improvements"—such as cutting a tree, driving a spike, or erecting a small structure—on the lands they claimed. According to western guidebooks, the Preemption Act promised to protect settlers, whether real or fictitious, against unregulated real estate hustlers then working the American interior. Preemption rights ultimately increased entrepreneurial expectations in Minnesota, for provided a settler "improved" the land, he could buy it cheaply once territorial expansion reached him and then sell it quickly, at a nice profit, although such maneuvering involved some risk. Preemption rights also fueled business expansion into the trans-Mississippi West, first among fur traders and later through a host of merchants, millers, skilled craftsmen, "farmers, laborers, and professional men in search of a new home."[6]

The Northwest Ordinance specified that when designated territories reached the legal minimum population of sixty thousand Euro-Americans, they could take their place in the union. Once admitted, territorial residents enjoyed the many benefits associated with controlling their own local affairs, including protection of private property rights and a legal apparatus to justify Indian removals from lands Americans wanted for themselves. The government created law and order in newly organized regions, awarded inhabitants legal representation in Washington, DC, to negotiate Indian removals, and bestowed upon them other local rights, privileges, and obligations. Congress gave territories a standardized legal infrastructure and provided fiscal appropriations for post office communication with the outside world. These federal actions freed regions from isolation and linked them more closely to eastern markets. Territorial status also conferred upon residents a political body to enact local laws, to resolve local disputes, and to draft their own state constitution when population justified it. They received civil rights to protect freedoms of religion and the press, school land provisions for the education of young citizens-in-the-making, and a host of other laws over time that encouraged the migration of capital and entrepreneurial spirits who would pave the way for territorial expansion and statehood. By the time the first permanent settlers crossed over the Mississippi River into Minnesota during the 1830s and 1840s, the federal government had formalized enough of those rules that American and European immigrants felt they could rely upon them. According to an early historian, by claiming land titles and increasing "the trade and importance of the place" through an "influx of new settlers, some of them men of capital, education and influence," early Minnesota arrivals thus counted on the federal government to help them transform their "wilderness and unorganized society" into "the dignity of an established commonwealth."[7]

In defining the political organization of the western states, the Northwest Ordinance had expanded American territorial rights to lands north of the Ohio River, south of Canada, west of the Appalachians, and east of the Mississippi River. As Jefferson's "empire for liberty" expanded into the Mississippi River Valley during the nineteenth century, many restless whites moved west, seeking to acquire economic independence in places where land remained abundant and cheap and labor scarce and dear. By 1803, the United States had purchased the Louisiana Territory and population expansion had resulted in the admission of Ohio as the nation's seventeenth state. At the same time, American continental explorations exhibited a more imperial thrust. The most famous among those ventures, the Meriwether Lewis and William Clark expedition, involved a young military officer named Zebulon Pike. While Lewis and Clark pursued the Missouri River to its source in Montana and from there traveled westward to the Pacific Northwest, Pike followed the newly acquired Mississippi River to its junction with the Minnesota River. Once there, he made preliminary surveys of the lands now containing St. Paul–Minneapolis and laid the groundwork for later treaty negotiations with the Dakota Indians. During 1812, Louisiana took its place as the nation's eighteenth state, and with its admission the Mississippi River lay open to American trade and travel from the Falls of St. Anthony to the Gulf of Mexico.[8]

Natural population increases in North America and massive migrations from Europe contributed to American development as well, fostering an expanding domestic market in the young United States and prompting a brisk westward drive over the Appalachian Mountains. Between 1810 and 1850, this "tide of immigration, continuous not only from Europe but from the eastern United States," stimulated the transformation of the northern United States from a small republic of agriculturalists into a modern, market-oriented society focused on continental expansion and industrial production. As the valley of the upper Mississippi passed from the imperial protectorates of the Dakota, French, Spanish, and British nations into American hands during the first two decades of the nineteenth century, the market economy jumped the Mississippi River, carrying with it military personnel, fur traders, and other adventurers anxious to develop the region for the larger nation. They emerged as part of larger agricultural and urban-industrial processes that transformed Great Britain into the world's pre-eminent economic power, set Atlantic migrations into rapid motion, and prompted Americans to enter the race for the spoils of an international economy-in-the-making.[9]

Determined to prosper personally even as they built a powerful nation, politicians and businessmen in the young United States devoted themselves to the peopling of promising regions. Beyond laying the foundations for territorial, population, and market expansion, the federal government developed a system to consolidate Native American land, cajoling the Indians into selling it when possible, taking it by force when all other avenues failed. In the New Northwest, from Michigan to Washington, the federal war department purchased "military reservations" from Native Americans in a maneuver aimed at opening "immense tracts of rich and fertile soils" for permanent "white" settlement. By 1820, those land acquisitions included a nine-square-mile parcel at the confluence of the Mississippi and Minnesota Rivers in the northwestern quadrant that Pike had surveyed. With these early Indian treaties, the government signaled its intention to protect American fur traders and other risk takers in the region against various odds, including warfare and competition from "foreign" traders. Moreover, the government encouraged those associated with John Jacob Astor's American Fur Company to assist with further expansion. As one traveler observed during his pre-territorial trip to Minnesota, Astor's fur traders surfaced as "very useful and influential characters" in the business of land surveying and future Indian treaty negotiations. Along with personal relationships established through trade and familial ties—their households often "composed of an Indian wife and a full assortment of half-breed children"—many regional fur traders made themselves "well acquainted with the geography of the northwest and with the traditionary history of the Indian tribes."[10]

Completed in 1822, the Fort Snelling reserve sprang up as part of the federal government's strategy to protect promising regions for white settlement and entrepreneurial undertakings. As the "most northerly station maintained by the United States in the valley of the Mississippi," the Fort Snelling "fortification" stood atop a parallelogram overlooking the Mississippi and Minnesota Rivers and present-day St. Paul–Minneapolis. Its builders had adapted the fort for mounting cannon if necessary; however, "the walls were unprovided with those weapons," suggesting to one visitor that "the strong stone wall was rather erected to keep the garrison in, than the enemy out." Indeed, given the friendly relations between traders, military personnel, and the Dakota on whom American military families depended for fish and furs during the twenty-five years preceding the organization of Minnesota Territory, the bastion functioned principally as a fur-trading rendezvous, as a lodging house for itinerant merchants, and as a sawmilling operation for the fort and other infant enclaves developing along the eastern shore of the Mississippi. Moreover, its site would make an excellent sally-point for the trans-Mississippi West once fur traders and government agents negotiated future land cessions.[11]

Strategically located on bluffs overlooking the practical head of steamboat navigation at St. Paul and the waterfall at St. Anthony (later Minneapolis), Fort Snelling gave early arrivals access to commodities they could either consume themselves or sell to meet Atlantic world demands. The forests to the north contained animals they could hunt for food and for furs to wear and trade. Via the ten thousand lakes and rivers connecting early settlers with Minnesota's 52 million acres of land, settlers had access to other resources, including fish to supplement their diets and timber to house themselves. They could saw into lumber the surplus of Minnesota's 26,000 square miles of pine, aspen-birch, and hardwoods hugging the Great Lakes, the Mississippi River, and the tributary waterways northward to the Canadian border. With millions of acres of North America's best wheat-growing lands spanning northwestward into the Red River Valley and other grain-growing and prairie lands sprawling to the south and west along the Mississippi and Minnesota River systems, settlers could cultivate the soil, graze sheep and other domesticated animals, provide themselves with dietary staples, and manufacture flour, wool, and other articles for the international market. Natural endowments thus promised profits to those who exploited the commercial and manufacturing potential of the limestone bluffs that would shield business and residential districts from frequent floods, the waterways that stimulated travel and trade, the waterfall's power source for milling, and the wheat-growing lands that would lure farmers to the region.

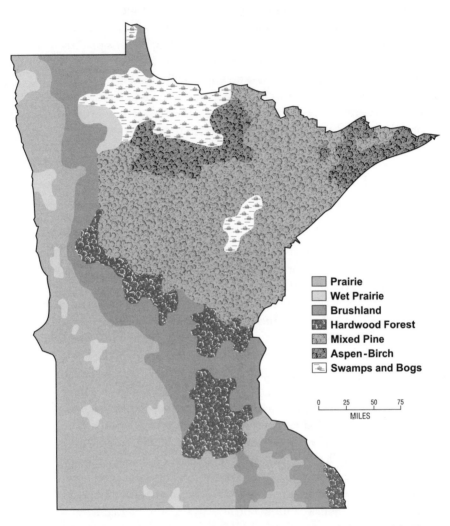

	Prairie
	Wet Prairie
	Brushland
	Hardwood Forest
	Mixed Pine
	Aspen-Birch
	Swamps and Bogs

0   25   50   75
MILES

Minnesota's settlers had access to abundant resources, from northern forests containing the hardwood, pine, and aspen-birch required for building their towns to millions of acres of North America's best grain-growing prairies that agriculturists could cultivate for home consumption and for export to meet Atlantic world demands.

Together, early Indian land cessions and the establishment of Fort Snelling attracted considerable attention among those seeking profits on this "verge of the civilized world." However, immigration to lands in and around St. Paul–Minneapolis remained light during the 1820s, with brutal winters, torrential springs, and primitive transportation networks initially precluding large-scale immigration. Interconnected rivers and lakes did allow for difficult but not impossible canoe and barge travel between late April and early November, however. Waterways thus supported communication, transportation, and trade routes during the summer and fall months for the few French, British, and American adventurers who filtered into Minnesota.

The Transportation Revolution and
Minnesota's Expanding Fur Trade

In nineteenth-century Minnesota and elsewhere throughout the developing North American West, would-be entrepreneurs, far removed from population centers and markets, confronted a formidable obstacle: the need for cheap and reliable transportation to link the region's people, resources, and businesses to the wider market economy. Without this essential, few enterprises could aspire to more than local significance. Thus, through all stages of development, Minnesota's history intertwines with the story of the transportation revolution and the networks it created, first through rivers and roads, later via rails.

During the first half of the nineteenth century, the transportation revolution made industrial expansion beyond the Appalachian Mountains possible, further inspiring American dreams of competing with Great Britain and continental Europe. Between 1815 and 1840, more than 1.25 million Euro-Americans crossed over the Appalachian Mountains into the Ohio River system. With tributaries stretching as far north as western New York State and as far south as North Carolina, the Ohio River Valley lay open to migrants willing to drift, paddle, and sail downstream to Pittsburgh, Cincinnati, Louisville, St. Louis, or New Orleans. By the time the migrant tide swelled into the Mississippi Valley, technology made it possible to go upstream as well. Settlers and tourists alike swarmed aboard the steam-powered vessels then revolutionizing the country's waterways.[12]

Seeing the connection between the federal government, the transportation revolution, and further expansion, one Minnesotan observed, "The United States had little authority over this region until 1812." Soon after, however, the introduction of steam power transformed American transportation, opening new business prospects, inspiring manufacturing and agricultural establishments in the interior, and increasing the expansion of riverboats and population beyond the eastern seaboard's settled regions. Following the 1815 Treaty of Ghent, which officially banished French empire builders from North America, the U.S. federal government implemented laws to lower the risks associated with American and British competition. By 1816, guidebook authors reported that Congress had excluded foreigners from the American "Northwestern Indian trade" and had established the military post at Fort Snelling "for the encouragement of [American] citizens." Together, these policies paved the way for American "traders, missionaries, and soldiers [to] penetrate into the western wilderness" in order to achieve dominance over the New Northwest.[13]

Following the introduction of steam-powered boats on the Mississippi River in 1815, the Mississippi and Ohio River Valleys boomed and urban enclaves along both rivers flourished. The early experiences of Ohio River settlers and entrepreneurs quickly revealed the wisdom of creating cities first, to provide jumping-off points for interior expansion. Consequently, early migrants built towns into which they hoped to lure capital that would help them build larger business networks. Next they beckoned farmers, who would foster urban populations by providing both the raw materials for manufacturing and distribution and a market for finished products. Traveling by steamboat during the 1820s and 1830s, migrants accelerated the industrial and agricultural development of commercial cities such as Pittsburgh, Cincinnati, and St. Louis. From National Road connections at Wheeling, Virginia, Ohio River traffic flowed upstream toward the Allegheny and Monongahela River junction at Pittsburgh, downstream along Ohio's border course toward Cincinnati, and thence onward to Cairo, Illinois.[14]

Steamboats prompted more rapid settlement along the Ohio River's circuitous path and along the Mississippi itself. From the Cairo junction, many people boarded steamers headed south for New Orleans. Others followed the river north for another 150 miles to St. Louis, the booming young city that emerged as the entrepôt into the trans-Mississippi West. Strategically located on the great north-south highway, St. Louis opened up land along many tributary rivers and lakes for travel, trade, and settlement. Jumping off from St. Louis, passenger and freight traffic could head some sixteen hundred miles northwest (at least during high water) along the Missouri River into present-day Montana, or continue to steam northward.

Along the Upper Mississippi's 800-mile fur-trading corridor, steamboats opened up new travel and trade between St. Louis and the practical head of navigation at St. Paul. According to one Minnesotan, when the first steamboat arrived from St. Louis, in 1825, "loaded with stores for the fort," its success in reaching the mouth of the Minnesota River opened the Upper Mississippi to steam navigation, "the mightiest agent in making the then wilderness blossom as a rose." Without further Indian land cessions to entice permanent settlement, however, the enclaves near the fort took several decades to "blossom." He remembered that winter service remained "irregular" throughout the pre-territorial period, for "only stray boats would make trips to this region, whenever they could get loads that pay." During 1826, a Fort Snelling employee reported "much rejoicing over the arrival of two officers *from below* [by dog sled] who had returned from a furlough, *bringing the first mail received for five months!*" The officers also brought basic dietary staples: flour, salted pork, tea, and sugar. This situation lingered until sufficient business and population justified regular packet lines in 1847 and Minnesota's first stagecoach service in 1849. Still, with increased consumer goods shipments going north and west and agricultural products and furs pouring south, steamboat competition reduced the cost and time of upriver shipments by an estimated 90 percent between 1820 and 1830. Moreover, during the 1830s, traders and settlers reduced the costs of reaching the wider world as new towns, including Davenport and Dubuque, Iowa, and La Crosse, Wisconsin, sprang up all along the northern Mississippi pathway. Traveling by foot, horse, dog sled, barge, and canoe to these larger places, early Minnesotans could board steamboats heading south.[15]

At the same time, northern east-west travel quickened along the canals that linked the eastern United States with the Great Lakes. The completion of New York's Erie Canal in 1825 and the inauguration of steamboat travel on the Great Lakes facilitated travel and shipments from New England and New York into Cleveland and Detroit. During the 1820s and 1830s, American fur trading operations flourished between Detroit and other Lake Michigan ports, including those emerging at Milwaukee and Chicago. In pursuit of furs, timber, and then farmland, immigrants pushed themselves into the Great Lakes region, a few reaching Minnesota's eastern shoreline along Lake Superior. Increased migration resulted in the creation of Wisconsin Territory in 1836. The new territory comprised lands from Lake Michigan to the Mississippi River, opening up possibilities for permanent white settlement along the Mississippi's eastern shoreline at St. Paul and St. Anthony. Michigan joined the American union during 1837 as the nation's twenty-sixth state. Thereafter, Wisconsin and Minnesota lay open to fur traders anxious to exploit untapped forests as they made their way from Lake Superior to the interior.

As increasing numbers of fur traders ventured from Michigan and Wisconsin to Minnesota during the 1830s, they used their eastern market experiences and credit connections to work the region for personal gain. Between 1830 and 1838, while they waited with fort personnel for the inevitable treaty negotiations with Indians dwelling on the Mississippi's eastern shoreline, they embarked upon "improvements" on lands they hoped to claim. Many forged alliances with centuries-old kinship networks, bonding with Dakota and Ojibwe families from whom they learned the arts of trade reciprocity and gift giving. Some ventured into the region as part of Astor's American Fur Company or other mercantile networks long established in the French and British empires. Still others arrived with connections to entrepreneurial steamboat captains, storekeepers, and assorted Fort Snelling personnel as well as to other traders conversant with businessmen situated along Minnesota's waterways. Once established, they sent for family members, friends, and other associates. During pre-territorial years, many who succeeded along this remote reach of the American nation became well versed in the survival techniques necessary for later developments.[16]

Arriving in Minnesota during 1832, Norman W. Kittson exemplified the kinds of success that men of small means and big dreams could achieve in remote but promising regions. Born in Sorel, Lower Canada, in 1814, Kittson had no money, but at age sixteen his abilities in trade and penmanship netted him employment with American Fur. The company sent Kittson to Wisconsin, where he proved himself an excellent and reliable trader, making money for himself as well as for the firm. Subscribing to the "whole theory of the fur trade, based upon good faith between employers and employed" and entrusted with "goods amounting to hundreds of thousands of dollars, nay millions" (including supplies of flour, corn, pork, tobacco, and other articles required for yearly operations), Kittson's "fidelity and honesty" earned him an increasing sphere of influence. By 1832, he operated an American Fur post on the headwaters of the Minnesota River; then he spent a year on Iowa's Red Cedar River. During 1834, he ventured north to Fort Snelling, where he acquired a clerking position with the fort's sutler (storekeeper), an appointment he maintained through 1838. Kittson's position at Fort Snelling sent him tramping northward to survey promising timber and wheat-growing lands, at the same time expanding his trade with the region's Indian, French, British, and American fur traders. As he prospered in small ways, Kittson made "improvements" on some of these lands—cutting timber, building log huts for trading purposes, and investing in larger trade and transportation networks. He also made important business connections at and around the fort with military personnel and other American Fur associates such as Henry Hastings Sibley.[17]

Although he arrived in Minnesota two years later than Kittson had, Henry Sibley emerged as the pre-eminent member of Minnesota's early commercial and political vanguard. Born in Detroit during 1811, Sibley could claim long-standing family connections to the building of the young United States. His grandfathers had participated in the Revolutionary War, and his father, one of only two lawyers established in Detroit during the first decade of the nineteenth century, had emerged as a delegate for Michigan Territory during 1820–21 and thereafter as a U.S. district attorney and a Supreme Court judge. Sibley's older brother had graduated at the head of his West Point class, but Judge Solomon Sibley had another career in mind for young Henry: a mirror of his own. Thus, once Henry finished the equivalent of high school, the judge hired an Episcopal clergyman to teach his son Latin and Greek, followed by two years' training in law. At the end of this education, Henry declared himself the "black sheep of the family" and told his father that he found the study "irksome" and, moreover, that he "longed for a more active and stirring life."[18]

During 1828, Sibley took a clerking position at a sutler's store located between Lake Huron and Lake Superior; however, "not fancying the occupation," he soon quit. In the spring of 1829, at age eighteen, he took another clerkship—this time one that would provide a steppingstone to a business of his own—with the American Fur Company post at Mackinac, Michigan. "Long the chief entrepot of the fur trade for the country bordering [the Great] Lakes as well as for the Mississippi valley above Prairie du Chien [Wisconsin]," American Fur's Mackinac post dominated the vast region of the New Northwest. Meanwhile, the British Hudson's Bay Company—"a veritable empire in extent"—controlled the entire trade north of the American boundary line. Joining the throng of French, British, and American fur traders "self-banished from civilization" at Mackinac, Sibley soon discovered that although the "contest for the possession of the Indian hunters' products was fiercely maintained, there existed a broad line of demarcation between the requirements of social life and the stern demands of business." Sibley moved seamlessly into this friendly yet "pugilistic" world. With reading and penmanship skills in short supply among men willing to live and work in the outback, Sibley's business abilities, political connections, and education allowed him to rise quickly in the firm.[19]

By 1830, Sibley had made important connections throughout Michigan and Wisconsin, ultimately partnering with influential *métis* (French-Indian) fur traders in Wisconsin who oversaw four American Fur trading stations located between Prairie du Chien and Fort Snelling. Taking advantage of new opportunities along this 300-mile fur-trading route during the years that followed the 1830 Indian Removal Act, Sibley made money for himself, for his Prairie du Chien partners, and for American Fur.[20]

From savings acquired during his early employment, Sibley invested in

American Fur during 1834, becoming both a partner in the company's western headquarters in St. Louis and the western division's primary agent in Minnesota. Leaving Prairie du Chien in October 1834, "all mounted, with one led horse, which was used temporarily by an old Winnebago [Ho-Chunk] Indian, who was engaged as a guide," Sibley made his way through the largely uninhabited region. He eventually reached the bluff that would become St. Paul and then traveled overland to the Minnesota River and his new post at Mendota. Located at the confluence of the Mississippi and Minnesota Rivers across from Fort Snelling, the "group of log huts" that constituted Mendota disappointed young Sibley, but he soon settled in. Sharing his new lodging with a métis family, he survived on "salt pork and bread, acquired some knowledge of the Sioux [Dakota] language," and purchased the residents' "entire interest in the fur trade at the four posts." Over the next two years, trading profits allowed him to construct Minnesota's first private and "spacious stone warehouse for transacting business [and providing] accommodations for lodging [his] numerous guests." Hospitably received by all the Dakota he encountered, Sibley soon married into one of their families. He also nurtured important friendships at Fort Snelling, emerging as one of the region's most trusted and capable fur traders, a "very useful and influential character" for those anxious to negotiate further Indian land cessions along the eastern Mississippi shoreline at St. Anthony and St. Paul. That task got under way in 1837, as part of Wisconsin Territory's expanding acquisitions.[21]

Land Acquisitions for "White Settlement" and American Expansion

During 1837–38, with assistance from fur traders such as Norman Kittson and Henry Sibley, the federal government negotiated further treaties with Native Americans living in the future towns of St. Paul and St. Anthony. The treaties resulted in part from a "memorial" submitted to the president by "citizens of settlements near Fort Snelling," who offered up a long-understood rationale for further land cessions. They argued that, having been "permitted to make improvements and retain unmolested possession of them for many years," they "believed the land belonged to the United States, and that the settlers were only exercising the privileges extended to them by the benign and salutary laws which have peopled the western country with a hardy, industrious and enterprising class of citizens."[22]

By the treaties—"a $450 annuity for 20 years [purchased] for just $9,000!, a very snug sum"—federal government agents induced the Dakota and Ojibwe Indians to cede all their lands east of the Mississippi River for "white settlement." Sibley sneered that "the boasted paternal regard for the poor Indians [was instead] but one [in a] series of iniquity and wrong"; however, Sibley himself, along with other American Fur traders and Fort Snelling personnel, profited handsomely in the years that followed. For example, the treaties allowed Kittson to expand his operations. Continuing to trade in furs throughout his tenure at Fort Snelling, Kittson resumed his employment with American Fur in 1839. When Astor's firm failed in 1842 and Pierre Chouteau, Jr. & Co. purchased its western headquarters in St. Louis, Kittson's profits allowed him to finance a fur trade operation of his own. Choosing nearby Cold Springs as his location, Kittson built up financial capital and partnered with other fur traders and friends at the fort. By 1843, news of his success—including the fur trader's "active, strong, and elastic body, and constant absorption in exacting and harrassing business"— reached Pierre Chouteau in St. Louis. Very soon, Chouteau coaxed Kittson back into his corporation's service, offering him all the business he could handle, not only at the Minnesota River's headwaters but also in the firm's trading networks along the British possessions.[23]

Through his Minnesota trade between 1837 and 1843, Kittson made money for himself and Chouteau; further, he gained entrance into and valuable information about the promising agricultural regions of the Red River Valley. By 1847, he had also embarked on a profitable trade with the Red River agricultural settlement, organizing a 125-cart brigade to sell furs and bring goods to St. Paul. From the capital and expertise he accrued, Kittson made numerous investments in the territory between St. Paul and Britain's Fort Garry (now Winnipeg, Manitoba). He also invested in St. Paul itself, purchasing a large townsite addition for a trifling sum by later standards: four hundred dollars for lands that soon formed the main business section at St. Paul's Lower Levee, the principal steamboat landing for boats traveling northward from St. Louis.[24]

Henry Sibley profited in similar ways. Lands he purchased in the wake of the 1837–38 treaty negotiations provided collateral to finance his operations. Continuing to build up his trading network, Sibley acquired positions as a regional Indian agent and gained enormous power over Minnesota's fur trade. He also acquainted himself with newer migrants who ventured into the region during the late 1830s and early 1840s—particularly cash-poor traders and merchants eager for access to investment networks.[25]

Kittson's and Sibley's initial fur trading activities connected them to influential economic, political, and social networks throughout Wisconsin, Iowa, and Minnesota, but their dominance in the region lasted only briefly before others encroached upon them. According to one Minnesotan, these upstarts included Fort Snelling's employees, "keen fellows, looking eagerly on, and waiting for a good chance to seize on some of the rich territory so soon to be open to the impatient speculator." Indeed, Fort Snelling's military personnel and their families had emerged both as the region's first permanent settlers and as some of its earliest entrepreneurs. As the 1830s closed and military expeditions dwindled, several fort residents saw a chance for personal gain along the Mississippi River, where the power potential of the Falls of St. Anthony conjured up images of the prosperous manufacturing town of Lowell, Massachusetts. Wearied by the monotony of a military life with few opportunities for armed confrontation, they ventured into trade, commerce, and milling.[26]

Knowing that manufacturing start-ups require more capital than do merchandizing activities, Fort Snelling personnel commenced their first milling businesses with government supply contracts for lumber and flour, combining early earnings with capital raised in places like Boston and Lowell. Although their plans predominately centered on the milling of lumber and grain, Minnesota's aspiring millers hoped to employ the textile model to lure investments. As they borrowed money and manufacturing techniques from Massachusetts, Minnesota's fledgling milling entrepreneurs followed in the footsteps of their eastern predecessors. Businessmen there had powered American industrialization with cascading waters that churned natural resources from Maine to Virginia into lumber, flour, paper, thread, and cloth. By 1837, Minnesota's millers supplied lumber and flour to both the U.S. Army and the small populations gathering along the banks of the Upper Mississippi.[27]

Arriving at Fort Snelling from Pennsylvania in 1837, twenty-two-year-old Franklin Steele would exemplify the ways in which young men could turn government contracts into economic independence and manufacturing success. Employed as the fort's sutler (replacing Kittson), Steele waited patiently for Congress to finalize treaties with the Native Americans who legally held the lands containing St. Anthony. He had already explored the pineries of the Northwest and had erected a small mill at St. Croix Falls, Wisconsin. As the treaty signing approached in 1838, the young milling entrepreneur canoed down the St. Croix River to Stillwater, Minnesota, raced to Fort Snelling, and tramped onward to St. Anthony, where he secured his claim just hours before other would-be manufacturers arrived. One competitor for the St. Anthony claim, upon finding Steele "at breakfast in a sufficient shack," demanded, "What can this mean, Mr. Steele!" Calmly, the new town's proprietor replied, "I am in possession of this land by preemption right."[28]

After his coup d'état, facilitated by inside information received from friends in Wisconsin and the fort, Steele used his sutler position to obtain more government contracts, thereby building the nexus for Minnesota's milling future. At first he sawed his own timber by hand and floated it downriver to the fort. By 1847, when military and then settler demands exceeded his capacity, Steele pitched the falls' water-power potential to acquaintances in the Northeast. With sufficient capital support from investors in Boston, Steele was ready to build on land purchased with proceeds from his government contracts. He turned his manufacturing vision into reality by constructing a dam across the river to Hennepin Island—one of three islands that connected St. Anthony with present-day Minneapolis. On Hennepin Island, Steele built four crude sawmills, employing a dozen or so men to manufacture lumber for Fort Snelling and other downriver points. With this increased lumber production, he entered into business dealings with local fur traders and other influential merchants, benefiting from the capital and mercantile expertise of his downriver neighbors. By the time he met Reverend Neill in 1849, Steele had acquired the capital he needed to transform St. Anthony from a scenic destination for weary travelers into an eastern-shore milling district along the northern Mississippi. In his ventures, he mirrored associations between merchants and manufacturers who had, several decades before, launched American industrialization along East Coast rivers.[29]

On the waterfall's western shore, similar milling developments were under way. With the U.S. Army's approval, Colonel John Stevens built flouring and saw mills along Fort Snelling's northern boundaries (present-day Minneapolis). This area was still off-limits to legal American settlement in 1848, so Stevens agreed to employ the mills for Fort Snelling's use only. As territorial status neared, however, he winked at the dozen or so illegal claimants who had established farms near his own. Supplying Stevens with wheat, oats, and other products for grinding, the small agricultural nucleus foreshadowed Minneapolis's evolution in the years following legal settlement of the trans-Mississippi West. Although milling activities depended on large cash outlays, millers at St. Anthony–Minneapolis would witness their profits rise with the federal government's recognition of their land claims and then with the benefits conferred by territorial status.[30]

Among those who followed Kittson, Sibley, and Steele into Minnesota, other former American Fur employees emerged as St. Paul's first merchants and bankers. Sometimes Sibley, other fur traders, and Fort Snelling personnel cooperated; sometimes they competed. Regardless, during the 1840s their activities nurtured profit-oriented centers along Minnesota's major waterways. They created retail and reshipping services at the St. Paul and Mendota villages, constructed small lumber and flour mills at the Stillwater, St. Anthony, and Minneapolis enclaves, and erected other trading posts at stopping-off points along the Mississippi, Minnesota, St. Croix, and Red Rivers. Many started their enterprises with credit extended by American Fur. Thereafter they bartered, sold, and trucked their furs, hides, and lumber. Traveling to St. Louis and other established trade centers, they procured food and sundries for the coming seasons—journeying in the late winter for early spring sales and then again throughout the summer and fall for the approaching winter months. These supplies saved many new settlers from privation during long winter seclusions. And the profits made on the precious goods that fur traders, merchants, and steamboat captains provided drew others into the competitive market emerging along the northern Mississippi River.[31]

With their various affiliations, Reverend Neill's "ignoble" collection of enthusiasts share many characteristics of merchants examined in the works of American economic and business historians. According to the classic statement by Joseph Schumpeter, similar impulses had guided American entrepreneurs since before independence. Emerging as the most innovative agents in the American economy, these far-sighted men left a pioneering trail along which a "swarm of imitators" followed. That swarm soon fueled city-building schemes and competition among contenders attempting to dominate the region economically and politically.[32]

During the late 1830s and early 1840s, the experiences of several fur traders illustrated these trends, not only sparking competition among traders, millers, and others who descended upon Minnesota but also influencing their strategies for expansion. Minnesota's early merchants and fur traders managed vast trading territories. Initially, most lived above their stores, employed few personnel (the largest engaging perhaps a dozen young men), and maintained highly personal connections. Technological and population constraints limited their early accumulations. The wealthiest among them amassed but $15,000 in personal and real estate property by 1849—a pittance compared to affluent eastern merchants. Although they paid dearly for transportation, communication, and provisions, they spent less on lodgings and real estate. Anticipating that real estate values would escalate with territorial status and statehood, they exhibited an attention to and knowledge of the larger American political process. Moreover, they took a keen interest in the city-building maneuvers of businessmen in places like Chicago, where speculative ventures and entrepreneurial investments had powered the Great Lakes port into a boom town. Sensing that economic and political ambitions would synergize in the days ahead, they also attached themselves to political networks throughout Wisconsin, Illinois, Iowa, and Missouri.[33]

The politically astute entrepreneurs who joined Kittson, Sibley, Steele, and other fur traders and military personnel understood that expansion would soon come to the region. They thus developed similar strategies despite their diverse backgrounds and unequal footing in terms of education, experience, and tangible resources. Those interested in trade (first in furs, later in whiskey, and finally in commerce for American urban-industrial and agricultural expansion) clustered at St. Paul because it opened for private settlement first. Those inspired by the waterfall's manufacturing potential made their way to St. Anthony or crossed the Mississippi into Minneapolis, where they waited for Congress to pass the preemption law that would open the trans-Mississippi West to permanent settlement. In each place, they "improved" the lands they hoped to acquire, especially prime real estate located along river embankments. Socialized as self-interested, go-ahead North Americans, early traders, merchants, and millers entered Minnesota with a "vigor and industry" common among their contemporaries. On lands converted from Indian tribal ground to tracts for white settlers' personal gain, they fashioned a profit-oriented landscape, hoping that one day they would emerge as the leaders of a "magnificent state beaming with riches." Their various activities also set the stage for Euro-American settlers who followed during Minnesota's territorial period.[34]

One of those newcomers, Henry Mower Rice, zigzagged his way to St. Paul from various stations and outposts. Born into a middle-class Vermont family in 1816, Rice studied law for two years before a Michigan attorney drew him west to Detroit in 1835. Rice found employment as an assistant engineer with the State of Michigan, working for two years on the Sault Ste. Marie Canal and other public projects. He gained valuable experience in transportation, business, and government, but like many self-starters he lacked the requisite capital for a quick ascent in already-crowded Detroit, where real estate prices had escalated beyond his means. During 1839, his quest for opportunities pushed him beyond the limits of American domination and into Minnesota. As an American Fur agent in charge of Chouteau's Ho-Chunk and Ojibwe trade, Rice commanded a territory stretching from Lake Superior to the British possessions. Along his lines of influence, he met other traders tramping over the Red River Valley and made business connections that soon tied him firmly to the region.[35]

By the close of the 1840s, Rice owned a vast expanse of land along the Mississippi River, particularly on townsite additions near St. Paul's Upper Levee, the major reshipping access point for trade with Fort Snelling and other interior locations along the Minnesota River. Rice leveraged his St. Paul possessions by purchasing a townsite addition with a friend, aspiring grocer John Irvine. Working together on various trading and merchandizing strategies, Rice and Irvine expanded their businesses and real estate

holdings at St. Paul. They also strengthened their political and social positions by donating some of their lands for the erection of businesses,
churches, and public meeting places during 1848 and 1849.[36]

As Rice and Irvine expanded into general merchandizing and distribution in St. Paul, other all-purpose merchants, including Henry Jackson, entered the region during the 1840s. A Virginian by birth, Jackson undertook
a peregrine route before settling on St. Paul. Already thirty-eight years old
in 1843, Jackson had failed in several business enterprises as he made his way
from Virginia through the Ohio and Mississippi River Valleys. Landing at
St. Paul, he erected a small log store near the Lower Levee, hoping to prosper from increased steamboat trade and to find the upward mobility that
had eluded him in larger and more competitive towns like Galena, Illinois.
Enjoying small successes, Jackson invited his old friend William Hartshorn
into a fur-trading partnership at St. Paul.

Along with Rice, Irvine, and Jackson, Hartshorn played a role in transforming St. Paul from a traditional fur-trading post into a commercial hub
for expansion. Others joined them, surveying the townsite for real estate
turnovers and building a two-story hotel complete with a "right smart tav-
ern," for everyone knew that "no one would want to go to a town that had
no good hotel." These efforts also attracted reliable physicians, carpenters,
teachers, and others who wanted to participate in the town's expansion. Of
course, expansion required more capital, and it also increased the risk of
failure as entrepreneurs dipped into their profits to fund larger-scale businesses. Historical precedents guided these entrepreneurial traders, however,
just as they had guided millers in St. Anthony and Minneapolis.[37]

Traditional Traders Turned
Commercial-Political Expansionists

By the 1840s, St. Paul had emerged as the focus for expansion into Minnesota. With the fur trade thriving in and around St. Paul, business with
St. Louis merchants multiplied. Pursuing increased trade, entrepreneurial
steamboat captains reached farther to the northwest, making more frequent
trips. By 1847, the Galena Packet Company established a regular schedule
of steamboats between St. Louis and St. Paul. As steamboat captains and
merchants invested in St. Paul, they established all-purpose stores and trading networks that played an indispensable role in supplying the demands
of Minnesota's seedling population. Merchants undertook risks associated
with meeting these consumer demands because they envisioned swelling
returns on their initial investments. Few in number, suppliers commanded
high prices for the staples they furnished—provided they lost little of their

inventory to freezing temperatures, waterway accidents, and the frequent robberies that beset river routes. From those who survived these risks of travel and trade, some emerged as prominent political agitators for the establishment of Minnesota Territory.[38]

Among the experiences of those who prepared the way for Minnesota's entrance into the wider American political economy, William Hartshorn's illustrates the kinds of trade in which Minnesota's riparian village populations engaged as the territorial announcement neared. It also reveals how economic decisions ultimately enhanced or diminished social and political positions. In common with many of his colleagues in the unorganized portions of the Upper Northwest, Hartshorn ventured in several businesses before finding success, in his case as a partner with Henry Jackson in a St. Paul general store. Born in Vermont in 1794, Hartshorn wandered west during his youth—a trek that eventually carried him to St. Louis in the 1830s. He worked for American Fur for a decade, and when Pierre Chouteau acquired the company's western interests, Hartshorn continued his apprenticeship with the St. Louis division. There he met other western opportunity-seekers working the region near St. Paul.

Hartshorn had hoped to take part in the developments that placed St. Louis at the center of northwestern expansion; however, as he neared his fiftieth year in 1843 he still lingered as a bit actor. Consequently, when all-purpose merchant Henry Jackson offered him the chance to earn higher profits in the less-settled regions of Minnesota, Hartshorn moved to St. Paul. Traveling up the Mississippi River on one of the few steamboats that ventured so far north during the fall of 1843, Hartshorn took both a stock of goods from St. Louis and August L. Larpenteur, a twenty-one-year-old clerk who had immigrated to Missouri three years earlier. Jackson soon partnered with Hartshorn in a fur-trading venture, a general store at St. Paul, and other posts along the Mississippi River.

After a modestly successful two-year stint, the opportunities presented by new settlement freed Hartshorn from his reliance on Jackson, and he dissolved the partnership. Taking young Larpenteur with him, Hartshorn branched out on his own, in 1845 opening William Hartshorn & Co. in St. Paul. On nominal returns from the first year's business, Hartshorn hired several younger fur trade associates to manage other posts along the Mississippi, St. Croix, Minnesota, and Red Rivers. As part of his general merchandizing operation, Hartshorn also made frequent trips to St. Louis for supplies, traveling via steamboats in the summer and fall and on foot, horse, and sled during the late winter and early spring.

By 1848, population expansion allowed Hartshorn to turn a snug little trade in the Upper Northwest despite the constraints he faced along the liquid highways that separated St. Paul from suppliers in established southern and eastern markets. Winter freezes prostrated activities in the sparsely populated region, condemning its residents to more than five months of isolation. Springtime relief came slowly—from St. Louis, Chicago, and elsewhere in settled North America. As ice gradually disappeared on the northern Mississippi River and along the channels of Lake Superior and as mails and commodities finally arrived in St. Paul, residents reconnected with the world beyond through the efforts of steamboat captains and regional merchants like Hartshorn.

Running accounts with prominent Indian traders along the contours of Minnesota's rivers supported Hartshorn's primary fur business at St. Paul, and his general store situated above the Lower Levee supplemented his income with reshipping services and general merchandizing. Ledger notations for 1847–48 indicate few large cash receipts for the goods and services he provided, but his customers balanced their accounts one way or another. Some purchased supplies with quitclaim deeds on their properties in and around St. Paul. Others exchanged labor for goods. One man tended Hartshorn's cow (the only domesticated animal in St. Paul) for oats, dried fruits, salted pork, and drink brought upriver from St. Louis. Some chopped his wood for products to finish moccasins and other garments— ribbon, silk, and thread procured from New York City and other Atlantic ports. Still others plowed his small field for powder, hardware implements, paper, and ink carried north from New Orleans and St. Louis. Chief Wah Co Tah of Red Wing paid for goods with furs and fish, while others bartered lumber and grain products from their infant mills at Stillwater and St. Anthony. These exchanges, together with deeded property and currency on hand, gave Hartshorn a small portion of the wealth he sought during his five-year tenure in St. Paul.

In the meantime, St. Paul's population and trade reached a size that warranted regular steamboat packets and federal government expenditures on postal services for the young village. Fort Snelling had offered some post office service since the 1820s; however, people interested in the region's development knew that each refinement in communication, travel, real estate, and trade prompted further settlement and ultimately promised profits to those who obtained the first appointments. Henry Jackson received the postmaster's commission, and the new designation transformed his general store into an information center for regional inhabitants. As the town's first permanent communication outlet, Jackson's shop housed his family, his friends, and the town's mail. By 1847, it also served as the principal meeting spot for people with ambitions for Minnesota. Early residents received communication from the outside world through Jackson's store. Protestant missionaries held services there, hoping to convert the region's Indians to the white man's faith. Although French Catholics had established a chapel a decade earlier, St. Paul's first missionary schoolteacher, Harriet Bishop, used Jackson's store to inaugurate Protestant American training for the few Euro-American and Indian children who lived in the village. Most important of all, successful traders, retail merchants, and milling proprietors gathered there for discussions about Minnesota's political future as an American entity.

The assorted functions housed in Jackson's small outlet prompted further developments as Minnesota's population expanded beyond his abilities to meet consumer, religious, educational, and political demands. For example, fur trader Henry Rice built warehouses along St. Paul's steamboat landings to stock more supplies. When family members and friends arrived during the late 1840s, wives, daughters, and sisters started the Saint Paul Circle of Industry, a women's charitable sewing institution. This group sought to raise funds from St. Paul's merchants to erect another small building for public meetings and educational and religious purposes for the village's Protestant population. The women took pride in the fact that "the first payment on the lumber for the first school house was made with money earned with the needle by the ladies of this circle." Circuit riders also arrived to give periodic sermons, while Protestants organized a temperance society to beat back the "whiskey hoe-down," the former means of raising funds.[39]

By the end of 1848, St. Paul's townsite plats encompassed nearly ninety acres housing some four hundred residents on the land claims entered at the St. Croix Falls' sales office. Still, these numbers constituted an insufficient population for inclusion in the new state of Wisconsin, even if they did form an important nucleus for the future. Unwilling to risk his profits on St. Paul's "potential," Hartshorn sold his real estate holdings and headed east to Stillwater. He soon regretted the decision.[40]

When he left St. Paul in 1848, storekeeper Hartshorn gambled on Stillwater because he thought its location on the border of the newly created state of Wisconsin favored ventures in business and politics. Unfortunately for Hartshorn, when Minnesota received territorial status in 1849, the settlements at St. Paul and St. Anthony–Minneapolis, not Stillwater, emerged as focal points for expansion into the Upper Northwest. Larpenteur— Hartshorn's former clerk turned storekeeper in his own right—expanded his St. Paul business fourfold while Hartshorn's Stillwater trade shriveled, driving him back to St. Paul in 1851. By then, territorial expansion had increased property values, and, once again, Hartshorn found himself a small-time actor in a maturing western market. According to a newspaper sketch about him, "though at times well off, [Hartshorn] was over-reached to an extent that kept him in reduced circumstances most of his life."[41]

On the other hand, storekeepers Jackson and Larpenteur continued to prosper, especially when St. Paul's territorial real estate boom quadrupled the value of the properties they had purchased from Hartshorn prior to his departure. Moreover, Jackson emerged as an influential political broker given his strategic positions as local information exchange agent, real estate mogul, "justice, postmaster, hotel-keeper, naturalizer of foreigners," social mediator, and several other "functionaries combined in one."[42]

As they prospered from trade with the few thousand Dakota, Ojibwe, Euro-American, and cross-blood groups scattered throughout the region, St. Paul's merchants and St. Anthony–Minneapolis's millers attracted others into competitive undertakings along the northern Mississippi River. According to one early resident, by "bending all their influence and energies to the benefit of the infant metropolises, and draw[ing] population and traffic hither," early Minnesotans transformed themselves from parochial traders and millers into political advocates for the creation of Minnesota Territory.[43]

The Quest for Territorial Status

By 1848, Minnesota's merchants and millers had achieved a measure of economic success on the margins of the expanding American empire. These early accomplishments nurtured their dreams of linking Minnesota's enterprises to the wider United States, with its vast, beckoning, swelling markets. On entrepreneurial impulses and government activities, Minnesota's vanguard had expanded St. Paul and Stillwater into villages populated by some four hundred residents each and St. Anthony into a hamlet containing several dozen people. They had acquired better mail service as well as a land office that safeguarded real estate acquisitions against new opportunity-seekers who arrived while original tenants departed on winter provision and trade missions. By the end of the 1840s, as scheduled steamboat packets regularly reached St. Paul, the city offered jobs in commercial houses that supplied credit and sold food and clothing imported from St. Louis and elsewhere. Meanwhile, lumber and flour mills in Stillwater and St. Anthony furnished manufacturing opportunities.[44]

The expansion of American railroads had also energized further development. By the end of the 1840s, railroad trunk lines reached the Ohio River Valley and the Great Lakes and had just started their thrust into the Mississippi River Valley. On more than 8,500 miles of track, railroads provided swift transit to jumping-off points for migrants heading northwest into Oregon Territory (acquired in 1846) and southwest into the recently annexed Mexican territories. As railroad connections neared Chicago, many western migrants traveled at least some distance by rail, along lines that reduced travel times between New York and Chicago from six weeks in 1800 to just under one week in 1848. By then, railroads traveling westward hauled four times as much freight as canals for about the same capital and labor costs. Moreover, those expenses promised to decrease further once tracks expanded west from Chicago.[45]

By 1848, these interlinked transportation arteries had carried some four thousand Euro-Americans into Minnesota and the Dakotas, the region's first wave of American settlers. Skulking along the outer limits of American society, Minnesota's Euro-Americans knew that further expansion would require backing from the federal government. This same reality had driven American territorial expansion since the adoption of both the Northwest Ordinance and the Constitution in 1787. With both a sixty-year legal process well established and industrialization and commercial agriculture heading west, Minnesota's entrepreneurs understood the enterprise they hoped to undertake. But first they needed federal status to build an appropriate infrastructure. Once in place, this prerequisite would allow them to connect their ambitions with the wider urban-industrial processes that had already transformed Great Britain and had begun to reconstruct continental Europe and the American Northeast.[46]

Before Wisconsin gained statehood on May 29, 1848, Minnesotans had enjoyed some of the benefits of being, technically, residents of Wisconsin Territory and thus living within the organized American realm. In 1848, however, Congress admitted Wisconsin without them. As one congressional member declared, Minnesota's small population derived from its "hyperborean region," which made it "unfit for settlement." With Wisconsin's western boundary set at the confluence of the Mississippi and St. Croix Rivers, Congress thus cut adrift those living within the triangle between Stillwater, St. Anthony, and St. Paul. Finding themselves "out in the cold" as an unorganized political anomaly, Minnesotans focused on the only conceivable solution to their quandary: agitation for their own incorporation as a U.S. territory.[47]

Minnesotans had witnessed rapid economic development in other regions granted territorial privileges during the first half of the nineteenth century, including Ohio, Missouri, Michigan, Illinois, and Wisconsin. With government appropriations for improved communication, transportation, industry, and trade, Cincinnati, St. Louis, Detroit, Chicago, and Milwaukee had quickly matured from lake- and river-side villages into bustling western metropolises with expanding populations. Minnesota's entrepreneurs sought similar opportunities for wealth and influence, but Congress consistently rejected their applications for territorial status. The refusals always focused on one central issue: an insufficient white population. Government expenditures for infrastructure development cost thousands, then millions of dollars, and without a plentiful population, Minnesota seemed to federal leaders an unacceptable capital risk.[48]

During the summer of 1848, as Minnesota's vanguard, "big with expectations," appealed to influential friends in the older Northwest, they found an important champion in the Senate—Illinois's Stephen A. Douglas, a free-soil supporter and the emerging advocate of popular sovereignty. Douglas had long promoted the creation of Minnesota Territory. Finally, as the conclusion of the Mexican War extended American land holdings to the Pacific and the annexation of Texas expanded slavery into newly acquired southern territories, Douglas had the political rationale to justify the expenditure. Embarking on an all-out campaign for his northwestern friends, Douglas promoted the region's wealth-generating potential. He and several others argued that in Minnesota "the 'elements of empire [are] plastic and yet warm,' and need only the right men to mould them into a prosperous State." Douglas also assured his senatorial colleagues that the region contained "somewhere between eight and ten thousand people," omitting the small detail that Native Americans represented more than half the total.[49]

Emboldened by Douglas and others who wanted to open Minnesota for resource extraction, "the right men"—fur traders Sibley and Rice, miller Steele, merchants Jackson and Larpenteur, and other regional entrepreneurs—held two meetings: one at Jackson's information and retail outlet in St. Paul in July 1848, the other at Stillwater in August. At these assemblies, Minnesotans deliberated various strategies for securing territorial status, including those echoing Senator Douglas's goal: to balance the expansion of southern slave territories with free-soil northern ones. Sixty-one men gathered at the Stillwater convention, where they agreed to send a representative—on behalf of the citizens of "Wisconsin Territory"—to Washington, DC.[50]

At a special election on October 30, 1848, territorial supporters chose their delegate: the popular and trustworthy Henry Sibley. Senator Douglas advocated Mendota as the new territorial capital and encouraged Sibley along the same course. Sibley, however, was nobody's fool: he had long recognized St. Paul's strategic location. During January 1849, the seasoned trader and local politician took his Wisconsin seat in the House of Representatives, presented his case, and soon prevailed. Sibley argued that he and his colleagues had passed through traditional Indian society and the channels of mercantile empires and now hoped to participate in the northwestern thrust of American expansion to the Pacific. On March 3, 1849, the U.S. Congress approved these goals. As larger sectional crises picked up momentum, Minnesota became a legal American territory and St. Paul emerged as the gateway for immigration into the region.[51]

In keeping with the provisions of the Missouri Compromise of 1820, Minnesota entered the American domain as a free-soil territory. With one stroke, the enabling act opened suffrage to all free white males then inhabiting the region. It protected their property rights and guaranteed access to abundant, cheap lands. The national government granted provisions for Indian treaty negotiators and land sale officers who would first purchase, survey, and register land titles and then sell parcels at public auction for a minimum price of $1.25 per acre. Speculators often drove up prices, but squatters—protected by the Preemption Act—avoided these competitive bidding wars. Once agents had surveyed the land and put it on the market, squatters received the same rights as other purchasers: they could pay $1.25 per acre and then sell their property at whatever price the market would bear.

Territorial status gave Minnesotans representation in Washington, DC, a standardized legal infrastructure, and fiscal appropriations for post office communication with the outside world. Providing for a legislative assembly, it also furnished Minnesotans with a political body to enact local laws and resolve local disputes. Congressional representatives parceled out school land provisions for the education of Minnesota's young. Territorial status secured civil rights—although a limited set for women and none at all for Indians. With all these statutes safeguarded by the force of the American Constitution, territorial status also encouraged the westward migration of other like-minded and restless spirits.

The enabling act framed the new territory's boundaries. Employing conventional land-surveying wisdom, territorial limits followed the contours of rivers. In this case, the Missouri River—the Mississippi's great northwestern artery extending from St. Louis to its source at Fort Peck Lake in present-day Montana—guided the Congressional decision. With Wisconsin and Lake Superior bounding its eastern limits, British possessions constricting its northern reach, and Iowa marking its southern boundary, Minnesota Territory included present-day Minnesota and the Dakotas east of the Missouri River's connection to the White Earth River. Euro-Americans now considered this land to be their own, an assumption they soon demanded Native Americans accept as well, willingly if possible, by force if necessary.

Finally, the act designated St. Paul the temporary seat of government and provided for presidential appointment of the territory's executive and judicial officers. The newly inaugurated Whig president, Zachary Taylor, soon nominated nonresident party faithfuls for principal political positions—the offices of governor, secretary, three justices, U.S. attorney, and marshal. His choices, together with the fur traders' Jacksonian traditions—including free-soil democracy, Indian removal, and universal white male suffrage—set the stage for the political life of the region.

In the weeks that followed, news finally reached the small cluster gathered in St. Paul: not only had fur-trading Sibley prevailed in Congress, his success meant that enthusiastic journalists, speculators, politicians, and settlers would begin to arrive the moment the Mississippi River's northern reaches thawed. For the moment, military land claims excluded Minneapolis from permanent settlement, but people in St. Paul and St. Anthony suffered no similar restrictions. Town lots were theirs for the taking.

Minnesota Territory emerged during a period of rapid national expansion and fierce competition for new settlers. Consequently, entrepreneurs at St. Paul–Minneapolis quickly moved to lure settlers into Minnesota and away from other western enterprises, such as California's gold-digging enclaves. Like other boosters of the day, they focused first on the construction of urban centers, where they hoped to accumulate the population and capital required for statehood and the corresponding American political and social structures. Beyond that lay the wealth they planned to generate into larger-scale financial, wholesale, and industrial developments, commercial agriculture, and ultimately the bigger business of railroad construction.[52]

When St. Paul's fur-trading and Free-Soil Democrat Henry Rice returned from labors in Washington, DC, where he sought to give the territorial cause "a new influence in the estimation of persons abroad," he celebrated the territorial announcement by erecting a large boardinghouse hotel near the Lower Levee. One admirer observed that Rice had already built other "warehouses and business blocks in his addition" and "donated lots to several churches and public institutions, besides considerable sums of money" in an effort to "divert trade and commerce from other points hither, and influence men of capital and energy to invest here largely." In these institutions, Rice expected to host land speculators, business investors, and new immigrants such as the Reverend Neill. Rice and John Irvine also gave away some of their Upper Levee lots to serve as sites for schools and a public park, cultivating an attractive community to lure ambitious young men and their families. Along the waterfall at St. Anthony, New York merchant Anson Northup erected a similar boardinghouse hotel for the New England lumbermen he planned to receive in short order. Celebrating their accomplishments and preparing for expansion, Minnesota's founding merchants and millers knew they had set the stage for townsite boosting, political hustling, and, hopefully, a territorial boom.[53]

As they explained the history that had made their meeting with Neill possible, Minnesota's territorial vanguard emphasized that they had not migrated to cultivate the soil but rather to profit from the American market economy. To realize these ambitions, they needed more people, more capital, and stronger ties to the wider nation.[54]

Together with other jubilant residents, the region's entrepreneurs thus welcomed Edward Neill and other opportunity-seekers into the fold. In the years that followed, from 1849 to 1855, the young missionary would witness profound changes in Minnesota. As new settlers joined those who had paved the way, the expanding Euro-American population began transforming the region from a fur-trading frontier zone into an urban-centered district for the expansion of American commerce, industry, and agriculture. As one of them later observed, "The period from 1840 to 1849, may be called the arcadian days of Minnesota. The primitive, easy-going simplicity of the people, isolated as they were, from the fashions, vices, and artificial life of the bustling world, was in strange contrast with the jostling throng of immigration that poured in a few months later, changing their steady-going habits and plain manners into a maddening, avaricious race for gold."[55]

1849–1855

Minnesota's Territorial Start-Up and the Race for Riches

DURING THE SPRING OF 1849, some eight hundred residents and squatters along the confluence of the Mississippi and Minnesota Rivers at St. Paul, St. Anthony, and the Fort Snelling reserve welcomed the season's opening of steamboat navigation to the newest U.S. territory. With it came the first of an anticipated multitude of new arrivals who promised to settle in the region, provide labor, bring capital, and emerge as customers for the articles Minnesota's merchants and millers planned to provide. During the territory's first season, white male representatives of earlier Atlantic migrations dominated the passenger lists of small steamboats carrying voyagers and cargo northward into Minnesota. These men included the usual assortment of mid-nineteenth-century travelers: fur traders, merchants, and millers joining family members and friends already established along the Mississippi River; journalists anxious to scoop the latest American territorial story; speculators touring the area for possible real estate investments; Free-Soilers and Whigs sent to work the region for their political parties; Catholics and Protestants on missions to convert Indians and others to their religious faiths; and a host of other restless spirits chancing a fresh start in the West.[1]

By 1855, the small enclaves had increased their numbers nearly six-fold on city-building schemes that transformed St. Paul, St. Anthony, and Minneapolis into focal points for permanent settlement and expansion into the trans-Mississippi West. During these early years, Minnesotans understood the need to focus on urban developments first—preeminently in buying and selling real estate but also, over time, in establishing credit services as well as in building roads, bridges, and businesses centered on the transfer of goods and services. Agitators for territorial status guided the transition while other men, anxious to support their efforts, soon joined them.[2]

Minnesota's earliest urban boosters had two primary objectives: first, to overcome competition for settlers from other new territories such as Oregon and California and, second, to build adequate urban infrastructures to lure capital and immigrants away from other urban contenders. In the meantime, they moved forward with commercial and manufacturing plans as they waited for the federal government to purchase millions of acres of Indian land. Following this acquisition, when residents would no longer need military personnel to protect them from perceived Indian threats, boosters also expected to acquire the Fort Snelling reserve for Minneapolis millers. All this done, they could then hope to link their roads and waterways to larger eastern and southern markets and to attract agriculturalists and railroads into their realm.[3]

Early residents in St. Paul and St. Anthony sought to surmount all these barriers quickly, for their more established neighbors in Wisconsin, a mere twenty miles away, might sweep over the border and devour the territory's timber, wheat, and other coveted prizes. Worse yet, wealthy investors in established centers like Chicago and New York might ogle the same treasures as part of the railroad empires they planned to build west to the Pacific Ocean. By the time the Mississippi River opened for navigation in 1855, however, residents of St. Paul–Minneapolis had made strides toward safeguarding themselves against these encroachments. Indeed, when the first steamboat arrived with passengers looking to inspect the region in 1849, these developments were already evident.[4]

Inspecting the Gateway Towns for Territorial Expansion

While territorial residents prepared St. Paul's Lower Levee for the arrival of the season's first steamboat during April 1849—building hotels to accommodate visitors and settlers, stocking shops to feed them, and marshaling real estate, furs, lumber, and other articles to sell them—several dozen men from points east and south readied themselves for the northwestern trek into the newly organized territory. As they wended their way toward Minnesota, these first arrivals absorbed important lessons about the unfolding market economy as practiced at the nation's margins. Sixty years had shown that American territorial expansionists—unimpeded by kings and nobles, encouraged by the federal government, and sustained by vast reaches of fertile soil—had a chance to become their own lords on the sparsely populated fringes of American society. They had seen that commercial agriculture and rural society interacted synergistically with industry and urban centers. Indeed, they had witnessed firsthand that in the business of turning the wilderness into commercial farmland it paid to construct towns that served, first, as jumping-off points for the interior and, later, as commercial hubs. Profitable hubs, however, required efficient transportation links to larger American and world markets. In the past, waterways had met this need, and the Ohio and Mississippi River systems had served entrepreneurs well. But by the time St. Paul emerged as a territorial gateway, Americans had begun to see the future in terms of railroads and the newly perfected electric telegraph, a trend that did not escape the notice of those anxious to explore opportunities in Minnesota.[5]

On April 9, 1849, the steamboat *Dr. Franklin* inaugurated the journey that many territorial immigrants would take to Minnesota's gateway at St. Paul. These travelers steamboated their way north along the Mississippi River from St. Louis, the burgeoning city that had long captured the river trade of the West. While the Great Lakes city of Chicago now threatened its dominance, having emerged as part of the North's emphasis on railroads and industrial expansion, in those early days St. Louis still represented Minnesota's connection to the outside world. St. Paulites, in particular, benefited from their position at the head of steamboat navigation for the Mississippi River system, while Minneapolitans would enjoy their close connection to Minnesota's territorial capital as they looked to northwestern expansion.

As the first group of Ohio River migrants (including young pastor Neill) waited for the northbound steamer to carry them to St. Paul, they saw the energies that young American and European immigrants had brought into the region during the 1840s. St. Louis, as the nexus for travel and trade to the north and west, exemplified this energy. According to one traveler, at the St. Louis pier they encountered "busy merchants and steamboat agents" along with "a string of drays, coaches with vociferous drivers, and people who had come to welcome an arriving or speed away a departing friend."[6]

Once onboard the *Franklin* at St. Louis, Neill finally met some of his fellow travelers—several of Minnesota's "ignoble" fur traders, merchants, and millers heading back with supplies for hungry settlers who had been deprived of many articles for several months. A throng of eager speculators seeking to make fortunes on rapid real estate turnovers also joined them. These traveling companions spent the next fourteen days following the Mississippi River's 800-mile corridor northward from St. Louis to the little-known village called St. Paul.

Severe weather, fires onboard the wooden vessels, and collisions with jutting trees, sandbars, unanticipated embankments, and other boats could affect the journey's length. Additional delaying factors often beset impatient passengers: during these early years, steamboats provided western settlers with their communication link to the outside world, and voyagers soon learned that "boats landed wherever there appeared to be the least excuse and even at times where there were none." When the *Franklin* anchored near obscure settlements, travelers noted that the "business between the Captain of the boat and the agent of the line, the landing and receiving of passengers, the loading and unloading of freight, caused delays of an hour or more." Moreover, many passengers took advantage of these stopovers, wading ashore and scrambling up embankments "to make a hurried visit to the business part of the towns," where they inquired into real estate prices and trade opportunities. Many seasoned travelers recognized these phenomena from earlier days, when canal-building schemes in New York, Ohio, and elsewhere inspired similar activities throughout the Old Northwest.[7]

After slogging northward for two weeks aboard the *Franklin*, crowded with passengers, merchandise, and livestock, at one of these stopovers Neill met an old friend, newspaperman James Madison Goodhue. Goodhue had trekked west after a brief stay in Chicago, traveling short distances by rail and then onboard coaches, barges, and anything else that could withstand the weight of the printing press he hauled. Determined to print the first story on the territorial announcement, Goodhue hailed the *Franklin* at Red Wing, Minnesota, and convinced the captain to hoist his press to the summit of the steamer's already top-heavy load for the final fifty-mile junket to St. Paul.[8]

Neill and his fellow passengers caught their first glimpse of St. Paul as the boat rounded a bend a half-mile downstream. The captain informed them that the scraggly village resting on a commanding bluff some hundred feet above the river's edge was St. Paul. The sight broke sharply with the heavily wooded terrain the travelers had beheld for many miles. Less than half a mile square, the village had fewer than four hundred residents, a few all-purpose shacks, and two sloping embankments that made steamboat landings possible. St. Paulites had named the first landing, at the north end, the Lower Levee. As the steamboat chugged toward that spot, the passengers formulated their impressions of this gateway to Minnesota, noticing "crowds of people lounging about waiting the arrival of the boat."[9]

The moment locals heard the boat's whistle, a hullabaloo commenced. As at other stops, the spring's first steamboat chime gave St. Paulites the "signal for a general rush to the landing" and "constituted the town's greatest holiday of the year." Neill now knew the routine. He disembarked with his friend Goodhue, not only to look around at the three or four buildings that composed "the business part of town" but also to catch his breath and take stock of the remote place now his home. Alas for Reverend Neill—as Harriet Bishop, St. Paul's pre-territorial schoolteacher, had warned the Presbyterian Church—the town's little flock needed a shepherd badly. Bishop and her co-religionists soon swept Neill away despite his inclination to reboard the *Franklin* and flee with it. By the time the *Franklin*'s captain trumpeted his imminent southern departure and mumbled that the next steamer should arrive in a week or two, Bishop had already ushered Neill into his boardinghouse hotel. The moment for escape had passed. As it turned out, Neill remained in St. Paul for the rest of his days.[10]

When Goodhue, St. Paul's first booster newspaperman, emerged from the steamboat into the small mob at the landing, he felt nothing of Neill's dismay at the absence of piety. Instead, he and others celebrated the village's transformation, a zeal Harriet Bishop acknowledged. Recognizing Goodhue and others as prospective residents, she likened both the returning merchants and the new arrivals to "steamboats, all determined to make [their] mark on the history of Minnesota."[11]

Two weeks later, when fur-trader-turned-territorial-champion Henry Sibley and his entourage returned to the "hoorays" of an even larger crowd, Goodhue reported that Minnesota's foremost promoter hardly recognized the place, what with the "rapidity of building and the miraculous resurrection of every [imaginable] domicile." Applauding the entrepreneurial ambitions of Minnesota's founders and new residents, Goodhue reported that "piles of lumber and building materials [from mills upriver] lie scattered everywhere in admirable confusion—stores, hotels, houses, are projected and built in a few days." He also announced, "California [and its gold are] forgotten, and the whole town is rife with the exciting spirit of advancement."[12]

Implicit in Goodhue's observations lay a dynamic reality: though an early arrival, he found entrepreneurial energies already hard at work, everywhere apparent in the very "piles of lumber and building materials" he found "admirable." Fired by visions of Minnesota's future, these groundbreakers embarked on construction activities that set the stage for speculation and quick real estate turnovers as well as for tributary industries: credit, legal, and commission networks to sustain the region's anticipated population expansion and economic development.

For prospective settlers, the first tour that circulated beyond the Lower Levee's "principal business district" got under way at the southern end of town, at St. Paul's Upper Levee. Fur-trading merchants and warehousemen Henry Rice and John Irvine had platted this townsite addition. Based on building, trade, and real estate turnovers, Rice had already emerged as

St. Paul's wealthiest merchant, a position that allowed him to buy Irvine's share in the addition and more inland property. At the Upper Levee, Rice's warehouse, Irvine's grocery, and several multipurpose shops had popped up to provide provisioning and reshipping services for increased passenger and freight traffic headed to interior locations, including Fort Snelling, Minneapolis, and St. Anthony.[13]

Several visitors trudged the muddy mile to the Upper Levee, where they encountered a small group of New England lumbering and milling entrepreneurs, mostly from Maine, who had traveled through the Great Lakes chain. Once on Minnesota soil, they inspected the hardwood forests hugging Lake Superior's shoreline in the northeast and the pinelands on the Mississippi River's eastern shores. At the river's source, Lake Itasca, they jumped aboard barges and sailed two hundred miles south to the cascading waterfall at St. Anthony–Minneapolis.

Built "for the encouragement" of American boosters and builders, Fort Snelling signaled the federal government's commitment to western expansion and the protection of Euro-Americans' property as well as a promise to remove barriers to expansion. These "barriers" included Native Americans like those depicted in the foreground of this painting by Henry Lewis.

Bending the ears of the prospective settlers, these lumbering New Englanders talked up the advantages of making early real estate purchases upstream at the Falls of St. Anthony. As part of the Fort Snelling reserve,
Minneapolis technically remained closed to nonmilitary personnel, but the
aspiring had seen that several squatters already prospered there. These illegal homesteaders provided timber and grain to John Stevens, the army
colonel who had founded the "water city" with his crude saw- and grist-
mills. Franklin Steele, the Pennsylvanian who in 1847 had first harnessed
the St. Anthony waterfall, told the lumbermen that he, Rice, and other
Free-Soilers planned to protect the preemption rights of the Minneapolis
squatters, allowing them to purchase the lands they had settled for $1.25 per
acre rather than making them bid competitively against the future speculators who would soon descend upon the region.[14]

Rough-and-tumble as St. Paul appeared, new arrivals who departed its
Upper Levee to survey the upriver villages at Minneapolis–St. Anthony
soon discovered they had left behind Minnesota's most sophisticated town.
Reaching the clearing at Fort Snelling's encampment, prospective settlers
came upon fewer than two hundred soldiers, a few lumbermen and Indian
agents, assorted Red River traders, and others who had traveled the ten-
mile road connecting St. Paul with the fort. Hiking upland some five or six
more miles, they eventually reached John Stevens's recently built house and
mills—their construction approved, Stevens bragged, by the government
for use by the army families stationed at the fort. When several under-
whelmed speculators declared that they had no interest in lands still barred
to investment, Stevens directed them to the Mississippi River embankment
that would lead them to eastern shorelands for sale at St. Anthony.[15]

As the tourists reached the impassable waterfall that divided Minneapolis from St. Anthony, they found both hamlets situated, like St. Paul,
on commanding limestone bluffs overlooking the Mississippi River. On the
western shore at Minneapolis, unoccupied prairie pastures stretched as far
as the eye could see. East across the river, St. Anthony's banks and bluffs
roared with activity. As the visitors traveled by barge across the eight hundred yards between Minneapolis and St. Anthony, they saw three small
islands—first Hennepin, then the larger Nicollet, and finally the minuscule
Boom—which parted the Mississippi's waters into channels harnessed to
screeching sawmills. On the eastern shore, they climbed the embankment
to the bluff above, where they discovered the St. Anthony settlement and
its population of perhaps two hundred.

Many early tourists departed after inspecting the primitive waterfall
town at St. Anthony, returning to St. Paul because—if nothing else—the
territorial capital initially offered better returns on their real estate invest-

ments. Yet some stayed, joining those who were damming the falls to power the hoped-for milling boom. Here again, another dynamic reality emerged. Having witnessed varying degrees of industrial prosperity among their friends and colleagues in New England, many of the men who ventured to Minneapolis–St. Anthony had long ago abandoned physiocratic doctrines that all wealth resides in land. Instead, they heartily agreed with the historical process that Adam Smith had observed in early industrial Great Britain, that "the most opulent nations generally excel all their neighbors in agriculture, as well as in manufactures; but they are eminently more distinguished by their superiority in the latter than in the former." This reality they planned to employ at St. Anthony and, later, at Minneapolis, once settlers gained legal title to their land claims.[16]

Faith that the future would see the manufacturing reality come to pass drove waterfall residents onward despite the fact that, for the moment, much of the nearby land lay closed to them. Minneapolis–St. Anthony's early entrepreneurs planned to mill all the lumber and grain needed by St. Paul, thereby ousting their competitors along the St. Croix River at Stillwater. Once booming on escalating local consumption, they planned to attract the capital and laborers needed to help send lumber and grain products elsewhere. Ideally, this capital and labor would aid them in building a diversified manufacturing sector, complete with tool-making shops, machine works, and integrated factories like those at water-powered cities in the Northeast. In time, they hoped, the business generated by steam-powered mills would also attract railroads into a manufacturing axis capable of capturing all the riches of the northwestern interior. In the interim, however, their ambitions centered on profiting from the supply and distribution services provided by their neighbors at the territorial gateway, St. Paul.[17]

Creating a Distribution Center at St. Paul

Galvanized by Smithian energies of their own—that "it is not from the benevolence of the butcher, the brewer, or the baker, that we expect our dinner, but from their regard to their own interest"—St. Paulites built their small trading outpost into a distribution center of some note during the territory's first season. Incorporated by the act of 1849, St. Paul emerged as the territory's capital and the seat for Ramsey County—named after Minnesota Territory's first governor, Pennsylvania's Alexander Ramsey, who arrived in May onboard the steamboat *Dr. Franklin No. 2*.[18]

Fur-trading entrepreneurs such as Norman Kittson and Henry Rice invested wisely on the $1.25 acres they had purchased at the Lower and Upper Levees and in townsite additions extending farther inland. As enthusiasm about territorial prospects escalated, they soon doubled and then tripled their original real estate investments. They sold parcels to speculators, transportation agents, arriving merchants, lawyers, government officials, and anyone else who wanted to participate in the territory's "speculative spirit" and "advancement." New property holders built stores, warehouses, real estate agencies, and boardinghouse hotels, selling off some parcels to others. Consequently, arriving and departing speculators and settlers made rapid returns on their investments. Their building projects also created for St. Paul's bustling business and residential centers a focus to lure those who hoped to profit from the Lower Levee's southern trade with St. Louis and the Upper Levee's south- and northwestern business beyond St. Paul.

By August 1849, St. Paulites had built "hotels enough and a good tin shop" as well as some eighteen retail outlets and twenty-five groceries. They also boasted of "several excellent ministers and one good school." Now, they required a few more things: better mail service (more than once every other week), more steamboats and stagecoaches bursting with immigrating capitalists and farmers, and government approval for roads and bridges to connect them with the West. According to one spokesman, "We go for a bridge most distinctly; and for a liberal appropriation of the Sioux [Dakota] lands when ceded, to furnish funds for building it on the most substantial plan."[19]

The first year's real estate transactions promised to bring St. Paul closer to its founders' vision. Property turnovers accompanied a tripling of St. Paul's Euro-American population, from some 400 in 1849 to 1,280, twice the total residents claimed by both St. Anthony and Stillwater, St. Paul's chief competitors for population and capital. By 1850, census takers recorded that St. Paul contained more than 21 percent of the entire territory's population of 6,077 Euro-Americans. The rest distributed themselves thinly across the vast expanse of land, from Stillwater to St. Anthony and as far west as the headwaters of the White Earth River in present-day North Dakota.[20]

Many of these new arrivals acquired choice real estate in St. Paul, including Connecticut's Lyman Dayton, a fur-trading merchant turned St. Paul realtor. Like Dayton, a number of these new arrivals had connections with the territory's earliest fur traders and merchants. Joining their family members and friends, they bolstered the vision first formed by fur traders Sibley, Rice, and Kittson and others who now included Governor Ramsey, journalist-booster Goodhue, preacher Neill, and Henry Rice's attorney brother Edmund. They, too, called for immigrants, but now, with "more than enough" merchants crowding the hotels, they focused on welcoming farmers into the region. "Every man in Minnesota who raises a cabbage, a bushel of potatoes, or any other produce for sale, has his labor protected by a high, natural tariff against the competition of farmers abroad," they implored, further emphasizing, *"there is no danger of glutting the market. Cultivate all the land you can."*[21]

Unfortunately for the early boosters who hoped to profit from hinterland cultivation, few farmers migrated to Minnesota between 1849 and 1851. Instead, more would-be town builders and political promoters appeared. Some of them had attained modest affluence before heading west, but, like before and since, many more entrepreneurial spirits had fled waning opportunities or business failures back home. Undeterred by past disappointments, they yearned to make a new beginning in a bustling place like St. Paul, open to migrants hungry for economic, political, and social mobility. Once sufficiently prosperous, some hoped to send for family members and friends to join them, while others expected to jump back into larger markets, either in La Crosse and Prairie du Chien, Wisconsin, the way other fur traders had done, or downriver in Dubuque and Davenport, Iowa, Galena, Illinois, St. Louis, Missouri, and larger merchandizing networks.[22]

These entrepreneurial migrants arrived from near and far. Initially, foreign-born immigrants came to St. Paul from interior fur-trading posts in the Old Northwest. Later they arrived from entrepôts girdling the settled United States and Canada from New Orleans to Savannah, New York, Boston, Halifax, and Montreal, and thence into young cities such as Cincinnati, St. Louis, Chicago, Milwaukee, and Toronto. Many migrants who eventually found their way to St. Paul already had connections with its merchants. Despite the influx, the young town needed more people, especially laborers to haul, store, and stock the merchandise arriving from below. Thus, during early settlement days, St. Paul's residents greeted anyone—regardless of connection, nationality, religious affiliation, or birthplace—who could employ his brawn or knowledge, adapt his skills, or use his innovative powers to nourish business in the territory.[23]

Creating a Milling District at St. Anthony

From 1849 to 1851, early alliances between miller Franklin Steele and young Maine millwright Ard Godfrey sparked a small but significant flurry of milling activity at the waterfall. During 1850, St. Anthony's population climbed to 660, making it Minnesota Territory's second-largest town, at long last allowing residents to boast that their population surpassed that of sawmilling rival Stillwater. Several New England lumbermen and merchants joined Steele at his mills, while others like New Yorker Anson

Northup, builder of the town's first boardinghouse hotel and other retail businesses, pursued other ventures. By 1851, waterfall residents had organized boom companies—the St. Anthony, Mississippi, and Rum River, for example—to capture northern timber, saw it, and then float the lumber downriver to larger Mississippi markets. In that same year, residents established the waterfall's first newspaper, the *St. Anthony Express,* an enterprise used to advertise the manufacturing potential at St. Anthony and Minneapolis. These activities enlarged Minneapolis's little enclave to perhaps fifty people by 1850. As other millers and merchants joined Steele in his efforts to unite the two aspiring milling centers by ferry, early partnerships quickly ensured common interests in and around the falls.[24]

Like manufacturers before and after them, millers at Minneapolis–St. Anthony faced the harsh reality that manufacturing start-ups take time to launch, require adequate labor, and demand plentiful, patient capital—three essentials in short supply in the territory. These challenges forced waterfall residents to draw on the resources of both capitalists in Boston and New York and friends and associates in St. Paul. Over time, waterfall millers grew to resent the influence of St. Paul's investors, whom they increasingly perceived as the architects of "the mighty incubus resting upon us, the most strenuous rivalry of a sister city [at St. Paul], which has spared no efforts to retard our progress, and to divert from us the streams of immigration and capital." For the moment, however, they had little choice but to endure these agonies: few investors outside the territory wanted to chance their capital on places still connected with lands closed to permanent settlement. Happily for waterfall residents, this situation was destined to change.[25]

Acquiring the Indian Lands, 1851–52

Among the many tasks that absorbed the attention of Minnesota's new territorial governor, "compensation" to towns not chosen as the territorial seat surfaced as the first order of business. A Whig from Harrisburg, Pennsylvania, Alexander Ramsey believed in political compromise between the parties. Self-styled as a humble descendant of Irish stock, "unaided but by his own genius and character, and the friends whom he gathered around him," Ramsey knew that economic profits and political support might flow from St. Anthony and Stillwater millers provided he bequeathed to them significant gifts.[26]

Thus, St. Anthony received the endowment for the University of Minnesota, complete with plentiful lands, from the territory's first legislature. Established on February 13, 1851, the university promised, among other things, to instruct young men in the practical arts of American legal, business, and agricultural pursuits. It would also serve as a place to train men and women for their roles as teachers of young citizens-in-the-making. Minnesota's territorial businessmen-politicians shared an affection for the idea that governments should nurture public education, particularly since earlier urban-industrial developments in Britain and the American Northeast had shown the prudence of such a course. Thus, Steele, Ramsey, Rice, and Sibley invested in the project, and the Minnesota legislature vowed to open the university's doors to the men and women of the territory the moment funds permitted the erection of an elegant new building. For its part, Stillwater acquired dubious distinction as the center of the territory's soon flourishing prison population. Beyond these two places, however, no other village population warranted any recompense, and so they got none, save the promise of a county seat once they too gathered enough settlers to bolster further expansion.[27]

Having completed the business of compensating St. Anthony and Stillwater for their political losses, Governor Ramsey turned to a more pressing matter: removal of the Dakota and Ojibwe Indians then occupying 85 percent of the territory's land. In cooperation with the commissioner of the Indian Department in Washington, DC, Ramsey hoped to negotiate treaties so that Euro-Americans could begin to profit from the region's natural resources, particularly wheat-growing lands in the trans-Mississippi West. Ramsey and other northeastern migrants had seen Rochester, New York, ascend rapidly by harnessing its water power for flour manufacturing: they hoped to imitate that success at St. Anthony and Minneapolis.[28]

To make real his visions of Minnesota's commercial and manufacturing greatness, Governor Ramsey soon effected the "speedy removal" of the Indians who stood in the way of white settlement. His actions reflected the all-important partnership the federal government had launched with businessmen and settlers to promote American industrial expansion. In 1851, St. Paul booster Goodhue articulated both the twenty-year policy guiding American Indian removals and the escalating "impatience" he witnessed among those who waited for consummation of the land acquisitions. Writing from his newspaper office at the Lower Levee, Goodhue announced, "Our population is pressing hard upon the Indian possessions. Saint Paul, increasing in buildings, in business, and in population with magic rapidity, looks earnestly across the river for the unceded [Indian] lands." Reporting that "the wigwam is in sight of our office—beholding our progress with amazement," he also proclaimed, "the welfare of the Indians requires their speedy removal from a neighborhood that makes them daily more dependent, and in which they learn the vices but attain none of the virtues of civilized life." His latter pronouncement resonated with arguments used elsewhere to justify removals so Euro-Americans could get on with the business of rapid expansion.[29]

During the summer of 1851, accompanied by Luke Lea, commissioner of the federal Indian Department, Governor Ramsey steamed up the Minnesota River some one hundred miles to negotiate the Treaty of Traverse des Sioux. With the Indian Removal Act in place since 1830, the governor had precedents to guide the negotiations; he also benefited from the "hearty cooperation and assistance" of traders who had long-established relationships with Minnesota's Indian leaders. That hearty cooperation soon gave Ramsey "unbounded influence" over the treaty arrangements. He completed the first, for territory in northwestern Minnesota, on July 23, 1851. Ramsey negotiated a sum of $1.665 million, with $1.3 million of that held in trust by the U.S. government, on fifty annual payments plus five percent interest to commence on July 1, 1852. On August 5, 1851, he concluded a similar treaty for lands in southwestern Minnesota. For these, the government promised to pay $1.4 million, with $1.2 million of that amount held in trust to defray the expenses of moving the Dakota to new Indian territory. When he tallied it up, Ramsey had purchased 45 million of Minnesota's 53.5 million acres for a little more than $3 million (less than seventy cents an acre). As part of Minnesota's investment portfolio, he soon deposited that money in a New York bank. In exchange, the region's Native Americans received swamps and other lands deemed worthless for American agri-business. The treaties moved the Dakota from the Mississippi's shores to lands south of the Minnesota River, some thirty miles distant from Fort Snelling. The Ojibwe would move later, once the government made provisions for an Indian reservation on the territory's northwestern fringe.[30]

After vigorous celebration with his friends in the territorial capital, Ramsey bustled off to Washington, DC, to obtain the treaty's final signatures from Millard Fillmore, inaugurated as president in July 1850 following Zachary Taylor's death. Rejoicing that the "Indians' days [in Minnesota] are numbered," residents in St. Paul and St. Anthony–Minneapolis spent the winter and spring planning for the coming season's events and for the flow of immigrants and capital they expected to arrive at spring thaw. They put forth their revised wish list, including "a good road, capital, men, industry, [and] large hotels," for indeed, local boosters exclaimed, "The Almighty never yet opened a scheme of human enterprises and speculations as grand as that of which St. Paul is this moment the center."[31]

The impending removal of the Indian obstacle to expansion also released speculators, developers, and other St. Paulites to increase pressure on property holders still indifferent to rapid development. These included the traditional French-Canadian fur traders and trappers who had not joined in St. Paul's real estate and land development schemes. With treaty signatures confirmed, many old residents wanted to leave anyway, to remove themselves to a place upriver where they could continue to enjoy their chosen lifestyle: the Indian trade, trapping and fishing, and kin-centered agricultural community building. In short order, many French-Canadians sold their properties to St. Paul realtors and quit the place altogether. Very soon, others from the settled United States and Canada, and from Ireland and elsewhere in war-ravaged Europe, took their places.[32]

Now, with fur trader Sibley representing Minnesotans in Congress, squatters in Minneapolis agitated for another sort of removal: that of military personnel occupying the 35,000-acre Fort Snelling reserve. Although the decision conflicted with his own ambitions for Mendota, the Mississippi-Minnesota River fur-trading hub he continued to maintain, Sibley complied with the Minneapolitans' wishes. During the 1852 congressional session, he convinced the federal government to pass a bill that sliced 26,000 acres from the Fort Snelling reserve, leaving just 9,000 acres for military purposes. The act contained no preemption clause; however, with the larger Preemption Act established for a decade, Congress authorized the immediate survey and sale of the reserve lands at public auction. Passage of the act also gave Henry Rice an opportunity to enter the political stage as the advocate for settlers in the trans-Mississippi West. Rice joined St. Anthony's Steele and others in the fight to secure preemption for the multiplying number of squatters now residing in Minneapolis. At the same time, ever-vigilant in their promises to those who would gather there, territorial legislators designated Minneapolis the seat of newly created Hennepin County, complete with a land-sale office quickly visited by local preemptors, business-oriented Free-Soilers, and other westward-looking investors.[33]

By the time northern rivers opened to steamboat navigation in the spring of 1852, these small but significant population removals and vast and decidedly vital land acquisitions increased interest in Minnesota Territory significantly, evidenced by escalating immigration into St. Paul, St. Anthony, and Minneapolis in the years that followed. Some newcomers came to cut timber or to clear the acreage now available for farming, but most came to profit from in-town ventures, including speculation in St. Paul's rapidly developing real estate market. In subsidiary businesses, some hoped to join the service-oriented economy, providing banking, legal, provisioning, and transportation services to new speculators, investors, and immigrants. Some sought to plunge into milling activities at the waterfall. Still others planned to purchase cheap townsites in the open country, where waterways would readily link them to St. Paul and Minneapolis–St. Anthony.[34]

So powerfully did these hopes attract speculators and settlers that Minnesota's land offices had already issued nearly eighty thousand letters patent in 1851. Public land titles with warrants (certificates of purchase) rose from minuscule numbers in 1849 to 2.5 million acres. Booster literature emanating from St. Paul–Minneapolis informed potential investors and immigrants that Minnesota would "make not less than 12,000,000 acres of public lands available on the market by 1852." Unhappily for newspaperman Goodhue, he never saw this ballyhoo culminate in his adopted home. The cholera epidemic that swept over the Midwest in 1850 carried him away with it in 1852. By the time he died, however, he and his fellow Minnesotans had paved the way for American Manifest Destiny "to overspread and to possess" another region—through persuasion and negotiation when possible, by force when not.[35]

Peopling the Newly Acquired
Indian Territory via the Transportation Boom

With Indian land cessions negotiated, Minnesotans soon profited from the national economic and transportation boom that transformed the northeastern United States between 1850 and 1855. As increasing numbers of investors and immigrants headed west to Minnesota Territory, some of them now came at least some distance by railroad, on lines expanding from 9,000 miles in 1850 to more than 31,000 in 1860 (with most construction preceding 1856). Transportation entrepreneurs—anxious to profit from the new technology, the liberal state charters, and the promise of federal land grants in the same ways earlier canal builders had—launched the railroad-building boom.[36]

Between 1852 and 1855, Americans linked most of the United States north of the Ohio River and east and south of Chicago, dramatically lowering the costs associated with rail travel and increasing the profits of those who carried agricultural products out of the hinterland and manufactured products into it. By 1853, the year Congress authorized the transcontinental railway survey, Baltimore and Ohio trains reached the Ohio River system. During 1854, east coast lines ran from Chicago to Rock Island, Illinois, thereby completing the first railroad connection to the Mississippi River and facilitating increased expansion beyond it. As more immigrants and tourists from the New England and Middle Atlantic states boarded railroads heading west along these routes, the once-dominant National Road, canal systems, and Great Lakes chain slipped into a protracted period of decline, as did Mississippi River traffic south of St. Louis.[37]

By the 1850s, westward-pushing railroads allowed immigrants to board at Rock Island any number of Mississippi steamers bound for St. Paul—the 350-mile trip reducing their travel time on the river to a few days compared to more than two weeks from St. Louis. Some immigrants continued south to St. Louis and the Missouri River connection to Oregon Territory, while others linked up with Mississippi River travelers heading north. These immigrants swapped stories about the roads, waterways, and railroad tracks they had journeyed on from settled regions into the wilds of the Upper Mississippi Valley. Railroad travelers told riverboat passengers about the speed with which they had traveled, if somewhat less comfortably than their riverine counterparts. Steamboat travelers told railroad passengers about professional gamblers who swarmed the riverboats between New Orleans and St. Louis, snatching away immigrants' limited cash savings and molesting them at every port. Thus, although Southerners introduced the phrase "Cotton Is King" in 1855, many of these northbound travelers had decided against settling in the slave-holding South, what with its riverboat gamblers, its trade limited to one cash crop, its labor competition from slaves, and its few railroads. Instead, they had determined to trek into the free territories and states of the north and southwest. In these places railroad connections promised to provide opportunities for faster and safer passage into economic independence, political participation, social mobility, and even great wealth for whites who participated in commercial agriculture and the construction of urban enclaves.[38]

Along with the expanding railroad network, increased immigration from both the Americas and Europe set the stage for the peopling of Minnesota. As European immigrants joined those swelling the young nation through natural increase, the U.S. population expanded from 23 million in 1850 to nearly 31.5 million a decade later. During 1854 alone, 400,000 immigrants arrived in the United States. Continuing turmoil in the British Empire and Europe provided the context for this rapid out-migration, while reduced fares from Liverpool to America—dropping from twenty dollars per passenger in 1850 to as low as ten dollars during 1854—lured many onto Atlantic steamers bound for the United States and Canada.[39]

During the 1850s, restless spirits migrated from near and far, but nowhere more so than from famine-ridden Ireland and politically turbulent northern Europe, particularly Prussia. Barraged by political unrest, religious persecution, and agricultural and skilled craft dislocations, the vast majority who arrived during the 1850s came not from Protestant enclaves but rather—for the first time in American history—in massive waves from Catholic Ireland, as well as from various Protestant, Catholic, and Jewish communities in German-speaking Europe. By 1854, anti-Catholicism, deeply embedded in the American experience, found a voice in the Know-

Nothing Party, which rose to national prominence as the Whigs collapsed and the Democrats turned their attention to the Southern cause. The movement from anti-Catholicism to anti-Semitism required no great leap in the northern United States. New immigrants, choosing like many before them to leave their beleaguered homes for America's apparent opportunities, soon found themselves confronting additional struggles on this new continent, struggles that threatened to engulf them in hostility. Many Europeans had destinations in mind when they arrived—principally the eastern seaboard and the settled Midwest, where they met friends and family members who had traveled on earlier ships. But some Catholics and Jews searched for homes beyond established communities, in places that would welcome them no matter their faith. Increasingly they followed the railroads, chasing after the many American and Canadian immigrants who had answered the call of John B. L. Soule's 1851 editorial in the Terre Haute, Indiana, *Express*, "Go West, young man, go West"—particularly after Horace Greeley, the famed New York *Tribune* editor, circulated the words with the added incentive, "and grow up with the country."[40]

Among the many millions of native- and foreign-born migrants who swarmed over the country between 1852 and 1855, enough men, women, and children joined travelers to Minnesota to make an enduring imprint. Moreover, the territory's established residents certainly welcomed these immigrants—for their labor, their capital, and whatever else they could provide—no matter their nationality, religious bent, or birthplace, at least initially.[41]

St. Paul's commercial hub pulsed with new energy as steamboat arrivals at the Lower Levee climbed from 119 in 1851 to 455 in 1854. Minnesota's population spiraled from 6,077 in 1850 to nearly 25,000 at the end of 1854. Figures for St. Paul leapt from 1,280 to more than 3,000, its inhabitants an increasingly diverse collection of North Americans, Irish, Germans, and assorted other immigrants from the British Isles and northern and central Europe. As New Englanders wended their way into the same westward-pushing railroad systems, they too swelled Minnesota's population. Some fanned out into the timberlands; others beat a path from St. Paul to the waterfall, increasing St. Anthony's population from 660 to 1,000. Anticipating future preemptions, they also enlarged Minneapolis's population from 50 to 300.[42]

As St. Paul's missionary schoolteacher Harriet Bishop watched these new immigrants come in greater waves, she gushed over their arrival, arguing that they had traveled "not from the fossilized haunts of old fogyism, but from the swiftest blood of the nations." Additionally, once arrived, they joined other community members in business ventures, potluck dinners, reading circles, chapel- and synagogue-raising projects, and political debates. They undertook the risks associated with these little-known places because they hoped to profit from their endeavors, staking claims for neither Know-Nothings nor Southern Democrats but rather for future parties that promised to bolster their dreams.[43]

Amelia Ullman's experience illustrates both the kinds of trials immigrants endured and the opportunities some found in Minnesota during this early period of expansion. A Jewish Bavarian, Ullman arrived in New Orleans during 1852 by way of Liverpool, England. The eighteen-year-old immigrated with her new husband, French-born Joseph, an aspiring twenty-five-year-old Jewish merchant. They had experienced religious persecution in Europe, had witnessed the huddled masses in industrial England, and now carried little more than a bundle of hopes for a better life. Prior to their wedding, Joseph had asked Amelia about her dowry, hoping that her father could subsidize their passage to America. Amelia had responded, "I know not how much he has; but I do know that I shall take nothing from him as he has a large family to care for." She added, "In America, though, any one who will work and be economical can earn money for themselves. We are young and can honestly earn a competence, so I shall go with you to the end of the world." Over the next three years, Ullman discovered just how far the world stretched.[44]

Once on American soil, the Ullmans searched for opportunities along the Mississippi River, a path many Jewish Bavarians followed. They first trekked from New Orleans to St. Louis, where they found a "graveled river bank piled high with a mass of merchandise; bales of cotton, hogsheads of sugar and molasses, stacks of wood and great stores to be transported to the military posts and new settlements up the Mississippi and Missouri rivers." There, Joseph joined a group of fur traders heading north. By 1855, he and another young Jewish Bavarian, Isadore Rose, had established a store at St. Paul. On a hope and a prayer, Joseph sent for Amelia.[45]

Amelia Ullman traveled from St. Louis to St. Paul with the few articles that she and Joseph had acquired, including a newborn baby and a recently arrived younger sister. With no male friends or older family members to accompany her upriver, Ullman reported that the journey "was neither an easy task nor a pleasant experience [even] to a young woman familiar with American life, and was specially trying to me, new to the land and customs." Of St. Paul, she knew nothing more than its name, noting that she had to go into several St. Louis shops "before [she] found a person who could inform [her] in what State or Territory it was situated." Soon enough, Ullman and her charges boarded a small steamer filled with twenty other passengers, the mails, and a full cargo of freight and livestock, and she found herself coasting by a relatively "barren wilderness." On that northern voyage, she questioned the prudence of her pledge to follow Joseph to the end of the world, for surely he had found it. When at last she debarked at St. Paul, however, the town residents took to Ullman immediately. Soon she knew why: "New residents were much sought for the struggling new towns, and any one who came with the intention of becoming a settler was sure of a hearty welcome."[46]

Embraced by her new community, Ullman later recalled, "we were not many, and a community of interests made us all well acquainted." Among other impressions, she described the landing as "most animated through the anxiety of each merchant to be the first to have his goods ready for sale, for people bought with avidity and upon the first opportunity what they had been deprived for months past." She also remembered that the transfer of real estate "became frequent" and that "values rapidly increased" beyond the means of some new settlers, while another pioneer observed, more in sorrow than anger, "You new comers have raised the prices of things so that what we used to get for ten cents now costs a quarter." On these inflated prices, Ullman had to spend her "quarters" and first several months as a permanent boarder at one of the town's hotels, until Joseph moved the whole family into a room above his store.[47]

This view by S. Holmes Andrews shows St. Paul before Euro-Americans completed the bridge that soon connected St. Paul with West St. Paul via "Harriet [Bishop's] Island," named for St. Paul's first permanent, Protestant missionary-schoolteacher.

At her first lodging, Ullman shared her table with Governor Ramsey's sister; an ambitious Pennsylvania merchant named Charles Elfelt; many young steamboat captains, speculators, retailers, and overland express agents; and other questing immigrants. The usual breakfast and supper at the American House Hotel "consisted of bacon, potatoes, biscuits, and tea," Ullman remembered, "with soup and pie, made from dried fruit, the additions that distinguished dinner, the mid-day meal, from the other two." Refrigerated shipping lay in the future despite the plethora of winter ice, and long voyages from St. Louis spoiled much of the food bound for Minnesota's young towns. Writing home, Connecticut's Sarah Fuller complained, "I had *two or three peaches* the other day, the first I have ever seen in St. Paul. Brought from below—they tasted very well here, but would not have tasted well at home."[48]

Despite these difficulties, customers yearning for a slice of beef, a juicy peach, and a dollop of unspoiled butter to distinguish the potatoes and biscuits of one meal from another created a market that supported many business start-ups. Once fed, consumers demanded more shoes, clothes, furniture, livery stables, steamers, and mail, to name but a few goods and services, thereby buttressing their communities' entrepreneurial drive for expansion.

After each long winter isolation, steamboats finally brought the scarce goods that residents craved. They also carried business and social contacts to the many men, women, and children who gathered along the landings, eagerly awaiting their arrival. Huddled with others at the Lower Levee, Ullman noted that "we knew not only most of the inhabitants and every building by name" but also what those inhabitants and buildings meant to St. Paul's future. Bankers loaned money and provided credit, steamboat captains brought goods, and retailers stocked them. Each steamer also delivered family members, friends, strangers, and capital. All promised to give Minnesota's new towns the resources required to build schools, religious meeting places, and city government offices for future security and expansion.[49]

As summer passed into fall, women and children pitched in at the landing, stocking homes and stores for the winter months ahead. They wrote about the ways in which they helped men inventory and distribute various staples: the "flour in barrels from mills at Prairie du Chien; the crackers from St. Louis; the bags of potatoes from the South; and the [longed-for] butter jars from Ohio." They undertook these tasks as community ventures, so that people like Mr. Coulter, for example, could busy himself "for several weeks, killing cattle and packaging away the beef in salt and sawdust for consumption during the winter." All residents worked, at least part of the time, in roles that were not gender specific, assisting with another round of "laying up" the community's summer stocks. Then, as supplies ran out and Coulter's meat passed the point of no return, the cycle recommenced. When husbands headed for St. Louis or the East—on foot, by horseback, and via stagecoach—during February and March, women tended the stores. Some of these women, unable to endure winter isolation, traveled with their husbands, as Amelia Ullman did. But whether they went or waited, everyone in the community saw seasonal business reopen with the thaw's first steamer, among its cargo the returning traders and new immigrants.[50]

American Fur's former employees, including St. Paulites Henry Rice and Lyman Dayton, provided the financial services that helped early residents through the first few winters. They sold goods on credit, made small loans for purchases of land and building materials, and introduced newcomers into business, political, and social networks. With the signing of the Treaty of Traverse des Sioux, however, new immigration surpassed their abilities (and desires) to continue offering these services. Sustained demand for more capital and credit soon provided new opportunities for those looking to enter the sphere of territorial banking.[51]

Linking St. Paul's Commercial Emporium
with the Wider Market

In the wake of Indian removals, two former American Fur Company partners decided to open a banking house at St. Paul. The first of the two, Charles Borup, a forty-one-year-old Danish-born merchant, had arrived in St. Paul in 1849, bringing with him his sixteen-year-old nephew, George Oakes. During 1851, Borup and his young clerk advanced bills of exchange, the lifeblood of commerce in the cash-poor, ante-bellum United States. Like other backcountry merchants, Borup saw further opportunities to prosper in emerging centers like St. Paul. By 1852, Borup induced his brother-in-law and George's father, Charles H. Oakes, also a former American Fur partner, to join them. Arriving that year from Vermont, the senior Oakes advertised money to lend, and by 1853 Borup and Oakes opened a bank. Once partnered in a limited liability company, they campaigned to increase Minnesota's supply of credit, a strategy that promised to line their pockets and create stability for their friends in St. Paul. During their first operational year, Borup and Oakes enjoyed a virtual monopoly on private banking in the territory, but soon their profits lured more people into competitive banking. Three other loan office partnerships formed in St. Paul during the winter of 1853–54, and by November 1854 five new credit and loan offices opened for business.[52]

St. Paul's credit suppliers located themselves near real estate offices and other service businesses that sprang up to support the speculative market at and near the Lower Levee. Private banking underpinned construction and speculation by the real estate, legal, insurance, and building-trade operators entering into business start-ups at both the Lower and Upper Levees.[53]

Banks fueled more than speculation; they financed the expanded trade engendered by St. Paul's development. Some bankers concentrated on rapid developments, speculating in hinterland properties and other high-risk ventures. Others, with an eye toward long-term, lower-risk investments, parceled out most of their funds to residents anxious to build retail shops, homes, schools, churches, and larger transportation and communication businesses that promised to lower the costs and anxieties associated with life in the wilds of Minnesota. No matter the strategy, early bankers, investors, and speculators helped create a commercial nexus that pulled more immigrants to St. Paul and the larger region. Promoting the expansion of St. Paul, St. Anthony, and Minneapolis, many new territorial bankers hoped these loans would help locals participate more fully in the lucrative steamboating trade that would link them to railroads at Rock Island and to the city of St. Louis. For example, Canada's Alexander Cathcart and Pennsylvania's Charles Elfelt borrowed money from established banks to open all-purpose retail houses in St. Paul. These stores soon connected the town's consumers with suppliers at downriver points in Iowa, Illinois, and Missouri. As they expanded their networks, Cathcart and Elfelt emerged as the principal purveyors of dry goods and groceries, including fancier items such as coffee, cloth, ink, pepper, sugar, and tea. Seeing their success, a swarm of dry goods competitors descended upon St. Paul.[54]

As the years passed, continuing strong demand for consumer goods led new entrepreneurs away from laboring for others and into bids for economic independence. Borrowing money from Borup, Oakes, and others, neophyte businessmen opened retail stores, commission houses, and overland express agencies at St. Paul. As young merchants prospered and tested the market, they found increasing demand that garnered larger profits on whatever scarce goods they procured from the world beyond, including the vegetables ("mostly spoiled on arrival") and the butter and salted pork ("dubious in color") that served early immigrants' basic dietary needs.[55]

Sustained demand inspired residents to agitate for government appropriations for communication and transportation improvements throughout the territory. Requests ranged from more post office facilities and better service to road-building projects that extended from St. Paul overland to Fort Snelling and thence into the trans-Mississippi West. Once realized, those improvements shortened the link between consumers in Minnesota's hinterland and their emerging suppliers in St. Paul. With connections expanding nationwide, these merchants could now procure goods more cheaply, not only from downriver points in St. Louis but also elsewhere through railroad networks established at Rock Island. Each new transportation link with the South and East diverted agricultural immigrants and skilled workers away from other booster regions, leading them to the potentially lucrative resource hinterland where Minnesota's urban residents hoped to develop further supply networks for even more expansion.

Constructing an Overland Express Network into the Trans-Mississippi West

Few entrepreneurs profited more from St. Paul's new linkages with hinterland consumers and eastern and southern suppliers than overland express agents who serviced the farmers and settlers fanning out on the prairies. Among those who hoped to prosper from this trade, Vermont's James C. Burbank emerged as the most successful. Prior to his arrival in St. Paul at age twenty-seven, Burbank had failed in several ventures, including logging. By the time he reached Minnesota in 1850, these failures had taught him valuable lessons about the market economy, particularly the virtue of government contracting as a viable strategy to start and expand a business. He had also absorbed the importance of strict cost accounting, of long-term investment, and of maintaining a healthy cash flow. At St. Paul, Burbank sought opportunities requiring little in the way of fixed costs for such things as buildings and stock.[56]

Several fur traders at St. Paul's levees, particularly Norman Kittson, introduced Burbank to the financially promising field of overland express. Burbank soon discovered that profits flowed from two strategies: doing business on a cash-only basis and exploiting slow but steady expansion where cultivated lands and existing settlements justified the trip, first in Wisconsin, Illinois, and Iowa and later in Minnesota. His operation would initially provide mail, passenger, and freight service between St. Paul and Galena, Illinois, the latter selected for its status as the most prosperous river city north of St. Louis at the time. Although other young entrepreneurs helped to fuel expansion into the interior, Burbank's decision to attach himself to experienced entrepreneurs—and thus to benefit from their knowledge about government contracting in remote Minnesota—confirmed his place among the region's emerging business elite.

Burbank started his business—the "North-Western Express Company"—as a "pioneer messenger" charged with carrying a mail contract for the territorial government. He departed St. Paul on September 21, 1851, for his first overland trip—toward the east, not the west—traveling an old mail route by way of Hudson, Black River Falls, and Prairie du Chien, Wisconsin, and thence southward to Galena. His first cargo consisted of one mailbag, and, according to witnesses, "the amount of express freight entrusted to him he carried in his pocket." Many believed North-Western would fail, and soon, but Burbank's government contract allowed him to adopt a cash-only policy that served him well as immigrants filtered into Minnesota.[57]

From 1852 to 1854, as North-Western Express services moved steadily southward into Iowa and Illinois and farther inland from the Mississippi River, Burbank's business increased rapidly. He headquartered his operation in St. Paul, then opened an outlet in St. Anthony for further expansion. Carrying St. Paul's merchandise as well as the waterfall's lumber and flour products westward into the interior, he soon enjoyed the economies of scale inherent in larger undertakings. During March 1854, escalating profits allowed him to lease a wharf boat to move passenger and freight traffic along Minnesota's interior waterways. Increased income from his well-established and lucrative cash-only business permitted further expansion—into grocery, forwarding, and commission services. At the same time, he met increasing demand from immigrant travelers between Galena and St. Paul by providing cheaper and safer, albeit bumpier passages than those offered on the Mississippi River. The land route enabled immigrants to retain some of their small savings for their arrival in St. Paul, and by the time river navigation opened in 1855 Burbank had emerged as the region's most trusted and reliable overland express agent. In the meantime, as he and fellow transportation agents built their networks, other entrepreneurs, particularly in St. Anthony, constructed roads and bridges across the Mississippi River, seeking to connect their milling ambitions with the developing hinterland population.[58]

Bridging the Gap Between St. Anthony and Minneapolis

Combined with the benefits of St. Paul's expanding distribution center and overland transportation systems, Indian land acquisitions in the trans-Mississippi West transformed St. Anthony and Minneapolis. While Minnesota's few agricultural settlers cleared land and planted crops, lumbering continued to attract entrepreneurs to the falls. One of these was Maine millwright Ard Godfrey, who, after signing various memorandums of agreement with Franklin Steele between 1849 and 1852, made St. Anthony his permanent home. There he helped Steele raise the small fortune ($30,000) required to build the first real commercial sawmills at the falls. By 1854, their joint venture's success allowed Steele and Godfrey to sell selected interests at the falls to other entrepreneurs from near and far, freeing up some of their profits for heavy speculation in real estate and myriad investments in ferry boats and bridge-building enterprises at St. Anthony–Minneapolis.[59]

As several of St. Anthony's millers invested in projects at and near the falls, small-scale developments commenced across the river, where preemptors waited for Henry Rice and Franklin Steele to aid them in safeguarding their claims. Like Steele and others in St. Anthony, Minneapolis millers borrowed money from friends, from northeastern investors, and, increasingly, from St. Paul bankers such as Borup and Oakes. These funds allowed them to purchase rudimentary machinery for small-scale industrial developments. Together with friends in St. Anthony and St. Paul, the millers also launched an ambitious bridge-building enterprise that would finally connect the two waterfall manufacturing hubs, an essential step in their quest for freedom from the "mighty incubus" at St. Paul.[60]

In 1852, the territorial legislature granted a charter for the Mississippi River Bridge Company, which would construct and oversee a connection between St. Anthony and Minneapolis. Several waterfall boosters undertook the task, among them former Fort Snelling employees Franklin Steele and John Stevens and St. Paul merchant Henry Rice. Between 1854 and early 1855, entrepreneurs at St. Anthony and Minneapolis constructed the first wire suspension bridge across the Mississippi River, capitalized in large measure by the bridge company's own investment returns. On January 23, 1855, in the dead of winter, they completed the single-arch toll bridge and opened it for traffic, prompting a large-scale celebration at the waterfall.[61]

Braced by southern comfort procured from whiskey shops in St. Louis, draped in furs purchased in St. Paul, and shod with mukluks manufactured locally, residents left St. Anthony's St. Charles Hotel and pranced over the new bridge, whooping, coughing, and swigging their way into Minneapolis. Two months later, Congress approved the Preemption Act for squatters on Minnesota's former Indian lands. Moreover, by settling the Ojibwe Indians on a reservation at the northwestern fringe of the territory along the Blue Earth River, the federal government authorized the early dismantling of Fort Snelling. With these important steps accomplished, the territorial legislature approved the 1855 act that incorporated the City of St. Anthony. Bestowing their gratitude upon Godfrey for the roles he had played in the waterfall's development and the successful preemption claims, residents elected the millwright as St. Anthony's first mayor. Two decades would pass before St. Anthony and Minneapolis merged permanently, but 1855 marked the first tangible connection between them, and for waterfall residents, the suspension bridge celebration symbolized commitment enough.[62]

Gazing into the Expansionist Future

Throughout the developing and still largely isolated West, business creators and town builders faced enormous risks during the early 1850s. No place revealed this truth more starkly than the territory along the northern reach of the Mississippi River, where winter ice paralyzed, spring floods obstructed, and summer droughts impeded travel and trade for months each year. Moreover, as St. Paul–Minneapolis's young enthusiasts transformed their small, multipurpose shops and specialized businesses into larger undertakings over time, the volume of business taxed their traditional structures. Many firms in fact collapsed, ruining their proprietors. Some failures quit the place, taking up residence farther north and west or returning whence they had come.[63]

Despite the many hardships Minnesota's urban enthusiasts endured, a sufficient number of their businesses survived, inspiring many residents to boast that they had in part achieved the advancement Minnesota's founders

Signifying the early connection between St. Anthony and Minneapolis, the bridge built across the waterfall in 1855 provided ample reason for milling town residents to celebrate. This painting by Ferdinand Reichardt offers a picturesque view of the wilderness outposts early in their development into a manufacturing center.

envisioned. As observant migrants connected themselves with wider American developments, they noticed that entrepreneurs and government officials who participated in the expansion of immigration, capital, industry, and transportation prospered. Conversely, those who eschewed these developments floundered. Indeed, as the market economy swept over Minnesota during the territorial start-up, it created a permanent business-oriented landscape that thoroughly engulfed the region, so much so that one minister traveling into the hinterland declared, "a man of practical, good sense knows there are possibilities and exigencies in Church work in which the priest or Bishop must be a man of affairs and wise in the intricacies of business, or he will be sure to fail." Further, with most of the region's migrants focused on real estate rather than on timber cutting and soil cultivation, population expansion created a sustained demand for men of practical affairs. The surging needs for capital, goods, and transportation generated incomes for those who provided the services and products required.[64]

By the time river navigation opened in 1855, Harriet Bishop's "human steamboats" had completely transformed St. Paul, St. Anthony–Minneapolis, and the territorial back country. They had attracted speculators and immigrants from the Americas and Europe who had augmented the territory's population an average of 55 percent annually between 1849 and 1854. Through cooperation, competition, and promotion, town dwellers in St. Paul–Minneapolis had also surpassed all nearby rivals in reaping the riches of Minnesota's Mississippi River trade.[65]

With this early prosperity and population increase, Minnesota's residents postulated that St. Paul and the territory stood a good chance of attracting railroads very soon. After all, they reasoned, waterways had built Chicago into a sizeable city that expanded rapidly after railroads arrived in 1848. By 1855, Chicago had two thousand miles of railroad track radiating outward in every direction, including the extension to the Mississippi River at Rock Island. Members of the Great Lake city's "smart set" had enormously increased their personal wealth and political clout by attracting railroads. Emerging as an east-west railroad hub and a large-scale commercial and manufacturing distribution center for the country north and west of it, Chicago could now challenge long-dominant St. Louis for the bounty of the northwestern interior.[66]

The 1854 railroad connection with the Mississippi River completed an important east-west linkage for the expanding Atlantic world economy. Cruising the river northward from Rock Island to St. Paul, one excursionist remarked that "the march [of the steam locomotive] has rendered Fort Snelling nearly useless" as an agency charged with protecting private property in the region. Continued immigration from Europe into the Americas also promised to solve the market economy's North American "labor problem"—its need for sustained numbers of workers to expand production and consumption.

That year, 1854, Minnesotans experienced another internationally significant event: representatives in British North America signed an all-important Canadian Reciprocity Treaty with the United States. Long protected as British colonists, Canadians had always refused to sign a free-trade agreement with the United States. In addition, as Americans began to build railroads during the 1840s, Canadians feared that their more aggressive neighbors to the south might attempt to annex them, especially when they considered their own population of 1.5 million compared to the United States' more than 17 million. With anti-annexationist sentiments running high in Montreal, powerful merchants there closed the border to free trade. In retaliation, Americans put up tariff walls of their own. But as Canadians struggled to realize their own dreams of urban-industrial expansion with less and less assistance from the British Empire, they increasingly looked to the south for support. The treaty promised to reopen the border for American investment in Canada, the Great Lakes to free trade, and American markets to Canadian agricultural products. For Euro-Americans in St. Paul–Minneapolis, it also placed international forests and Red River Valley soil within the grasp of entrepreneurs who perceived a sustained demand for the region's timber and wheat products.[67]

Understanding the implications of railroads, immigration, and free trade, Minnesota's urban boosters now believed that nothing could stand between them and the riches they coveted most. In particular, they sought "personal gain and self-aggrandizement" for the roles they planned to play in Minnesota's transition from traditional riparian dependence into railroad networks. Casting further out, they visualized statehood and the bigger business of connecting their emerging commercial and manufacturing centers with hinterland producers and consumers. Over the next six years, as Minnesota entered into its first large-scale economic boom, further expansion would test the entrepreneurial acuity of the men whose profit-oriented impulses had spurred the territory's early success.[68]

1855–1861

Territorial Expansion and
Minnesota's First Economic Bust

WITH TREATIES NEGOTIATED, lands open for settlement, bridges built over the Mississippi River, hinterland roads under construction, and profitable opportunities unfolding throughout St. Paul, St. Anthony, and Minneapolis during 1855, Minnesotans crested the wave of a national immigration, commercial, and manufacturing boom. Over the next several years, they also embarked on the bigger businesses of building railroads and applying for statehood, and they bankrupted themselves on the credit notes, liens, and railroad bonds they had used to fuel rapid expansion on the eve of the 1857 financial panic. Minnesotans' first humiliating experience with the market economy's tendency to inflate boom periods into large-scale busts forced them to confront the reality that their newly created state had outgrown the management abilities of many of its founders. Like their counterparts in the Old Northwest during the 1830s canal-building boom and bust, many Minnesotans overextended themselves into insolvency, particularly on speculative schemes that they had touted as evidence of success. But appearances deceive. As the economic depression overwhelmed Minnesotans between 1858 and 1861, many experienced the vagaries associated with city-building schemes that outran development of the region's potential natural resource economy.[1]

As the United States entered a dangerous new decade and the State of Minnesota lay in financial ruins, a few vigilant entrepreneurs managed to maintain their composure. Having successfully steered themselves through the transition from traditional fur-trading networks into the early phase of Minnesota's industrial economy, these businessmen emerged as the region's new urban elite. As the first entrepreneurial shake-out in the towns' short histories got under way, these men pulled power from some of the region's founders, many of whom now struggled to ward off foreclosure proceedings. In St. Paul, the successful included James Burbank, Norman Kittson, and newcomer William Davidson. In Minneapolis, William D. Washburn arrived to compete with, and then oust, St. Anthony's Franklin Steele. Their ascendancy commenced during 1855, as the nation's immigration and railroad boom moved west toward Minnesota.[2]

The National Immigration and Railroad Boom

As approximately 500,000 European immigrants annually joined those swelling the nation through natural increase, the U.S. population expanded from 23 million in 1850 to more than 31 million a decade later. Alert to the potential benefits associated with increased immigration from famine-ridden Ireland and revolution-ravaged northwestern Europe, the New York Immigration Commission leased Castle Garden during 1855. Located at the tip of Manhattan, Castle Garden became a reception center for arriving immigrants—and a bonanza for railroad, steamboat, land office, and other immigration agents seeking to profit from American territorial expansion. Although Castle Garden emerged as the most significant port for such agents, other reception areas soon surfaced along the Atlantic seaboard and throughout the interior. At every North American entrepôt, regional ambassadors set up shop to capture some of the restless souls searching for hospitable communities. Minnesota's young territorial government had no cash to spare for such endeavors, but steamboat captains, railroad companies, and other private citizens interested in Minnesota's future swiftly compensated for that deficiency. At the same time, family members and friends already settled in Minnesota came forward to help their eager kin, sending representatives to way stations, writing newspaper articles, and even convincing local capitalists to lend immigrants money for transportation into the wilds of Minnesota.[3]

With the assistance of transportation lines and various new immigration agencies, millions of North Americans and Europeans fanned out from the east and into the west. Some 135,000 of them chose Minnesota, increasing the young territory's population by 112 percent annually between 1855 and 1857. Drawn by the promise of land, trade, products, and cheap, reliable transportation, arriving immigrants expanded Minnesota's population from some 16,000 at the close of 1854 into more than 150,000 on the eve of statehood in 1857. During the same period, St. Paul's population increased from 4,000 to 11,000. With passage of the Preemption Act confirming investments in the trans-Mississippi West, St. Anthony's and Minneapolis's populations surged from approximately 800 to 3,500 and 400 to 2,800, respectively. By the time special census takers surveyed Minnesota during the summer of 1857, the Stillwater settlement, eighteen miles upland from St. Paul, had conclusively lost the race for population increases, commercial and manufacturing expansion, and urban supremacy in the territory.[4]

Whether native or foreign born, the vast majority of immigrants who arrived in Minnesota during the first wave in 1855 came to join families and friends already established in St. Paul–Minneapolis. Immigrants traveled by the most established route—the Mississippi River corridor—some wending their way northwest onboard trains to Rock Island, others steaming northward from New Orleans and St. Louis. Amelia Ullman recalled that these immigrants followed the trail of earlier speculators and business enthusiasts, many of whom "had the year before made purchases of real estate in [St. Paul] or vicinity, and [now] came up to look [over] their investments to see what could be done in the way of 'booming.'" *The Song of Hiawatha*, Henry W. Longfellow's 1855 publication, motivated others, stirring immigrants' imagination about the laughing waters at Minnehaha Falls. Indeed, Minnesota's industrial propagandists employed this poem to

Many of the western-bound immigrants arriving at New York planned to travel at least some distance by rail. During the national immigration and railroad boom between 1850 and 1857, Americans built railroad tracks as far west as Rock Island, Illinois, where travelers met Mississippi River steamboats that would carry them north to St. Paul and beyond.

lure people to the little-known manufacturing towns now connected by the Mississippi River's first wire-suspension bridge. Many others followed the path of Joseph and Amelia Ullman—simply traveling north and west in search of better opportunities than they had known in their native states and provinces. Once arrived, immigrants joined in the activities that transformed St. Paul, St. Anthony, and Minneapolis from bustling villages dominated by fur traders, merchants, millers, and speculators into young cities forced to accommodate families, increasing consumer demands, and growing economic, social, ethnic, and political diversity.[5]

As rail, river, and road migrants swapped accounts of their travels between 1855 and 1857, Minnesota's mass of returners and arrivers soon transmitted news about the market economy's influence over the developing Northwest. They noted in particular the ways in which Chicago now challenged its St. Louis rival "by stretching her long iron arms" into the western states and territories. As eastern railroads headed west from Chicago, towns like Rock Island expanded while those like Davenport, left with nothing but waterways, soon withered or folded. By the time Chicago-based railroaders built a bridge over the Mississippi into Dubuque, Iowa, in 1856, others speculated that "it is useless to deny it—[river dependent] Galena has seen her best days. The omnipotent [iron] horse goes thundering past with only a curious, birds-eye side glance." Of course, as steamboat passengers probed more deeply into Minnesota after giving Galena a sideways glance, they noticed other things as well. One, a Bostonian traveling in 1857, observed that "not one in ten who comes West is satisfied with the country; but on the contrary wishes himself back again. But he has come West, and hates to own himself fooled, so pockets the shilling (when he can get it) and lets as big fools as he flock to the West" on the promise of railroads.[6]

Railroad expansion also accelerated the twenty-year legal shift from traditional business partnerships to incorporation, complete with the hierarchical structures in finance, purchasing, marketing, distribution, and development necessary for such complicated and capital-intensive enterprises. A liberal and uniform bankruptcy law had been in place for more than fifteen years, and, further, limited liability clauses in the incorporation law protected stockholders' personal property against the many fixed and floating costs that threatened to topple a mighty enterprise like railroad expansion. With all these factors, the nation's first "big business" lured more capital investment into its realm than any other entity in American history.[7]

Indeed, at first blush many would-be Minnesota railroad pioneers judged the financial risks and managerial headaches involved in railroad construction to far outweigh the benefits associated with such a venture. The prodigious costs of road beds, rolling stock, machine shops, warehouses, office buildings, and backward and forward linkages into fuel sources and marketing and distribution networks could daunt the most daring and dwarf the resources of even the most prosperous entrepreneur, already laden with such heavy burdens as real estate debts. Even if Minnesotans could overcome all these problems, actual railroad operations involved a nightmare of floating costs attended by the vagaries of supply and demand in labor, in passenger and freight traffic, and in political patronage, plus other uncertainties such as grumbling farmers, striking laborers, and bellyaching customers all along the line.[8]

Railroad construction along thousands of miles of the underdeveloped, sparsely populated American West offered stark lessons. Nevertheless, Minnesota's entrepreneurs and politicians eagerly accepted the risks because the depth and breadth of the possible prizes seemed to outweigh the costs involved in getting those railroads. Rice, Steele, and others who sought capital infusions for their iron horse plans met some of the new *millionaires* who had emerged since the term entered the American lexicon in 1840. Indeed, many of Minnesota's fur traders had worked for millionaire John Jacob Astor. Moreover, in once-unlikely places such as Chicago, some Minnesotans had witnessed both the fortunes that William Ogden and other local businessmen had made on railroads and the expansion of capital, immigration, and industries associated with their westward thrust. Many of Minnesota's entrepreneurial hopefuls had also seen what happened to Mississippi River colleagues who either dissipated their resources with too many investments in outmoded networks or spread themselves too thinly on new ones. In Davenport, for example, businessmen's revenues had shriveled, often into foreclosure proceedings. These impressions about railroads would apply to the future of St. Paul–Minneapolis as several territorial entrepreneurs undertook plans to promote their construction. In the meantime, the Mississippi River trade would help to pull more immigrants into the region so that Minnesotans could one day launch railroad endeavors of their own.[9]

Hauling Passengers and Freight into Minnesota from Rock Island's Railroad Hub

Anyone positioned to link his operations to phenomenal railroad growth had an excellent chance to make a substantial fortune. For example, while the river still dominated transportation north of Rock Island, steamboating offered outstanding opportunities to realize enormous profits by plowing earnings into potential railroad hubs. Several far-sighted steamboat captains seized the moment, profiting from passenger and freight traffic and making money on some of the valuable properties they had purchased at embankments between Rock Island and St. Paul. They launched steamboat packet companies 350 miles south of St. Paul at Rock Island, at the 285-mile mark at Galena, and at the 200-mile mark at Prairie du Chien. On profits, packet company entrepreneurs bought property, offices, depots, and bigger and better boats. They took out larger and splashier advertisements, boasting of their many river and rail connections, luxurious new private rooms, and a host of other traveling comforts.[10]

Between 1855 and 1857, a young Ohio steamboat pilot named William Fuson Davidson typified small-vessel owners working the region alongside the larger and more "opulent" ships then plying the Mississippi River. Unlike many riverboat captains, Davidson held few sentimental attachments to the great, zigzagging river, and he recognized the diminishing prospects for the Mississippi's share of the northwestern trade. Consequently, he embraced the deepening vision of many nineteenth-century entrepreneurs: that the future of the American West resided in railroad expansion from Chicago and Milwaukee, not in river-borne southern trade with St. Louis and New Orleans. Accordingly, Davidson invested cautiously, primarily in secondhand boats, buying ragtag skiffs cast aside by riverboat captains who sought larger specimens. As he prospered in the Mississippi's Wisconsin trade, Davidson plowed his earnings into choice pieces of property along docks in Prairie du Chien and La Crosse. At these locations, he met the aging Hercules Dousman—a Wisconsin fur trader and merchant heavily invested in some prime real estate along St. Paul's levees and St. Anthony's waterfall embankments.[11]

On the basis of his mounting trade throughout Wisconsin, Davidson joined forces with Dousman in La Crosse as Milwaukee-centered railroads thrust their way west toward that city during 1857. Through Dousman and other Wisconsin businessmen, Davidson met some of Minnesota's foremost entrepreneurs, including fur trader Norman Kittson and overland transporter James C. Burbank. Soon Davidson began to work the 145-mile stretch between La Crosse and St. Paul, making arrangements with various merchants anxious to participate in the railroad connections approaching the downriver city. At the same time, he entered into "draw-back understandings" in which Milwaukee-based railroads paid him to turn over his freight to them rather than to their competitors. Drawbacks and other secret tariff agreements with westward-pushing railroads gave Davidson the cash and connections he required to buy more skiffs and further real estate holdings in Wisconsin, Minnesota, Iowa, Illinois, Missouri, and elsewhere—as well as to gobble up weakened lines whose owners had overextended their resources between St. Louis and St. Paul.

The upsurge in steamboat trade also provided opportunities for other transporters, including Burbank, whose North-Western Express Company boomed on increased overland transportation demands between Dubuque and St. Paul. From his pocket of mail in 1851, Burbank built an overland stagecoaching business that carried government mails, passengers, and freight for St. Paul's bankers, merchants, and residents, offering regularly scheduled service to Galena by 1855. Adhering to his original formula, Burbank continued to expand his company on government mail contracts and cash-only business dealings. On cash-and-carry transactions—particularly lucrative during the winter months—North-Western Express emerged as the region's most reliable and successful overland carrier company, dominating transportation between northern Iowa, St. Paul, and the Minnesota interior. At St. Paul's levees, Burbank entered into exclusive arrangements with many steamboat companies for the transfer of their freight and passengers into hinterland areas. During 1857, the *Minnesotian* reported, "Although a high tariff is charged by this Company, it is in fact the only safe and certain mode by which money and valuable goods can be brought into Minnesota." Burbank expanded his net earnings from nothing in 1851 into a phenomenal $1 million by 1857, on an unprecedented $2.4 million in business during that year alone.[12]

His domain increasing year after year, Burbank decided that North-Western Express had expanded beyond his abilities to manage it. Needing a partner he could trust with clerical details and the firm's mounting cash receipts, he hired his younger brother Henry, a twenty-two-year-old who left wage work in New York to tramp west on the promise of his older brother's success. As it turned out, Henry had a better eye for groceries than anything else. As a result, Burbank decided to follow the example of Norman Kittson, who had remained in the Indian trade. Through the Canadian reciprocity agreement, Kittson profited from connections to Hudson's Bay Company (HBC) representatives headquartered at Winnipeg, Manitoba. These business dealings, Kittson assured Burbank, would only increase. After calculating the risks, Burbank decided to move northward into the potentially profitable HBC monopoly market developing along the Red River trail between St. Paul and Winnipeg. He pushed young Henry into this hinterland, stationing him at St. Cloud, a town seventy-five miles northwest of St. Paul. Burbank chose this promising spot for its intersections with the Mississippi River, the Red River cart trail, and, if all went well, one of the land-grant railroads recently incorporated in St. Paul. Henry established a strong grocery business in St. Cloud during the summer of 1857. James plowed the profits back into overland express, buying more oxen, horses, and stagecoaches to work the reciprocity zone from St. Paul into St. Cloud and thence northward to Winnipeg.[13]

As steamboats and stagecoaches—overflowing with passengers, freight, and mail—crowded St. Paul's levees between 1855 and 1857, the commercial town throbbed with diversity and change. When the editor of the New Haven, Connecticut, paper *Palladium*, Charles F. Babcock, toured St. Paul during 1855, he reported on the "ample streets, upon which are all kinds of buildings of moderate pretensions," claiming that "the city bears all the marks of youth, for it is but six years old—and yet it appears full three times as large as your town of Fair Haven—I mean in respect to the number of its buildings." In addition to this observation, Babcock noted that despite Indian removals, he encountered cross-blood women and Native American men in the streets of St. Paul and St. Anthony, indicating the enduring quality of the fur trade and its importance to connections with downriver St. Louis.[14]

Babcock witnessed the early transition. During 1855, the Lower Levee received cargo from 560 arriving steamboats, a considerable figure despite the fact that the river opened on April 17 and closed on November 20, the second-shortest season since 1844. But the next year's arrivals surpassed even these numbers: during the 212 days that preceded Minnesota's coldest winter on record, 857 steamboats wheeled into St. Paul. The next astonishing year, Mississippi River traffic escalated again, and St. Paul's levees accommodated 1,026 arrivals from New Orleans, St. Louis, and Rock Island in a record 198 days. Moreover, in this last spectacular year an unparalleled 216 boats chugged their way to St. Paul's Upper Levee from the Minnesota River Valley. Along with delivering eager passengers to the expanding territory, the steamboat trade fostered a commercial explosion at St. Paul's levees.[15]

St. Paul's Expanding Commercial Levees

Modeled after the winning formula that had placed Cincinnati, St. Louis, and now Chicago at the center of regional commerce, St. Paul emerged as Minnesota's most important and diverse town. New immigrants raised its population from 4,000 to 11,000 between 1855 and 1857. Along with Kittson, Burbank, Davidson, and other successful entrepreneurs, the town had drawn additional newcomers, including the Ullmans and very soon young James J. Hill and Maurice Auerbach. During 1856, local boosters bragged that in just two short seasons, "the speculative spirit of the day, joined with ample opportunities presented by the fertile territory [has attracted] capital from the East, and [has done] much to accelerate the growth of St. Paul." The evidence included 52 attorneys, 31 real estate dealers, 14 bankers, 13 architects and builders, 6 newspapers, 5 fire and life insurance agencies, and numerous other retail shops and transportation services.[16]

As new immigrants made their way to boardinghouse hotels on arrival, they noticed other things as well. For example, Amelia Ullman reported that St. Paul had "no streets, properly speaking." Once settled into "temporary" lodgings—where the "initial week turned into months before [they] built their own homes"—Ullman and other immigrants daily found in "the dining room the most interesting collection of steamboatmen, bankers, speculators, and frontiersmen of every type [and nationality]." Leaving the hotels, they wandered along what passed for streets, these thoroughfares filled with the "rush and hurry of business" of every kind and, according to another new arrival, the "untaught brats" who waited to usher them into retail outlets lining the streets leading back to the levees.[17]

No matter their birthplace, nationality, or first impressions, entrepreneurial immigrants soon learned that soaring demands for food, clothing, and building materials offered the chance for sizeable returns among those who undertook the risks associated with travel and trade. During the open season, ambitious young men like Charles Elfelt steamed down the Mississippi River with Davidson and others, bringing back quantities of dry goods that soon allowed Elfelt to establish one of the town's leading business houses. Enterprising merchants like Joseph Ullman traveled by Burbank's "mail coach" or "sled" to Galena and Dubuque between February and March, procuring food and drink to tide over St. Paul's residents until spring thaw. Others from various places soon followed, and by 1856 St. Paul required a city directory to advertise all the new businesses developing in and around the young city.[18]

Among those who increased the demand for goods and services in the territory, nearly two thousand Irish immigrants—mostly Catholic—took up residence in St. Paul between 1855 and 1857. They arrived from famine-ridden agricultural areas in their rocky homeland, from congested tenements in Dublin, London, Boston, New York, and Philadelphia, and from coal-mining communities in Pennsylvania's anthracite and bituminous regions. The city's established, if modest, Catholic community drew many of these Irish settlers. Although pamphlets hailing Minnesota's agricultural potential had poured into the Northeast, immigration agents had all but failed to impress native-born migrants as well as Irish and other foreign-born immigrants with the promise of farming. Once at St. Paul, the Irish chose to stay in town rather than return to the slogging tasks of clearing and cultivating another soil that might starve them. Moreover, they realized that, given their numbers, they might become an important economic and political bloc in St. Paul.[19]

Beyond the draw of the Catholic Church and the critical body of immigrants sustaining it, many of these new arrivals settled on St. Paul because the booming town offered opportunities to unskilled laborers. Many cash-poor Irish (along with other similarly impoverished immigrants) found work as waiters in boardinghouses, as servants in the homes of emerging elites, and as laborers on the levees' docks. At the very least, boardinghouse hotels and private residences provided *relatively* clean lodgings, and the chance to gobble a biscuit, a potato, or a slice of greasy bacon and gulp a cup of hot tea. Moreover, in a town rife with entrepreneurial enthusiasm, many arriving immigrants noticed that even the "untaught brats" made money on the escalating demand for laborers at the levees' transportation agencies, retail stores, and warehouses. Indeed, with the town in its infancy, workers scarce, wages relatively high, and future prospects rosy, many laborers and aspiring entrepreneurs deemed St. Paul infinitely better than crowded city sweatshops, dirty and dangerous mines, and isolated regions. As they met entrepreneurs in hotels and homes, at the docks, and during drives around town, other opportunities soon emerged.[20]

For example, entrepreneurial hopefuls such as Canada's eighteen-year-old James J. Hill soon learned that shops along the Mississippi levees needed not only day laborers but also anyone with clerking, cashiering, and bookkeeping skills. In short supply throughout the developing West, anyone with writing and arithmetic abilities soon found plentiful office work, commercial expansion placing a premium on employees who could monitor costs and cash flow. When Hill arrived in St. Paul during 1856, he had neither experience nor capital. At first he worked scrubbing docks, loading warehouses with goods, running errands along the Lower Levee, and driving wagons around St. Paul. When grocers at the docks discovered Hill's other talents—the penmanship he had learned in an Ontario schoolroom and the cost-cutting measures he grasped—they put the young man to work as a clerk. Inside the office, he wrote letters to suppliers and customers, kept the books, and, when needed, scrambled to unload freight.[21]

Like Hill, a Canadian of Irish and Scottish ancestry, many arriving Irishmen worked their way into and then up through retail stores; newspaper chains; land-surveying offices; steamboat, overland express, parish, political, and civil-service networks; and eventually railroad contracting and construction companies. Another example, Charles Boyle, an Irish Catholic laborer who arrived by way of Pennsylvania's bituminous coal mines, acquired jobs as a land surveyor for the young city and as a civil engineer with the newly incorporated railroads. Bolstered by the success of earlier immigrants, he and others who had received appointments in the city sent for family members and friends.[22]

While the Irish settled into many laboring, professional, and business callings, arriving Germans soon learned that they had fewer obstacles to overcome than some of their counterparts, at least in terms of skilled human capital. Uprooted by political, religious, and industrial rather than agricultural chaos, many Catholic and Jewish Germans who descended upon St. Paul were middle-class merchants and farmers, skilled craftsmen, and the laboring elite. Boarding steamboats at New Orleans, many followed the path traveled by Joseph and Amelia Ullman. Others arrived circuitously, having jumped onboard railroads that took them to Chicago and Milwaukee, where they often encountered other German-speaking people who planned to travel west. From there, many embarked on eastern railroad systems heading for Rock Island, for northwestern soil, and for urban jobs in St. Paul–Minneapolis and other villages popping up in Minnesota and elsewhere.[23]

St. Paul's German-speaking population wended into Minnesota from Protestant, Catholic and Jewish villages in Europe and from German Protestant communities in the American South, the Middle Atlantic states, and other developing enclaves, particularly those in Missouri, Illinois, Iowa, and Wisconsin. Once in St. Paul—some of moderate pretensions, others penniless—many Germans fanned out into the hinterland, but a substantial number stayed in the booming commercial hub, contributing their capital and skills to a community desperately needing both. Among those with capital, some set up or entered into established fur-trading networks or grocery, dry goods, hardware, and other retail stores near the levees. Others launched banks and legal, real estate, or additional offices conducive to the territory's diversifying market economy. Skilled German workers soon dominated building trades, the teamsters among them hauling lumber and other building materials to St. Paul's work sites. Germans also set up boardinghouse hotels, saloons, restaurants, smithies, shoe-making shops, millineries, breweries, and livery stables. The latter employed arriving laborers—not only Germans but also Americans, Canadians, Irish, and the trickling flow of British Islanders, French, and Scandinavians. One member of this clamoring throng, a young Prussian Jew named Maurice Auerbach, arrived, like Hill, with nothing more than a few coins in his pocket, but his clerking abilities and dry goods experience soon gained the attention of established merchants, who hired him into their own dry goods store.[24]

No matter the newcomers' nationality or previous home, St. Paul needed them. Merchants put them to work, seeking out those who had capital or special talents to develop. Together with others already on the scene, successful immigrant businessmen invested in other spheres—churches, schools, and meeting places such as the Germans' *Turnverein*—and sent their children to these community institutions. For example, on the success of their retail outlet, the Ullmans set up a Hebrew school, helped to found and finance St. Paul's first synagogue, and created a social network for Jewish families scattered throughout town. German speakers joined French and Irish Catholics at mass in the "red brick" chapel, complete with a belfry built on fund-raising activities. When St. Paul established its board of education in 1856, German merchants won their bid to make German the town's second official school language. Regardless of denomination or ethnic group, the town's emerging business elite bought front-row pews, donated large sums for the construction of religious and educational institutions, and governed the boardrooms of both. They also participated in city-building projects to enhance St. Paul's urban attractions and tried to solve the escalating problem of water pollution along the river—not only from steamboats and mills but also from the "infirmities" of horse-drawn vehicles, "wild dogs," and "cows that swim across the River daily of their own accord."[25]

Together, native and foreign-born residents created a "never ceasing whirl" of business activity at Minnesota's reception areas, so recently prepared along St. Paul's Lower and Upper Levees. By 1857, however, credit notes and liens generated much of that "whirl." Amelia Ullman—now an established resident bustling about the levees, waiting to greet the many friends and strangers arriving in St. Paul—remembered that "every new person appeared to have money; but *mostly in coin,* they spent it freely" and quickly. Having exhausted their meager savings, these new residents sought credit, and businesses sprang up each season to meet this increasing demand. Banks provided "rapid circulation of credit notes" to assist many thousands who arrived "somewhat low on funds." Other businessmen loaned money for the "speedy" erection of new buildings and storage facilities to house speculators and immigrants, commercial and manufactured goods, offices and stores. Still others in land-holding and insurance businesses assisted with the "quick appreciation of real estate," while merchants loaned money for the "frenzied hauling, stacking, and storing" of imported products for "immediate and future sale."[26]

Transportation agents assisted in untangling many of the bottlenecks created by this increased activity. Along with steamboats, stagecoaches carried into and throughout the region the never-ending stream of passengers and freight, including all the lumber required for interior construction projects. They departed with merchants who needed to make yet another quick trip to procure goods for anticipated demands, their pockets full of promissory notes and deeds which they hoped to exchange for credit from their downriver suppliers, what with capital so "very scarce" in St. Paul. Transportation entrepreneurs also guided lumbermen into the woodlands and helped float logs downriver to the St. Anthony–Minneapolis booms.[27]

As St. Paul's distribution hub vibrated with energies flowing from increased steamboat and stagecoach traffic, the demand for groceries, dry goods, building materials, and other products and services spiraled upward, as did the use of credit for their purchase. With more promissory notes circulating each day, many millionaires-in-the-making also purchased "handsome carriages and first-rate horses," various baubles and trinkets for their new parlors (whether in homes already constructed or merely in the planning stages), and the services of superlative architects, lawyers, and brokers. As town lots acquired for $75 in 1855 sold for $1,500 in 1857, these would-be millionaires also invested in business and residential building. In 1857, Amelia Ullman recounted St. Paul's changing landscape and the elites who now dominated the town's business and political life: "in a desirable situation overlooking the river are several well built dwelling houses; Gov. Ramsey and Mr. Charles Elfelt have their homes there. Mr. Rice has the best house up there and Mr. Dayton, who is the owner of much of the land and who has given his name to the bluff, lives in the largest of the houses." Rapid construction transformed St. Paul from a few meandering dirt paths into a five-mile-square emporium focused on competition that would yield present and future prospects.[28]

During the three-year boom, resident investors built 517 homes and shops, 70 business houses and manufactories, six churches, four "luxury" hotels, and four private schools, all, as many observed, with "much evidence of opulence" for such a young western town. According to several eastern tourists and reporters, the most important element in St. Paul's transformation derived from "the public spirit of its leading business men [who] put their hands deep into their pockets to improve and advance the place." Indeed, six percent of St. Paul's families now held nearly 50 percent of its prime real estate. The city's ascending elites—men such as banker Charles Borup, fur trader–politician Henry Rice, realtor Lyman Dayton, and others—also invested in tourism, building St. Paul's "first-class" Fuller House, a five-story brick hotel "surpassed by very few in this country," particularly in its cost vis-à-vis its location. Originally estimated at $30,000, complete with furnishings, the final bill arrived for nearly $200,000, a princely sum in those days.[29]

With St. Paul's official incorporation during 1856, many new entrepreneurial elites served on the common council's board, working to structure the city they planned to dominate. They wrote laws to regulate steamboat docking and travel as well as various western nuisances, including prostitutes and the "wild roaming of livestock and other animals." They agitated for and secured a city marshal and police power to protect their ornate new homes and businesses. They allocated funds for pauper relief, and they established a board of health to regulate the expanding market demand for better meat, vegetables, and other products prone to spoilage.[30]

Those who had helped incorporate the city also set to work on plans for the education of its children. As the board of education's directors, they designed and built four public brick schoolhouses between 1856 and 1857. Additionally, when Reverend Edward D. Neill sought funds to establish Macalester College (organized in 1853), he turned to St. Paul–Minneapolis's main real estate holders. By 1856, Neill had raised $8,000 for the cause; thereafter he shared Macalester's boardroom with the college's principal endowers: St. Paul's Alexander Ramsey and George Becker (an attorney associated with Henry Rice's brother, Edmund), St. Anthony's Franklin Steele, and other local nabobs. As Macalester's subscribers and trustees, urban businessmen made clear the college's mission in its first brochure: "In a country so youthful, the demand is for practical men, rather than complete scholars." To help practical young men learn the art of western business, Macalester offered a wide range of courses, including civil engineering, chemistry of the arts and agriculture, mechanics, geology, constitutional history, and mercantile law and ethics.[31]

As St. Paulites constructed their commercial city, no Hausmann or L'Enfant laid out boulevards and esplanades. Instead, businessmen and residents built where they pleased, constructing offices and homes higgledy-piggledy, along embankments and on plains and hills that still confuse neophyte travelers weaving their way into St. Paul's business center. This rapid and haphazard construction nevertheless created a permanent commercial landscape for St. Paul, with boosters claiming that town merchants had recently invested capital amounting to nearly $1 million. Although other national cities, particularly expansive Chicago, dwarfed St. Paul and its financial-commercial accomplishments, within its immediate region the town had made tremendous strides. More importantly, rapid development inspired its entrepreneurial vanguard to perceive only the sky as the city's limit. In their quest to outdistance St. Anthony and Minneapolis, St. Paulites also invested in a hoped-for manufacturing boom. They poured $100,000 into three sawmills, $12,000 into a flouring mill, $10,000 into a sash, door, and blind manufactory, and upwards of $30,000 into other small-scale factories, foundries, and smithies "to promote the mechanical and milling arts." Meanwhile, entrepreneurs upstream at the waterfall sawed, ground, hammered, dammed, and forged their way into larger-scale milling and manufacturing activities.[32]

St. Anthony–Minneapolis's
Expanding Manufacturing Emporiums

With a commanding position at the head of steamboat navigation, St. Paul's transportation and merchandizing entrepreneurs captured the lucrative Mississippi River trade; however, the upriver waterfall offered comparable opportunities to those who quickly moved to harness its power potential for manufacturing. Thus, while St. Paul's increasingly diverse residents busied themselves with commercial expansion at the Lower and Upper Levees, New Englanders fortified their stronghold through chain migrations dominated by Maine's lumbermen and manufacturing-minded families. Other young hopefuls from the Northeast—including William D. Washburn, William Eastman, and John Sargeant Pillsbury—followed Franklin Steele's lead, descending upon St. Anthony and Minneapolis during these years.[33]

The plans of the waterfall's aspiring manufacturers differed from those of St. Paul's commercial entrepreneurs in one important essential: they required more money for their start-ups, a fact which soon compelled them to seek outside capital to finance their larger ambitions. Mindful of northeastern manufacturing models as they pursued riparian rights to the Mississippi River waterfall, two groups quickly dominated activities on either side of the falls. Franklin Steele, now financially backed by New York capitalists, acquired most of St. Anthony's prime milling real estate. Pennsylvania-born Robert Smith, Steele's predecessor at Fort Snelling, quickly gobbled up 25 percent of Minneapolis's milling district for himself and friends in Wisconsin and Maine. In short order, Steele, Smith, and their respective business associates controlled the future of the young waterfall towns. At the same time, William Eastman, a young man raised on paper milling along New Hampshire's Saco River, leased land from Steele to grind grain on Hennepin Island. He also acquired some property on Nicollet Island, where he established a successful sawmilling operation.[34]

By 1854, St. Anthony's New York backers decided to send an agent to oversee their investment in the former Fort Snelling storekeeper, whose expanding sawmills had yet to produce expected profits. Appointing Ohio's Richard Chute to the post, the investors encouraged him to establish a water power company there. They instructed Chute to secure rights to use the waterfall for irrigation and to develop other manufacturing establishments on both the St. Anthony embankment and along the eastern shores of

Hennepin and Nicollet Islands, both largely owned but already heavily mortgaged by Steele. Other aspiring manufacturers had taken similar chances on real estate and water power in New England. Some had succeeded, but many more had failed. Steele hoped to join the ranks of the former, particularly given the success some flour millers had enjoyed through rapid developments in Buffalo and now Rochester, New York. Besides, he reasoned, he had the added benefit of an inside track with local free-soil politicians in St. Paul.

On information obtained from Henry Rice and other territorial legislators, Steele exchanged mortgages for the capital required to "improve" vast tracts of land in Minneapolis. The moment government land offices put these lands up for public sale, he planned to claim preemption rights and make his purchase. As early as 1851, Steele conveyed his Nicollet Island property to Wisconsin's Hercules Dousman as collateral for a loan. Mendota's Henry Hastings Sibley also held title to some of Steele's landholdings as security against other loans. With various mortgages (and thus financial interests) in the hands of friends inside the territorial legislature, Steele gained the assistance he required. Backed by political muscle, Steele also headed the effort to secure water power for his eastern-shore sawmills. These prospects glittering, Chute took up permanent residence in St. Anthony in 1855. Together with Chute and St. Paul's Henry Rice and John Prince (both formerly employed by Pierre Chouteau), Steele established the St. Anthony Falls Water Power Company. The group elected Steele as president and Chute as company agent. During 1856, the company received a perpetual corporate charter from the territorial legislature, capitalized at $160,000.

In the meantime, Robert Smith formed a partnership on the waterfall's western shores. Then residing in Wisconsin, Smith also approached friends and business associates in the territorial legislature, hoping to secure riparian rights to the Minneapolis embankment and to the western shores of Hennepin and Nicollet Islands. Smith had previously obtained a loan from a prosperous land agent in Wisconsin, Maine-born Cadwallader C. Washburn, a successful businessman with strong family and political connections in New England. The portly Washburn knew and utterly disliked Free-Soiler Steele as well as his fur-trading confederate, Henry Rice. When Smith, Steele's major competitor, approached Washburn about the investment opportunity, he gladly jumped onboard. Alas, with business and political careers flourishing in Wisconsin, neither Smith nor Washburn wanted to move to remote Minneapolis or provincial Minnesota. But Washburn had an excellent solution to their managerial problem: two men from Maine—his cousin Dorilus Morrison, a first-rate sawmiller, and his younger brother, William Drew Washburn, a recently minted attorney. During 1856, the four associates established the Minneapolis Mill Company. Through Smith's connections they too received a perpetual corporate charter from the territorial legislature, also capitalized at $160,000.[35]

With corporate charters and riparian rights confirmed, the owners of the St. Anthony Falls Water Power and Minneapolis Mill Companies set to work, cooperating on a V-shaped dam to divide the flow of water between them. The companies' owners completed this project between 1856 and 1857; however, their cooperative efforts, and managerial similarities, ended there.[36]

From first to last—as it labored "under the mighty incubus" of St. Paul and the management of Steele and Chute—the St. Anthony company adopted *ad hoc* policies toward milling expansion, allowing renters free rein over water and land use. These guiding principles quickly expanded St. Anthony's population—from 800 in 1855 to more than 3,500 in 1857—as questing millers hoped to prosper on Steele's and Chute's liberality. Their efforts increased the value of Minnesota's then most lucrative product—lumber— the supply of which St. Paul's builders devoured. On this sawmilling boom, the range of entrepreneurial activities expanded rapidly. As just two examples, manufacturer John Orth of France established the town's first steam-powered brewery and lumber mill along St. Anthony's embankment and merchant John Sargeant Pillsbury of New Hampshire opened a hardware store to provide the nails and other products required for milling and building expansion.[37]

The St. Anthony company adopted liberal policies because its owners hoped to generate quick profits so that Steele could settle his debts. These policies inspired rapid manufacturing expansion, but as land on the waterfall's eastern shore escalated in price, proprietors spent their earnings on machinery and on more land to keep up with development. As a result, the company generated insufficient funds for the dividends Steele had envisioned. Moreover, rather than paying off his debts, Steele used some of his earnings to leap into the potentially lucrative business of railroads, spreading capital he obtained from mortgages into more land purchases and railroad bonds. With others, he also entered the businesses of building larger mills and an ornate home and founding churches, schools, and benevolent fraternities to attract more immigrants (and consumers) into his developing manufacturing town.[38]

Unlike their rivals in St. Anthony, the principal owners of the Minneapolis Mill Company embarked on no major installations along the western shores of the waterfall. Instead, they adhered to a strict plan centered on promoting the waterfall's long-term manufacturing potential in both lumber and grain. They restricted leasing agreements to water use in the central milling district and confined land use to mills and mill maintenance only, limiting the canal's water distribution system to manufacturing.

Seeking advice regarding the company's plan, kingpin Cadwallader C. Washburn lumbered back to New England during the final consummation of the Minneapolis Mill Company charter. He visited the New York flour manufactories then transforming Buffalo and Rochester into mighty empires. There he learned many new tricks about processing wheat into flour. Next he toured the famed waterfall-powered textile mills at Lowell, Massachusetts. There he retained the services of an experienced engineer to help the Minneapolis Mill owners design a proper water distribution system for the western shore. By the time he descended upon the family homestead during 1856 to spirit young William Drew away from his law books, C. C. Washburn knew precisely what he wanted to do in Minneapolis: buy out his eight partners, exchanging land for ownership of water rights and the more lucrative opportunities associated with water power; arrange financing to consolidate ownership among the four principals; and build no major operations until the company realized its first dividend.[39]

When William Drew Washburn permanently removed to Minneapolis in 1857, the two waterfall companies had completed the V-neck dam and the western-shore town's population had increased from 300 in 1855 to just over 2,800—60 percent of its residents formerly of Maine. Welcomed into the town designed for his management, W. D. Washburn immediately set up a legal office. Although his older brother's schemes appealed to his own sensibilities, twenty-six-year-old W. D. had a few ambitions of his own, including a political appointment in this remote country—compensation for his unfortunate position as youngest in the family hierarchy. Finding the legal market already glutted by downriver attorneys swarming over the territorial capital, W. D. consoled himself with the fact that, for the moment, he could pursue lumbering, the only other business he knew, while attending to the managerial obligations attached to his family's interest in Minneapolis Mill.[40]

As the company owners consolidated their plans, they attracted other like-minded entrepreneurs similarly anxious for long-term gains on Washburn's solid manufacturing strategy. In 1856 Minneapolis had received official sanction as a town; thereafter, residents embarked on building projects similar to those in St. Paul and St. Anthony, erecting homes, churches, schools, and businesses to accommodate the expansion of timber and flour milling.[41]

While St. Paul's commercial entrepreneurs procured credit and bought, sold, distributed, and transported goods throughout the region, and St. Anthony's millers sawed up a storm and tumbled their lumber downriver to eager St. Paulites, and Minneapolis's manufacturing visionaries contemplated diversified developments in logging operations and flour-milling activities along the river's western shoreline, railroad and statehood enthusiasts beat a path toward the new territorial capital. Driven by fears that "Boston and New York capitalists [are undertaking efforts] to grasp the trade of the Upper Mississippi country by means of a system of railroads," residents throughout the territory ignored the fact that as early as 1855 capital, "as usual," had become "devilish[ly] tight" in the West. Overshadowing all other pursuits, the desire for both railroads and statehood, present from the beginning, rose to a frenzy during 1856 and 1857. By the time it engulfed the territorial capitol building, the governorship had passed through several hands. While ex-governor Alexander Ramsey took up residence at his new $200,000-plus estate overlooking the Mississippi River, St. Paul's William Gorman stood at the capitol door to receive the railroad enthusiasts. By 1858, the governor-elect for the new state, fur-trading Henry Sibley, had to deal with them.[42]

Minnesota's Expanding Railroad Vision

Rapid immigration expansion, economic development, and urban success between 1855 and 1857 finally emboldened Minnesota's territorial founders to undertake the larger enterprises of railroads and statehood. Casting beyond confirmation of statehood, Minnesotans hoped to induce the federal government to support their ongoing plans for railroad developments. These they knew would entail considerable struggle from dream to realization, as agriculturalists accelerated the clearing of northern forests and the planting of seeds in the cities' wheat-growing empire. Railroads promised to carry large numbers of settlers into the hinterland and to haul plentiful raw materials into the developing cities that would serve it.[43]

On the heels of the federal government's first large grant for railroad construction—an 1850 right-of-way designated on lands in Illinois, Mississippi, and Alabama to connect Chicago and Mobile—Congress expedited other endowments for railroad development, ultimately including in its plans Minnesota Territory's so-called "Great Railroad Land Grant of 1857." Anticipating the windfall of a land grant—and ignoring historical precedents, danger signs, and warnings alike—Minnesota's railroad enthusiasts continued to pursue expansion between 1856 and 1857. The territorial legislature chartered some twenty railroads during these two years, on the hope that, "without the intrigues of external influence," at least one would bear fruit. According to local papers, with these railroads largely capitalized by resident investors, land speculators, "rife along the line of proposed roads," hoped to "accumulate immense fortunes," buying "land by the acre, laying off a town, and selling it by the foot."[44]

Among the many railroad and townsite boosters, few pitched themselves into the effort more energetically than did Ignatius Donnelly. A self-proclaimed advocate of Pennsylvania's emerging "Republican" cause, Donnelly departed his home state with a prophetic mission, descended upon St. Paul during the summer of 1856, and, after "procuring a little credit," undertook a grand plan for Nininger, a munificent railroad city soaring in his lofty imagination but nowhere else. Launching the *Emigrant Aid Journal,* Donnelly hoped that the country's many *Weekly Times* would "profusely circulate" news about Minnesota's prospects "among merchants, business men, and others residing east, thus aiding the onward march and future greatness of our present embryo State."[45]

On March 3, 1857, Congress answered Minnesota boosters' pleas, granting lands for railroad construction—12 million of Minnesota's 53.5 million acres. On these, Minnesotans pledged the credit of their future state toward building four railroad lines extending from various locations to the territorial borders. The land bill made no definite grant: Congress denoted general routes, making the territory and future state of Minnesota the federal government's trustee and agent for railroad purposes. Minnesota could sell granted lands only as railroad building progressed, and those not sold for the act's purposes within ten years would revert to the United States. By the time Minnesota's railroad land grant passed Congress—complete with prohibitive construction obligations—others had followed young Donnelly into St. Paul, including a correspondent for Minnesota's new Winona *Republican.* The paper's lead story conveyed the delirium that had possessed the entire territory: "All are anxious to see what yet another new spring will bring in the way of prosperity to St. Paul and Minnesota." The newspaperman observed, "Politicians, Railroad men and proprietors of town sites are as plenty as blackberries in August. There is pulling and hauling this, that and every way, and all have their eye open to the main chance ahead." Further, he reported, "Railroad maps and maps of Minnesota are in great demand; the latter marked with lines in every conceivable direction, each line representing a Railroad, with towns all along each route, and a station upon almost every quarter section."[46]

Throughout the spring and summer of 1857, as residents, speculators, and new immigrants congregated in St. Paul hotels to pore over railroad maps and townsite plans, real estate and other statistics seemed to support the notion that St. Paul–Minneapolis had emerged as undisputed railroad termini for lines from major eastern and southern cities. Indeed, neophyte speculator David Merritt boasted to his son back east of his ability to lend money in St. Paul at between "30% and 36% per annum interest," while others told distant family and friends similar tales about Minnesota's new opportunities in real estate and railroads. For example, calculating the value of lands located between St. Paul and the mouth of Lake Superior acquired by Minnesota's millionaires-in-the-making in 1855, John Gilman wrote his fiancée, Helen, that just one year later St. Paul properties were now "worth 300 percent" more than the original purchase price.[47]

Businessmen, workers, educators, religious leaders, and politicians all set their minds to the "main chance ahead." Lizzie Fuller encouraged her brother back east to study hard so that he "might prepare for college and find a suitable position in the business world," preferably as a manager of one of St. Paul's emerging railroads. Other parents, siblings, and friends said the same, including teen booster Truman White, who reported that on anticipated railroads, "the citizens of St. Paul are trying to raise enough money to build a bridge across the Mississippi River[.] They have 30,000 dollars now, an amount that shows St. Paul is bound to be a great City."[48]

Lest the female and teen capitalists lose out on the "mighty big chances to realize" on church, school, millinery-shop, and other enterprises, booster women and children clambered aboard the railroad ride, too. Wives of prominent St. Paul merchants dashed about town raising funds for church-building schemes and charitable causes, and many invested these donations in the "speculative spirit" of the day. For example, the Ladies' Benevolent Society of the First Baptist Church, charged with raising funds to build a new church, procured $350 in private donations from those "opening their pockets" for yet another excellent community cause. By mid-1857, the Ladies proudly reported that a "portion of the funds were some months since invested in wild lands which have at least doubled their value since investment." The remainder, they boasted, had been "loaned on call." Rejoicing in the activities of the Benevolent Society and other community fund raisers, teen booster Sarah Cavender exclaimed, "although our city has grown so rapidly, me thinks it is yet in its infancy, and destined to be one of the largest and most flourishing cities on the Mississippi!" Of course, not everyone agreed with these sentiments. Reverend John Pope worried about his own church Ladies, as well as Minnesota's teenage speculators, who stood about street corners shouting, "Corner lots! Mighty Big Chance to Realize!" Unfortunately for Pope, few citizens found his appeals as beguiling as what the Ladies had accomplished.[49]

Other nervous Minnesotans cautioned citizens against their continued emphasis on rapid urban expansion, pointing out that eastern capitalists had ceased to invest in western railroad schemes after financial distress in

1855 signaled trouble on the horizon. About farmers, the anxious declared, "not generally political economists, however intelligent they may be; they will prosper only where *they pay for everything as soon as they buy it.*" Regarding railroads, the nervous advised, "let those who want the trade of our valley build them. Produce enough to make railroads pay to this valley. Neglect to do that, and railroads will not pay. [Eastern] capital will make your railroads for you, as soon as they are worth making." Expansionist schemes had preceded and contributed to the depression that followed the panic of 1837, they declared. They also pointed out that wily capitalists had learned their lesson on earlier canal-building projects that bankrupted Ohio and other parts of the country. Sagacious advice, indeed; however, railroad enthusiasts ignored it, correctly pointing out that eastern capitalists had retrenched, curtailing their investments in the risky venture of building railroads along lines of hoped-for settlement, where an initial outlay promised to take years to realize a return.[50]

Ambitious to construct the most important commercial and manufacturing towns northwest of Chicago, boosters in St. Paul–Minneapolis finally convinced fearful preachers, farmers, laborers, entrepreneurs, government officials, and others that railroads promised to clear all their start-up debts more quickly than any other project. After all, they exclaimed, Minnesota's young towns "now matched, and even surpassed the past, present, and future prospects of Chicago, Toledo," and other western cities. Indeed, as more immigrants scurried to St. Paul, Minnesotans claimed that their expanding river trade had already "toppled Galena and Dubuque." Newspapermen reminded territorial residents that Chicago had used waterway networks to nurture agricultural production during the previous decade; with railroads, the metropolitan corridor for that cultivation had expanded exponentially. "Chicago had a population of 4,470 in 1840," they declared, and "after its tremendous growth, and railroad building intrigues [between 1848 and 1850], it possessed 27,786 souls." Now that Chicago's industrial distribution center had extended its reach westward to Rock Island, eastern interests promised to swallow up Minnesota's profits unless locals built their own railroads first. Besides, boosters insisted, railroad expansion had nothing in common with earlier canal-building fiascos. Instead, they declared, "the iron horse" was "leading the United States westward to the Pacific Ocean and into wealth and glory" without end.[51]

In the summer of 1857, despite a two-year shortage of capital in the western territories, the powerful lures of railroads and expanding immigration thrust Minnesotans into their next grand scheme: agitation for statehood and all the associated appropriations, government contracts, and revenues that would follow. The territory's 150,000 residents more than adequately fulfilled one of the admission requirements, and Minnesotans prepared to present their petition to Congress for admittance as a free state. However, jealousies over land-grant handouts turned into personal hostilities between those with economic interests to the south and west of St. Paul–Minneapolis and those who stood to profit in areas north and west toward the Red River Valley. Over nearly six months of bickering, name-calling, and mudslinging, Minnesotans spent hundreds of thousands of dollars on lengthy proceedings to draft their state constitution. Finally, the territory's legislative representatives and entrepreneurial vanguard signed a mutually agreed-upon Minnesota State Constitution on August 29, 1857. Inauspiciously, they completed the task just five days after newspapers announced the suspension of the Ohio Life Insurance and Trust Company's operations, the failure that signaled the arrival of the 1857 panic. Unleashed by frantic depositors withdrawing funds from New York banks and distressed creditors calling in loans, the panic soon overshadowed Minnesota's "grand" state constitution.[52]

Following the panic, chaos ensued. As financial distress spread west during the winter of 1857–58, it fed upon Minnesota's crisis-in-progress. But the state's railroad boosters disregarded the gathering storm, even when they learned, on March 27, 1858, that their railroad pet, the Minnesota and Pacific, had collapsed into bankruptcy. According to local papers, "without means or credit" the railroad could not "even pay [its] employees." Regardless, boosters cried, "If a railroad isn't built, Iowa and Missouri will capture all the emigrants!" Alas, "all the emigrants" had stopped dead in their tracks, many of them already foundering under the weight of the deepening financial depression.[53]

On the eve of statehood, abandoned by eastern banks yet undeterred by either market realities or the impending crisis over slavery, Minnesotans had also undertaken a dangerous expedient. They turned to their only other source of revenue: the emerging state government.

The Panic of 1857 and Minnesota's Expanding State Commitments

As Minnesotans staggered into 1858, other problems signaled trouble in the territory, including the convening of the "new state legislature" in March 1858, two months before Congress approved statehood. The state legislature stayed in session for five long months to address both the continuing financial "rickety times" in Minnesota and the railroad issue. As one participant remembered, "the first Legislature of the State of Minnesota was not composed of men of talents, experience or sound judgment such as the emergency [required]." The session cost more than $430,000, funds not easily collected from taxpayers deeply in debt. Revenues continued to shrink as inflated properties left more and more delinquent taxpayers financially strapped. Making matters worse, the territorial government had hired only a few officials to collect these taxes and had provided no additional means to enforce payment. To resolve the multiplying problems, the Minnesota legislature issued bonds to defray its expenses. Beyond this measure, the legislature also passed a free banking bill—whereby state banks could deposit railroad bonds as security for the promissory and other notes they issued—on the hope that investors in St. Paul could lift the region out of its financial slump.[54]

As members of Congress fought over admitting yet another free state, Minnesotans went forward with their railroad plans, ignoring the several among them who warned about "bungling" the process of statehood on the "folly of our blind course, so entirely occupied with railroads bound for glory." By then, however, the skeptics' appeals fell on deaf ears and even the fainthearted caved in to the argument that railroads would save and vindicate Minnesota. During March 1858, Minnesota's statesmen decided to fund four proposed railroads: the Minnesota and Pacific Railroad Company (already bankrupt as a non-land-grant road); the Transit Railroad Company; the Root River Valley and Southern Minnesota Railroad Company; and the Minneapolis and Cedar Valley Railroad Company. Minnesotans entrusted these companies with building a primary railroad system for the new state and divided among them the 12 million acres granted by Congress. The legislature then added a constitutional proviso for "special bonds" bearing seven percent interest, payable semiannually, to aid the four companies in the construction of their railroads. This proviso translated into a $5 million "loan of public credit," backed by the state's faith in the companies. The legislature promised to issue loans in $10,000 batches as construction progressed.[55]

When the legislature presented the proposed bill to its constituents for their approval during April 1858—one month before Congress approved statehood—14,981 territorial voters said "yes," with almost unanimous endorsement from those in St. Paul–Minneapolis. Only 1,634 residents voted against the proposal to loan the entire credit of the state to the four railroad companies. The companies soon set to work, letting construction contracts posthaste.[56]

In the meantime, territorial status came to an end. On May 11, 1858, after a two-month congressional debate, Minnesota passed into statehood. With this significant step achieved, an internal system devoted to land-grant railroads activated, and a free (i.e., unregulated, and in this case "wildcat") banking policy enacted, the new state's politicians and railroad men believed they could lessen the financial panic's effect in Minnesota. They infused the proposed railroad system with their expansionist dreams of spreading the influence of their commercial and milling centers into the northwestern regions of the United States and Canada. Minnesotans in general, and residents of St. Paul–Minneapolis in particular, thus placed enormous weight on the railroad system hatched in 1857.[57]

Much to Minnesotans' mortification, however, the panic continued to engulf the West, and by May 1858 the financial crisis toppled their regional plans. Ignoring the "memoranda of doubtful accounts," the bankruptcy and foreclosure notices, and the region's general despair, Minnesota's territorial politicians and businessmen encouraged further speculation on the free banking act's circulating notes backed by railroad "special bonds." Having just planted their first crop, many farmers failed immediately on the rapidly depreciating bonds. Already struggling, town-centered businesses soon followed, exposing the problems that rapid and debt-nourished success had engendered.[58]

In October 1857, St. Paul's Lizzie Fuller informed her sister back east that "Excepting the Marshall's and Truman Smith's, there are no business failures yet, but they must come if these times keep on." By November, they had come with a vengeance. Maria Madison made hopeful observa-

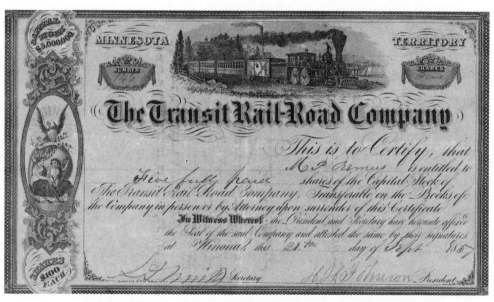

Despite the panic of 1857 and the economic depression that followed, Minnesotans translated their desire for locally controlled railroads into a $5 million "loan of public credit." To fuel railroad construction, the new state legislature issued "special bonds," which unfortunately became worthless in no time.

tions that "we have obtained information, upon the most reliable authority that Messrs. J. C. Winter and J. Frost King, wealthy northern capitalists, have completed arrangements for banking in the city on an extensive scale, and no apprehensions of a sum upon them need to be entertained." When Winter and King arrived, however, they bore insufficient capital to keep their banking houses open. During her visit with Madison and other family and friends that month, Miss Moseley stressed that "tight" failed to convey the alarming nature of Minnesota's "financial cholera," instead likening the territory's afflictions to "the difference between the Frenchman's rheumatism and gout." The harshest of market realities had descended upon Minnesotans: David Merritt never collected on his "30% and 36% per annum" loans, and the Ladies Benevolent Society lost its $350. By March 1858, one local attorney reported that Minnesota's "many millionaires" now found themselves "nearly all bankrupt, our brilliant and fanciful wealth of 1856 vanished into thin air." Moreover, many of those "considered the most wealthy and solvent men in St. Paul [in 1856–57] could not now [in 1858] get credit for a barrel of flour, or even a grocery bill of three dollars."[59]

The "special bonds" proved disastrous, worsening a financial situation already made precarious by the credit notes and liens that had funded territorial and urban developments. Deeply in debt, Minnesotans had no crops and industrial products to sell and no capital to offer their creditors as the financial panic destroyed public and individual confidence in western railroads and "inflicted widespread and acute distress" throughout the nation. With neither the capital resources nor the requisite experience to sustain the new state's agricultural and industrial capacity, Minnesotans foundered under the weight of railroad construction. In just two catastrophic years of operation, the Railroad Loan Bill issued $2,275,000 of the state bonds to Minnesota's four original land-grant railroad companies. But before the end of the first year, all four had defaulted on their loan payments and ended their careers in foreclosure. The legislature reorganized the companies, but in the deepening depression each defaulted once again. The state confiscated their roads, franchises, and other assets, and the "special bonds" became worthless.[60]

Unfortunately for Minnesotans, the railroad bonds continued to circulate throughout the state. By the end of 1860, most local banks had failed, and Minnesota's entire credit structure collapsed. As one shrewd observer noted, Minnesotans had succumbed, along with the rest of the country, to "an overgrowth of banks, and an overtoppling of credit on the overgrowth." Debtors fled the region. During 1860, census takers recorded 172,000 resident Minnesotans, including 2,369 Indians, hardly the sustained boom anticipated earlier. The decision to move forward with rapid expansion took down railroads, banks, stores, factories, and farms, and many entrepreneurs with it. In 1860, those losses included pioneering banker Charles Borup, a once cautious investor who had succumbed to the region's speculative fever. Teen capitalist Truman White reported "the startling news" to his cousin in Ohio, exclaiming, "a well-known and respectable citizen has jumped off the bridge" into the depths of the Mississippi River, leaving behind a widow, several children, and but $20,000 in depreciated property, less than the capital he had arrived with in 1851.[61]

Minnesota's Big Business Bust

At first, many of Minnesota's territorial founders blamed their descent from boom to bust on eastern capitalists and on London, the world financial capital where all nineteenth-century panics started. Those responsible resided within territorial borders, however: much to their own peril, many economic expansionists had chosen to disregard the very realities that had prompted them to seek entrance into the larger national market. At the same time, they had ignored both the competitive forces and the history of industrialization that had caused many an aspiring entrepreneur to overextend resources and thereby overproduce, overbuild, and oversupply the market. As one historically minded Bostonian observed on his tour of St. Paul–Minneapolis, Minnesotans had benefited from the long-established U.S. policy of "bestowing patronage" upon its territorial start-ups—"the government [paid their] political expenses, [built their] roads, and [gave them] a fair start in the world." Along with their "fair start," Minnesotans also benefited from larger Atlantic world forces, including a tide of European immigration that promised to solve their pressing need for agricultural, commercial, and manufacturing laborers. In addition, the rapid westward expansion of railroads and the recently negotiated free-trade treaties between the United States and Great Britain's Canadian colonies quickly pulled immigrants into the Mississippi River trade system and drew the Red River Valley into the American market economy.[62]

Minnesotans lost so much control over their financial destiny in so short a period of time that young Joseph Wheelock, the state's commissioner of statistics in 1860, reported "All the schemes of the day, the value of property, the business enterprises were founded on [optimistic] ratios of growth in population." Furthermore, he grumbled, "lands were bought to supply the demands of an immigration which promised to absorb an empire in its augmenting train. Rates of interests were [also] adjusted to a scale of expectation that was extravagant indeed." Much to their chagrin, Minnesota's youthful enthusiasts had managed to repeat the earlier mistakes of young states bankrupted on canal expansion after the panic of 1837.[63]

The $5 million railroad loan extravaganza bankrupted Minnesota within six months of statehood. By May 1860, the state auditor sold forfeited special-bond bank stocks at seventeen cents on the dollar. St. Paul's town lots depreciated from $5.8 million in 1857 to less than $5 million in 1859; St. Anthony's and Minneapolis's fell much further, from $2.5 million to $1.1 million. Gloomy business prospects caused Minnesota's property valuations to deflate from nearly $50 million to $35 million in the same years. Private and corporate indebtedness stood at $330,000 in state debts, $2,275,000 in contingent railroad debts, and other county, city, and record debts—a total of $9 million, the equivalent of one-fourth the value of private property owned in the state. Immigration to the West virtually stopped, and steamboat arrivals declined from a high of 1,068 in 1858 to 808 in 1860. Few American states had ever experienced such a colossal bust.[64]

As the depression engulfed store after store, industry after industry, and farm after farm, even apparently "going concerns" like the St. Anthony Falls Water Power Company came within an eyelash of failure. Betting their future on the infant railroad companies, politicians and entrepreneurs in St. Paul–Minneapolis overextended themselves to such a degree that many firms failed. Others spent the next ten years struggling to recuperate their losses. Franklin Steele and his water power company associates, for example, expended most of their energies searching for capital to pay back eastern creditors and nearby friends such as Wisconsin's Hercules Dousman, St. Paul's Henry Rice, and others in St. Paul–Minneapolis. Richard Chute spent his time in New York, Washington, and Boston looking for investment capital. Eventually, Chute even encouraged Steele to make a trip to Europe in search of funds.[65]

By 1860, newly arrived (and indebted) farmers had plowed fewer than 25,000 acres for commercial wheat production, even though the commissioner of statistics recorded 21,500 farms with 464,000 acres under cultivation in corn, oats, potatoes, and wheat for local consumption. Infant mills in St. Anthony, Minneapolis, and the now shriveling Stillwater had sawed barely enough wood to meet the region's demands. Many associated with the St. Anthony Falls Water Power Company, in particular, had plunged their earnings into land speculation rather than into manufacturing improvements. Minnesotans produced no articles for export, save furs and fish, and they imported most of their consumer items and all of their breadstuffs. Consequently, the 1857 panic merely expedited a looming crisis already in progress. The nation had another Ohio on its hands, and most people recognized it.[66]

In 1861, summing up the manifold problems Minnesotans had suffered since 1857, Henry Rice—then representing his state in Washington, DC—scribbled a note to Franklin Steele: "One thing I do see is that *all* of the Old settlers in Minnesota are *ruined* hopelessly. I fear Hard times have only just commenced, and yet the people are all crazy. [Alexander] Ramsey left on Friday, or Saturday. My brother Edmund is in Phila., but for what I do not know. Becker thinks of removing to Bayfield [Wisconsin], Stetzer & Mower have gone there already, and others are going." Fur traders and military personnel had seen the opportunities in the towns they founded; however, many lacked both the psychological stamina and the economic and political skills required for the larger leap into railroads and other long-term projects. Steele exemplified the worst among them. In his lust for Minneapolis lands, milling supremacy, and the entire region's riches, he spread himself too thinly and squandered his hold over the milling district he hoped to monopolize. Decried for lacking political savvy and economic integrity, he lost the respect of his neighbors when he fled to avoid paying taxes on his property. Although he retained much of his personal property, Steele frittered away the two things many of the region's aspiring entrepreneurs coveted most: control over his business and the gratitude of a region he helped to found and promote. Those treasures would fall to other entrepreneurs, the ones who had neither lost their heads in the quest for rapid riches and glory nor abandoned their obligations to the communities that nurtured their dreams and, indeed, had come to depend on them.[67]

Minnesota's Ascending Entrepreneurs

Despite the very real financial emergency Minnesotans now faced, entrepreneurs—both long resident and newly arrived—had carried St. Paul–Minneapolis into a new phase of development by exploiting the hinterland, its resources promising to increase their wealth and regional influence. When Charles Francis Adams toured the river towns during September 1860, he remarked, "Though people are obviously not rich, none seems very poor." St. Paul, St. Anthony, and Minneapolis had managed to survive while other towns failed. In fact, for every person who left Minnesota between 1857 and 1861, another immigrant took his or her place, forsaking crises elsewhere in the larger nation.[68]

Throughout the financial crisis, fur-trading Norman Kittson had continued in his role as Hudson's Bay Company agent in St. Paul. As such, he enjoyed a government-sponsored monopoly in British North America that underwrote his expansion into the Red River Valley and allowed for handsome profits on the American-Canadian reciprocity agreement. When other businesses in and around St. Paul collapsed, Kittson used his HBC seed capital to finance small loans in exchange for property mortgages calculated on preboom figures, gaining title to prime St. Paul, Minneapolis, and hinterland real estate. He employed the same strategy for steamboating opportunities, snatching up lines to expand into interior waterways. During 1858, he joined forces with James Burbank; together they soon dominated the transportation arteries—both river and road—into northwestern Minnesota.[69]

In 1859, St. Paulites rewarded Kittson's success as government contractor and surviving entrepreneur by electing him mayor. At the same time, political ally and state investor Henry Rice continued to wield influence in the state senate, making connections with capitalists elsewhere. Henry Sibley employed his territorial appointment to secure some of his investments in a gaslight company; as president, he arranged for exclusive business agreements with St. Paul's city government. In addition, Sibley, Alexander Ramsey, Wisconsin's Hercules Dousman, and others profited from mortgages they sold, particularly those centered on wide-ranging properties (and foreclosures) belonging to the bankrupt Franklin Steele.[70]

Like the generation of men who preceded them in the fur trade, William Davidson and W. D. Washburn had attached themselves to Burbank, Kittson, Sibley, and other surviving and politically connected entrepreneurs. In so doing, they set themselves apart from the rank and file by building traditional, small-scale enterprises into firms that expanded on government contracts and general prosperity during the boom. During 1858, Burbank's reputation as the most reliable overland transportation agent in the region—and his connections with Kittson—won him a lucrative HBC transportation contract that sustained him through the financial depression. Following Burbank's lead, Davidson used cash-only strategies and special agreements with railroads to build up his cash flow. Those tactics soon gave him the leverage required to gobble up competitors along the Mississippi River, firms sinking under the weight of increasing fixed costs on warehouses, steamboats, and real estate. Young Washburn devoted his energies to Minneapolis Mill, agreeing to wait until he received his first dividend from the parent company before venturing elsewhere. Patrolling family investments constantly, he ousted lessees who failed to pay their rent.[71]

With neither mounting debts nor cash-flow problems, Minnesota's surviving entrepreneurs sought and won government contracts and bought land and businesses at foreclosure sales. Their cautious strategies matched those employed by some earlier entrepreneurs along the Atlantic seaboard and in western cities such as Cincinnati, St. Louis, and now Chicago. An emphasis on specialized services and products in markets with sustained demand (including those associated with government entities), combined with a focus on long-term expansion, allowed them to achieve the economies of scale required for larger leaps. Despite the panic, Minnesotans still needed passage and communication into and out of the region, still needed freight and mails hauled and shipped. Reputable steamboat pilots and express agents persevered to provide these services. Minnesotans still needed to feed, clothe, and house themselves. Solvent forwarding and commission merchants, millers, and established agriculturalists procured, manufactured, and extracted to meet these needs.[72]

Those who successfully maneuvered from traditional trading networks into firms fully integrated in the market economy between 1858 and 1861 slowly induced economic recovery in Minnesota. As their businesses survived the many crises brought on by rapid expansion, they married, had babies, built houses in town, helped establish private charity networks, and immersed themselves in the region's social and political life.[73]

While the larger United States collapsed into the Civil War, Minnesota's ascending entrepreneurs stood ready to capture the land-surveying, transportation, and supply contracts that federal and state governments thrust into the northern economy during the early 1860s. An exogenous factor in the region's development, the Civil War stimulated investment in Minnesota and other resource-rich areas far removed from battle but linked closely enough with the northern war effort to supply it with timber, grain, soldiers, and other supplies. Wartime demands not only rescued Minnesota but also inflated the price of its products. The larger community—internal as well as external to the state—supported the entrepreneurial efforts of Kittson, Burbank, Davidson, Washburn, and others because their government contracts and private businesses promised to stabilize the region for resource extraction and future railroad development. The first opportunities arrived with the war's outbreak, when increased demands for timber and wheat products created a federal customer anxious to provide the capital surge on which Minnesota's urban entrepreneurs could build.

1861–1868

Civil War Contracts and the Revival of Minnesota's Economy

AS INTELLECTUAL DESCENDANTS of the eighteenth-century Enlightenment and the philosophies of Adam Smith, Minnesotans had learned to equate progress with wealth creation. By the time they joined the American nation in 1858, the railroad had emerged as the symbol of both. Touring Canada and the United States during the Civil War, Englishman George Tuthill Borrett wrote to his father that Americans, more than any other people, understood the "all-important influence" of railroads: "They civilise with the steam-engine and the telegraph—the Bible is left to follow—and these two pioneers of civilisation [tow] worldly prosperity" in their wake. Comparing the American quest for private gain to the Canadian colonists' continued reliance on the British Parliament for economic development, Borrett further claimed that American ideas and institutions justified their laws that encouraged development by releasing the nation's creative energies. "On the American side," he wrote, "the egg is prematurely hatched, the foetus artificially developed, and yet, the wheels run easily, the machinery is well-oiled; there is less hitch or clog about it than in Canada."[1]

St. Paul–Minneapolis's entrepreneurs understood the railroad's wealth-creating potential well enough in theory, but by 1861 they had failed to profit from that knowledge in any practical way. Instead, they had learned the painful lessons of "prematurely hatched" railroad schemes. As elsewhere in the industrializing United States, successful railroads depended upon finding capital enough to build them and commerce enough to make them pay. Despite high transportation and communication costs in out-of-the-way areas such as Minnesota, insufficient products and consumers constituted barriers that frustrated the state's railroad-hungry residents. Between

1861 and 1865, the Civil War rectified both problems. Government contracts enriched Minnesota's surviving urban entrepreneurs, and various federal acts pushed more immigrants into the hinterland north, south, and west of St. Paul–Minneapolis. Larger national events thus ushered in a sea change, though this outcome was not evident in the early spring of 1861.[2]

Although Henry Sibley, Henry Rice, and other Democratic faithfuls dominated territorial politics throughout the 1850s, Republicans carried nearly two-thirds of the state in 1860. Committed to the Union cause but far removed from combat, urban entrepreneurs found themselves strategically positioned for the war effort. Between 1861 and 1865, several turned wartime exigencies and inflation into highly profitable ventures. During the three years that followed, they also completed the intrastate railroad network envisioned a decade earlier. Entrepreneurs who successfully managed the leap from traditional to modern enterprise between 1861 and 1868 revived the region. They also learned to employ their skills as political brokers and big business executives, and their efforts catapulted St. Paul, St. Anthony, and Minneapolis into trajectories carrying them toward their future as cities structured for long-term industrial expansion.[3]

Entrepreneurial Beneficiaries of the Civil War

Though at its outbreak few imagined and fewer still wanted to fight a prolonged and bloody civil war, the conflict arrived at a propitious moment for northern industrialists and Minnesota's aspiring entrepreneurs. Minnesotans quickly mustered over nine hundred men, hoping that, as the first western state to offer volunteers, they would be rewarded for their early participation. Very soon, the federal government responded, authorizing contracts that stimulated capital investments in northern waterways and railroads. Wartime preparation also escalated demand for raw materials from Minnesota's hinterland, where earlier expansion had planted some 150,000 immigrants for timber extraction and commercial wheat production. Federal contracts therefore promised to foster wealth-creating ventures among Minnesotans who had survived the financial panic of 1857, provided they could manipulate these opportunities.

Larger phenomena had combined to assist in this effort through 1861, including the Atlantic world's sustained demand for products to feed, clothe, and shelter expanding populations. The *1860 Census of Manufactures* recorded $2.4 million invested in Minnesota's 562 infant mills, where 2,125 workers produced lumber, flour, and other articles valued at just under $3.4 million—a modest sum, but a vast increase over 1850's minuscule numbers. Minnesota's population reached 172,000 in 1860, including 2,639

Indians—the grand total well under predictions yet a significant change from the 6,077 Euro-Americans recorded and some 12,000 Indians estimated in the 1850 census. With Euro-Americans dominating the business-oriented landscape and with signs of economic recovery evident in St. Paul–Minneapolis, the influx of immigrants promised to buttress the impact of population increases once Minnesota inched its way out of the financial depression.[4]

Between April 1861 and July 1862, the federal government sparked Minnesota's economic recovery through contracts, appointments, and incentives. These inducements sustained several transportation, commercial, and milling enterprises launched during the late 1850s, including Davidson's La Crosse and Minnesota Steam Packet Company, Washburn's Minneapolis Mill, St. Paul's Minnesota and Pacific Railroad, and Burbank's North-Western Express. But even these surviving entrepreneurs knew they faced competition for the resources of their own hinterland. As established railroads in Chicago and Milwaukee completed lines through Illinois, Iowa, and Wisconsin, they threatened to vault the Mississippi River and expand their commercial, manufacturing, and population networks westward into Minnesota's forests and wheat-growing prairies. Should Chicago's reach extend so far, entrepreneurs in St. Paul–Minneapolis feared they would lose control of their railroads and the waterfall's "abundant motive power" as well as the "facilities for cheap distribution" that promised to provide a "surplus to eager markets on both banks of the great [Mississippi] and its tributaries." Thus, during 1861, even the most prosperous Minnesotans found themselves at a disadvantage vis-à-vis states with established cities connected to sufficiently populated and productive hinterlands. As a result, local entrepreneurs soon moved to exploit opportunities before others beat them to it.[5]

Like the fur traders, merchants, and millers who preceded them, Davidson, Washburn, and Burbank had entered the territory during their twenties and early thirties, connecting themselves to the region's established businessmen and politicians. Having ascended the ranks over the course of a decade, they shifted into larger-scale operations during the Civil War while people like Franklin Steele, Henry Rice, and Ignatius Donnelly temporarily absented themselves from Minnesota. Steele removed to Philadelphia to raise funds; Rice served the state's interests as a Democratic senator in Washington, DC; and Donnelly carried Minnesota's Republican torch into the House of Representatives.[6]

Between 1861 and 1862, Davidson emerged as "the old man of the river," standing atop Minnesota's transportation food chain. When war broke out in the spring, he acquired government contracts to carry soldiers and provisions between St. Paul and other regional railroad hubs. These contracts subsidized the development of his Northern Line, a fleet of steamboats plying between St. Paul and St. Louis. Drawbacks and excise tax "refunds" helped him initiate rate wars aimed at weakened steamboat lines and fledgling barge operations. As he consolidated failed enterprises into his Northwest Packet Company, connecting St. Paul with Dubuque, Iowa, Davidson gained a virtual monopoly over freight and passenger traffic between Minnesota and the east and south. His fortune bred additional successes in St. Paul as suppliers scrambled to furnish the steamboat captain with volunteers, mails, timber, wheat, and other provisions for the northern war effort.[7]

Despite his deserved reputation as the most dangerous predator along the Mississippi's headwaters, "Commodore" Davidson had begun to forfeit his transportation monopoly from the moment of his first arrangement with the La Crosse railroads. No one appreciated that fact more than Davidson himself. Unlike many riverboat captains, he recognized the diminishing prospects for the Mississippi River's share of the northwestern trade. Thus, he launched steamboat rate wars to maximize profits while he could, at the same time moving his investments into one of St. Paul's railroads. The Civil War provided impetus for this shift, but Davidson still awaited the development of products that would make railroad investments pay.[8]

The federal government also declared its intention to subsidize lumbering when it opened up the new state's pine forests for wartime production. Politics once again came into play, this time thanks to C. C. Washburn, who as a leading Republican had delivered Wisconsin and Minnesota for the party and had earned a spot in the White House inner circle. Choosing credible allies to meet the Union's wartime needs, President Lincoln bestowed the appointment of Minnesota's surveyor-general upon C. C.'s brother, thirty-year-old lumberman-attorney William Drew Washburn. While political loyalty swayed Lincoln's decision, Washburn's management techniques, which had maintained Minneapolis Mill's profitability during the state's financial crisis, also earned him the appointment. With this assignment, lumbering opportunities in Minnesota suddenly multiplied, giving Washburn a "chance to realize" returns on sawmilling operations and Davidson new possibilities to profit by shipping Minneapolis Mill's lumber. Aware that political patronage conferred economic benefits upon those who employed appointments wisely, Washburn handed the firm's management over to his capable cousin, Dorilus Morrison, and tramped northward to survey Minnesota's pinelands. According to one observer, "through the influence of [his] senior brothers, and through their capital," Washburn thus "succeeded in securing large quantities of pine lands by reasons of the knowledge and power coming from [his] position."[9]

When Washburn ventured into Minnesota's northern timberlands, he set himself apart from those who had preceded him by eschewing *ad hoc*, seat-of-the-pants tactics in favor of the strategic business plan his older brother had formulated for Minneapolis Mill Company. Benefiting from his government appointment, W. D. made investment choices that promised long-term returns. First, he purchased pinelands along the Mississippi River from its wellhead at Lake Itasca south to the Minneapolis Mill Company's dam. Wartime inflation quickly boosted the value of the land and its timber, and as Washburn cleared the forests for his own operation he also sold off some of his real estate. Next, he sought to control timber processing from the northlands to his dam site by encouraging other government-appointed surveyors to set up operations along the Minneapolis shoreline. He offered them generous leasing agreements—provided they adhered to the firm's policies promoting the waterfall's manufacturing potential. These agreements restricted proprietors' land use to mills and mill maintenance and required that they secure permission before diverting any of the water elsewhere, endorsements W. D. rarely granted. In this way, he attracted sawmillers who shared the Minneapolis Mill vision.[10]

In March 1862, on rapid and profitable land turnovers, the young surveyor-general and Minneapolis Mill associate formed William D. Washburn & Co., a timberland operation headquartered along the waterfall's western shoreline. He sent large quantities of cut timber to the Minneapolis boom, selling some to the government through local sawmillers and floating the rest farther downriver to customers throughout the Mississippi River Valley. Within a few months, wartime inflation and increased demand generated sufficient returns to hoist Washburn into his own lumber business.[11]

During the summer of 1862, Washburn opened a lumberyard and erected Lincoln Mill, the sixth sawmill located on the Minneapolis Mill dam. In keeping with the mill company's enduring business strategy, he reinvested 30 percent of his net earnings from real estate, Lincoln Mill, and William D. Washburn & Co. in the parent firm's improvement fund. Minneapolis Mill soon generated revenues that allowed W. D. Washburn, his brother Cadwallader, their cousin Morrison, and their partner Robert Smith to tighten control of the parent firm. Recognizing that long-term profits lay in milling, the Washburn-Morrison-Smith team exchanged their Minneapolis real estate for other stockholders' shares in the company. By the middle of the decade, they had realized C. C.'s original vision: the four manufacturing planners owned the entire stock of Minneapolis Mill.[12]

By the time the river opened for navigation in 1862, Davidson's federal transportation contracts and Washburn's timber-surveying appointment had stimulated enough business to interest eastern capitalists in the state's bankrupt railroads, particularly the Minnesota and Pacific. Headquartered in St. Paul, the railroad promised plentiful profits on land grants stretching north along the Mississippi River and west to Dakota Territory. On March 10, 1862, by an act of the Minnesota legislature, the newly incorporated St. Paul and Pacific Railroad (SP&P) seized the twice-forfeited rights, properties, and franchises of the Minnesota and Pacific line. The next day the company's board of directors—including St. Paul attorney Edmund Rice, St. Paul banker James E. Thompson, and St. Anthony Falls Water Power Company agent Richard Chute—met for the first time. Moving to exploit the new opportunity, the board elected Rice president and Horace Thompson, James Thompson's younger brother and banking associate, treasurer. While reorganization was one thing, reinvigoration was quite another. Despite their desire to control the company without the "intrigues of foreign [capital's] influence," the railroad as yet had neither sufficient passengers nor adequate freight for survival, never mind success. Only months after its reorganization, these realities and the SP&P's costs forced its new owners to admit that the local road needed eastern support.[13]

In a desperate attempt to stay afloat, SP&P directors approached eastern investors, exchanging some ownership for a then-sizeable $700,000 loan to build a line from St. Paul to Watab, some eighty miles away. New York's Samuel Tilden and Russell Sage provided the needed capital because they believed in the railroad's promise; they also concluded that Minnesota's hustlers had mismanaged their enterprise and that proper administration would set things right. The capital infusion bought the construction team a little time, but after pouring money into timber and rolling stock for the first ten miles between St. Paul and St. Anthony, the SP&P's directors lacked capital to complete the next seventy miles of track. Thus, Edmund Rice entered the company into a $1.2 million mortgage on June 2, 1862—this time with the Litchfield brothers, influential Brooklyn investors. The mortgage added another burden to the existing $2 million bond issued to cover earlier construction and equipment costs.[14]

To bring eastern investors onboard, Minnesotans forfeited ownership in the SP&P. However, for the first time in the state's short railroad history, local residents secured control over their vision: the railroad would remain in St. Paul, and they could continue building westward. Within weeks, the strategy paid off. As winter slipped into April and sirens heralded the season's first steamboats, one of Davidson's barges towed the locomotive *William Crooks* up the Mississippi River from La Crosse. Meanwhile, one railroad tie followed another as the SP&P reached St. Anthony. On June 27, shipping merchants at the Lower Levee received a collection of passenger cars. By noon the next day, railroad superintendent William Crooks had the cars lined up behind his namesake engine. Two hours later, nearly one hundred guests joined Minnesota's lieutenant governor, St. Paul's mayor and aldermen, and the railroad's directors to inaugurate the line. With the railroad, St. Paul—the "precocious child of the prairie"—passed into an industrial adolescence; St. Anthony–Minneapolis followed shortly thereafter.[15]

Leaving St. Paul at 2:30 PM on June 28, the *William Crooks* stopped briefly in St. Anthony and re-entered the capital in time for dinner at six—a swift twenty-mile excursion compared to the standard, full-day journey up and down the river. After a five-year wait, Minnesotans celebrated their first railroad connection: a modest accomplishment when measured against expansive predictions and an equally expansive faith. Nevertheless, just as in 1855, when the wire-suspension bridge across the Mississippi River had signified the commitment between St. Anthony and Minneapolis, the ten-mile line gave Minnesotans a railroad—and for now, one sufficed. With the first railroad link complete, residents of St. Paul–Minneapolis chugged one step closer to their founders' vision. Freed from total dependence on waterways, they could turn their towns into a metropolitan axis with abundant transportation arteries, numerous financial and commercial houses, and scores of milling establishments linked to agricultural producers and consumers in the developing hinterland.[16]

A few elated residents called for the St. Paul and Pacific to consecrate this pivotal moment in Minnesota's history with a "general jubilee"; however, no one protested when the road's directors announced that "appropriate ceremonies" would have to wait until the company could sustain a twenty-mile line northwest to Anoka. After all, Minnesotans possessed intimate knowledge of the railroad's frailties, especially given the distressing liaisons they had carried on with various enterprises in the all-too-recent past. Thus, on Sunday, June 29, a battle near Charleston, South Carolina, and speculation about the Union's future took precedence in local papers while two paragraphs covered the previous day's railroad coronation in St. Paul. More apology than eulogy, the "Opening of the Railroad to St. Anthony" painfully reminded Minnesotans of the price they had paid for statehood and industrial change. But no matter their troubles, residents found encouragement in the SP&P's promise to forge ahead with construction activities as rapidly as possible despite financial anxieties and the Civil War.[17]

Cautious enthusiasm prevailed through the next two months despite the nation's deepening involvement in the war. However, a local fracas between Indians and Euro-American settlers confirmed the wisdom of the wait-

and-see vigil. After years of frustrating privation, unanswered pleas for assistance, and the realization that Minnesota's legislators had detoured annuity payments into failed banks and the state's railroad sinking fund, Dakota Indians finally resorted to violence. On August 18, 1862, a large group of Dakota surrounded a Minnesota River trading village near the Lower Sioux Agency. Both sides suffered casualties, and frightened inhabitants throughout the state found themselves briefly entangled in a second, more immediate war.[18]

By October 1862, the Dakota War had ended, but racial strife had permanently severed the fragile ties between Native and Euro-American cultures. On December 27, Henry Sibley—long-time self-styled friend to the region's Native Americans—telegraphed news from Washington, DC: by order of the president, Minnesotans could execute "38 Indians and half-breeds" for their participation in the uprising. Further, the Minnesota legislature removed both Dakota and Ojibwe people from settled areas, tramping them to swampland reservations along the Minnesota-Ontario border between Red Lake and Lake of the Woods. These punishments resulted in a wartime expedient: the federal government reclaimed a large chunk of the Fort Snelling reserve for military operations, curtailing economic development south along Minneapolis's shoreline. While Washburn's mills kept humming, other Minneapolis investments went into limbo.

Uncertainties caused by the Dakota War delayed railroad construction beyond St. Paul to St. Anthony; however, by the time newspapers published the St. Paul and Pacific's "Time-Table No. 1" on October 14, 1862, those same quandaries served to lift the hinterland out of its troubles. Final Indian removals awarded Minnesota's Euro-Americans what they had desired all along: complete control over the region. The conflict also created new opportunities. James Burbank, for example, obtained state and federal contracts to transport soldiers and supplies into the southern Minnesota war zone. During the next two years, he profited enormously, using his operation to plant settlers and investments along the lines of future railroad expansion. Summing up the outlook for Minnesota's opportunity seekers, a local business directory noted: "If Saint Paul ever attains the metropolitan destiny which her people confidently expect, it must be from the growth of the country adjacent and north and west of her particularly, and when her railroads are built and her merchants become merchant *princes* in liberality, public spirit and forecaste—from the country south of her also." Again, government contracts played the critical role: just as they had assisted Davidson's Mississippi River business to the east and south, they also aided Burbank's transportation network developing to the north- and southwest.[19]

Burbank initially built on contracts from the British-owned Hudson's Bay Company. This foundation allowed North-Western Express to expand into transportation, storage, shipping, grocery, and wholesale clothing businesses on hinterland trading networks between 1858 and 1862. With the federal and state government's wartime largesse, he pushed those lines farther inland, along the future paths of the state's land-grant railroads. By the outbreak of the Dakota War, Burbank's thriving business had emerged as the logical candidate for federal agents to favor as they inspected the region for transportation contractors.[20]

The Minnesota legislature awarded Burbank's firm a major contract: control over the state's overland networks, including the shipment of people, supplies, mail, and furs to and from hinterland regions south and west of St. Paul–Minneapolis. With this guaranteed income, Burbank invested in larger-scale, limited liability corporations, including those connected with Davidson's expanding La Crosse and Minnesota Steam Packet empire and Kittson's far-reaching steamboat lines.[21]

Seeking to branch out on his own after the Dakota War, Burbank sold some of his interest in North-Western Express to his brother Henry and other associates. He then formed J. C. Burbank and Co., an exclusive government contractor for transportation and supply focused particularly on grain and other provisions. With the government's stake in his success assured, Burbank ventured more deeply into other shipping partnerships. His several forwarding and commission lines soon reached from St. Paul into the Red River Valley and Dakota Territory, all along the proposed routes of Minnesota's land-grant railroads. By 1865, in addition to Red River steamers and other endeavors, he worked over seven hundred horses and two hundred men along his expanding lines of influence. The firm carried Minnesota's Civil War volunteers to La Crosse and Rock Island, where they boarded Davidson's steamboats heading south to St. Louis. Both men profited enormously, and they developed an appreciation for each other's talents, not only in business but also in marshaling government funds to promote and broker local interests.[22]

Abundant wartime commerce provided Burbank and his partners with valuable experience in negotiating the leap into larger enterprises. Employing time-tested cost-cutting measures to ration his government seed capital and separating business and marketing roles to complement each partner's expertise, Burbank parsed the firm into manageable divisions. New branch operations controlled specialized retail shops, land-sale offices, and warehouses at strategic points along the Mississippi, Minnesota, and Red Rivers, with Burbank overseeing the company from St. Paul. His brother Henry watched over the St. Cloud business while new partners

108   CIVIL WAR CONTRACTS

Amherst H. Wilder and J. C. Merriam ventured into real estate, wholesaling, and forwarding and commission opportunities in St. Paul–Minneapolis. Each time Burbank established a hinterland outlet along roads, rivers, or proposed rail routes, he bought local real estate to enlarge his physical plant and to fuel further developments. As he ran out of relatives, he employed many of St. Paul–Minneapolis's young climbers. His networks set the stage for several Minnesotans' entry into postwar railroad operations through decisions foreordained in 1862, when the federal government announced incentives that pushed some 80,000 immigrants into Minnesota during the three years that followed.[23]

Between May and July 1862, the federal government passed the Homestead, Pacific Railroad, and Morrill Acts, each of which further stimulated Minnesota's economic development. This legislation extended the settlement process begun with the ordinances of the 1780s and multiplied the attractions that lured agricultural settlers to Minnesota's wheat-growing lands. Enhancing the 1841 Preemption Act, the Homestead Act formalized the idea that lands should go to actual settlers at the lowest possible price. The Pacific Railroad and Morrill Acts promised to subsidize the cultivation and increase the production of the region's soil. These laws—together with wartime inflation and rising national demand for Minnesota's timber, wheat, and wool products—renewed people's hopes for a prosperous and secure future while facilitating repayment of ante-bellum debts.[24]

The acts' detractors cautioned that land give-aways not only encouraged dangerous speculations like those that had embroiled the nation in the financial panics of 1837 and 1857 and imperiled one of the government's most lucrative revenue sources but also imposed unjust costs upon residents of older regions, especially in the southern slave states. With southern obstructionists out of Congress and the Civil War stretching into a second deadly year, northern members pushed the bills through, arguing that homesteads promised to stimulate agricultural production, stabilize northern communities, and pull war-weary residents away from the Confederacy.[25]

Passed on May 20, 1862, the Homestead Act offered U.S. citizens— current and prospective—a once-in-a-lifetime deal: 160 acres of the public domain in exchange for an eighteen-dollar filing fee and a promise to maintain residence for five years. Bolstering that generous grant, on July 1 President Lincoln signed the Pacific Railroad Act, incorporating the Union Pacific Company. Subsidized with federal lands, the company promised to build a rail line from Nebraska to the Central Pacific Railroad, thereby forming the nation's first transcontinental line. Pledging immense tracts of public land to support western railroad construction, the act envisioned three transcontinental routes; the northern one promising to traverse lands in Minnesota, from the Wisconsin border at Lake Superior west to the Pacific Coast. Then, on July 2, Congress passed the Morrill Act, extending the federal commitment to commercial farming along western immigration and railroad routes. Government lands would subsidize state agricultural colleges, where agronomists could teach farmers about the latest technological advances in American agri-business. By the end of 1862, these vast promises—160-acre homesteads, transcontinental rail routes, and state agricultural colleges—demonstrated the federal government's dedication to agricultural development through a dual approach, stimulating settlement and underwriting railroad construction along lines of western cultivation.[26]

Between 1863 and 1865, on the strength of earlier successes and promised riches, Minnesotans embarked on plans to draw immigrants, capital, and railroads into their expanding business and political webs. They launched a period of corporate reorganization and competition that stimulated the development of an intrastate railroad network; new rail-to-river shipment services and forwarding, commission, wholesaling, and distribution businesses at St. Paul; larger manufacturing projects in Minneapolis; and extensive reshipping ventures northward from the Falls of St. Anthony.[27]

Minnesota's Homesteading Immigrants

As potential homesteaders wended their way west during the Civil War, Minnesota's population increased by 45 percent—from 172,000 to nearly 251,000—between 1862 and 1865. By the latter year, immigrants restored St. Paul's population to its pre-panic total of 13,000 and increased Minneapolis's from 2,800 to 4,600. Arriving from near and far, these immigrants buttressed the impact of earlier migrations; as both producers and consumers, they also increased opportunities for business expansion throughout the region. Accordingly, in an 1864 address to the national House of Representatives, Ignatius Donnelly declared that, "with nearly one billion [acres] of unsettled lands on one side of the Atlantic, and with many millions of poor and oppressed people on the other, let *the people of the North* organize the exodus which must come, and build, if necessary, a bridge of gold across the chasm which divides them, that the chosen races of mankind may occupy the chosen lands of the world." Answering his call, many immigrants invested their futures in Minnesota, increasing St. Paul's assessed property valuations to $2.7 million and Minneapolis–St. Anthony's to $924,000. In the hinterland, where prices had climbed from $1.25 an acre to more than $7.00 on lands near proposed rail lines, immigrant investments raised the possibility of millions more. Expansion in St. Paul–Minneapolis bolstered Minnesota's coffers with tax revenues that provided $202,000 of the $261,000 collected statewide during 1865. Small in comparison to the totals in nearby Wisconsin and Illinois, these sums nevertheless offered tangible signs that Minnesota had recovered from its earlier setbacks, evidence that lured more immigrants into the region.[28]

The immigration tide that had swept through Illinois and Wisconsin prior to the Civil War rolled steadily over Minnesota. Between 1863 and 1865, tens of thousands of new settlers arrived on steamboats from La Crosse, debarking at St. Paul for passage into the north- and southwestern parts of the state. Before long, like elsewhere in the western United States, competition for these immigrants—whether entrepreneurs or laborers or farmers—culminated in the creation of "land companies." Bombarded by increasing numbers of steamboat and express company delegates, pineland agents, railroad representatives, and real estate speculators, western immigrants began hiring themselves out as "invented" or "temporary" homesteaders. Paying for their land claims with the sponsoring agent's funds, they promised to maintain a productive agricultural residence until the title matured, a period that lasted anywhere from six months to the full five years, at which point they turned their lands over to the employing agency. Among such agents in Minnesota, politically astute steamboat captains, express company delegates, and lumbering entrepreneurs made the first substantial gains.[29]

In the strictest legal sense, homesteading "deals" represented an enormous fraud practiced upon the federal government; however, Americans had used land claim "inventions" long before the Homestead Act as a way to stimulate production, consumption, and business expansion. Indeed, land laws reflected an outmoded ideal of rural self-sufficiency long after farmers and new immigrants had embraced the market economy. By 1862, Americans had devised methods of cheating the land laws in the same ways that they had worked out Indian removals for private gain. Federal agents looked the other way provided homesteaders and land agents remained within the bounds of decorum, which usually meant staying inside the state claimed as their residence. The land-company logic seemed self-evident to nineteenth-century nation builders, particularly with the United States facing immanent disunion. By promoting rapid real estate turnovers, land-company agents peopled the underdeveloped West with farmers who could meet northeastern demands for wheat, timber, wool, and other agricultural commodities. While cash-poor farmers often found themselves stuck within an unyielding system of "debt peonage," many who settled Minnesota lands acquired under the Homestead Act managed to prosper on a few mild winters, banner crops, escalating demands, and wartime inflation. But some abandoned the project for opportunities elsewhere, moving to St. Paul–Minneapolis or exploring other of the developing nation's urban and rural locales.[30]

Swift homesteading turnovers stimulated other investments, particularly among those who had learned to manipulate the expanding American political economy. Washburn's workers cut timber for Minneapolis millers. Burbank's employees supplied outposts with settlers, provisions, and trade. New entrepreneurs in St. Anthony–Minneapolis manufactured farm machinery. Transportation agents and railroad companies sold land on relatively reasonable terms. St. Paul–based freight-forwarding agents distributed water, wood, and coal throughout the region. Entrepreneurs built warehouses, elevators, and larger shops and mills to accommodate the increased flow of immigrants and commerce. Local capitalists opened banks and insurance companies secured by New York and Philadelphia houses to safeguard these ventures. Through such activities, Minnesota's urban-based entrepreneurs also stimulated business that promised to enrich the state's urban and rural residents rather than absentee speculators. Minnesota's legislators, most thoroughly entangled in regional business networks themselves, assisted in the effort by reorganizing and incorporating railroads and other firms that promised to accomplish long-standing expansionist plans.[31]

The state's struggling railroads benefited immediately from immigration promotions and rapid real estate turnovers. Railroad construction and farm development required patient and plentiful capital before anyone could hope to reap the riches of the fertile but sparsely settled Red River Valley. Renewed immigration into Minnesota, along with the assistance of Edmund Rice's brother, Senator Henry M. Rice, prompted outside financiers such as Edwin Litchfield and his brothers to invest in the struggling sp&p. Their capital injection quickly culminated in construction of the twenty-mile line to Anoka, completed on December 30, 1863—the first railroad push toward the Red River Valley.[32]

With the St. Paul and Pacific's connection to Anoka an accomplished fact, Minnesota's legislators stepped forward to bolster further construction. On February 6, 1864, following corporate machinations and legislative hustling in St. Paul, the state approved a special act that secured an additional $3 million in bonds for construction projects aimed at the Red River Valley. Leveraging the political decision, sp&p president Edmund Rice embarked on investment strategies to strengthen the railroad's position in Minnesota. During the spring of 1865, he acquired more money from the Litchfield brothers, who by then had sent the youngest, Egbert, to St. Paul to manage their investments. The Litchfields' capital propped up the rail-road's coffers and accelerated construction into the state's already populated agricultural regions.[33]

At the same time, William Davidson aligned himself with other local nabobs to exploit southwestern Minnesota's market opportunities and to deflect intruding foreign capitalists. During 1864, along with express agent Burbank, lumber baron Washburn, milling expansionist Steele, ex-governor Sibley, and banker-negotiator Thompson, Davidson reorganized the bankrupt Southern Minnesota Railroad Company. Relaunching it as the Minnesota Valley Railroad (MVR), the new firm's executives and principal stockholding directors subscribed $473,000 of the $500,000 in capital stock authorized by the state legislature. Through the MVR, Davidson and his allies hoped to connect Minneapolis's sawmilling operations to estab-lished lumber markets in southern Minnesota, Iowa, and Nebraska and to link the wheat-growing corridor along the Mississippi, Minnesota, and Missouri Rivers to hungry consumers in the United States and Europe. Their shift from informal, traditional partnerships to the incorporated MVR came at a fortuitous moment, for in 1864 larger national events prompted Minnesota's state legislators to endorse all the schemes put forth by the reorganized railroad.[34]

That summer, the federal government once again raised entrepreneur-ial expectations in Minnesota, this time by moving forward with transcon-tinental railroad plans. During the early phases of the Civil War, Maine's state legislature had awarded Josiah Perham a charter to build the "People's Railroad" west from Portland. Perham initially prohibited mortgages and limited the purchase of shares to but one per investor; not surprisingly, these restrictions attracted few venture capitalists. As plans for the People's line started to disintegrate, friends, among them Henry Rice, persuaded Perham that the railroad required a congressional charter, complete with sensible financing and provisions to build through Minnesota to the Pacific Northwest. At the same time, associates of Canada's British-owned Grand Trunk Railway tried to gain control of the young road, inspiring fear that, without congressional support, the dream of a northern, American-operated transcontinental route would evaporate.[35]

On July 2, 1864, Congress safeguarded Perham's vision by approving an act to create the Northern Pacific Railroad Company (NPR), a Wisconsin corporation empowered to build from Lake Superior to Washington Ter-ritory's Puget Sound. As the road's promise drew more and more home-steaders to Wisconsin and Minnesota, St. Paul–Minneapolis businessmen-politicians sought to lure NPR contracts into their expanding regional plans. Senator Henry Rice and ex-governor Alexander Ramsey stepped forward to spearhead the effort, which included creation of a state immigration board.³⁶

In founding the Minnesota State Board of Immigration during 1864, officials followed strategies employed by more established states, formalizing the important role business and government cooperation would play in peopling the state and expanding the nation. Minnesota's board devoted considerable space in its early guidebooks to advertising the promise of agri-business and to touting the increasing significance of St. Paul and Minneapolis as the unfolding commercial and manufacturing "emporiums" for the "New Northwest." Promotional literature attempted to lure settlers not to a hardscrabble, hand-to-mouth existence along the frontier but rather with the riches they would enjoy as the agricultural sector of an integrated urban-rural network of farms, railroads, shops, mills, and factories supplying markets near and far. In crafting whitewashed versions of Minnesota's bounty, its "healthful climate," and other fictions, the state legislature worked with steamboat entrepreneurs like Davidson, overland transporters like Burbank, pineland realtors like Washburn, and reorganized railroad boards. Together, they hoped to draw more people and capital and thus to attract additional railroad construction, economic opportunities, and political patronage for themselves and their friends.³⁷

As Englishman Borrett journeyed two hundred miles by railroad from Chicago to La Crosse and then another two hundred upriver to St. Paul during 1864, he marveled at the "chronic state of fidgets" induced by federal acts and local promotional campaigns. "Men and women of every age, babies in arms, females almost as numerous as the males, crowd the cars, stuff the steamboats, overwhelm the omnibuses, and storm the hotels!" he exclaimed. Once in St. Paul, Borrett declared, "agriculture increases its area, and every day sees new settlers arriving and fresh lands subjected to the plough [while] commerce follows in its wake. Being on the highway of the Mississippi, the great artery of the North West, the city must rise in importance with the development of the country, and the signs of St. Paul's future rise are already visible."³⁸

With signs of "progress" manifest in St. Paul, immigrants swarmed over Minnesota during 1864 and 1865. At the end of this period, the state's land registrars had recorded nearly 10,000 new homestead entries. Meanwhile, various railroads constructed 210 miles of track shadowing the overland and water routes built by Minnesota's entrepreneurs. As Davidson, Burbank, Washburn, and others prospered by these connections, they channeled some of their earnings into St. Paul and Minneapolis, erecting new business blocks and donating funds to educational, religious, and other social institutions. They also jockeyed for government appropriations and for positions inside city and state politics.[39]

As greater numbers of immigrants settled on farms, acres under cultivation for commercial wheat soared from 25,000 in 1862 to more than 1.2 million at the end of 1865, for the first time placing the young state on the nation's list of important grain suppliers. On wartime inflation, Minnesota's per-bushel wheat prices rose from an average of 50 cents in 1862 to 75 cents in 1863 to beyond $1.50 by the end of 1865, a three-year increase with few precedents in the developing West. Enjoying sustained demand for timber and wheat, Minnesota residents settled debts and generated state and federal revenues—through property as well as income taxes following the nation's first income tax law, passed on August 5, 1861. Homesteaders bought more land and more equipment—the mowers, reapers, threshers, and other farm implements required to achieve the economies of scale that would transform their modest human capital into agri-business. They purchased this equipment, along with food, lumber, clothing, and other articles, in St. Paul–Minneapolis, where a multiplying population of entrepreneurial hopefuls developed the wholesaling, manufacturing, and service-oriented networks required for larger-scale consumption. Plowing some of their earnings back into expansion, St. Paulites and Minneapolitans knew that if they could sustain railroad development they had a real chance to triumph over other regional boosters.[40]

During 1865—with the Civil War finished and immigrants and capital pouring into the state—Minnesota's transportation entrepreneurs got on with the business of building railroads, aiming to transform St. Paul and Minneapolis from riparian towns into hubs for industrial expansion.

Minnesota's Postwar Railroad Builders

Between 1866 and 1868, railroad expansion launched the rise of big business in Minnesota and linked its cities with an agricultural hinterland that produced and consumed commodities on which urban opportunity seekers hoped to capitalize. Although the federal government had championed railroad enthusiasm by donating millions of acres to the cause, land-grant builders understood that "free land" came with certain obligations. In addition to prohibitive construction schedules, land-grant charters included a significant caveat: the government could seize lucrative acreage if builders failed to complete the lines on time. Further, in most cases, railroad companies had to show "sufficient" construction progress before they could sell any of their lands for townsite expansion and agricultural production—sales critical to stimulating freight and passenger traffic and making railroads pay. To meet these challenges, Minnesota's new rail-roader-politicians renegotiated their construction timetables through 1873 and made "sufficient progress" in stimulating interest among both investors and actual settlers.[41]

Under the care of Burbank, Davidson, Washburn, and their associates, the Minnesota Valley Railroad opened its line from the state capital into the southern suburb of West St. Paul on August 24, 1866. Spanning the Mississippi River via a conveniently located bridge, the MVR immediately drew trade away from the horse-and-wagon express companies that had enjoyed a near-monopoly on business between St. Paul and its cross-river agricultural communities. As an insider, Burbank suffered nothing: he had sold his express interests before any trains thundered over the bridge. In the next year, the MVR completed another forty-eight miles, from West St. Paul to Belle Plaine. As the locomotive's speed proved attractive to the majority of settlers traveling into southern Minnesota via West St. Paul during 1867, the iron horse overwhelmed its express and steamboat competitors for passenger traffic. Again, insider Davidson suffered no loss, having already sold off many of his steamboats. As the state's increasingly robust and ubiquitous rail system wove a path through Minnesota's timber and wheat-growing districts, it captured freight traffic as well. By the end of 1867, railroads had snatched the bulk of the state's freight business—with the exception of Davidson's Mississippi steamboat trade south toward St. Louis—on lines that expanded from 210 miles in 1865 into an increasingly productive 429-mile network centered on St. Paul.[42]

The MVR co-opted much of the lumber traffic previously carried by steamboats plying the Minnesota and Missouri Rivers, particularly after it completed 90 of its planned 121 miles of track between St. Paul and Sioux City, Iowa, in 1868. Under indefatigable railroad promoter Edmund S. Rice's direction, however, the reinvigorated SP&P played an even more pivotal role in the state's river-to-rail conversion. While southwestern Minnesota offered quick returns for local capitalists engaged in the MVR, the Red River Valley promised the wheat-growing bounty that had enticed immigrants, capital, and railroads into St. Paul–Minneapolis from the beginning. With "food cheap, land the same, house-rent not yet high, labour extremely scarce, and wages good enough," expanding railroads had the potential "to populate the country ten times as fast as [Civil War] immigration."[43]

On behalf of the SP&P, Rice had already parlayed family connections into legislative authority to issue $3 million in preferred stock. This issue culminated in the formation of a separate, subsidiary company, the First Division of the St. Paul and Pacific Railroad (First Division), under the presidency of Rice's trusted colleague and friend, attorney George Becker. Charged with building a main line road from St. Anthony more than two hundred miles northwest to Breckenridge, a village strategically situated along the Red River at the Dakota border, the First Division immediately passed into Edward Litchfield's capable hands. He agreed to finance construction of the main line as well as a branch line extending from St. Paul some sixty-six miles north to St. Cloud, the North-Western Express hub located just three hundred miles south of the Canadian border. Following the original act that established the First Division, a second provided for another land-grant line—an extension branch from St. Cloud to Minnesota's northern border at the town of St. Vincent.[44]

From its original junction at St. Anthony, the St. Paul and Pacific built northward along the Mississippi River. In September 1866, the firm opened its branch line from St. Paul to St. Cloud, thereby appropriating much of the riverboating trade along the Mississippi's northwestern shoreline. On inside information, Kittson and Burbank had already moved their Red River steamers farther north and west. A year later, the First Division achieved a similar feat on the river's eastern banks, completing its branch line to Sauk Rapids. At these intersections, each sixty-six miles from St. Paul's milling "suburbs" of St. Anthony and Minneapolis, the SP&P companies renegotiated their land grants for cross-road connections: first and foremost among them an intersection with the proposed Northern Pacific Railroad route, running from Lake Superior through Minnesota, into Dakota Territory, and thence westward to the Pacific Northwest.[45]

The genesis of a second intrastate road transpired during 1867, the year the British North America Act granted Canadians their political independence. Knowing that newly independent Canadians would soon embark on their own transcontinental railroad schemes, SP&P directors held a special stockholders meeting to map out ways to pull northern wheatgrowing riches down a proposed Canadian Pacific Railroad (CPR) branch line from Winnipeg to the international border, through St. Vincent, and then into St. Paul. On the strength of this scheme, the state legislature gladly renegotiated the land grants, rescheduling their completion for 1878.

From St. Cloud, the SP&P planned to construct a northern extension, connecting first with the NPR main line near Fargo and then with the proposed CPR branch line along Minnesota's border at St. Vincent. From Sauk Rapids, the First Division intended to build north to Brainerd, where it also planned to meet the NPR line. Moving ahead with its original charter, during 1868 the First Division completed 51 miles of its main line, which would run from Minneapolis (rather than St. Anthony) 207 miles northwest to Breckenridge. Together, these lines decimated steamboat and express competition; further, they promised to pull northern Minnesota and the entire Red River Valley into a network of farms and towns focused on St. Paul–Minneapolis. Once again, Kittson and Burbank had already moved their boats farther north and west.[46]

By 1868, Minnesota's railroad builders had made great strides in constructing an intrastate railroad network with its hub at St. Paul. However, to maximize the benefits of this local work they needed to link Minnesota's lines to national ones. Consequently, MVR and SP&P directors undertook important steps to negotiate all-rail routes to Chicago and Milwaukee. With eastern railroads pushing into Iowa and the MVR constructing southward in 1868, Minnesotans would soon make their first through-connection to Chicago. Indeed, by 1869, via branch lines north from Sioux City, Iowa, shipments from St. Paul–Minneapolis could reach Chicago's railroad depots within thirty hours. At the same time, Milwaukee-based lines promised to provide a more direct route to Chicago. To that end, during 1867 the Minnesota legislature authorized the newly incorporated Milwaukee and St. Paul Railway (M&SP) to purchase the bankrupt Minnesota Central and all its rolling stock, equipment, immunities, and privileges— but not its land grants. During 1868, the M&SP started building a short line between La Crosse and St. Paul. With a competitor's connection looming, SP&P directors approved various stock issues to supplement their earlier mortgages, putting forward a special $6 million offering to finance a hoped-for connection with the Chicago and Northwestern (which they completed to Eau Claire, Wisconsin, in 1868). SP&P directors and others incorporated the St. Paul and Chicago Railroad (SP&C) as the first link in that chain, electing Edmund Rice chief executive officer.[47]

As president of both the SP&P and the SP&C, Edmund Rice approached his senator brother Henry to enlist the infant board of immigration in promoting local railroad lines. With the legislature's support, the board planted newly authorized agents in Milwaukee and Chicago, their salaries jointly funded by the state and the railroad companies. State immigration agents tailored their advertising pamphlets to attract the "right sorts" of homesteaders: displaced agricultural and factory workers from the British Isles, northern Europe, and the more populous regions of the United States, those anxious to "settle upon fertile prairies, and become prosperous and influential citizens."[48]

New stock offerings and immigration promotions fostered tangible increases in railroad construction and settlement along company lines. Additionally, expanding production and consumption networks strengthened many struggling railroad firms, including the Lake Superior, which had curtailed its construction plans after Lyman Dayton's unexpected death in

1865. By 1868, as more immigrants entered the region and additional funds surfaced, capital infusions culminated in the reorganization of the Lake Superior company. Directed by its new president, William Banning—a Delaware transplant who had emerged as an important St. Paul banker—the Lake Superior completed thirty miles of track along its land grant, tracing northward from St. Paul toward connection with the Great Lakes system at the port of Duluth, 155 miles distant.[49]

By the end of 1868, Minnesotans had completed 560 miles of track throughout the state and could look forward to Chicago-based railroads opening all-rail routes into St. Paul–Minneapolis during the next year. At times St. Paul–Minneapolis's new railroad executives cooperated, at times they competed, but between 1866 and 1868 their collective efforts prompted land-sale promotions and passenger and freight rate discounts that ultimately lowered the costs associated with living in Minnesota. As each company built bridges, depots, grain elevators, machine shops, and other industrial enterprises in St. Paul–Minneapolis and along their land-grant tracks, they contributed directly toward the peopling and agricultural maturation of the state. Further, they generated expanding linkages—backward to raw materials and forward to marketing and distribution. Adhering to the time-tested symbiosis between urban and rural development, Minnesota's transportation entrepreneurs pulled their agricultural hinterland into St. Paul–Minneapolis by using established networks—rivers, roads, and now railroads—to stimulate production and consumption to benefit their own urban markets. Railroads also lowered the cost and time associated with reaching larger suppliers and customers in Chicago, Pittsburgh, New York, and other established centers on the eastern seaboard and beyond.

On the strength of derived and anticipated demand for the region's wheat and timber products, transportation linkages also created new opportunities at St. Paul–Minneapolis, where an increasing number of anxious residents had congregated to profit by gathering, dispatching, and producing the goods and services their intrastate railroad network required. With the 1857 panic and the Civil War over, the postwar boom promised to carry many of these survivors into the Twin Cities' limelight. Agreeing with Minnesota board of immigration agent Hans Mattson that "the remoteness of our State from the East, and the cost of transportation render the development of [commerce and] manufacturers an objective of the highest importance," emerging urban entrepreneurs such as St. Paul's James J. Hill and Maurice Auerbach and St. Anthony–Minneapolis's William Eastman planned to take part in and profit from the Cities' expanding regional prominence. Just as the previous generation's entrepreneurs had attached themselves to prosperous fur traders and transportation, merchandising, and milling pioneers, these young hopefuls connected themselves to Minnesota's new industrial entrepreneurs—Norman Kittson, William Davidson, James Burbank, C. C. and W. D. Washburn, Edmund Rice, George Becker, and other urban railroaders who had linked Minnesota more closely with the Atlantic world's expanding markets.[50]

1866–1872

The Post–Civil War Boom and the Rise of the Cities

DURING 1866, St. Paul's commissioner of statistics, J. W. McClung, warned that Minnesota's recently acquired wartime wealth "must not be locked up in safes, nor stowed away in barrels, boxes, and hogsheads." Rather, he insisted, "it must bestir itself in works of public improvement, and with the plastic hand of enterprise, machinery and artistic skills, go out into the hedges and highways to create wealth, develop values, employ labor, and open the paths of commerce." Once done, he predicted, "the building of our railroads will not only draw wealth and immigration to the City, but will hold them there by a surer tenure than the rope of sand we spun in 1857."[1]

A new generation of enthusiasts quickly answered McClung's call—collecting, forwarding, and manufacturing wheat and timber from the increasingly productive hinterland and meeting the growing demands of regional railroads and consumers for fuel, machinery, food, clothing, building materials, and other articles. These efforts further nurtured the impact of Minnesota's economic recovery and the state's expanding railroad construction. Joining the rest of the northern United States in a seven-year economic boom, Minnesotans transformed St. Paul into the region's transportation, distribution, wholesaling, and financial center and Minneapolis into a manufacturing nexus for large-scale production. Using local politicians' clout, Minnesota's new urban industrialists learned how to block the moves of—as well as encourage cooperation with—wealthy and influential outsiders according to the needs of the moment. Although still somewhat inexperienced in big business, Minnesotans nevertheless discarded the remnants of their riparian past.[2]

Between 1866 and 1872, St. Paul and Minneapolis developed bustling depots, towering grain elevators, elongated warehouses, multistoried office blocks, soot-covered streets, overflowing sewers, and increasingly conspicuous boundaries between diverse socio-economic clusters. As railroaders completed their intrastate transportation network, several opportunity seekers seized new openings in fuel supply, wholesaling, flour milling, and large-scale manufacturing. These developments stimulated interest among immigrants, eastern capitalists, and locals anxious to profit from the expansion of Chicago-based railroads and the Northern Pacific transcontinental project. Increased business catapulted St. Paul and Minneapolis from relative obscurity onto the list of the nation's most productive urban centers. By the time Philadelphia's Edward Young inventoried real wage statistics in Europe and the Americas during 1871, St. Paul–Minneapolis also ranked within the top ten places to live in the industrialized world, thanks in large measure to the cities' dominant positions in the transportation, distribution, and manufacture of the nation's food supply. Minnesota's urban innovators and railroad builders had achieved these changes on optimism engendered by the Civil War's conclusion.[3]

Opportunities and Challenges along
St. Paul's Expanding Levees, 1866–68

Wartime demands and inflation provided the impetus for Minnesota's journey from economic collapse to postwar prosperity, but urban industrialists faced a number of new challenges as they bridged the gap from waterway dependence to railroad-based expansion. Reversing trends associated with the 1857 fiasco, some entrepreneurs had outgrown Minnesota's capacity to house their businesses. For example, Civil War profits allowed Joseph Ullman to expand his merchandising business on minks and other regional furs into larger marketing networks in Chicago and New York. As he spent more and more time in the two larger cities' wholesaling districts, Ullman decided to pack up his growing family and move east. While he maintained an outlet in St. Paul, when he moved his headquarters to Chicago during 1866 he avoided middleman costs by establishing a direct link with New York and European buyers. Chicago also offered various social advantages over St. Paul, including a larger Jewish community and better Hebrew schools. Other St. Paul–Minneapolis entrepreneurs made similar leaps, returning to markets that had eluded them during their start-up years. But their success in larger eastern cities inevitably pulled business away from Minnesota competitors.[4]

Additionally, when eastern capitalists looked west for the "next Chicago," they found several towns—including St. Paul, St. Anthony, and

Minneapolis, but also Kansas City, Omaha, Sioux City, and Minnesota's own Lake Superior port at Duluth—clamoring for recognition, capital, immigrants, railroads, and trade. As a result, several observers cautioned that St. Paul–Minneapolis's continued regional dominance depended upon the "public spirit" that had guided economic recovery between 1862 and 1865.

Notwithstanding these challenges, on January 1, 1866, the *Pioneer Press* rang in the New Year with confidence for the first time in nearly a decade. Its editors declared that St. Paulites had emerged from the Civil War "fresh, vigorous, energetic, hopeful, determined, wealthy—just gathering up our wonderful energies [for a] glorious future." The newspaper reported that one St. Paul investor had recently sold a prime business corner for $13,500, netting a $4,500 profit over the price he had paid in 1860. Similar lots had changed hands with a $10,000 profit, the *Pioneer* claimed, while prices for choice street frontage had escalated from $100 to $1,000 per foot. Moreover, realtors now listed "abundant and cheap" lots for those seeking excellent returns near the main thoroughfares connecting St. Paul with its "suburbs" of Minneapolis–St. Anthony.[5]

Railroad construction, government sponsorship, capital investments, and entrepreneurial energies contributed to the city's vigorous new spirit. Minnesota Valley Railroad directors James Burbank, William Davidson, and Henry Sibley increased the capital of their St. Paul Fire and Marine Insurance Company, stimulating further transportation investments throughout the region. With passage of the nation's banking act in 1864 and uniform bankruptcy legislation in 1867, J. E. and Horace Thompson stabilized the First National Bank, where MVR directors deposited their earnings and dominated the board. Henry Sibley and others established the Minnesota Savings Bank and the St. Paul Chamber of Commerce. Active promoters of St. Paul, these overlapping business owners charged the chamber with increasing the city's manufacturing capacity to compete with—and hopefully rival—Minneapolis's expanding milling operations, while other entrepreneurs incorporated the St. Paul Manufacturing Company to stimulate investments in city factories. As president of the St. Paul Gas Light Company, politician Sibley acquired an exclusive charter to lay pipes and fittings, soon equipping the businesses and homes of his friends. By 1867, these and other infrastructural improvements increased St. Paul's capital investments to $30 million, compared to $10 million in 1864.[6]

Not all profits fueled infrastructure upgrades. During the late 1860s, Davidson built a $100,000 mansion (equivalent to $2.5 million in 2000) on Dayton's Bluff. Burbank erected a similar home along Summit Avenue, the emerging boulevard for St. Paul's industrial elite. Along with other homes, these structures made the city a more attractive place. Further, as principal directors of the city's newly created board of education, St. Paul's civic leaders encouraged the construction of a new high school, complete with a business department to train teen capitalists in bookkeeping, correspondence, mercantile law, and other "useful" commercial skills. Established entrepreneurs also bolstered the coffers of St. Paul's business college, founded in 1866, making donations for textbooks, endowing a scholarship fund, and offering apprenticeships. Successful businessmen further "opened their pockets" to build social centers for their employees. Davidson established the St. Paul Music Hall Association, an institution designed to provide "amusements" for the city's expanding class of salaried and wage workers. Davidson also wheedled like-minded businessmen, including Thompson, Burbank, Sibley, and Amherst Wilder, to purchase stock in the Music Hall and in other public meeting places. In addition, elite wives hosted parties at which upwardly mobile professionals and white-collar workers could meet and mingle with "the people [they] wanted to know."[7]

In expanding society-page columns, the city's leaders advertised various parties and social functions—their contribution to St. Paul's new urban "sophistication." These and other ventures coalesced to encourage young entrepreneurs "to invest their futures" in the city. Indeed, residents and tourists credited St. Paul's elite for their "beautiful, growing, prosperous" city. By "accumulating and using wealth in manifold avenues toward comfort and even luxury," Burbank, Davidson, Rice, Thompson, and other established businessmen had created a community with "throbbing trade, comfortable homes, [and] all the institutions of modern civilization grouped into urban life."[8]

As each improvement stimulated more expansion, entrepreneurial energies gathered throughout St. Paul—nowhere more so than along the Lower Levee between the Mississippi River and the St. Paul and Pacific's railroad tracks. There, young men like James J. Hill jockeyed for position in warehousing, forwarding, distribution, and fuel supply networks for Minnesota's river-to-rail conversion. Hill's ascent along St. Paul's levee both reinforced and refuted stereotypes regarding the nineteenth-century transformation from traditional to industrial enterprise. Emerging from his ten-year clerkship into his role as a businessman just as Horatio Alger Jr. published *Ragged Dick,* Hill proved that opportunities existed for men of big dreams, slim means, and entrepreneurial skills.[9]

Although a classic representative of the "rags to respectability" myth, Hill never rescued the boss's daughter to escape the daily grind. Like Andrew Carnegie, Hill ascended through all the phases of entrepreneurship, working hard, rejecting offers from people whose visions collided with his own, learning the arts of brokering and political patronage, and rising from respectability to great wealth on shrewd maneuvers. Also like Carnegie, Hill embodied the exception rather than the norm. Regardless of position along the social spectrum, few succeeded on such a scale during this period of vast technological change and rapid economic development. Indeed, Hill's career became the stuff of legend, both during and after his own time, but his rise also signaled an important shift in entrepreneurial expectations after the Civil War, a change that lured many young dreamers into places like St. Paul–Minneapolis during the late nineteenth century.

Throughout the Civil War, Hill remained in St. Paul, avoiding military service because of a childhood injury that had partially blinded him. In the land of the blind, however, this one-eyed man truly emerged as a king in the changing business world. Recalling an early encounter, one Minnesotan described Hill, at age twenty-four, as a young man with a "juvenile, inno-cent and kindly looking face as you ever saw." He added, "No man would suppose that he could grow up and accomplish what he has done, grab a

To meet demands during the Civil War, young James J. Hill built a warehouse that could accommodate both steamboat and railroad shipments. The first building downriver from the steamboat in this photograph by Benjamin Franklin Upton, the warehouse gave the aspiring transportation entrepreneur access to St. Paul's "throbbing trade," Minneapolis's "flour men," and customers in all directions.

continent, grid-iron it with railroads, and do the men and the things he has so easily done." But several established entrepreneurs noticed young Hill's qualities—his determination, his cost-accounting skills, and his grasp of the "investment mentality" required for entrepreneurial success. Between 1856 and 1866, with neither capital invested in St. Paul nor family obligations to occupy his attention, Hill economized, husbanded his earnings, and assisted his employers with cost-cutting measures, ascending from dockworker to bookkeeper for one of the levee's most successful wholesale grocery firms. As opportunities materialized between the railroad tracks and the river, Hill symbolized the kind of person capitalists, casting about for trustworthy young climbers, considered an acceptable risk.[10]

Hill so impressed William Davidson that he offered the young bookkeeper a job in his transportation empire during the Civil War. But Hill declined the proposal, ostensibly out of loyalty to his employers at the Lower Levee, although he soon revealed the real reason he had turned down the mighty "old man of the river." While the Commodore owned more St. Paul real estate and more corporate stock in regional steamers, barges, grain elevators, banks, insurance companies, and railroads than any of his local rivals, Hill had his eye on a bigger prize than a job with Davidson. Just as Davidson had rejected the glamour of the river for larger railroad profits, Hill had visions of building a transportation empire to Asia. Davidson's political and MVR connections offered fewer opportunities to realize those dreams than did Edmund Rice's Democratic Party affiliations and the St. Paul and Pacific Railroad. Moreover, like many young men in St. Paul, Hill's "ambitions now reache[d] toward a business house" of his own. Thus, in all his dealings as a bookkeeper, Hill cozied up to Edmund Rice, George Becker, and anyone else involved with enterprises that promised to expand alongside the Pacific-bound railroad. By 1866, several people stepped forward to assist the twenty-eight-year-old striver.[11]

On February 6, 1866, James J. Hill redefined his future when he rented a freight house from the SP&P's First Division and entered the competitive world of transportation and wholesaling along St. Paul's Lower Levee. Having witnessed many failures between 1856 and 1865, Hill discerned that most businesses floundered when their principal owners tripped over the fixed costs that devoured cash flow. He thus resolved to build his own business on other people's money—renting rather than purchasing real estate and building warehouses, trading information and expertise for capital investments. The First Division warehouse gave him access to the levee's entire reshipping industry, plenty of room for his own business, and a dock for boats to work regions still untouched by railroads.[12]

Ultimately, Hill's plans meant competing against Davidson, and in no time he found schemers willing to assist him in launching a transportation, storage, and commission business. William Wellington and George Blanchard, employee-associates in Davidson's North West Packet Company of Dubuque, Iowa, offered information and capital provided Hill ran the warehouse, purchased flour and lumber from Minneapolis millers, and arranged rail-to-river reshipping at St. Paul's levee. As superintendent of Davidson's lines, the treacherous Wellington knew of his employer's plans to undercut competitors. With Davidson's attention spread across many businesses, Wellington wrote Hill that they could beat him at his own game: "the old man will go for all that flour at Minneapolis, but place him where he cannot give *inside* rates nor *draw backs*—and he is disarmed at once—and I will do this if I have to carry the freights for nothing." After Hill drummed up business from railroad customers in Dubuque, Milwaukee, Chicago, and St. Louis and negotiated with the Minnesota "flour men," Wellington kept his promise. In exchange for Hill's time and energies, Blanchard and Wellington provided the young man with the capital required to underbid Davidson and to purchase a line of boats. SP&P directors abetted the process as well, for through young entrepreneurs like Hill they planned to enhance their position vis-à-vis the irascible Davidson and his cohort operating the MVR in southwestern Minnesota.[13]

On April 1, 1866, with warehouse space, products, customers, capital, boats, and relatively silent partners in hand, the young entrepreneur formed James J. Hill and Co.—St. Paul's newest transportation, storage, and commission business. Because of tardy customer payments, Hill struggled during his first operational year. But on January 15, 1867, his efforts paid dividends when the SP&P granted him exclusive reshipping rights on the railroad's wheat, flour, lumber, shingles, lathes (a machine for working wood and metal), and assorted general merchandise heading downriver. The SP&P also installed a dock extending 250 feet below its new elevator, including a side track leading directly into the lower floor of Hill's warehouse. Writing to railroad companies in Milwaukee, Chicago, and elsewhere, Hill boasted, "the arrangement will give me more room than there is at the La Crosse, Wisconsin depot, and a larger landing on the river—the whole of the St. Paul Public Levee. I am going to be situated to accommodate the Millers at the Falls and up the road, and I find already they are anxious to take advantage of it." Anxious indeed: Hill procured 30,000 barrels of wheat to start his spring season, and on successful negotiations with the Chicago & Burlington, the Illinois Central, and other westward-pushing railroads, he crowed that he had secured "all the fat for our mutual lines going to points for which our lines compete at all," including through-freight in wheat, flour, salt, pig iron, and coal and other lucrative shipping contracts.[14]

Possessing many of the things he required for a prosperous future, Hill took a bride—a young Irish waitress named Mary Therese Mehegan. Before the marriage ceremony, Hill sent Mehegan to a finishing school in Milwaukee to learn the etiquette required for life inside larger social circles. Gendered expectations had changed with urban development and St. Paul's prosperity: no longer would the Amelia Ullmans trek to the steamboat landing to unload earthenware jars and other freight. Instead, like Mary Mehegan, Minnesota's aspiring women would receive training in the social graces deemed imperative for familial success. On August 17, 1867, educated in the arts of household management, Mary Mehegan became Mrs. James J. Hill. Thereafter, she governed the servants who toiled inside the house the Hills built in "Lower Town," St. Paul's emerging bourgeois quarter north of the business district. One month later, Hill pushed himself more deeply into the St. Paul and Pacific's network.[15]

On September 16, 1868, Hill formed another general transportation business, this time with a partner, Egbert S. Litchfield, the youngest of the Brooklyn brothers associated with the SP&P's capital infusions. With railroads approaching from Milwaukee and Chicago, the partners leased another freight depot along the Mississippi River. In the year that followed, Hill then partnered with Norman Kittson, Hudson's Bay Company agent and former mayor of St. Paul. Through Kittson, Hill gained absolute control over the HBC's fur shipments between Winnipeg, St. Paul, Chicago, Detroit, and New York and absorbed important lessons in negotiating with both the government and the region's political operators. By the end of 1868, as transportation entrepreneurs expanded Minnesota's railroad network into an increasingly cohesive 560 miles of track, thirty-year-old Hill emerged as a businessman in his own right, with established freight-forwarding networks stretching from St. Paul to the south, east, north, and west.[16]

While Hill and others tied their fortunes to expanding St. Paul and Pacific networks, William Eastman and fellow hopefuls worked with Davidson, Burbank, the Washburns, and assorted regional businessmen ambitiously seeking manufacturing supremacy at the waterfall.[17]

New Manufacturing Opportunities and Challenges at the Waterfall, 1866–69

As the *Pioneer* touted St. Paul's "glorious future," it also boasted that the "business season" for the manufacturing "suburbs" upriver at Minneapolis and St. Anthony "is about to open with great earnestness, with all the elements of wonderful prosperity." In 1866, hinterland farmers cultivated 895,000 acres and produced 9.5 million bushels of wheat, enough to feed regional residents alone for at least three years. Beyond sawing nearly 62 million feet of lumber and producing 20.5 million shingles and 11.9 million laths, waterfall entrepreneurs had brought about "a great exportation [79,000 barrels] of flour to New York and Boston," supported by "paper and woolen mills in full blast." These activities—along with those of ironworks, foundries, and machine shops—signaled an enormous change from ten years earlier, when mills at the falls had manufactured neither enough lumber to meet local needs nor enough flour to feed regional residents.[18]

Like their neighbors in St. Paul, residents of St. Anthony and Minneapolis invested in their communities, stimulating further development while railroaders built the intrastate system between 1866 and 1868. St. Anthony received its city charter in 1866, Minneapolis followed suit in 1867, and citizens elected water-power owners Richard Chute and Dorilus Morrison, respectively, as mayors. During 1867, Minneapolis Mill owners Morrison and C. C. and W. D. Washburn invested in new saw, flour, woolen, and paper mills and joined the Minnesota Millers Association in cooperative grain purchasing efforts. Waterfall residents established a Union Board of Trade to stimulate wholesaling ventures to compete with—and hopefully oust—their commercial rivals in St. Paul. Morrison and W. D. Washburn founded the *Minneapolis Daily Tribune* to advertise the interests of the waterfall cities. Millers opened banks to stimulate further investments and, together with Sibley, Rice, and other St. Paul entrepreneurs, encouraged the establishment of a state reform school between the cities so businesses could employ low-cost inmates for building projects. Mirroring St. Paulites' efforts, Minneapolitans founded a board of education in 1867, electing W. D. Washburn and other local elites to direct it. Together with associates in St. Paul, waterfall businessmen also organized the University of Minnesota's board of regents, establishing a permanent endowment in 1870. With the Morrill Act stimulating agricultural innovations in the West, St. Anthony hardware merchant John S. Pillsbury funded the university's new experimental farm. Ever in competition with their St. Paul neighbors, water-power owners constructed lavish homes and their wives hosted parties and charitable events to build cohesive communities.[19]

Networks in Minneapolis and St. Anthony encouraged aspiring entrepreneurs such as New Hampshire's William Eastman to embark on larger projects associated with the waterfall's manufacturing potential. Whereas James J. Hill required few resources and relatively little time to launch his business in St. Paul, continued manufacturing success in Minneapolis–St. Anthony depended on increased waterfall capacity, a project requiring long-term efforts and ample capital. However, anyone proposing to expand the falls' potential had an excellent chance of marshaling the required financial support. Eastman had purchased shares in Minneapolis Mill upon his arrival in Minneapolis during 1854, but in 1859, at the age of thirty-eight, he relinquished his connection to the firm. Drawing on his experience in a family-run New Hampshire paper mill, Eastman acquired leases from the water-power companies and launched St. Anthony's first paper mill and Minneapolis's first flour and woolen mills. His diversified milling success increased the revenues of Minneapolis Mill and the St. Anthony Falls Water Power Company. These accomplishments, combined with the viability of Eastman's proposed tunnel-building project, inspired St. Paul's John Merriam, a former partner in Burbank's North-Western Express, to help Eastman buy the land he coveted. Minneapolis Mill directors provided other resources for his scheme, replacing older cement tubes with stronger iron pipes to direct the western shore's water flow, for example.[20]

Like Hill, Eastman developed an expansive vision during the Civil War. On profits from sustained wartime demands for flour, wool, and paper, he pushed to make the Mississippi River waterfall a "Lowell, Massachusetts, of the West," albeit one centered on flour production rather than on textiles. By the mid-1860s, save for the highway between the bridges spanning the two branches of the Mississippi, maple-covered Nicollet Island remained virtually untouched by the rapid development on either side of the waterfall. Its possibilities for industrial improvements captivated Eastman, who, having witnessed millers harnessing the rapids from Mount Washington's Saco River during his teen years, held great faith in water power. Once arrived in St. Anthony, he devised a plan that utilized Nicollet Island to create vast milling sites along both sides of the waterfall, a vision he perfected during the Civil War years. He would excavate a tunnel in the soft sandrock behind the falls, conducting the river's flow to water wheels positioned to make the full head of the waterfall—some forty feet—available for larger-scale manufacturing. Experience at other waterfalls supported his plan. He needed only one thing to move it forward: capital, and plenty of it.[21]

Franklin Steele's financial problems laid the foundations for Eastman's rise. Despite wartime profits, Steele's St. Anthony Falls Water Power Company collapsed during 1865, and a Wisconsin investor gained title to Nicollet Island in exchange for one of the company's mortgages. On September 17, 1865, Eastman bought the island's mortgage for a trifling $24,000—half of that his own savings—and formed his tunnel-building company. He acquired the remaining capital from John Merriam, who divided his interest with two silent partners, North-Western associate and St. Paulite Amherst H. Wilder and Minneapolis lumberman-miller William Judd. Wilder had reinvested his express company dividends throughout Minnesota—in real estate ventures, in wholesaling start-ups, and in milling improvements. Immersed as a stockholding director in various St. Paul–Minneapolis enterprises and always on the lookout for other opportunities, Wilder deemed Eastman and his Nicollet Island plan excellent risks. Judd, a Minneapolis Mill lessee and aspiring flour-milling entrepreneur, went along for the ride.[22]

As part of the Nicollet Island purchase, Eastman and his partners sued the St. Anthony Falls Water Power Company for water rights at the falls and demanded that Chute and Steele level the firm's dam. With Steele living on the East Coast, the company's financial affairs had fallen to Richard Chute. Although a capable businessman, Chute had failed to keep the company afloat; now pushed to the wall, neither he nor Steele had a choice. The dam came down, and Eastman obtained water rights for his subterranean tunnel project, which would extend from the south end of Hennepin Island to the south end of Nicollet Island.[23]

Eastman and his engineers crafted the tunnel design at a favorable moment in Minneapolis history, for wartime inflation had prompted wheat prices to soar "from 10 to 20 cents per bushel over any other state." Once the Civil War ended, Eastman and his associates stood to reap substantial profits from their property investments and the flour mills under construction on the Minneapolis Mill dam site. By the time Wilder and Merriam purchased Burbank's interests in North-Western Express in 1866, Eastman had acquired access to Wilder's wide-ranging networks in government contracting, real estate investments, overland express, wholesale groceries and clothing, and other forwarding and commission businesses. That same year, Cadwallader C. Washburn provided additional impetus for milling capacity expansion and augmented the Minneapolis Mill Company's interest in the project.[24]

Increased wheat production and flour-milling revenues inspired C. C. Washburn to use some of the company's water power for flour-milling expansion. In 1866, he constructed the 66-by-100-foot, six-story Washburn "B" Mill, the largest flouring manufactory west of Buffalo, New York. Built on the south side of Eastman's projected canal and furnished with the best available machinery, the entire structure—building and equipment—cost Washburn $100,000. While representing an enormous sum for a western manufacturer, the investment gave the "B" a capacity of 800 barrels a day, three times more than that of any other mill at the waterfall. As the Minneapolis Mill Company's absentee owner, C. C. Washburn leased the "B" for a five-year period, at $12,000 per annum, to two transplants from Maine, George Brackett and Eastman's then-silent partner, William Judd. By 1866, the thirty-year-old Brackett had risen from a lowly position as a

Minneapolis butcher boy to become one of the waterfall's most important mill managers, operating Eastman's first woolen and flour mills. Judd, meanwhile, had surfaced among the throng of Minneapolis lumbermen anxious to buy into manufacturing schemes at the waterfall.[25]

Eastman's decision to partner with western-shore investors in the Minneapolis Mill Company's manufacturing plan came at the right moment, particularly once Wilder, Merriam, and Judd liquidated some of their assets, dropped other projects, and officially joined Eastman during 1867. With large-scale manufacturing in mind and capital and strong management behind the project, Minneapolis Mill granted Eastman and Co. a perpetual lease of 250 horsepower of water for a nominal fee. The small investment paid off quickly. During 1867, profits from increased business prompted Minneapolis Mill to issue its very first dividend: $20,000, divided among Dorilus Morrison and C. C. and W. D. Washburn. An excellent return on investment—nearly 20 percent, a measure taken seriously by

During the post-Civil War boom, St. Paul's "manufacturing suburbs"— Minneapolis and St. Anthony—pulsed with activity. Envisioning the "glorious future" ahead, entrepreneurs not only expanded their efforts in milling timber and wheat but also initiated construction to increase the power potential of the waterfall, shown here in a photograph by Charles Alfred Zimmerman.

Minnesota's new breed of entrepreneurial financiers—this windfall had resulted from further backward and forward linkages to the expanding industrial economy. After Eastman constructed the first tunnel on the Minneapolis side of the river, western-shore mills also prospered, with the
Washburn "B" immediately benefiting from increased water flow.[26]

As Eastman's hydraulic project moved forward, both the Minneapolis
and the St. Anthony water-power companies endorsed the scheme; however, since St. Anthony's sawmillers had supplied no capital for the plan,
they had to wait until Eastman finished the western-shore tunnel before
getting one of their own. Eastman started on the east-side development
during 1868, and all went well until the Mississippi River flooded during
the following spring. The tunnel collapsed, and within moments the river
swallowed all the St. Anthony mills in its path.[27]

The tunnel collapse foreordained the consolidation of Minneapolis and
St. Anthony into one city. Changes in the market sealed St. Anthony's fate:
over the following two years, wheat replaced lumber as Minnesota's most
lucrative product. Increased immigration into North America, growing
consumer demands for wheat, imminent completion of the transcontinental railroads, and innovations in milling techniques placed flour at the
center of Minneapolis expansion. Perceiving this shift, Minneapolis Mill
owners combined interests while the St. Anthony Water Falls Company,
its owner Steele nearing personal bankruptcy, collapsed on declining lumber revenues.[28]

Between 1869 and 1871, Minnesota wheat production boomed, federal
and state governments stepped in to assist waterfall residents with recon-
struction, and the city of St. Anthony, vexed by the tunnel's collapse and as-
sailed by floods and fires, crumbled. In the meantime, W. D. Washburn pre-
served his lumber interests by consolidating operations on the western shore,
and the capably managed Minneapolis Mill Company drew the attention of
the Northern Pacific Railroad. Hoping to share in the riches of Washburn's
flour-manufacturing scheme, NPR owners awarded railroad track construction contracts to Minneapolis millers. At the same time, St. Paul's railroaders moved to fortify their own position, while the state legislature assisted
both cities by reorganizing local railroads to help them raise the capital required to complete their 1873 land-grant obligations before Chicago-based
roads vaulted the Mississippi and swallowed hinterland profits.

Connecting St. Paul–Minneapolis with Other Expansionists

During April 1869, on the promise of wealth-generating expansion beyond
Minnesota's borders, the state legislature reorganized and refinanced the

Minnesota Valley Railroad into the St. Paul & Sioux City Railroad (Sioux City). Under the new plan, local entrepreneurs still dominated the company's financial affairs, but in the wake of the Eastman tunnel collapse William Washburn and other Minneapolis millers terminated their association with the road. Focused on rebuilding the waterfall's manufacturing districts, they instead connected their interests to NPR expansion. In their place, a new generation of entrepreneurs—John Merriam, Amherst H. Wilder, and others intimately connected with investments in St. Paul—joined the previous generation's Henry Sibley, Horace Thompson, William Davidson, and James Burbank on the Sioux City's new board. These shifting alliances set the stage for more intense urban rivalries between the two cities in the days ahead. For the moment, however, under the aegis of the reorganized Sioux City, engineers and laborers connected St. Paul and Minneapolis with a new bridge over the Mississippi River, erected a freight house for shipment exchanges between the railroad and Davidson's steamboats, built a new railroad bridge into West St. Paul to link the Sioux City with other St. Paul–centered lines, and completed construction between St. Paul and Sioux City, Iowa.[29]

On September 29, 1869, the Sioux City's first northbound train entered St. Paul, inaugurating the road's line to southwestern Minnesota as well as the city's first through- (albeit roundabout) connection with Chicago-based railroads. With this accomplishment, increased immigration and capital flowed steadily into the state, and the Sioux City grabbed most of southern Minnesota's wilting riverboat trade.[30]

Meanwhile, the SP&P commenced construction of a 148-mile line that promised to connect with the Chicago, Milwaukee, and St. Paul Railroad (CM&SP) building northwest from La Crosse, Wisconsin—giving St. Paulites their first all-rail link to larger northeastern systems. In addition, the First Division main line expanded another 60 miles westward during 1869, reaching the 111-mile station at Morris, its scheduled intersection with a proposed NPR branch line. Also that year, the Lake Superior company constructed 47 miles of track between St. Paul and Duluth, thereby completing nearly half of the 155-mile line that promised to link Minnesota's two most important ports: St. Paul's Mississippi River hub at the Lower Levee and Duluth's Great Lakes connection with New York.[31]

With Minnesota's internal railroad network well under way and direct communication with Chicago imminent, the directors of the SP&P, First Division, and Lake Superior turned their attention toward the railroad that promised to unite their northern ambitions—the Northern Pacific. One of the 1862 Pacific Railroad Act's three beneficiaries, the NPR remained the only incomplete transcontinental line, its land grants scheduled for forfeiture in 1873. Minnesota's founders had envisioned a transcontinental route for more than a decade when Henry Rice joined a finance committee's 1869 excursion to Ogontz, Jay Cooke's country residence near Philadelphia. Several St. Paul–Minneapolis bankers and railroaders had already courted the famous Civil War bond negotiator, and as early as 1868 Cooke himself had solicited British, German, and Dutch capitalists to invest in the land-grant road. Now, with the NPR charter in the hands of the Pennsylvania Railroad's J. Edgar Thompson and other northeastern capitalists, Cooke hoped to garner sizeable profits from the American transcontinental route while also building feeder and forager lines into the prairie provinces of newly independent Canada, where a shortage of freight had bankrupted the young country's Grand Trunk Railway.[32]

Unfortunately for Minnesota's railroad enthusiasts, early discussions about the NPR's headquarters centered on Superior, Wisconsin, not Minnesota's infant port at Duluth. In response, indefatigable Henry Rice and other St. Paul railroaders worked to lure Cooke away from Chicago- and Milwaukee-based lines, offering the NPR "friendly" arrangements with the St. Paul and Pacific, First Division, and Lake Superior companies. With such seemingly malleable friends in Minnesota, Cooke readily assented to act as the NPR's fiscal agent, knowing that he would have the chance to absorb the young state's lucrative land-grant roads en route to the larger riches of the Red River Valley, the mining resources in the Rocky Mountains, and the timber products of Oregon and Washington. The promise of the midwestern hinterland had already prompted highly competitive and often redundant "trunk line" routes from the eastern seaboard cities of Philadelphia, New York, Boston, and Montreal to burgeoning settlements in the West, particularly Chicago. By the 1860s, Americans had emerged victorious against their Canadian counterparts in the "great trunk-line wars" waged between the New York Central, Pennsylvania, Erie, and infant Canadian Grand Trunk for the bounty of the western prairies.[33]

This victory, together with the 1869 completion of the transcontinental route joining the Union Pacific and Central Pacific railroads at Promontory Point, Utah, attracted other capitalists interested in expanding northwestern lines to the Pacific Coast. With Jay Cooke overseeing the NPR's financial arrangements, the Minnesota State Legislature expeditiously moved to assist with completion of the line from Duluth to the Dakota border. By a joint resolution in May 1870, Minnesota authorized the NPR to issue bonds and secure them by mortgages. Under Jay Cooke & Co., the NPR briskly negotiated $15 million in bond issues (equivalent to more then $3 billion in 2000) throughout the United States, Britain, and Continental Europe. Eastman joined other prominent Minneapolitans such as C. C.

and W. D. Washburn, George Brackett, and Dorilus Morrison as well as St. Anthony's Richard Chute in forming a construction company that eventually won the contract to build the road's first fifty-mile section. Anticipating great days ahead, Minneapolis millers bought land and built grain elevators and mills north and west along future NPR lines.[34]

During 1871, with Horace Thompson's support, First Division president George Becker secured an additional $15 million in bonds for the SP&P's extension from St. Cloud to St. Vincent and from Sauk Rapids to Brainerd. The NPR's Minneapolis-based construction team spent the summer completing the 165-mile branch road from Duluth to Morris, a feeder line into the SP&P's jumping-off point for expansion into the Dakotas. From Morris, the NPR contracted to carry passengers and freight northward to the international border—180 miles by coach and 610 miles by steamer to Winnipeg, located along the northerly flowing Red River. Also that year, the Lake Superior completed its 155-mile road from St. Paul to Duluth. Together with NPR connections from Duluth to SP&P lines, St. Paul–centered linkages gave Cooke access to 1,166 miles of track, more than half the state's total.[35]

The $30 million in bonds facilitated completion of the NPR's east-west line through Minnesota and provided Cooke and friends with the leverage required to absorb the SP&P, First Division, and Lake Superior companies. After negotiating the bulk of the NPR mortgages in Amsterdam, Cooke surreptitiously acquired majority interest in Minnesota's northern land-grant roads. He thereby consolidated more than 45 percent of the state's railroad lines, almost 700 of the 1,550 miles completed by the end of 1871. Millers in Minneapolis happily endorsed his scheme because a consolidated NPR promised to pull trade away from St. Paul and into their own city.[36]

Like entrepreneurs in St. Paul and Minneapolis and investors in the emerging transportation center at Duluth, Cooke coveted not only wheat-growing lands in Minnesota and Dakota and mining resources in Montana but also the prairies of Manitoba and Saskatchewan. Following Cornelius Vanderbilt, Jay Gould, and other railroaders who had carved up the American landscape through the great trunk-line wars, the Pacific railroad acts, and further industrial enterprises, Cooke took his place in America's "new nobility" of the Gilded Age by accelerating plans to devour both countries' agricultural frontiers. When the SP&P completed its 216-mile branch line from St. Paul to Breckenridge on October 25, 1871, he pounced. Unfortunately for Cooke, at least two groups belligerently opposed the NPR's dominance over the Minnesota-Manitoba wheat market: the seemingly irrational and paranoid Canadians and the increasingly hostile Sioux City directors, who by 1871 still included SP&P trustee Horace Thompson.[37]

By the time Cooke & Co. proposed an American-operated railroad linking Minnesota to Manitoba, Canadians declared that they had had enough of their pugnacious, grasping southern neighbors. After decades of trying to assert their economic independence from the United States and having only recently received sovereignty from British rule, Canadians planned to build something that would symbolize their newfound nationalism. However, in 1871, just four years after Canadian Confederation, Manitoba contained fewer than one thousand Euro-Americans, most of them representatives of either the Royal Canadian Mounted Police or the Hudson's Bay Company; the province had no railroads; and Winnipeg's entire manufacturing capacity consisted of a tannery and harness shop. Moreover, the Canadian Shield—the barren, rocky terrain along the Great Lakes between Winnipeg and its closest railroad link with a more developed Canada, in Toronto, some 1,300 miles distant—posed engineering challenges not faced by American railroad builders.[38]

With this geographical impediment and a diminutive industrial base, Canadians felt vulnerable to the more populous and powerful United States. A transcontinental railroad seemed to offer one solution to the problem of tying together their vast dominion—so much of it, like Manitoba, long on promise but short on people. Such a project would require time and lots of money, some of which would have to come from outside Canada. Still bruised and bankrupt from the great trunk-line wars, Canadians reasoned that building their own transcontinental line offered better chances for industrial success than placing themselves at the mercy of a new generation of American "annexationists."[39]

Thus, when Cooke tried to grab generous land grants made available by the British North America Act of 1867, he found Canadians determined to sever ties, permanently, with the Americans then managing their economic affairs through earlier free trade agreements that had opened up Canadian territories for American investment and the more powerful country's control. Cooke announced that the NPR, "being the natural allies of Canada and the Provinces," promised Manitoba farmers far greater profits via connections with surging American markets than anything their own infant government could provide. These "inducements" failed to impress many Canadians, among them the HBC's Sir John Rose, who declared himself "particularly exercised" about Cooke's designs on Manitoba and deeply suspicious of American interests in the young nation. Knowing full well that the Canadian prairies offered "two to three million dollars worth of sales and the establishment of a good market in the future," Rose feverishly worked to block Cooke at the border while simultaneously encouraging Canada's new Parliament to approve its own transcontinental railroad act.[40]

In the afterglow of the NPR's success in Minnesota, the proposed setback of an "all-Canadian" railroad route from Toronto to the Pacific Northwest unnerved Cooke enormously, for he had not expected such aggressive nationalism from Canada's young parliamentarians. Fuming over Rose's interference, Cooke decided to mount a seduction campaign aimed at Winnipeg's small collection of entrepreneurs. He promised enormous profits on their ventures provided they supported the NPR's bid to build the Canadian road, arguing that Rose "cannot bear that anybody should talk about Canada but [him]" and suggesting that they "fix the Canadian people quietly and get [the NPR's entry into Manitoba] settled." Many Winnipeg traders embraced Cooke's proposal, but his arguments left others unmoved. When he and fellow Yankee hustlers "offered assistance" to the proposed Canadian Pacific Railway project in 1871, politically minded Winnipeggers let out "one long, continuous howl, denouncing the scheme and its authors." While adversaries like Rose frustrated Cooke's immediate plans, NPR investors believed Canadians would come around eventually, especially when they realized "that our involvement brings wealth to them."[41]

With construction to the Canadian border just commencing in 1871, Cooke and his NPR co-conspirators convinced themselves that time and patience would eventually win the battle. In contrast, they adopted a stronger and more immediate response to the Sioux City's troublesome competition from St. Paul. Writing to his brother Harry during November 1871, Cooke acknowledged that "Merriam, Thompson, Drake, & Co. of the Sioux City road are powerful in politics in Minnesota" and "our enemies because we refused to [accept their] onerous terms [for consolidation]." Moreover, "because they think" the branches the NPR built "to Minneapolis and Stillwater to accommodate the trade of the State hurts St. Paul," Cooke snarled, "they have become ungrateful out there, and I feel it our duty to whip them." Like the proposed CPR project, however, a good thrashing would cost money, and plenty of it.[42]

Although consolidating the SP&P, First Division, and Lake Superior into the NPR's realm had strained the company's resources and a fight against the Sioux City, with its myriad allies in Minnesota, Chicago, and Milwaukee, carried enormous risks, Cooke forged ahead. After all, he reasoned, the NPR had benefited immensely from its Minnesota acquisitions, particularly the land grants. According to the state's railroad commissioner, the various roads Cooke had procured traversed "much of the finest wheat lands in America." By the end of 1872, the Minneapolis construction team completed the NPR's 252-mile main line—from its junction with the Lake Superior road at Duluth westward across the state and into Dakota. Now the Sioux City's land grants—and the possibility of seizing a near-monopoly on the entire state's resources—beckoned. With Minnesota's railroad land grants totaling nearly 12.3 million acres, Cooke could not resist the opportunity.[43]

Sioux City directors anticipated Cooke's expansionist plans, and during 1871 and 1872 Horace Thompson and other interested parties convinced many SP&P, First Division, and Lake Superior insiders that Cooke threatened not only the Sioux's interests but also their own investments in St. Paul. The next few years proved that, in assessing Canadians and Minnesotans, Cooke had underestimated both, including their desires for freedom from interlopers and the power of local solidarity. In 1872, the Sioux City moved forcefully, completing its connections to the Sioux City and Pacific, the Chicago and Northwestern, and the Dakota Southern, all of them with knowing directors opposed to the grasping Civil War bondsman and more than happy to assist St. Paul's entrepreneurs.[44]

As the NPR's traffic increased day by day, Minnesota's boosters drew ever closer to realizing their vision: dominance over all the products and profits their fertile wheat-growing region promised. But competitive posturing between Cooke & Co., Minneapolis-based construction teams, and St. Paul's Sioux City cohort increased rivalries between St. Paul and Minneapolis, with groups in each city duplicating the other's railroad-building efforts in order to siphon trade. As concern over these issues mounted, Minnesota's first railroad commissioner warned, "the prosperity of the state and the permanent prosperity of the railroads in a great degree depend upon each other. The state cannot be developed successfully without railroads, neither can the railroads be permanently successful unless the agricultural and other industrial interests of the state are prosperous." He also sparked the calls for railroad regulation by arguing that "there may be serious doubts whether competition, as it is claimed, works a permanent advantage to any community, or can be relied upon as a protection" for producers and consumers. He further noted that farmers had suffered tremendously at the hands of Chicago, Milwaukee, NPR, and Minnesota lines alike: "The masses of the people have complained so much of the exorbitant rates charged and of the discriminations made," he warned, "and ask nothing which shall injure, impair or destroy the railroad interests of the state, but they do ask that their agricultural products and manufactures shall be transported to market at reasonable rates." The state's political clout resided in St. Paul–Minneapolis, however, and hustlers there convinced local politicians that a hands-off policy guaranteed future profits for themselves and other Minnesotans.[45]

In part, the state legislature dismissed calls for more regulation because the companies had made good on their promises to link Minnesota's railroads to the larger nation. During 1872, the CM&SP announced the year's accomplishment: completion of the "only through route between St. Paul and Chicago without change, connecting the Milwaukee and St. Paul Road at Tomah, and for all eastern points." The direct link between St. Paul, Chicago, and New York gave Minnesotans what they had wanted all along: access to the American Northeast by rail rather than through the Great Lakes system. Steamboat and then railroad competition had reduced travel times between St. Paul and New York from eight to twelve weeks in 1849 to just under four days by the end of 1872. Railroaders had also placed something more at stake, a point First Division president George Becker underscored in response to regulatory threats, reminding capital city voters, "St. Paul is not the only point in this region where the river and railroad business of this country can be done [and] there is plenty of levee room in the Mississippi or the St. Croix river that can be had for the asking." Becker assured St. Paulites that "the managing officers of this company are Minnesotans and citizens of St. Paul, and are directly interested in the future growth and prosperity of this city," but, he warned, "they are men who will be governed [by the] interests of the corporation they represent, [and] shall not pay one cent of tribute for the privilege of doing business upon [their] own property and improvements." As Minneapolis's William Washburn became more deeply involved in railroad enterprises, he made similar threats, although his interests in the waterfall's manufacturing potential periodically induced him to call for regulation of Chicago- and St. Paul-based lines, so that Minneapolitans could capture the profits from railroad expansion. Unfortunately for Washburn and other western-shore boosters, wheedling in St. Paul triumphed over caterwauling in Minneapolis.[46]

By the end of 1872, a 1,900-mile rail network connected St. Paul–Minneapolis to Duluth in the north, Sioux City in the south, Chicago in the east, and Breckenridge in the northwest. The grid covered much of the state, extending Minnesota's trading season from six months into twelve and launching greater opportunities for St. Paul merchants and Minneapolis millers. Railroad competition had forced many to consolidate their interests to ensure profitability, but, like Cooke, Minnesota's urban industrialists wanted more. Thus, Minneapolitans sought improved milling methods while St. Paul's entrepreneurs integrated vertically—backward more deeply into land and fuel sources and forward into marketing networks for wholesale distribution.[47]

St. Paul's "Throbbing" Distribution Hub

While St. Paulites and Minneapolitans undertook railroad expansion between 1869 and 1872, European immigrants continued to pour into North

Prepared for the Minnesota Railroad Commissioner, this map reveals the construction that accompanied the post-war economic boom. "Like spokes of an enormous wheel," railroads radiated outward from St. Paul and Minneapolis in every direction for thousands of miles.

America. Tallying newcomers and natural increases, the U.S. population swelled to nearly 40 million in 1870, and with westward expansion the country's gravitational center shifted from the Atlantic seaboard to forty-eight miles northeast of Cincinnati, Ohio. By 1870, Minnesota's population reached 440,000, pulling the state from the bottom of the nation's population list to number 28 out of 37. Although most Minnesotans still lived east of New Ulm and south of St. Cloud, railroad construction promised to push immigrants farther west and north into the Red River Valley. In 1869, lumber remained Minnesota's most profitable industry; however, homesteaders cultivated nearly 1.8 million acres on more than 46,000 farms, where plows and harvesters devoted 60 percent of farming efforts to commercial wheat production. During 1869 and 1870, Minnesota's wheat yield reached 18.8 million bushels, providing sufficient business to keep St. Paulites busy hauling passengers, merchandise, and machinery in and freight tonnage out, as well as to absorb Minneapolitans in filling elevators, grinding grain, bagging flour, and shipping barrels for local consumption and export.[48]

At the same time, the British North America Act of 1867 opened new opportunities to "assist" Minnesota's newly independent northern neighbors in entering the industrial world. Although annexationist fears gathered momentum among Canadians, the act stimulated interest in transportation and distribution networks in St. Paul, where Norman Kittson, James C. Burbank, and others had developed a substantial trade with sparsely populated but potentially bountiful Manitoba. Younger entrepreneurs such as James J. Hill and Maurice Auerbach also benefited directly from these larger connections, on business that allowed them to launch more comprehensive networks.[49]

Hill expanded his warehousing business into coal land purchases in Iowa, steamboat networks in the Red River Valley, and other related transportation enterprises. As with previous undertakings, he enlisted established entrepreneurs to help broaden his operations. In entering the fuel supply business, for example, he relied upon Chauncy Griggs, a Civil War veteran who had made money supplying railroad companies' increased demands for wood and coal. By the time he merged interests with Hill in 1869, Griggs had invested heavily in Iowa coal lands. During August 1870, the partners moved to saturate the region with cheap coal, plowing some of their profits into more land purchases.[50]

By 1871, together with Norman Kittson, Griggs and Hill connected their fuel business to the expanding settlements along the Red River. Like Jay Cooke and others who coveted both the American West and the Canadian prairies, Hill and Griggs sought to span the international divide. To that end, they joined forces with George S. Acker, a local hustler who had forged direct links to Pennsylvania's anthracite coal mines. St. Paul's William Dean fashioned similar connections with iron manufacturers in his hometown of Pittsburgh, Pennsylvania, drawing on these relationships to supply local distributors. Once local dealers lowered the costs associated with procuring coal and iron, railroads relied on them for provisions. Hill continued to partner and expand, using Acker's capital and connections to purchase, with Kittson, a steamboat appropriately named *The International*. During May 1872, Hill and Acker formed a coal business partnership with several entrepreneurs in Duluth and Iowa. In no time, Hill had gained access to the entire local transportation network, connecting his aspirations with the Mississippi River trade at St. Paul, the Great Lakes system at Duluth, the international market from St. Paul to Winnipeg, and all regional railroads.

Maurice Auerbach and other St. Paul wholesalers used similar connections to expand their trading networks after fire destroyed Chicago's wholesaling district in 1869. Prior to 1857, no wholesaling houses had existed west of Chicago, a lacuna that prompted St. Paul retailers to diversify their interests. At first, most merchants bought supplies in Galena, Illinois, stocking their retail houses twice a year via Mississippi River shipments. Seeing profitable opportunities, a few gradually embarked on wholesaling, the most successful among them the dry goods concern of Justice and Forepaugh. While their annual business never exceeded $25,000 through the end of the Civil War, the Chicago fire, expanding rail transport, and hinterland demands for direct access to wholesale houses increased possibilities to profit in wholesaling and distribution. Spinning off from Justice and Forepaugh, Auerbach launched a business of his own.[51]

Starting with a small inventory in 1868, Auerbach exploited railroad connections to drum up business for his dry goods concern. By 1872 his firm employed nearly fifty workers to sew articles in gingham and print departments, supervise shop floors, sell wares throughout the region, and oversee hinterland retail outlets. As he established direct linkages with larger wholesaling houses in Chicago and New York, Auerbach joined the owners of other grocery, drug, clothing, and hardware concerns in the rapid construction of St. Paul's wholesaling quarter, investing in larger business blocks that pushed retail and residential districts farther inland. City government assisted with this expansion by incorporating the St. Paul Water Company. Financed and managed by local entrepreneurs, the company constructed a fully integrated waterworks north of St. Paul, at Lake Phalen. When the company installed sewers to service the wholesaling district, the city hired a fire department, hoping to protect local wholesalers from large-scale catastrophes like the Chicago fire.[52]

Writing from St. Paul to his uncle in Boston during 1869, recently arrived George Aaron Chapin exclaimed, "The country is growing [so] fast, it must outstrip the East, in business of all kinds [because] so much building is required for the emigration [flood]." Within one year, city wholesalers had captured the region's business to such a degree that Stillwater entrepreneurs appealed to their Minneapolis counterparts for aid in curbing St. Paul's influence. Writing to Minneapolis lawyer William Lochren, Stillwater merchant J. W. Castle announced, "The people of this city last evening passed resolutions. They will not buy nor trade with St. Paul by Wholesale or Retail & also today stopped all our papers from that city [because of the] hostility of the St. Paul people to our R.R. [and business] enterprises." Despite this bluster, by the time railroads completed a direct link to Chicago in 1872, St. Paul's wholesalers had gained wealth enough to quash Stillwater's ambitions.[53]

In addition to building banks and stores, St. Paul's wholesalers helped James Burbank organize the St. Paul City Railway. This horse-drawn street railway system inaugurated movement toward residential suburbs as the city's population expanded inland from the Lower Levee's wholesaling, banking, and transportation center. Working with other established entrepreneurs, wholesalers also contributed to the $100,000 purchase of Como Park, a new railroad and residential district north of the city where elites planned to erect houses, public amusements, machine shops, locomotive works, and other facilities for St. Paul's expanding labor pool. These amenities lured more people to the capital city and increased the economies of scale associated with buying merchandise there.[54]

By 1872, St. Paul emerged as the undisputed hub for transportation, finance, and wholesaling in Minnesota, Iowa, Dakota Territory, and Manitoba, its size and population having expanded from five square miles with 13,000 inhabitants to 17.5 square miles with 25,000 residents. St. Paulites had converted multipurpose operations into ninety wholesaling houses specializing in dry goods, grocery, and hardware firms, complete with separate functions for both owners and directors and managers and employees and with divisions for finance, production, purchasing, and distribution. Driven by a record $17 million-plus in the jobbing trade that year, wholesalers joined St. Paul's industrial elite in chamber of commerce initiatives to encourage and underwrite manufacturing investments. St. Paulites boasted of their eighty-eight factories employing one thousand workers who manufactured $1.6 million in products. But while developments in St. Paul significantly altered the city and the habits of its hinterland consumers, they also accelerated enterprises in Minneapolis, where waterfall entrepreneurs had commenced transformations that rapidly dwarfed the capital city's heralded manufacturing accomplishments.[55]

Innovations in Food Supply: Minneapolis "Patent Flour"

While St. Paul's entrepreneurs expanded into larger fuel, wholesaling, and banking activities associated with railroad expansion, Minneapolis flour millers joined other innovators in the transformation of the nation's food supply. From 1870 to 1872, Minneapolitans not only drew the American center of flour manufacturing away from upstate New York; they also absorbed St. Anthony and its lumbering activities into a larger and more competitive manufacturing city. Viewing these changes, residents and tourists alike commented that Minneapolis–St. Anthony "must have been a very wild and beautiful place twenty years ago, but all its picturesqueness is gone now; the river is cut up with dams, and choked with immense numbers of logs; its banks are lined with mills [and] bustling activity." Many also observed, "if it only had the advantages of River and Railroads, it would beat St. Paul [and] there is a great rivalry between the two cities."[56]

As the nation's population center shifted to the Midwest, the heart of technological innovations pushed westward as well, particularly into Chicago, where entrepreneurs had assembled to build railroads, agricultural machinery, commodity exchanges, stockyards, meat-packing houses, and mail-order firms to meet the consumer appetites of an expanding hinterland population. In 1867, George Pullman incorporated his Palace Car Company, making railroad travel into the wheat-growing West infinitely more comfortable. Three years later, Gustavus Swift perfected the refrigerated railroad car, opening up possibilities to ship from Chicago to points east dressed beef as well as Armour and Company's pork, packaged in the plant Philip and Herman Armour had added to the original Chicago Grain Commission during 1867. Augmenting these examples with Henry J. Heinz and L. C. Noble's food-packing company in Sharpsburg, Pennsylvania, American innovators took a giant leap forward in supplementing the nation's diet, providing products that soon replaced much of the "salted" food early Minnesotans found so unappealing.[57]

Minneapolis's transformation into a large-scale food supplier commenced in 1870, as C. C. Washburn increased his efforts to make flour milling more profitable. Brackett and Judd, their attention diverted by the NPR construction project, had failed to generate profits on their Minneapolis Mill lease. Terminating the association in 1870, C. C. cast about for new partners, making an excellent investment when he joined forces with George Henry Christian, the fourth son of an Irish miller. Arriving from Alabama in 1865, Christian started his Minneapolis flour-milling career as a buyer for a New York merchant, but when Washburn offered him an interest in the "B" mill in 1870, he folded his own business to join the firm. The Washburn concern had also recently employed an excellent journeyman miller, John La Croix, who described a process he had observed in France, one that would produce a better quality flour. Inspired, Christian reached into his own pockets, eventually developing a machine that churned out genuinely superior flour.[58]

Laying the foundation for modern flour-milling practices, the process involved the invention of the "middlings purifier," which eliminated the impurities in winter wheat, improved the quality of manufactured flour, and increased the yield from wheat harvests. Christian obtained a patent for the invention, but—like so many American innovations—word of its successful application soon spread throughout Minneapolis and elsewhere. Other would-be flour millers devised their own machines, including John Sargeant Pillsbury's nephew Charles, a young businessman who had moved to St. Anthony in 1869. Charles purchased an abandoned stone mill, acquired a generous leasing agreement from the faltering St. Anthony Falls Water Power Company, and proceeded to challenge Washburn's preeminence at the falls.

By 1870, competition between the Washburn and Pillsbury mills had perfected the process that catapulted Minneapolis "patent flour" onto the world stage. Immediately recognized as far superior to the flour manufactured throughout New York, patent flour launched a boom on both sides of the waterfall. Pillsbury constructed another large mill to rival the Washburn "B," and other enthusiastic entrepreneurs erected smaller mills and tertiary businesses, including barrel and bag manufactories. Flour milling success also wrote the final chapter in St. Anthony's independent existence. In 1870, with W. D. Washburn's prodding, the Minneapolis Board of Trade recommended annexation, emboldening Minneapolis entrepreneurs such as Washburn and his associates to branch out into railroad construction projects and wholesaling start-ups centered on the consolidated waterfall city. The following year, while Minneapolis Mill achieved a record $1 million investment along the western shore, a sheriff presided over the St. Anthony Falls Water Power Company's foreclosure sale. During 1872, Minneapolis absorbed the eastern-shore town, expanding the consolidated cities' borders from four square miles with 7,600 inhabitants to a sprawling 20-square-mile urban-manufacturing center with nearly 24,000 residents. In the years that followed, flour millers on both sides of the river would dominate the waterfall's future under Washburn's manufacturing plan, to compete more effectively with St. Paul.[59]

The Ascent of the Cities

By 1872, St. Paul–Minneapolis had emerged as *the Cities* of the New North-west. In his annual address, St. Paul's mayor argued, "the great feeders of our trade and commerce—the hundreds of miles of railroads that are net-working our State and developing its wealth, shows the importance of ren-dering all the aid we can to these [city-based] corporations, [taking] liberal action in all matters connected with growth." Between 1866 and 1872, St. Paul's commercial entrepreneurs had funneled some $30 million into the city, making it the largest growth center northwest of Chicago. Investments in Minnesota's manufacturing establishments climbed to $12 million, with $6.8 million (compared to $358,000 in 1860) ventured in Minneapolis alone. Throughout the state, its population now 500,000 strong, start-up mills, factories, locomotive works, and other industrial enterprises em-ployed more than 12,000 workers to produce in excess of $23 million in commodities for local consumption and eastern and southern export. At the same time, Minnesota's more than 46,000 farms produced a river of wheat on which both cities planned to expand their influence. Just ten years earlier, Minnesota had but ten miles of railroad and no exportable wheat.[60]

By 1873, connections with larger railroad networks promised to enhance the Cities' position vis-à-vis other regional rivals, but as eastern capitalists penetrated Minnesota they also threatened local control over the region's riches. Relatively inexperienced in big business intrigues, entrepreneurs in St. Paul–Minneapolis found themselves confronted with new and more dangerous competitors. Desire for expansion, however, pushed them into alliances with Jay Cooke and other eastern hustlers; once connected with outsiders, state railroaders built 1,350 miles of track between 1869 and 1872. Through this brisk construction, Minnesota's railroad companies met most of their land-grant obligations, receiving from the state alone over 12 mil-lion acres—a profit-generating area larger than Massachusetts, Rhode Is-land, Connecticut, and half of New Hampshire combined. In seven years, the state's railroads had increased their income from $157,000 to more than $4.6 million (earnings much lower than those in Illinois and other estab-lished states but significantly higher than Minnesota's earlier railroads could boast). Lucrative construction contracts for this expansion fell mostly to businessmen based in St. Paul–Minneapolis; in turn, those local con-tractors plowed many of their profits into citywide investments and re-gional developments.[61]

Beyond external threats to the Cities' regional hegemony, rapid immi-gration and continual increases in railroad construction, commercial farm-ing, passenger and freight traffic, and manufacturing developments taxed

Minnesotans' abilities to manage their cities' transformation. As competition for and demands upon available resources escalated, railroads, industries, and consumers placed heavier burdens on the infrastructure needed for urban development and on the Mississippi River basin's capacity to house swelling distribution and manufacturing facilities. As trains rumbled into St. Paul laden with more passengers and freight tonnage each year, industrial accidents, fires, water pollution, and other problems proliferated. Slapping up wooden structures to meet increased demands, many entrepreneurs quickly depleted their cash flow and opted not to insure their property, a decision that proved costly when fires swept through the warehousing district. Similar problems attended businesses at the waterfall, with floods and other natural disasters limiting its water-power potential. Canal and dam builders continued to devise ways to preserve the falls until the industries could convert from water- to steam-powered manufacturing.[62]

Despite industrial growing pains, Minnesota's urban entrepreneurs sought to fulfill their predecessors' visions by expanding into the interior before larger, external systems could invade the region. Hometown residents—dependent upon these businesses for their livelihoods—supported the managerial and technological innovations of successful entrepreneurs headquartered in St. Paul–Minneapolis. City residents bought bonds to assist with infrastructure improvements, and entrepreneurs donated funds to flood and fire victims. Both cities cooperated to save the Falls of St. Anthony, and, with its constituents' blessing, the state legislature authorized further railroad construction.[63]

Finally, with a 1,900-mile railroad network centered on St. Paul–Minneapolis, the "plastic hand of enterprise" had reconstructed the Cities from hinterland outposts into magnets for further commercial and industrial expansion. Aided by government funding and incentives, Minnesota's urban-based enthusiasts had orchestrated the transformation. As this host of entrepreneurial dreamers embarked on new ventures—constructing railroad tracks, cutting and sawing timber, moving and milling grain, assembling and shipping machinery, negotiating government contracts, opening banks and insurance companies, selling city and countryside real estate, and creating networks to supply hinterland immigrants with fuel, groceries, dry goods, and hardware—they facilitated other Minnesotans' entry into the larger industrial economy.[64]

At the end of 1872, Minnesota's urban dwellers envisioned a promising future. Once railroads pushed into the Dakotas, Montana, and Canada's prairie provinces, residents of St. Paul–Minneapolis expected to manage and prosper from their wheat-growing, mineral-rich hinterlands. City planners encouraged the development of more parks, public buildings, and health and educational programs to beautify St. Paul–Minneapolis and to hopefully suppress the most egregious disfigurements of the more developed Northeast's industrial cities and to ameliorate some of the social inequalities that attended industrialization. In Minnesota, they intended to construct "ideal" western cities. The state's wealth-creating vanguard in St. Paul and Minneapolis also promised to generate more opportunities, not only for themselves but also for their less fortunate neighbors and for the newcomers they planned to attract. Unfortunately, another financial panic, followed by the nation's first industrial depression, was about to test their entrepreneurial skills once again.[65]

1873–1877

Industrial Depression and the Survival of St. Paul–Minneapolis

DURING THE SPRING OF 1873, optimism pervaded Minnesota as residents of St. Paul–Minneapolis speculated about their "inevitable" rise as the next great cities of the expanding American empire. Unfortunately, on September 18—just as the Minneapolis construction team completed the Northern Pacific extension from Minnesota's western border to Bismarck, North Dakota—Jay Cooke & Co. failed, signaling the panic of 1873. As Minnesotans collided with another mortifying financial panic and the larger nation collapsed into a four-year financial depression, railroads, banks, businesses, and farms fell into bankruptcy and industrial expansion ceased from east to west. Entering yet another phase in their connection with the larger market economy, entrepreneurs in St. Paul–Minneapolis had to channel their energies away from expansion and into structural reinforcements to safeguard the Cities against the United States' first industrial depression.[1]

Exacerbating the situation in Minnesota and the New Northwest, grasshoppers swarmed over Minnesota, Iowa, and the Dakotas, darkening the skies and devouring crops against which farmers had signed loans for more land and equipment to expand their commercial operations. The plague also diminished hinterland consumption, on which urban entrepreneurs had borrowed for anticipated expansion. Between 1873 and 1877, the insects returned each harvest for another feeding frenzy, annihilating crops and dashing residents' hopes throughout the region.[2]

Despite these problems, some entrepreneurs in St. Paul–Minneapolis who had managed to protect their investments during the postwar boom now consolidated their interests to safeguard the Cities' competitive position and thus their own. Several dozen of the Cities' bankers, wholesalers, millers, and transportation entrepreneurs not only survived the depression but even prospered by it. By 1877, urban investors and managerial innovators saved themselves from failure and paved the way for one of the most profitable railroad takeovers of the nineteenth century, allowing forty-year-old James J. Hill to transform himself from a fuel supplier with a $15,000 annual income into the Twin Cities' most aggressive and successful railroader. Notwithstanding the myths that surround him, Hill benefited from, rather than built, the Twin Cities. He distinguished himself as a broker of local interests and a shrewd business operator by building upon the urban *fait accompli* that pulled him into the limelight. Previously established entrepreneurs set the stage for that moment by preserving St. Paul–Minneapolis as a nexus for further expansion.[3]

The Panic of 1873 and the Long-Term Challenge

On the strength of more than 1,900 miles of railroad plus thriving immigration, trade, manufacturing, and farming within and beyond the state's borders, Minnesota's urban boosters had cause to believe themselves bound for wealth and glory during 1873. Pointing to the rise of Chicago, local forecasters predicted that "as the country expands, there must be one great city every four or five hundred miles—a center of trade, wealth, and opinion, a center political, commercial, and social." By 1873, St. Paul–Minneapolis had knocked out several regional competitors—including St. Anthony—in the battle for urban supremacy. Although Duluth and Kansas City threatened, entrepreneurs in St. Paul–Minneapolis could boast that they had pulled wheat production and regional consumers away from rivals in Davenport, Dubuque, Rock Island, and Stillwater and into their realm.[4]

During 1873, seven railroads headquartered their operations along St. Paul's levees, from which tracks radiated outward for hundreds of miles in every direction. In just ten years, traffic had increased from a few trains chugging between St. Paul and St. Anthony into hundreds roaring into the city daily and carrying thousands of passengers and a half-million tons of freight annually. Export grain receipts climbed from $2.8 million in 1870 to a record high of $6.5 million in 1873. The city's population increased from 20,000 to more than 30,000 during the same period, generating business that crowded every thoroughfare for miles around. Successful entrepreneurs watched over these developments from the palatial grandeur of their newly constructed Summit Avenue homes. James Burbank, William Davidson, Norman Kittson, and others donated hundreds of thousands of dollars toward the establishment of social, scientific, literary, religious, and political institutions. Railroad companies and private citizens expended not thou-

sands but millions of dollars investing in banks, wholesale houses, manufactories, waterworks, gaslights, street railways, and other "improvements."
They also spent part of their profits on elegant homes, fine churches, and
assorted ornamental structures. During the early 1870s, Henry Rice built a
$150,000 mansion, an expenditure ten times his total wealth in 1850 (the
residence's value equivalent to more than $3 million in present-day terms).[5]

St. Paul's First National Bank, under the direction of Horace Thompson, Norman Kittson, Henry Sibley, James Burbank, Chauncy Griggs,
Amherst H. Wilder, and other local investors, increased its capital to
$1 million, making it one of the most profitable banks northwest of St.
Louis. The city's wholesaling business climbed another $2.5 million, reach-
ing a new high of $19 million. Dry goods wholesaler Maurice Auerbach
launched the Merchants National Bank—a U.S. depository capitalized at
$500,000—and lured other prosperous St. Paulites, including Wilder and
John Merriam, into its boardroom. Considering the city's prosperity since
the Civil War, some speculated that if St. Paul "proved smarter and more
enterprising" than Minneapolis, it could emerge as the next great American emporium.[6]

Having annexed St. Anthony during 1872, Minneapolis boasted similar
achievements, leading its 28,000 residents to believe they had an excellent
chance of challenging St. Paul for supremacy over the wheat-growing
Northwest. Visiting in 1865, the famous *New York Tribune* editor Horace
Greeley had predicted, "Minneapolis has advantages enough in her enormous yet most facile water power to give employment to a population of
100,000 souls. It has no superior but Niagara and surpasses that inasmuch
as the pineries above the wheat lands all around are calculated to supply it
with profitable employment." Indeed, lumber production had climbed from
118 million feet in 1870 to 190 million feet in 1873, making Minneapolis the
third-largest lumber-milling center in the United States. And, having perfected the process of flour manufacturing, Minneapolis millers saw their
earnings surpass the most profitable mills in upstate New York. During
1873, six million bushels of Minnesota grain descended upon the city, and
the Washburn and Pillsbury mills, along with smaller establishments, produced 585,000 barrels of the nation's best flour, compared to 193,000 barrels
of inferior brands in 1870. Half of that output they now exported east and
south. Moreover, George Christian had just returned from France and
Hungary, carrying technological information that promised both to complete the foundation for modern milling practices and to increase yields
from the expanding wheat harvests. If Minneapolitans constructed a
"cheap, speedy, and regular transit between [their flour mills] and the commercial and manufacturing centers of the East [and] markets of Europe,"

many reasoned that they would also absorb St. Paul's commerce and trade on their march toward greatness.[7]

Israel Washburn Jr., brother to Cadwallader and William, theorized, "If Minneapolis can unite with manufacturing the trade and commerce of this region, she will become the great city; if St. Paul can supplement her extensive trade with many and successful branches of manufacturers, the prize will not pass from her grasp." But most Minnesotans argued that, although "one of [the nation's new] Emporiums shall grow up near St. Anthony Falls," the Cities would "inevitably" emerge in concert, for "as to all interests" St. Paul and Minneapolis "are as much one in fact as if they had grown together." Both had enough "local facilities and accommodation," they argued, "combined with wealth, sagacity, and energy" to ascend the heights as a united force.[8]

Fortunately for both cities, they also housed a few dozen shrewd entrepreneurs who understood the art of government cooperation and the difference between speculation and investment, for economic realities were about to test the nation's capacity for expansion once again. On September 20, 1873, just two days after Cooke & Co.'s failure, the New York Stock Exchange closed. The resulting economic depression embroiled Americans in four years of uncertainty made worse by the hundreds of millions of dollars invested in railroads and other large-scale industrial corporations. By the end of 1873, auditors settled Cooke's accounts at twenty-five cents on the dollar. On January 1, 1874, with $30 million in bonds issued, the NPR defaulted on its interest payment and declared bankruptcy.[9]

Between Cooke & Co.'s 1873 bankruptcy and September 1877, more than five thousand incorporated U.S. businesses failed, including the Minnesota railroads Cooke had absorbed in his quest for hegemony over the New Northwest. Untold numbers of small firms and farms collapsed as well. On April 6, 1875, the NPR's trustees, along with several Dutch bondholders, commenced foreclosure proceedings. Minnesota's SP&P and First Division trustees followed suit shortly thereafter. Work stopped on all Minnesota railroads: contractors sued for payments on services rendered, construction workers lost their jobs, and real estate "went begging" throughout the Cities and their hinterland. Eastern capitalists reorganized the NPR on September 9, but no further construction took place until after the industrial depression passed. As the SP&P and its First Division fell into receivers' hands, local nabobs lost managerial control over their railroads. The Dutch bondholders arranged temporary agreements to keep the trains running and retained John S. Kennedy and Company of New York to find a buyer for the $15 million in bonds they held in Minnesota's railroad corporations.

As the state's railroad commissioner tallied up construction in 1876, he noted that Minnesotans had built fewer than fifty miles of track since 1873.[10]

Increased agricultural poverty sparked national campaigns for currency inflation to ease farm debts in the West and South as well as for railroad and grain elevator regulations to lower farmers' transportation and storage costs. Oliver Kelley's Grangers lobbied for and gained regulations in Minnesota, Iowa, Wisconsin, and Illinois, and the Farmers' Alliance, founded in 1873, worked with them to place increased pressure on state and federal governments. Their combined efforts resulted in the triumph of the "Granger Laws" during 1877, when the Supreme Court's *Munn v. Illinois* ruling upheld the right of states to regulate railroads and set maximum freight-hauling rates. Consistent with long-standing American assumptions that laws should protect and promote competition, Chief Justice Morrison R. Waite argued that Chicago's railroads and grain elevators "stand in the very 'gateway of commerce,' and take toll from all who pass." Granger legislation sought to curb railroads and other monopoly-seeking institutions from limiting competition; by encouraging cooperatives, the proposed regulations simultaneously mobilized the larger community for the greater public good. The legislation boded ill for Minnesota's urban industrialists, but railroad enthusiasts in St. Paul–Minneapolis sought ways around the statutes so they could realize continued profits. With non-Granger friends in the state legislature, they managed to thwart regulation more often than not.[11]

Although ineffectual in the long run, the Granger Laws of 1877 demonstrated that something had gone terribly wrong with American industrial expansion. Labor strife along eastern railroad lines during 1877 only confirmed this impression. During the long depression's final summer, railroad managers accelerated labor disputes on most lines east of the Mississippi River when, without warning, they slashed wages by ten percent. Gaining strength since the 1860s, the Railroad Brotherhoods called for a strike. Ignited by the Baltimore and Ohio's wage cuts, the great railroad strike of 1877 resulted in violent confrontations between management and labor from the Atlantic to the Pacific Coasts, particularly in the streets of Baltimore, Pittsburgh, Chicago, St. Louis, and San Francisco. Federal troops stepped in before the conflict swept over the northern Mississippi River into Minnesota, but nervous residents in St. Paul–Minneapolis, already struggling to stay afloat, had new cause to worry about the future.[12]

Despite a four-year financial slump plagued by grasshoppers, mounting farmer protests, and increased social problems along the nation's rail lines, several dozen of Minnesota's urban entrepreneurs had managed to apply valuable lessons they had learned about the market economy. With lumber, they had a product to sell during booms; with wheat, they had one to sell no matter the economic climate. Perceiving these truths, several diversified their portfolios into transportation, banking, wholesaling, and manufacturing networks. Together, these associations promised to lower the costs of moving wheat into and out of the cities, of milling flour for local consumption and export, and of redistributing consumer articles back to hinterland producers. When railroads promised to accomplish those goals more economically than rivers or roads, savvy entrepreneurs invested in them. When railroads expanded too far beyond settled regions, however, these same businessmen studiously avoided them. Instead, railroad trustees negotiated agreements to keep transportation arteries open and flowing so they could continue to pull grain stored in hinterland elevators into Minneapolis and St. Paul for milling and redistribution to the east. Thanks to loans from Merchants Bank, wholesalers consolidated their interests by purchasing stock at liquidation sales, reselling it to hinterland retailers and consumers at reasonable rather than rapacious rates, knowing full well that customers rarely forgot or forgave the latter.[13]

Earlier investments in lucrative transportation, commercial, and manufacturing networks now placed Minnesota's successful entrepreneurs in an enviable position. Their new challenge centered on maintaining profitability to sustain wheat production and its associated businesses throughout the depression. The United States still had 40 million mouths to feed, and Minnesotans had developed the best food staple in the country along with transportation arteries to carry Minneapolis flour out of the region more cheaply than before. Moreover, European crop failures increased demand for Red River Valley grain products and Minneapolis flour. During the previous ten years, farmers had cultivated enough wheat to keep Minneapolis mills occupied. On postwar profits and inflation, Minnesota's taxpayers had also generated sufficient state and city revenues to divert some investments into citywide road, sidewalk, sewer, and other public improvements that had failed to keep pace with rapid expansion.[14]

As early as 1872, structural improvements had become an "imperative necessity" in both St. Paul and Minneapolis. The dirt streets that dominated the landscape turned to muddy quicksand during spring floods, and industrial waste foamed at the levees alongside sewage that "slobbered its way into the river." With the increasing number of new businesses compelling government development, St. Paul had already established a public works department, gas and waterworks companies, sewage systems, and a board of health; however, as both cities expanded rapidly, improvements invariably fell behind demand.[15]

While many residents had diverted their savings into consumption and bonds for railroad expansion during the boom, Thompson, Davidson, Burbank, Wilder, Auerbach, and other urban entrepreneurs had invested in utility companies that soon captured lucrative government contracts. One such business, the St. Paul Gas Light Company, acquired both exclusive privileges in city contracting and virtually unlimited powers to determine where and when businesses and residences received wrought iron pipe, gas fittings, and gas and steam services. With the utility under the management of Henry Sibley, a trusted friend and colleague involved in the First National Bank, the St. Paul and Sioux City Railroad, the St. Paul Fire and Marine Insurance Company, and the chamber of commerce, Thompson and others purchased bonds in Gas Light. Their investments earned them prompt service to supply their business needs and, moreover, allowed Gas Light to provide jobs for laborers and contractors then searching for work.[16]

Petitions among property owners increasingly "manifested a feverish impatience" for infrastructural improvements. By 1870, Minneapolis water mains extended into only seven or eight streets and most people still carried their water from wells. In addition, residents had instituted numerous lawsuits against the city for "alleged injuries by falling into Side walks and holes in the Street." These and other inducements prompted Minneapolis Mill representatives involved in city government to form their own boards of public works and health. With Minneapolis Mill associate George Brackett as mayor and W. D. Washburn presiding over the Union Board of Trade, city contracts and services not unexpectedly went to people with proven interests in the long-term viability of the milling district. At the same time, prominent residents in both cities called for more police protection to rid their business and residential neighborhoods of "riotous persons who infest the locality and [place] our property in great danger from fire and theft." City governments authorized larger police forces that not only protected investors' properties but also provided much-needed jobs.[17]

Between 1873 and 1877, both cities issued bonds to construct cedar-block sidewalks and cement-paved streets in high-traffic areas and to extend sewer systems, fire-fighting equipment, and gasworks throughout business districts and into wards whose citizens purchased the certificates. Not surprisingly, solvent and prosperous entrepreneurs bought most of the bonds and thus their businesses benefited from new services first. With banking colleagues such as John Prince running St. Paul's Board of Public Works and milling entrepreneurs like George Brackett overseeing Minneapolis's city government, local politicians soon employed the same cost-cutting strategies used in business. On the advice of Horace Thompson and other bankers, city officials called for lowered taxes to stimulate investment and for "strict economy and retrenchment," including the "rigid cutting off [of] all unnecessary expenses" unless authorized by taxpayers willing to fund them. Again, Minnesota's urban elites who purchased bonds for certain upgrades received them first, thereby raising the value of their business and residential properties and allowing them to hire more workers to keep up with any increased commerce the improvements generated. In turn, those upgrades allowed bankers, wholesalers, and millers to lower some of their fixed costs and then to reinvest in already profitable business networks.[18]

Sustained demand for wheat also provided laboring opportunities on large-scale farms, where prosperous commercial operators needed assistance in harvesting crops before the dreaded grasshoppers attacked. Swedish immigrant Arvid Person joined many other Minnesotans in this effort. He had lost his job as a carpenter when Stillwater's building boom collapsed during the depression. Writing his parents in 1875, Person claimed "the times have not been this bad since before the [Civil] War. The only activity [outside the cities] is in farm work. Everything else is at a standstill." His parents sent word that Person should return to Sweden, but despite the struggles he faced in Minnesota, he replied, "I really could not [live] in Sweden [now]. The Swedish customs are so different from those in America." Moreover, "it would be the Swedish laws that I could [no longer] endure, [where] one person [has] greater privileges than another." At least in Minnesota, he claimed, during hard times "we all ride alike, said the scoundrel when he rode alongside the King." Real wage statistics comparing the United States and Europe in 1875 supported Person's assertions. Far removed from and relatively untouched by eastern conflicts and buoyed by demands for Red River wheat, Minnesota remained, despite its many difficulties, a relatively good place to live throughout the depression.[19]

Of course, the profits associated with building city infrastructures, as well as the benefits conferred by the improvements, tended to circulate among the same collection of friends and colleagues within established economic and political networks. Even so, the larger community supported this self-serving graft because prosperous businessmen provided jobs, kept families fed, and offered products at reasonably competitive rates. For example, during the 1850s, Irish-born Charles Boyle moved his family to St. Paul from Pennsylvania's bituminous coal mines, working his way up from a laborer into a city surveyor and civil engineer. During the postwar boom, Boyle captured lucrative jobs with the city, the St. Paul and Pacific, and the Catholic Church. As he succeeded in small ways, Boyle hired his son Michael to work on a surveying team and borrowed thousands of dollars to purchase lands in and around St. Paul. When the panic of 1873 hit, it bankrupted the elder Boyle, and he returned to Ireland to look for work, leaving young Michael, then just seventeen years old, in charge of the family and its debts. Discovering "the financial & business outlook decidedly bad," Boyle found himself to be "in considerable trouble about father's business affairs. A good deal of ready money is wanted to meet some obligations, but is not forthcoming." Maurice Auerbach soon came to the rescue, offering Boyle a job. Employed as a picker in "feather [mattress] hell," a job without parallel "for pure meanness," Boyle remembered that, though unpleasant, the job kept his family afloat during the worst years of the depression. At the same time, as business improved, Boyle rose relatively quickly, from menial work to stock boy in the textile department.[20]

When the crisis lifted after 1878, Boyle declared his appreciation for the ways in which Auerbach and other successful St. Paul entrepreneurs had assisted his family and the larger community. "We have every reason to feel grateful to father's creditors for their behavior towards us during the last 4 or 5 years," he mused, for "his debts are not few nor some of the amounts small, but without exception every person he owed has treated us with a consideration which I did not believe a characteristic of human kind where money matters are concerned." Entrepreneurs' and investors' faith in long-term stability provided the impetus for that consideration, and beneficiaries like Boyle repaid their city's entrepreneurial elite with loyalty at the time clock, the cash register, and the ballot box.[21]

The St. Paul Syndicates

The 1873 panic, the NPR's collapse, and the bankruptcies that followed exposed weaknesses hitherto obscured in Minnesota's rapid development. However, several dozen entrepreneurs in St. Paul–Minneapolis overcame the many challenges presented by America's first industrial depression not only because they got lucky but also because they understood that railroads presented a means, not an end, to investment. Horace Thompson, president of St. Paul's First National Bank, trustee of the SP&P Railroad, and archenemy of Jay Cooke, refused to take the whipping Cooke so cavalierly claimed it his "duty" to inflict during earlier railroad consolidations. Moreover, Thompson perceived what the mighty war bondsman had chosen to ignore—that the only good railroad is one that pays. He further understood that more businesses survive through long-term investment strategies than by seat-of-the-pants speculation, even when both approaches stimulate rapid economic development and expansion.[22]

Backed by national deposits and investments from friends and associates on the St. Paul and Sioux City Railroad and First National boards, Thompson made most of his investments along railroad lines already built in settled regions. When the panic destroyed confidence in western railroads, banks, and other businesses, the Dutch bondholders' New York agents entrusted the sp&p and First Division to Thompson and his solvent, nay, prosperous bank. Thompson and others thus confirmed the Cities' capacity to overcome adversity, increasing St. Paul–Minneapolis's economic, political, and social standing throughout the region. At the same time, they proved the fallacy inherent in the assumption that large-scale corporations, once swung into action, can never fail. All-powerful Cooke had fallen at the height of his career, and no faceless sea of managers could save the npr from the consequences of his voracious appetite. At the other extreme, backwater Thompson and the entrepreneurs sponsored by his bank more than survived the depression—they and their ventures flourished throughout it.[23]

During the industrial depression, Thompson, Burbank, Auerbach, and other successful investors associated with St. Paul's banks and insurance companies proved that they understood one of the venture capitalist's most enduring principles: survival depends upon reliable information, and each penny that lowers the costs associated with gathering it is one well spent. Consequently, St. Paul bankers formed a syndicate, pooling information about debtors, creditors, and investment risks. During the 1840s, new credit bureaus such as R. G. Dun & Co. and Bradstreet's Mercantile Agency had opened their doors in New York. Now, as the scale and scope of Minnesota's business increased beyond investors' abilities to learn everything they needed to know about those seeking credit, bankers encouraged bureaus to set up shop in St. Paul, gladly paying the agencies to ferret out the information they required.[24]

When the National Protection and Collection Bureau opened an office in St. Paul during 1873, associates of the banking syndicate bought subscriptions to receive information about the region's merchants and millers. When business increased Minnesota's capital and population enough to justify a local establishment, R. G. Dun opened a similar office in St. Paul in 1875, followed by Bradstreet in 1876. Through moral suasion and public humiliation, many Twin Cities businessmen hoped to induce payment and avoid the costs of drawn-out legal proceedings. First National's bankers used the information to maintain the firm's $1 million in capital and to avoid risky credit seekers. Indeed, the bank enjoyed a $250,000 surplus during 1875, a remarkable sum given the ways in which other of the nation's financial institutions faltered under the weight of the depression. In addition, First National managed to pay handsome dividends to its stockholding directors, some of St. Paul's most successful businessmen among them: bank president Horace Thompson, transportation entrepreneur James Burbank, Red River trader Norman Kittson, Gas Light president Henry Sibley, coal supplier Chauncy Griggs, and wholesaling and milling investor Amherst H. Wilder.[25]

Jay Cooke might have winced if he read Mark Twain and Charles Dudley Warner's 1874 novel *The Gilded Age: A Tale of Today*, which satirized post–Civil War corruption and the speculative fever that had pitched the United States into the depths of depression. St. Paul's syndicated bankers, however, had confirmed that they did not exemplify the novel's searing lines, "Beautiful credit! The foundations of modern society. 'I wasn't worth a cent two years ago, and now I owe two millions of dollars.'" Thompson and his associates gained notoriety not from scandal, foreclosure proceedings, and embarrassment but from their abilities to avoid the excesses of "beautiful credit." Attaching their syndicated interests to directorships in St. Paul Fire and Marine, they also protected their investments against the lurking possibilities of failure by purchasing insurance policies from their own company. Bankers associated with First National and the St. Paul and Sioux City Railroad built up the capital of Henry Sibley's St. Paul Savings Bank; by the time the depression lifted the associates had ventured into a European steamship business to carry Minneapolis wheat across the Atlantic. More importantly, by the close of 1877 St. Paul had emerged as the region's undisputed financial center.[26]

Maurice Auerbach undertook measures to pull the city's wholesalers into the networks Thompson and his banking associates had built. By 1875, Auerbach's firm had emerged as the region's most substantial dry goods concern, and in that year he sold some of his interest to two new partners. With the help of Amherst H. Wilder, the venture capitalist who had provided the young wholesaler with capital to expand his firm, Auerbach launched the Merchants Bank. Merchants joined the syndicate, and very soon Auerbach was using credit information to safeguard his interests as well as those of other emerging wholesaling concerns. As a measure of gratitude toward Wilder and his associate, John Merriam, Auerbach hired Merriam's young son, William, as the Merchants' teller. Thus, by 1875 Auerbach, Wilder, and the Merriams had connected their overlapping interests and investments throughout the state.[27]

Auerbach also reorganized his dry goods firm under the name Auerbach, Finch, and Van Slyke, acknowledging the New York wholesaler who had invested in Auerbach's previous success. By 1877, the dry goods firm employed nearly one hundred workers—salesmen, shop floor managers, and laborers such as Boyle—and turned more than $1 million in business. Together with other wholesalers, Auerbach helped increase St. Paul's jobbing trade from $19 million in 1873 to more than $27 million at the close of 1877. Young workers in St. Paul developed a new hierarchy of labor, meas-

uring personal success alongside their employers' rise in stature. Employers rewarded them with competitive salaries and with credit to tide them
over during the depression. This paternalism also increased employee loyalty to their firms and to the cities that housed them.[28]

While St. Paul's overlapping networks of resident businessmen sustained the city through the crisis, many overextended companies capsized
under the weight of expansion. One struggling manufacturer lamented that
he very nearly required warehouse space to store his expanding non-
payment file. Businesses received debtor letters from near and far, all
announcing in some form "I have tried my best to raise the money [I owe
you], but could not do it" and promising to pay in the future—say in sixty
or ninety days. Those days passed, and rather than payment, the debtors
submitted further excuses: "We are obliged to say that we cannot meet the
note of $1,880.73 when due. We can scarcely keep our [own] mill running."
Inevitably these parties failed, while other creditors down the line continued to plead, "I am pretty hard pressed for funds at this time, and a re-
mittance of same amount will be very greatly obliged." Within weeks, those
firms folded, too.[29]

Hundreds of failures occurred while St. Paul's industrial elite amassed
great wealth; however, the city's general prosperity during hard times encouraged many people to move to or remain in St. Paul. The city maintained a population of 33,000 in 1877 (compared to 13,000 in 1865 and
20,300 in 1870), and local residents continued to shop and to invest in business and building projects. Diverting some of his multiplying wealth from
investment to conspicuous consumption, Kittson built a new mansion on
St. Anthony Hill. Admiring residents commented that it had emerged as
"one of the most beautiful and elegant homes in the city," a towering symbol of St. Paul's elites and the roles they had played during the country's
larger struggle. Commodore Davidson built a new Opera House for the
city's residents, and Summit Avenue dwellers shared the neighborhood
with several charities they helped establish, including the Orphan's Asylum
and St. Joseph's Academy. Elites also purchased bonds to build a new high
school, complete with a business department to train new arrivals in the
arts of the emporium's enterprises.[30]

Under Henry Sibley's leadership, the St. Paul Chamber of Commerce
had invested in manufacturing start-ups that now produced $5 million in
business each year. By 1877, the city boasted 97 groceries, 33 meat markets,
15 newspapers (including Ignatius Donnelly's newest entrepreneurial venture, the *Anti-Monopolist*), and hundreds of retail shops networked to more
than 100 wholesaling houses. Minnesota Stagecoach still ran services right
alongside the street railway Burbank had launched before his death in 1876,

and steamboats still carried pigs, wood, grain, and other products south, demonstrating that many Minnesotans now sustained any transportation network that paid, rather than viewing railroads as the only solution to high transportation costs.[31]

By 1877, bankers had enough capital to invest in further expansion among firms with capable managers. St. Paul banks averaged nearly $4 million in daily deposit balances and the same in daily discounts, the three national banks together aggregating more than $2 million in capital. The wholesaling business of Minnesota, the Dakotas, and Manitoba had decisively passed from Chicago into the hands of local houses in St. Paul, while successful firms arranged imports directly, thereby cutting out the middlemen associated with transfers. As St. Paul rose in prestige as a national banking and wholesaling center, Minneapolis millers undertook a few innovations of their own, not only actively securing the waterfall under the Minneapolis Mill plan but also confirming their city's position at the center of the world's flour-manufacturing stage.[32]

The Minneapolis Manufacturing Plan

Fellow waterfall millers observed one major strategy that contributed to Minneapolis Mill's success: C. C. Washburn's long-range plan included a fund for technological changes, but the absentee mill owner refused to use those monies to support "elegant" but unproven technologies. Like successful manufacturers before and after, Washburn insisted that the only good technologies were those that paid—particularly ones that promised to lower costs in established processes and markets. Once champions had proven new equipment and methods, Washburn spared no cost putting them to work under managers he thought he could trust, including his younger brother William. Alas, W. D. had overextended his reach by 1874 — on heavy investments in land, lumber, railroads, flour mills, real estate, wholesaling, a steam-powered street railway project, and sundry other enterprises, all backed by C. C. himself. When W. D. had to suspend his lumbering operation and the street railway company failed, C. C. temporarily confiscated W. D.'s properties, settled his debts, and reached into family networks for more funds. In response, other siblings in Maine warned that both western brothers sometimes labored "under a small delusion [that we] can pass $5000 notes as easy as a chicken can swallow a grasshopper."[33]

One of the greatest dangers to manufacturing establishments lay not in failure but rather in success. Early accomplishments at Minneapolis Mill threatened its owners' resources as they expanded more deeply into flour milling and consequently faced mounting capital costs. Over time, William

Entrepreneurial elites laid the foundations for St. Paul's future as the region's transportation, financial, and wholesaling center. By 1874, St. Paulites had built urban infrastructures to sustain the city's expansionist plans, including railroad bridges connecting urban residents and their bustling downtown with the undeveloped lands and bucolic countryside shown in this panorama.

Minneapolis's long-range manufacturing plan included schemes to topple rivals in St. Paul through the sale of abundant timber and wheat stored in warehouses on both sides of the river. The university's tower prominently displayed in the panorama's foreground trumpets another marker of the city's prestige, as the center of higher education and culture for the state.

Dunwoody—a successful Pennsylvania grain trader who moved to Minneapolis during 1869—convinced associates and competitors to pool their resources not only to meet these rising costs but also to make the milling district more profitable during the vexatious 1870s. By 1877, Dunwoody, George Christian, Charles A. Pillsbury, C. C. Washburn, and others had consolidated the interests of the millers associated with both Minneapolis Mill and the reorganized St. Anthony Falls Water Power Company, thereby improving on the manufacturing plan first formed by C. C. Washburn.[34]

By 1875, flour manufacturing emerged as Minneapolis's chief industry, thanks in no small measure to George Christian, the miller responsible for perfecting the earlier "patent" process that enhanced the position of the city's flour in national markets. Inspired by this initial success, C. C. Washburn decided to construct a larger-capacity mill, the Washburn "A," where he hoped to produce the best flour in the world. Embarking on the project, Christian traveled to Europe to study the continent's superlative machinery. As luck would have it, another Washburn brother, E. B., was then the acting U.S. minister to France and thus able to provide Christian with access to the best French mills. Once Christian had imported the finest French millstones to Washburn "A," Minneapolis's patent flour received resounding acknowledgment as the world's best. Again, Minneapolis Mill's success centered on blending the benefits of both political and economic contacts.[35]

French millstones further improved Minneapolis flour manufacturing, but Christian soon learned that even the best millstones could not compete with the techniques then under development along the east and west sides of the Danube River, in Europe's famous flour-milling capital, Budapest. For millstones, the Hungarians had substituted chilled iron rollers, which lasted longer and proved a better technology for the money spent. When Washburn and Pillsbury adopted the Hungarian method during 1874, Minneapolis millers completed the foundation for modern flour manufacturing. Soon recognized as the world's choicest, Minneapolis patent flour advanced from two dollars below the world market price to first place on the list. In the depths of the depression, Minneapolis millers had managed to inaugurate a flour-manufacturing boom. In no time, millers throughout the nation gathered their belongings and scrambled to St. Anthony Falls.[36]

On political hustling and industrial contacts, C. C. Washburn and Christian had ushered in the boom; however, during 1875 Charles A. Pillsbury and his brothers surpassed Washburn's achievements. Building their own "A" Mill, the Pillsbury brothers increased the profitability of Minneapolis flour through competition.[37]

Born in Warner, New Hampshire, in 1842, Charles Pillsbury graduated from Dartmouth at age twenty and thereafter engaged in a mercantile business in Montreal, newly independent Canada's financial center. Pillsbury carved out a tidy little business but—lacking experience and connections— he found the leap into larger networks difficult. When his uncle, John Sergeant, recommended he take a chance on the developing Northwest, Charles made his way to Minneapolis. Though unacquainted with flour milling when he arrived in 1869, Pillsbury purchased an interest in an abandoned mill from a man who had taken it as a debt payment. From these inconsequential headquarters on the eastern side of the Mississippi River, Charles searched for connections to make him *au courant* in every aspect of the business, including the grain trade. By 1870, he understood enough to launch Gardner, Pillsbury & Crocker and to purchase one-third interest in the St. Anthony milling enterprise. From the outset Pillsbury employed Christian's innovations in his mills, and by the time Minneapolis and St. Anthony consolidated during 1872, his Charles A. Pillsbury & Co. had emerged on top of the flour-milling heap.

In 1874, after federal government engineers helped Minneapolis residents reinforce the falls for future manufacturing expansion, Charles A. Pillsbury & Co. purchased an older mill on the river's eastern shore. Renaming the mill Pillsbury "B," Charles immediately adopted the methods employed in Washburn's "B" mill. Wary of the formidable cross-river competitor, the young miller cast about for allies to help him build a flour-milling empire. He found them in the people he trusted most: members of the Pillsbury family, which stretched from Minneapolis to New Hampshire. At Charles's request, his eighteen-year-old brother, Frederick Carlton Pillsbury, headed west from Concord, New Hampshire, taking up residence in St. Anthony during 1871. Fred began his western career as a clerk in his uncle John's hardware store, where he remained until 1875. Between 1872 and 1875, along with his uncle John and his father, George (the latter still residing in New Hampshire), Fred began investing in his brother's firm so that Charles could enlarge the operation's scope. Before long, Fred was the junior member of Charles A. Pillsbury & Co., and in 1875 he became a full-fledged partner in the family-run business. That same year, John Sergeant officially abandoned the hardware trade in favor of the firm. Three years later, George A. Pillsbury, father to Charles and Fred, joined the firm as well. Having served twenty-four years as purchasing agent for the Concord Railroad Company, George A. brought an important bit of expertise to the firm: his knowledge about transporting commodities. Soon the Pillsburys stood front and center in the developments that remade Minneapolis into the world's foremost breadstuff supplier.[38]

The Washburns, the Pillsburys, and the Christians (George and his sons) remodeled their mills, employed the new patent flour process, and entered into competitive battles for supremacy in the market. By the end of 1877, "Pillsbury's Best" won favor in all markets at home and abroad, quickly becoming the most recognized brand of flour in the world. Innovations gave Minneapolis a monopoly on the new process, and competition generated substantial profits on the economies of scale the large firms enjoyed. Their success stimulated other northwestern wheat-processing entrepreneurs to move to Minneapolis, along with barrel and bag manufacturers and assorted businessmen anxious to profit from flour. While the two largest firms—Washburn and Pillsbury—consolidated a number of smaller mills under their corporate umbrellas, other millers took steps to protect the interests of Minneapolis's large and small flour businesses, forming organizations for the "mutual improvement, benefit, information, and protection" of Minneapolis's patent flour.[39]

Grain trader William Dunwoody applied himself to problems associated with buying supplies for the Minneapolis mills as they increased their consumption of hinterland wheat. During 1866, George Brackett and 130 flour millers from Minneapolis and southeastern Minnesota had formed the Minnesota Millers Association. An offshoot of Chicago's Northwestern Millers Association, the cooperative first concentrated on protecting member firms from lawsuits initiated by holders of rival flour-milling patents. As the use of Hungarian chilled iron rollers allowed Minneapolis to gain a foothold in the national market, the millers then shifted their focus toward both reducing the expense of buying wheat and facilitating its transportation to the waterfall mills.[40]

During 1876, as manager and general agent for the reorganized Minneapolis Millers Association, Dunwoody brought Minneapolis's private buyers and agents together under one roof. This arrangement allowed members to set rates cooperatively and to buy all the wheat the city's seventeen strongest mills required. Thereafter, the association distributed it according to the capacity and contributions of member mills. The association penetrated all parts of the Northwest and made choice selections from grain fields sometimes still under attack by grasshoppers. Dunwoody soon initiated a system of grain storage elevators—purchasing some, building others—along the lines of railroad operation in areas with the most promising crops. By stabilizing the supply, grain elevators kept the mills in operation twelve months a year. Before long, the cooperative venture allowed Pillsbury and Washburn, in particular, to expand their operations by setting up mills in other towns along westward-pushing railroad lines. By 1877, the association had gathered enough momentum to warrant a trip to Europe for the purpose of arranging direct exports from Minneapolis to the Continent. The association remained in operation until Minneapolis millers grew profitable enough to establish their own large-scale grain elevators in the years that followed the depression. In the meantime, Dunwoody earned his place in the Minneapolis grain trade, and his stopgap measures allowed Minneapolitans to remain solvent until the city built systems that eliminated the need for purchasing agents.[41]

Through cost-effective flour manufacturing and pooling efforts, Minneapolis received 23,415 carloads of wheat at the waterfall in 1875 alone. In addition, shipments of flour rose from negligible numbers in 1870 to 27,275 carloads in 1875, yielding receipts that had expanded from virtually nothing into $4.5 million. Together, increased freight capacity and multiplying receipts confirmed Minneapolis's status as the nation's number-one breadstuff supplier.[42]

Increased flour production and federal dam improvements also revitalized the lumber industry and other local manufacturing establishments. As W. D. Washburn realized dividends on Minneapolis Mill, he put his sawmill and lumberyards back into operation. Others helped to reorganize St. Anthony Falls Water Power Company so the firm could continue to support efficient sawmillers on the eastern shore, such as former pineland surveyor Thomas Barlow Walker. Born in Xenia, Ohio, in 1840, Walker rose through the ranks from a country-store clerkship into teaching positions in mathematics. During 1862, while in Iowa waiting to hear about a position at the University of Wisconsin, he met a Minneapolitan who induced him to travel northward. Recognizing the waterfall's profit potential during the height of the tunnel-building project, Walker wrote his wife in Ohio, confessing, "I have found the spot where we will make our home." During 1863, the St. Paul and Pacific hired him to survey lands, and by 1868 the government had engaged him to survey northern pinelands. Buying as much property as his finances allowed, he switched to the lumber business, setting up shop on the St. Anthony shoreline as W. D. Washburn's most aggressive competitor. He suffered from eastern-shore floods and fires and shut down his mill during 1873 and 1874, but Walker had also built mills elsewhere in the state, along the banks of the Upper Mississippi River. When flour milling took off at the falls in 1874, he had the capital required to resume operations. Between Washburn, Walker, and others, Minneapolis's entrepreneurs produced more than 200 million board feet of lumber during 1875, surpassing the previous record, set just two years earlier.[43]

By 1876, C. C. and W. D. Washburn concluded that increased flour manufacturing warranted diversion of water power into the new industry; therefore, when sawmilling leases came up for renewal, Minneapolis Mill exercised its option, and soon the six western-shore sawmills came down. By 1877 their stone foundations were the only remnants of the city's pioneer mills. Within short order, Walker's Pacific Mill in St. Anthony dwarfed all others, save W. D. Washburn's sawmill and lumberyard on the Mississippi River's northwestern shoreline.

Minneapolis Mill Company's decision to dismantle many of the sawmills at the waterfall provided opportunities to branch out into other businesses that supported large-scale manufacturing. One venture included the cross-river competitors' newly viable woolen mills: Washburn and Morrison's North Star Woolen Mill Company and Charles A. Pillsbury's Minneapolis Woolen Mill, both reorganized during 1875. Stability and a population reaching 32,000 in 1875 revived other industries and stimulated Minneapolis millers to forge ahead with city improvements. They completely rebuilt the suspension bridge with heavier material, a wider roadway, and higher towers. The long, low, wooden structure soon became the bridge to new manufacturing concerns, especially those engaged in sawmilling and lumberyard operations. Minneapolitans also built a second bridge, a larger, iron-truss structure situated on high piers resting on the riverbed. Railroad companies constructed six other bridges throughout the city, and a young lawyer named Thomas Lowry reorganized Washburn's and Morrison's failed street railway company. The son of a Londonderry, Ireland, farmer, Lowry purchased the company with capital he had saved from earlier investments in Minneapolis. By the end of 1875, he had completed the first line of track and launched Minnesota's first steam-powered streetcar.[44]

During 1877, plow and harvester works, tool-making and machine shops, barrel and bag factories, iron foundries, roller mills, furniture makers, breweries, and many other manufacturing establishments popped up to support the various milling operations at the falls. On capital investments that reached $21 million that year, milling expansion provided new employment opportunities for journeymen millers, coopers, and various other skilled craftsmen. Minneapolitans also built a jobbing trade, the business expanding from $1 million in 1870 to more than $5 million during 1876. Many important wholesaling branches had no representation in Minneapolis, however, including the all-important dry goods business that had confirmed St. Paul's place as the Northwest's jobbing center. Thus, despite efforts to surpass St. Paul in wholesaling as well as in manufacturing, Minneapolis remained a milling town, albeit the focal point of the region's manufacturing future.[45]

Innovations in wheat milling also spurred the Washburns, Pillsburys, Christians, and others to establish additional commercial enterprises in the city. Prominent manufacturers and transportation investors organized banks, acted as their presidents, and dominated the boards in strategies similar to those used in the capital city, though their results never matched the capitalization of St. Paul's institutions. After his subterranean tunnel scheme failed, William Eastman envisioned a way to use Nicollet Island without destroying the waterfall: the lower part of the island could house a long row of shops, the upper portion, family dwellings. Eastman laid out and platted the residential neighborhood during the depression, building a home for himself and constructing sixty more from stone he had quarried along the island's lower levels. Other successful manufacturers soon built homes there as well, making the upper part of the island one of Minneapolis's most desirable residential districts. Business houses sprang up to serve the refined tastes of the city's rising flour-milling elite. Eastman organized a company to build the city's most elegant business block: the "Syndicate," a seven-acre structure completed over the next few years. At the same time, W. D. Washburn pushed for investments to complete the University of Minnesota's agricultural college. Entrepreneurial elites in Minneapolis and St. Paul supplied monies for the new scheme; in return, they emerged as the university's first board of regents.[46]

By 1877, Minneapolis Mill generated sufficient profits to enable W. D. Washburn to complete the state's first major railroad construction project since the panic of 1873—the Minneapolis and St. Louis (M&StL). This road provided a gateway from the St. Croix River to Minneapolis–St. Paul, continuing to Albert Lea, near the state's southern boundary. Influenced by the railroad's executive committee, composed of Washburn, John Pillsbury, and other prosperous millers, Minneapolitans bought bonds to support completion of the road to Albert Lea. At the same time, with the St. Paul and Pacific in a receiver's hands, its trustees granted the M&StL permission to run trains over the First Division's tracks in Hennepin County. This move assisted millers, shippers, and businesses in both cities, simultaneously generating revenues for the SP&P while legal battles hindered operation along its land-grant lines.[47]

Although M&StL completion gratified W. D. Washburn and his associates, another, more significant railroad rescue loomed in St. Paul, where Norman Kittson and James J. Hill had secretly instigated plans to acquire the bankrupt SP&P and its First Division subsidiary. That scheme flowered in the fall of 1877, mere weeks after farmers saw the last of the grasshoppers and just months before the four-year depression lifted.[48]

The St. Paul and Pacific Rescue Operation

On October 26, 1877, Minnesota's *Pioneer Press* announced that Norman W. Kittson and James J. Hill, along with "the heaviest capitalists in Canada," had initiated a "scheme" to "capture" the main and branch lines of the St. Paul and Pacific Railroad. The newspaper reported that the group (later known as "the Associates") had made the first formal offer to the company's Dutch bondholders earlier that month. Executed "with skill and secrecy," the proposed buy out promised to solve a pressing problem that still weighed on local taxpayers: the need to complete Minnesota's land-grant railroad before impending deadlines reverted millions of productive acres to the federal government. Now Hill, Kittson, and their undisclosed financial backers needed the community's support in placing pressure on locals who had instigated suits against the road.[49]

Seeking this crucial assistance, the *Pioneer* declared the scheme an all-out "rescue" operation, reminding residents that it not only promised to release Minnesota's most important roads "from the web of litigation which has so long obstructed their completion" but also guaranteed "an end to the complicated tangle of mortgages" on the state's various railroad lines. At the same time, the paper claimed, resumed construction would "encourage the actual settlement and cultivation" of the Red River Valley, still sparsely populated but rich in wheat-growing potential. These appeals inspired Twin Cities residents—particularly those holding the now-worthless 1850s railroad bonds—to rally to the cause. However, no one, including Hill, foresaw the ways in which the alliance—and the private ambitions of the Associates' principals—would alter relationships between the Cities and their hinterland in the six years that followed.[50]

The Associates intended to headquarter their entire operation at St. Paul, with absentee president George Stephen working from Montreal to sort out the bankrupt company's financial affairs. General manager James J. Hill would oversee the swift repair, completion, and operation of tracks on the main, branch, and trunk lines strung along the St. Paul and Pacific's land grants. Once they consolidated the SP&P and its First Division subsidiary, the Associates planned to undertake new projects, some privately funded from their land-grant profits, others fueled by the Canadian government, which had started to make plans for tying together its far-flung new nation. The first project targeted their most pugnacious rival, the reorganized Northern Pacific. The Associates envisioned building a competitive, westward-pushing line north of NPR junctions in Minnesota and the Dakota Territory. By constructing feeder and forager lines from the American side of the border into the wheat-growing provinces of Manitoba and

Saskatchewan, the Associates aspired to oust the ill-fated NPR from the region altogether. Further, Hill simultaneously hoped to render an all-Canadian transcontinental line an expensive redundancy. The blueprint promised mutual benefits to the American and Canadian associates, particularly Hill—the Canadian expatriate, St. Paul climber, and junior partner who had economic and personal interests in both countries. The scheme hinged on the Bank of Montreal's president, George Stephen, and his ability to negotiate monopoly guarantees with the Canadian government. Once won, however, the Associates knew they had the entire apparatus necessary for an enormous—and profitable—international system stretching to the Pacific Coast on both sides of the border.[51]

Driven by market perceptions from the moment he arrived in St. Paul during 1856, Hill had envisioned his own version of the railroad takeover as early as 1867, the year the British North America Act granted Canadians independence from British political rule. Newly autonomous Canada had rekindled Hill's childhood dream about building an empire to Asia, but he knew many years would pass before he could realize his ambitions. Therefore, prior to 1877, he trimmed his sails, quietly working on the scheme that soon convinced the men who became the Associates that, at the very least, they shared his growing "faith in the future of the Northwest." In many ways, the Associates' alliance came naturally, for these men shared not only future dreams but also similar pasts, wherein each had built a modest birthright into sizeable personal fortunes. As immigrants—Hill and Kittson both Canadian expatriates residing in St. Paul; George Stephen, Donald Smith, and John S. Kennedy all Scottish-born men living in their adopted North America—each recognized common qualities in the others, including a lust to leapfrog their pasts, make imprints on the nations that had nurtured their entrepreneurial talents, and gain access to international fortunes and fame.[52]

Throughout the 1870s, Hill laid the foundations for his ascent in St. Paul by learning how and with whom to deal and by acting as broker between various interests. During 1877, he started to integrate his wood, coal, and lubricating businesses vertically—backward into Iowa coal lands, forward into wholesaling, distribution, and marketing. His capstone achievement during May 1877, the incorporation of the North-Western Fuel Company, launched him into the presidency of a firm charged with the purchase, sale, and shipment of wholesale and retail wood, coal, "and fuel of every kind" and the construction, purchase, lease, and operation of dockyards and warehouses along St. Paul's Lower Levee. Between the North-Western Fuel Company and the Red River Transportation Company that he and Kittson now owned, Hill envisioned big returns along the northwestern borderlands once the rescued railroad completed its line near Manitoba at St. Vincent, Minnesota. His aging mentor Kittson, although invested in several other enterprises in St. Paul, agreed to go along for the ride. Once onboard, Kittson introduced Hill into wider investment circles, including those associated with Horace Thompson, the St. Paul and Pacific's trustee at the First National Bank.[53]

While Kittson and Hill carried enormous weight in St. Paul's financial circles, they possessed no direct experience in railroad finance, construction, and contracting. As Canadian-born, localized hustlers, they still inhabited spheres confined by the Red River Valley. Separately and together, their entrepreneurial zeal had carried them into the nexus of St. Paul's expanding business center and gained them reputable positions throughout the region. Known in Minnesota, Iowa, Dakota Territory, and Manitoba as trustworthy and hard-working transportation agents, warehousers, fuel suppliers, and steamboat shippers, each man had chosen his projects wisely. Their business acumen showed particularly in the development of the Red River Transportation Company, which had expanded their influence throughout the Red River Valley during the 1870s. But neither man had authority in larger financial circles. Even Hill's expanding businesses in 1877 yielded only $15,000 in profit, the largest annual income he had ever achieved. Thus, when Hill and Kittson—introduced by Horace Thompson—presented their buy out idea to Johan Carp, the Amsterdam-based attorney and Dutch bondholding committee agent rebuffed them. Carp's attitude changed during May 1877, however, when Hill and Kittson informed him they were backed by big money in Montreal.[54]

Hill first met Donald Smith during the winter of 1870, when he traveled from St. Paul to scrutinize the Riel Rebellion then interfering with the Red River Transportation Company's business. Pushing through a blinding blizzard, Hill ventured north as far as railroad tracks allowed, onboard a St. Paul and Pacific train to the NPR connection at Morris. From there, he made the rest of his 360-mile journey by dog sled. Along the way, he met up with Smith, then the Canadian prime minister's personal emissary investigating the rebellion. Stranded in drifting snow near Winnipeg, Hill and Smith discovered that they shared many traits, among them a desire to develop railroads in the Red River Valley. Smith liked Hill instantaneously, in part because Hill's ascent in St. Paul reminded him of his own rise from the hardscrabble terrain of northern Scotland, to a lonely Hudson's Bay Company post in Labrador, and thence into a pre-eminent position in the young Canadian nation. The meeting convinced Smith to introduce Hill into Montreal's financial circles once the timing seemed right, and over the next six years the two men continued to nurse plans hatched at their first rendezvous.[55]

In the meantime, Smith undertook the challenging task of convincing his younger cousin, George Stephen, who possessed the financial clout required to buy and build railroads, to join the scheme. Like the others, Stephen had ascended from obscurity. Born in his father's Dufftown, Scotland, carpentry shop, Stephen clawed his way through clerkships in London and Montreal and finally into the distinguished role as president of the Bank of Montreal. When initially approached by Smith, Stephen argued, first, that he had not reached his current position without managing his investments wisely and, second, that other investors deemed the St. Paul and Pacific a monumentally high-risk venture. In addition, the specter of the NPR's failure still lingered among many once-bold investors, not only throughout the British Isles and Continental Europe but also inside North America. Moreover, Stephen carried scars from his earlier, arguably unwise involvement in the Grand Trunk fiasco that had left him as battered and bruised as other Canadians crushed in the great trunk-line wars. Hit hard financially as well as psychologically by that encounter, Stephen suspected similar trouble with the St. Paul and Pacific scheme, particularly when he considered the financial depression, the lag time between construction and return on investment, and the determination of Minnesotans like the First Division's George Becker to expand the railroad along depopulated and, hence, risky, unproductive lines of cultivation.[56]

Over time, however, Stephen warmed slowly to Smith's western railroad scheme as he watched similar ideas incubate elsewhere in Montreal's financial circles. By 1874, as nationalistic sentiments percolated throughout settled Canada, Alexander McKenzie's government settled Stephen's mind by pushing the Canadian Pacific Railway Act through Parliament. To those who could build a transcontinental railroad across the young nation, the act promised all the riches of the Empire, including monopoly guarantees and the ultimate commonwealth prize—a peerage in the British realm.[57]

By the mid-1870s, Smith recognized that Hill's dreams meshed with those maturing behind the doors of the Bank of Montreal's presidential office. By the time Smith introduced Hill to Stephen, the calculating bank president also reckoned that Hill had something both he and Smith lacked—a desire to run actual railroad operations. While Hill had never managed a railroad before, he had demonstrated his abilities to compete successfully with rivals and to "put the axe to the root of every existing expense" in his other businesses. With their troika thus formed, Stephen, Smith, and Hill pulled Kittson into negotiations. Kittson had already approached Horace Thompson, who, as trustee for the St. Paul and Pacific's Minnesota bondholders and for the NPR, took the buy-out proposal to John S. Kennedy in 1876. Kennedy, the Dutch bondholders' representative in New York, did not take Kittson's information seriously until May 1877, when Johan Carp revealed that Kittson and Hill had unearthed a gold mine in the form of George Stephen and his powerful bank. Indeed, Kennedy wanted in on the action, having already laid the foundations for a takeover. Now, with the right "vulture" capitalist onboard, Kennedy reasoned that he could slip into the background, feed the Associates information about the Dutch bondholders (through Carp), and, once the Associates signed a contract, rise to wealth and glory inside New York's financial community. Unfortunately for Kennedy and the Associates, the negotiations started slowly: the Dutch refused several preliminary offers and rejected the October proposal that promised to launch construction.[58]

As Kennedy's negotiations with the Dutch bondholders dragged on during the fall of 1877, the Associates faced greater dilemmas than resistance to the deal, the most pressing among them the need to resume railroad construction on the line to St. Vincent before the land-grant clock ran out at the end of 1878. If the Associates missed the deadline, they would lose an indispensable component of their expansionist plans. Early on, the Associates had realized they needed Hill's influence in St. Paul to convince the Dutch they could both complete the St. Vincent branch line before the land-grant deadline passed and end problems with the NPR. With many friends in St. Paul and Minneapolis, Hill thus emerged as the logical person to coax the various parties into appropriate concessions and reconciliations. Hill chose to start with the *Pioneer Press,* masterminding the October 26, 1877, article quoted above. Once word spread via the press, Hill received letters of congratulations from people throughout the region, including Minneapolis flour-milling associates such as John S. Pillsbury, who by that time served as Minnesota's governor. In all these letters, the message remained the same: "What can we do to help you get the St. Paul and Pacific moving again?" Over the next twelve months, Hill had plenty of answers. The Associates needed to end the legal squabbles attached to various bankruptcies. Horace Thompson, along with other influential St. Paulites, intervened to smooth the way for arbitration.[59]

With Hill working behind the scenes in St. Paul during the fall of 1877, the tide turned unexpectedly and the Dutch finally acquiesced to the Associates' proposal. Among the other factors contributing to their decision, the 1877 wheat crop proved less favorable than predicted; grasshoppers had infested a few areas, making immigrants and investors nervous once again. More importantly, with the SP&P in the hands of a receiver and the international investment community reeling from the shock waves of the summer's railroad strike, the Dutch bondholders decided that they had endured enough. On January 5, 1878, they accepted the offer. The Associates crafted their own agreement, and on March 13, 1878, the bondholders signed the contract. Now, the Associates reasoned, they could keep their eyes on the prize: the reorganization of the St. Paul and Pacific and its First Division subsidiary into one consolidated firm, with four million acres of land grants at its disposal.[60]

While St. Paul bankers and wholesalers and Minneapolis millers stabilized the cities for long-term expansion, James J. Hill invested in one project only, and he armed himself to cut off the hand of any other grasper who coveted *his* railroad. Like many visionaries, Hill had laid the foundations for his ascent through maneuvers that placed him at the center of regional deal making. When the moment arrived, he seized it. On the project that now catapulted him into the limelight, Hill emerged as the "person behind the throne" of a coup d'état at least a year in the making. Moreover, grateful citizens viewed him as the local hero who snatched Minnesota's most important railroad from foreign hands. In fact, while Hill enjoyed the praise, others had already delivered Minnesota from foreign control. The next few years would test whether Hill or any other local nabob had the necessary stamina, entrepreneurial fiber, and political clout to keep it that way.[61]

1878–1883

The Triumph of Minnesota's Metropolitan Complex

WITH ST. PAUL CONFIRMED as the region's commercial center, Minneapolis flour at the top of the world market, the St. Paul and Pacific rescued from receivers' hands, and the industrial depression waning, Minnesotans entered a period of business competition and consolidation that stimulated the region's third economic boom. Competition of rival systems leveled the Twin Cities' provincial landscapes, and consolidation replaced them with a metropolitan complex incorporated into the international market and the industrial processes of a dawning bureaucratic age. With locals now firmly in charge of the state government and its associated benefits, Minnesota's urban industrialists looked across the border into Canada, where they hoped to exploit opportunities in international government contracting, business development, and resource extraction. The changes engendered between 1878 and 1883 matched and then surpassed those effected during the territorial period and the Civil War. As transportation builders integrated products of the northwestern borderlands into St. Paul–Minneapolis's distribution and manufacturing networks, they secured for Twin Cities residents the status they had coveted since the 1850s. St. Paul received recognition as one of the nation's top ten transportation, commercial, and financial centers, its domain extending west to the Pacific Ocean, north into Canada, south into Iowa and Nebraska, and east into western Wisconsin. The market endorsed Minneapolitans as the world's best flour makers and their city as the most significant manufacturing hub northwest of Chicago.[1]

The period commenced on January 5, 1878, the day the Associates—James J. Hill, Norman Kittson, Donald Smith, George Stephen, and John

S. Kennedy—made the Dutch bondholders an acceptable offer for the St. Paul and Pacific Railroad. The contract inaugurated one of the most profitable company turnarounds in railroad history. During 1910, as he reminisced about the takeover, Hill noted that "the capitalization of the lines purchased and built was approximately $44,000,000, and the deal a large one for those days." Large indeed, especially considering Hill's rapid ascent from a small businessman making an annual income of $15,000 into one of the major stockholders in a wealth-generating system that wrested a major facet of Minnesota's entrepreneurial vision from foreign control and made Hill a regional celebrity.[2]

The period ended on September 3, 1883, in a Twin Cities–wide celebration commemorating the Northern Pacific Railroad's "grand opening" of its transcontinental line to the Pacific Ocean. In just five years, Minnesota's railroaders had expanded 3,000 local miles of track into 10,000 miles, 2,054 of which represented the NPR's main- and branch-line arteries stretching from St. Paul–Minneapolis west to Tacoma, Washington, and Portland, Oregon. Symbolizing the grand achievement—and the cathartic nature of the celebration—Minnesotans closed the day's ceremonies with an enormous bonfire, kindled by thousands of "$5 Million Railroad Bonds," now unequivocally redeemed after twenty-five long years.[3]

The economic boom—and the competition it stimulated—induced number crunchers in both cities to compile lists upon lists to show that "their" city had emerged as the "great northwestern emporium." Ignoring some rather striking inconsistencies while laboring over the latest statistics, Minnesota's urban enthusiasts greatly amused visiting easterners. As one wry observer noted, "If one puts up a fifty thousand dollar church, the other sees it and goes twenty-five thousand better, besides sending to Brooklyn for a preacher. That, in effect, is the Minnesota Plan." Few rivalries demonstrated this "Minnesota Plan"—merely a microcosm of the American Plan—more than those gathering momentum in the wake of the Associates' 1878 railroad triumph.[4]

Reorganized Railroads
and the Reinvigorated Race for Riches

The Associates knew they faced enormous risks as they embarked upon their plans to reorganize the St. Paul and Pacific during 1878. They had to brave winter snow blockades, a "complicated web of litigation," and a "tangle of mortgages" associated with the road remaining "in the hands of Trustees until [they resolved] the foreclosures [that promised to take] a year, or maybe more." As president of the Bank of Montreal, Stephen advanced the Dutch $280,000, the small cash security demanded for the transaction. Unwittingly furnished by the bank's stockholders, the deposit bought the five Associates $6.5 million in aggregated railroad stock ($13 billion in 2000, when adjusted for inflation) and $33 million in bonded indebtedness (more than $54 billion in present-day terms), apart from floating obligations. The Associates divided the shares equally: Hill, Smith, and Kittson held one-fifth each, and Stephen retained the other two (half of that as Kennedy's then-undisclosed portion). Hill set to work on construction and operation, and the firm turned a $75,000 profit in its first operational month. The Associates received an immediate million-dollar offer, but Kennedy allowed them to decline it by keeping the operation afloat with short-term loans.[5]

Beyond negotiating the initial buy out, the Associates had many problem people to deal with, including Edwin Litchfield, a greatly vexed investor and "wary old bird"; George Becker, a stubborn stockholder and ousted SP&P president; J. P. Farley, the increasingly irascible receiver and the road's general manager; and a multitude of impatient contractors still demanding payment for previous work. Despite these problems, the Associates had trusted allies in Horace Thompson and Edmund Rice, who promised to "leave no stone unturned to bring about a reconciliation" between the contending parties. If they failed, the Associates had contingency plans "to handle, with or without gloves on," Litchfield, Becker, Farley, and anyone else who got in the way. They had not come this far only to lose the much-coveted land grant from St. Paul to the Canadian border. Governor John Pillsbury offered his support, agreeing to send a "friendly engineer to inspect the road and have it accepted by the state the day it is completed." Better still for the Associates, the NPR, reorganized and under eastern management, had its own headaches as its construction teams resumed work on the railroad's Minnesota lines that spring.[6]

All weather conditions and legal entanglements considered, the leap into 1878 went smoothly enough; that is, until the NPR directors surprised the Associates in June by shifting their gaze from Duluth to Minneapolis as the proposed site of their eastern terminus. Horace Thompson warned John S. Kennedy that the "local feeling in Minneapolis favors such a road, and I am also advised that the Mil[waukee] & St. Paul interests encourage it" because "the fertile lands, and local business are on the *west side of the river.*"[7]

If the NPR started rapid construction on the Mississippi River's west side, from Minneapolis to the two railroads' connection at Sauk Rapids, the Associates faced the harsh reality of gaining nothing more than local trade on the river's eastern side until they completed the line to St. Vincent at the

Canadian border. Hill advised Stephen and Smith that Minneapolitans planned to do everything in their power to effect the NPR decision because "they great[ly] fear that Saint Paul will in some way get ahead of them." But for St. Paul's Hill, Kittson, and Thompson, getting ahead of Minneapolis was precisely the point. Thus, they immediately swung into action their collective influence, arranging private meetings among St. Paul's prominent business leaders.[8]

As tension mounted through October 1878, Hill informed Stephen that St. Paul's businessmen had formed a "compact to ship absolutely nothing by the Milwaukee & St. Paul Railway until they abandon the West side line entirely and the N.P. as a connection." He further argued, "as St. Paul pays over three times as much freight as Minneapolis, you will see that [the Milwaukee road] will have to yield [to] public opinion, always the strongest lever" in such matters. Thanks to Hill's brokering skills, the Associates prevailed. On October 31, 1878, NPR director Frederick Billings offered a peaceful solution, observing that "it is almost a sin to [spend], in these days, money to build parallel roads" and cautioning that "it is the duty of us all not to let these two enterprises drift into endless war." The two roads reached a truce: the SP&P's acting trustees Horace Thompson and John S. Kennedy authorized the NPR to run trains over the shorter route from Sauk Rapids to St. Paul rather than via Duluth. Deeming St. Paul and Minneapolis "essentially one," NPR executives bundled up their Duluth office and headed to the region's center of transportation, wholesaling, and finance. The rivals ostensibly agreed to spheres of influence as well, with the NPR dominating east-west lines and the Associates the north-south route between St. Paul and St. Vincent. Of course, the companies' ideas about these spheres ensured further combat as each prepared to gain larger prizes throughout the region, including all the agricultural products associated with rapid settlement in Manitoba's Red River Valley.[9]

By January 1, 1879, construction workers had completed Minnesota's most important land-grant line from St. Paul to St. Vincent. Four months later, the Associates owned the entire property. On May 23 they relaunched the firm as the St. Paul, Minneapolis, and Manitoba Railway (Manitoba Road) and announced a new stock offering: $15 million, two million of which they retained for their trouble. By the end of the year, Minnesota had 3,000 miles of railroad, 800 more than in 1877. Once reorganized, the Manitoba Road's capitalization expanded quickly, enriching its rescuers beyond Hill's most "sanguine expectations."[10]

Soon, however, another battleground surfaced, again involving lucrative government contracts and land grants. Canada's Parliament passed legislation in 1878 authorizing bids to complete the Canadian Pacific Railway

(CPR)—begun four years earlier—by building west through Winnipeg to-ward Vancouver, British Columbia, complete with north-south lines head-ing straight into Minnesota. As Hill put the finishing touches on the line to St. Vincent and the five shareholders' earnings outpaced their wildest dreams, the CPR contract gave them an opportunity to capture all the riches of the Red River Valley on both sides of the border. Frustrated because it had taken four years to build the CPR from Lake Nippising, Ontario, through the Canadian Shield, and west to Winnipeg—this fact com-pounded by secessionist threats from disappointed British Columbians—the Canadian government offered to turn the CPR over to new owners who could finish the job quickly. Those proprietors would benefit from a once-in-a-lifetime deal: a $25 million cash grant; 30 million acres of land (com-pared to Minnesota's 12 million), tax-free for twenty years; a free gift of the 700 miles of previously constructed line; no competitive railroads for twenty years; and no regulation of rates until the CPR achieved a ten percent return on investment.[11]

Here was a prize truly worth maneuvering for, and Manitoba Road and NPR owners both launched all-out campaigns to win it. The battle soon pit-ted St. Paulites against Minneapolitans, Minnesotans against Manitobans, and ultimately American associates against Canadian co-conspirators. Canadians in general had already had quite enough of the NPR and its lin-gering association with Jay Cooke. Consequently, the NPR quickly fell out of the race. Thereafter, the company accelerated its dash toward the Pacific, leaving the Manitoba Road in the dust. But the Associates fretted little about the NPR's westward push, secure in their knowledge that the Cana-dians among them had the best shot at the unprecedented northern spoils offered for completion of the CPR. Launching their bid, they reminded Par-liament that the four then-disclosed associates were, in fact, all Canadians, even though expatriates Hill and Kittson lived in St. Paul. The rapid suc-cess of the Manitoba Road sealed the deal. By 1880, the Associates became part of "the Syndicate" that won the CPR contract in October, a stroke exe-cuted by Smith, Stephen, Hill, and Bank of Montreal vice-president Richard B. Angus.[12]

. Unfortunately for the expatriate Associates, the Canadian government had no intention of placing the CPR at the mercy of another American takeover. Just as construction crews completed the line to St. Vincent and the Associates eliminated the NPR as a competitor for the CPR contract, the Canadian government slapped up a tariff wall that virtually halted business between St. Paul and Winnipeg. Like their American counterparts, who had legislated tariff barriers against England in order to build their own manufacturing capabilities free from foreign competition, Canadians now hoped to protect infant industries from their aggressive southern neighbors. Despite the historical precedent, the new policy incensed James J. Hill.[13]

When Canadians enacted the tariff during April 1879, Hill sent what seemed like hour-to-hour appeals to his mentor in Montreal. But Stephen, negotiating behind the scenes for control of the CPR, cautioned that their investment strategies "should be based on principles of self interest. Nothing is to be gained by fighting the Government or anybody else for the pure love of the fun, but we must be always ready to defend ourselves, when attacked, against all comers, otherwise other people will soon trade upon our cowardice." By then, however, "self interest" and "all comers" conjured not a collective will but rather distinctive visions in the mind of each associate. In large measure, these personal definitions connoted the national loyalties through which each hoped to realize his private ambitions.

A Canadian by birth, an American by choice, and an empire builder by design, Hill envisioned completing American transportation networks that would reach Asian markets. Kennedy, a native of Glasgow, held similar ambitions in New York's investment banking spheres. For these two men, the United States more so than Canada seemed to offer opportunities for realizing their dreams. The American government had guided industrial expansion, but it had also let individuals work out the competitive details and grab the profits. As for Steven and Smith, these scions of northern Scotland coveted more than wealth and power. They yearned for the great British prize: peerages in the Empire for the roles they planned to play in the Canadian commonwealth's success. Knowing full well that Canada could afford only one large-scale railroad endeavor, they planned to capture all the profits and glory it would provide. Although they could build castles in the United States with the wealth generated by their part in railroad expansion, only in Canada could they win titles to grace them.[14]

A localized go-getter but relatively inexperienced in large-scale intrigues, Hill missed the larger meaning that long-time capitalist Stephen employed in his definition of self-interest. Further, Hill alienated fellow Canadians in Manitoba and elsewhere by seething openly about the tariff barrier for the next three years. Kennedy tried to mollify Hill by sending regular reports on the Manitoba Road's success. Smith, Stephen, and Kennedy all recommended that Hill take more time off from his operational duties, but he declined. After all, he believed they were assembling *his* imperial vision, and empire builders have no time for respite. Beyond that, Hill distrusted most people outside the Associates and the Syndicate, and even among the latter he feared possible defectors and interlopers.[15]

Hill had good company in St. Paul–Minneapolis, for the tariff barrier hurt wholesaling and flour-milling businesses as well. One of Auerbach's young representatives complained that "the infernal act cut off our business with Manitoba almost entirely. On account of the exorbitant duties, we lose $20,000 worth of sales at least this Spring." Indeed, Auerbach's concern lost a great deal more, as did many other wholesaling firms affected by Canada's new "National Policy." Canadians let raw products in cheaply; however, they placed goods such as cotton, wool, nails, screws, and engines under tariffs ranging from 25 to 30 percent, claiming they could manufacture many things on their own. As struggling firms capsized under the weight of tariff duties, many larger businesses in St. Paul–Minneapolis consolidated their interests to make up for trade losses and to remain competitive. They bought up stock and machinery at foreclosure sales and integrated their operations—backward more deeply into grain elevators and wheat lands and forward into distribution and marketing networks. But these new hostilities between Minnesota and Manitoba also boded ill for promoters hoping to make money hauling freight across national borders.[16]

Winnipeg residents and merchants suffered under the weight of the new tariff as well, but they endured the agonies in the hope that, one day, they would emerge as the Canadian equivalent of St. Paul–Minneapolis. During 1877, *Grip*, the Canadian satirical weekly, took out an advertisement encouraging people in Winnipeg and elsewhere to defend Canada's new isolationism against American aspersions: "WANTED—PROTECTION! You [Americans] this great truth should know, Countries alone by manufactures grow. The present's here; the lazy past is done, We'll have a country, or we will have none." All well and good, Americans replied, especially the bit about ending the lazy past. But with completion of the St. Vincent line encouraging immigration on both sides of the border, Americans found "few things more strange and inscrutable" than the new protectionist trumpets sounding off in ten-year-old Canada, "especially where [free trade] bring[s] wealth to them."[17]

Very soon, visitors touring the area noticed that farmers in Manitoba—anxious to acquire cheap products from nearby St. Paul rather than pay exorbitant freight rates from Toronto—had begun to abandon Canada. Even Montreal's David Currie claimed, "I found that Canadian farmers who have been living here for several years and were doing well, having become the owners of first class farms with considerable improvement made on them [have] recently taken land in [Minnesota] and Dakota, [particularly where the] Saint Paul and Manitoba have laid a track along the bank of the river [or are] erecting a large grain elevator." Currie believed these "Cannuck Yankees, few of them [adopting] the vaporing, spread-eagle jargon so prevalent among Western American pioneers," would return once "all the best lands in Dakota are appropriated." For the moment, however, he feared

Parliament had gone too far with its protectionist program, particularly given Winnipeg's long-standing relationship with St. Paul–Minneapolis.[18]

Despite such arguments against protection, several Canadians attempted to demystify the issue by explaining why they had "hardened" their "determination to achieve industrial independence, even if purchased at the cost of industrial isolation." Expressing sentiments shared by many of his countrymen, Canada's governor general declared, "It is our lot to emulate the United States; and Canada wishes to be their friend, but does not desire to become their food. She rejoices in the big brother's strength and status but is not anxious to nourish it by offering up her own body in order that it may afford him, when over hungry, that happy festival he is in the habit of calling a 'square meal.'" This response baffled Americans as well as investors in Britain and Europe, many of whom, like the Washburns, deemed Canadian economic policies "ludicrous" at best.[19]

But something else had caused Canadians to perceive the deck stacked in their favor at this particular moment. Canadian government officials, working quietly with Stephen on the CPR deal, believed they had found the perfect time to strike, during this period of renewed railroad construction and sustained demand for their wheat, especially since Stephen had a group of hungry and successful American railroaders in the palm of his hand. Unbeknownst to Hill, the Manitoba Road's very success had helped promote the new protectionist campaign. Now that the Associates offered immigrants extremely low rates for passage into Manitoba, Canadians felt confident in their ultimate success. As a reward, in October 1880, Stephen and his "Syndicate"—Smith, Hill, and Bank of Montreal vice-president Richard B. Angus—thus won the CPR contract handily.[20]

In the meantime, as immigration, investment, and wheat production surged on both sides of the border, Stephen persuaded friends and political allies that Canada (and the infant CPR) had more to gain than lose from the Associates' railroad enterprise in Minnesota. In fact, during 1879 Hill himself exclaimed, "You never saw more railway excitement than there is [throughout Minnesota, Dakota, and Manitoba] at present." Further, despite temporary setbacks in St. Paul–Minneapolis during the winter of 1879–80, business in both cities boomed on increased immigration. During 1880 alone, St. Paul–based railroads forwarded an unprecedented 15,000 tons of wheat, 7,000 tons of other grain, 910 tons of flour, 103,000 tons of lumber, and 177,000 tons of merchandise to their hinterland consumers. At the same time, tonnage heading east amounted to an equally exceptional 233,000 in wheat, 2,500 in grain, 14,000 in lumber, and 58,300 in merchandise. Compared to freight arrivals in Chicago, these figures represented but a trickle; however, in the region itself they constituted a torrential increase over business just ten years earlier. As Cecilia Hall, a Manitoba "maid-of-all-work," complained about the inconveniences caused by floods, customs officials, and other holdups resulting in staple shortages, she observed, "4,000 freight [cars] were delayed at St. Vincent; [then came into Winnipeg] at the rate of 4,000 per week, and still people [could] not get their implements, stores, &c. fast enough. We asked several times for some turpentine at one of the shops, and the answer always given [was] 'It is at the depot, but not unloaded.'" Those "4,000 per week" signaled a major transition at Winnipeg, including its population expanding from perhaps 1,000 people in 1877 to more than 10,000 during 1880, the number doubling again in the next two years.[21]

By 1880, on increased freight and passenger traffic Manitoba Road earnings had escalated to $3.7 million over $2 million in expenses, an operating ratio of 54. Combined, Minnesota's railroads reached $10.8 million in earnings over $6.6 million in expenses, presenting the state with profitable roads and an average operating ratio of 61, evidence that seemed to confirm the prudence of encouraging the "competition of rival systems." The Manitoba Road secured its final 2.3 million acres in land grants and made $5 million in land sales as increased wheat production in the Red River Valley allowed the firm to sell land at $2.70 per acre and profit from the swelling number of immigrants who settled along the road's lines.[22]

Hill became an American citizen in 1880, permanently tying his future to that of the United States. Continuing to invest throughout the Twin Cities and the region, he also helped stimulate increased employment opportunities. Calling in favors as he searched for "the services of a first-class Master Mechanic" and other workers for the railroad's shops and offices, he told friends throughout North America, "I know of no person in whose judgment I would have greater confidence [than yours to assist me], and have not forgotten the old adage—there is no use having a friend if you don't use him. Your kind attention to this matter will place me under a vast obligation to you, as I need a good man, and can give the right sort a good place." Hill soon returned the favors. The Manitoba Road had incorporated the St. Paul Union Depot in 1879; now, as a gift to the "pluck and enterprise" of supportive friends in the capital city, the company built it. The "elegant" structure cost the Associates a trifling $151,000 but won them untold friends in the city. Then, on April 16, 1880, as a show of gratitude for John S. Pillsbury's "friendly" assistance, Hill and his associates rescued the ever-troubled St. Anthony Falls Water Power Company. They paid $100,000 down (another excellent takeover price) and agreed to pay the remaining $300,000 in annual installments over three years. The Associates devised a new business plan for the corporation, complete with funds for expansion that promised to extend Charles A. Pillsbury & Co.'s reach. The Associates also broadened their investments into grain elevators, land agencies, lumber companies, coal establishments, and other enterprises in and around St. Paul–Minneapolis.[23]

With an operating income of $9.2 million over expenses of $4.3 million during 1883, the Manitoba Road boasted an operating ratio of 47.2, a moneymaking machine by any standard and finally a crowning example of Minnesotans' ability to make their railroads pay. The final plum—nearly four million acres in Minnesota land grants secured with completion of the St. Vincent line—made the whole deal more than worthwhile. At the center of this success stood cost-cutting James J. Hill, whose status with the Manitoba Road changed from general manager in 1878 to chief executive officer in 1883.

William D. Washburn observed Hill's gambits with increasing suspicion; nevertheless, he sought to lure the Associates into Minneapolis Mill investments, particularly after Franklin Steele died in September 1880. After all, he reasoned, the Associates could use a political ally such as himself. During 1878, Republican Washburn had out-maneuvered anti-monopolist Ignatius Donnelly for U.S. representative in Minnesota's third congressional district, despite the fact that his unabashed promotion of all things Minneapolitan had "caused many a strong Republican of St. Paul to vote for Donnelly." With Steele nothing more than a memory, Donnelly out of Congress, and his own popularity confirmed, William D. hoped to consolidate the Washburn and Pillsbury interests, including their railroads. In the meantime, the *1880 Census of Manufactures* confirmed the Minneapolis Mill owners' greatest hopes and dreams: wheat had finally surpassed cotton as the nation's most lucrative agricultural product, Minneapolis had emerged as a manufacturing center in its own right, and its millers' patent flour now sat proudly atop the world market.[24]

"King Wheat" and the Red River Valley Boom

During the five years between railroad redemption and the transcontinental celebration, Minnesota's railroaders and millers entered into a series of competitive, contentious, and even litigious adventures and initiated unparalleled railroad construction, immigration expansion, and business consolidation in the region. St. Paul–Minneapolis residents and local, county, and state officials generally supported the skirmishes between businesses "shrouded in the public interest" because they believed renewed competition would beget abundance. Throughout the final period in the Twin Cities' evolution from villages to central cities, Minnesota's railroad commissioners consistently argued that the state government should "give assurance to capital that might seek investment in [our] railroads." Thus, through a hands-off regulatory policy, legislators encouraged the "competition of rival systems" as the most expeditious way to accomplish what everyone seemed to want: "relatively" fair rates throughout the state, more immigration, and further capital investments in the region.[25]

As "King Wheat" vied with "King Cotton" for status as the nation's most profitable crop, renewed competition sparked a three-year regional boom. Immigrants continued crossing the Atlantic to join Americans pushing westward into the interior: the U.S. population surpassed 50 million during 1880 and that year Minnesota's climbed to 780,000, a 77.6 percent increase over 1870. Several hundred thousand additional Americans and immigrants reached the state between 1880 and 1883, while in excess of a million more pushed farther west into the Dakotas, Montana, Idaho, Oregon, and Washington and north into Manitoba, Saskatchewan, and Alberta. As immigrant business ventures permeated the region, observers argued that "the energy and enterprise of [St. Paul–Minneapolis's] merchants and manufacturers [makes them] deserve the fruits which they have won by their pluck and enterprise [for] despite hard times and grasshoppers they have overcome all obstacles." Indeed, by 1877 the entrepreneurial "pluck" of men such as St. Paul's Maurice Auerbach, William Davidson, and Horace Thompson and Minneapolis's William Eastman, Charles Pillsbury, and William D. Washburn had launched enough prosperity to make Hill's ascent possible. And, by the time the economic boom commenced in 1880, even wholesaling worker Michael J. Boyle could announce that his bankrupt father intended to return to St. Paul "in the fall if not successful in getting into business [in his native Ireland]," exclaiming, "father's decision is a sensible resolution! America is the country for a man to rebuild his shattered fortunes."[26]

Expanding railroad and business competition also pitted entrepreneurs, politicians, and Cities residents against each other. "Friendly" rivalries transformed into bitter contests for transportation systems and terminals, for population numbers, for investment capital, for business, educational, religious, and other social institutions, and for political supremacy over the Cities and their hinterland. As rate wars slashed costs, re-energized St. Paul–Minneapolis for large-scale investment, and prompted immigrants and opportunity seekers to inundate the region, Minnesotans argued that "the people of the Northwest, as all the world knows, are proverbially a business people, striving with energy to better their conditions of life." Provided they continued to see labor demands hoist real wages and new ventures improve living conditions, people in both cities saw every reason to fight for their share of the riches.[27]

As the larger nation turned the corner into the modern bureaucratic and consumer era of the 1880s, events conveniently concatenated to provide many other requisite conditions that fueled the race for the region's riches. More than ever before, regional business profitability fluctuated with the wheat harvest: happily for Minnesotans, the departure of grasshoppers coalesced with a few good winters and European crop failures that sustained the demand for northwestern wheat and Minneapolis patent flour. Minnesotans exclaimed that the rise of King Wheat had generated "immense land sales, bountiful harvests, [and] simply enormous" business opportunities throughout the region. As one urban resident observing the transition declared, "population and capital are flowing in like mighty flood-tides of the ocean, and the trackless wastes of yesterday are converted, as if by magic, into the waving wheat-fields of today."[28]

Immigrants traveled principally on NPR and CPR lines, but they also boarded Manitoba Road cars west from Grand Forks—shadowing the NPR's Fargo line, just seventy-eight miles to the south—for their trek into Dakota and beyond. Arriving via railroads in greater numbers each year, many newcomers did more than simply pass through, choosing instead to make Minnesota their home. Nearly 100,000 Minnesotans clustered within St. Paul and Minneapolis during 1880, and thousands more settled in the greater metropolitan area. By the time census takers surveyed Minnesota in 1885, the state's total population had reached more than 1.1 million, with St. Paul's climbing to 111,000 and Minneapolis's soaring to 129,000.[29]

With a bluster reminiscent of Minnesota's territorial days, the St. Paul and Duluth Road claimed that NPR and Manitoba Road developments had created abundant prospects for those seeking opportunities in the Northwest. But while "capitalists, ambitious to become monster wheat-growers, may combine to control railroad facilities, erect elevators, purchase machinery, and secure the cheap labor necessary to successfully operate their immense plantations [farther east]," the company claimed to lament the condition of the ordinary farmer, "who attempts to compete with them, or even to support or educate a family in their vicinity." Of course, "why bother with such impediments to success when you can settle along the lines of the St. Paul and Duluth Railway?" it begged.[30]

As competition for immigrants increased throughout the North American West, railroads took the most active role in promoting settlement along their lines of business and influence, placing immigration agents in all major European and American ports. The companies called for "laboring men, who earn a livelihood by honest toil, men of moderate means, who are earnest and enterprising, men of wealth and cultured tastes, who revel in Nature's bounty and desire homes in a beautiful and prosperous country." Most of all, they sought "the farmer, the stock grower, the artisan, and the tradesmen." To these they offered, "on long time and easy payments, fertile, undulating prairies" at an average price of $6.50 an acre, a rather enormous sum in 1882 compared to the two dollars and change commanded during 1880 or the eighteen-dollar filing fee for earlier homesteads.[31]

Despite escalating land prices, farmers, artisans, office workers, skilled craftsmen, railroad men, and other hopefuls came in droves. Their reasons seemed clear. For the most part, real wages kept pace with inflation during these years, especially in the Twin Cities. And lowered freight rates finally corresponded with railroad expansion, prompting Minnesota's railroad commissioner to declare, "this change removes a long-standing complaint on the part of wholesale dealers and shippers in Minnesota, who were at a disadvantage compared with Chicago shippers." Now relieved of those burdens, urban dealers passed the savings on to their hinterland customers.[32]

Steamboats got into the act as well. To those concerned about steep railroad rates, packet companies pointed out their rock-bottom Mississippi River transport fees. Immigrants and freight transfer agents effected a river revival, making William Davidson extraordinarily glad he had not abandoned his packet company investments altogether. With the South reconstructed and the industrial depression a thing of the past, St. Paul's river trade prospered, particularly after New Orleans rebuilt its harbor to accommodate large European steamships. Minnesota boosters like John Land claimed that although it took nine days to ship by river from St. Louis to New Orleans and only two days by rail from Chicago to New York, "the effect has been that each bushel is carried from St. Louis to the seaboard at New Orleans, for *six cents,* while the lowest point yet reached from Chicago to New York has been *twenty-two cents.*" *Ceteris paribus,* St. Paul shippers thus sent barges down the Mississippi to St. Louis and New Orleans. Further supporting this business decision, spokesmen for the American Society of Civil Engineers, gathered at St. Paul–Minneapolis for the ASCE's annual meeting in 1883, noted, "the problem of cheap transportation is never wholly solved." Indeed, they argued, because of their low freight charges, "water routes still have an important part to play, and first among them stands the Mississippi, the highway of the continent." Situated at the great river's navigational head, St. Paulites once again had the upper hand, declaring, "the grain of this country [will reach] the sea by the Mississippi—every thoughtful person understands this, simply because it is the *cheapest route it can take.*"[33]

As before, chain migrations dominated the peopling of St. Paul–Minneapolis and their hinterland; however, for the first time Scandinavians flocked to the region in large numbers. The floodgates opened with the assistance of Minnesota's Swedish-born Hans Mattson, who now worked northern Europe as an immigration agent for the state government, for Hill's Manitoba Road, and for other Minnesota-based railroads and steamboat packet companies. In part, Mattson's efforts flowed from increased competition for British Isle residents, a result of the new Canadian government's nationalist campaign. Writing to Richard B. Angus from London, England, during the winter of 1880, Manitoba Road immigration agent Molyneux St. John confided, "Emigration very largely depends, as you have probably been told by Mr. Smith and Mr. Stephen, on the action of the Canadian Parliament regarding the Pacific Railway project in which we [American and Canadian associates] are all interested." Within the year, he reported that Canadians had secured most British Isle immigrants. Consequently, Hill and other local hustlers encouraged Danes, Norwegians, and Swedes rather than Brits, Scots, and the Irish to fan out across the American prairies. Agreeing with Mattson that "Scandinavians make better farmers" than most other Europeans, Hill welcomed the shift. Swedish immigrants in particular descended in vast numbers upon Minneapolis's milling district, becoming the city's largest foreign-born population by the middle of the 1880s. In both cities, German numbers surpassed those of the Irish, although the latter maintained a strong presence in St. Paul. Despite language and cultural barriers, people in St. Paul–Minneapolis welcomed these new immigrants, just as they had previously hailed Irish Catholics, German-speaking people of various faiths, and other entrepreneurial spirits in times when demand outstripped the local labor supply.[34]

Railroad and immigration expansion into and beyond Minnesota transformed the Cities, where busy railroad terminals, wholesaling houses, financial institutions, and manufacturing enterprises pulsed with activity. At the same time, technological and business innovations increased the attractions of urban life in the West. Telephones quickened communication between local businesses. Light bulbs illuminated city centers, allowing manufacturers to produce goods twenty-four hours a day. Plumbing improvements brought "modern conveniences" to businesses and homes. Business consolidations and economies of scale lowered the costs of many consumer goods. The fields of engineering and business gained professional and academic prestige throughout the nation during this period, reflected, for example, in the founding of professional associations like the American Society of Civil Engineers during 1880 and the establishment of the Wharton School of Finance and Economy, the first of its kind in the United States, at the University of Pennsylvania during 1881. New etiquette books and advice manuals confirmed mounting social aspirations. High wages, plentiful work, an increased variety of consumer goods, and greater opportunities for social activities influenced both the psychology of work and leisure and the proliferation of new business and social clubs. Indeed, visitors reported, "it seems that every man, woman and child in [St. Paul–Minneapolis] are trying to do something to make [urban life] a success," whether organizing firms, attending new business colleges, buying items to

Advertising the many advantages of economic expansion from the Twin Cities to the north and west, the Manitoba Road's locomotive and cars race along the company-built stone bridge connecting St. Paul's busy transportation district, Minneapolis's ever-widening manufacturing center, and the lucrative wheat-growing lands of the Red River Valley.

reflect upward mobility, or establishing and joining the expanding number of professional and social "syndicates" developing in the Cities.[35]

St. Paul's "Universal Law of Commerce"

On railroads and the distribution of wheat, St. Paul's commercial empire swept over the region during the early 1880s. When booster John Land published an account of the city's advantages in 1883, he reminded readers near and far that "it is a universal law of commerce [that] all things being equal or nearly so, customers will go to the nearest market; and this is especially true of the wholesale business, else the retail merchants of Missouri and Illinois would continue to go to New York." With railroads "palmating westward into five great fingers," Land claimed that customers throughout the region now looked to St. Paul rather than to Chicago. As evidence he noted the rise in the jobbing trade, from $28 million in 1878 to more than $81 million just five years later. On this expansion, wholesaling had emerged as St. Paul's market niche by the end of 1883.[36]

St. Paul's wholesalers had to overcome a number of hurdles during these years, including floods and fires that threatened both business prospects and lives annually. Worst among these catastrophes, the Mississippi flood of 1882 swept away businesses and homes throughout the river's upper and lower valleys, leaving an estimated 85,000 people homeless. Save for the owner hearing the "5.15 alarm" and watching "most merchandise destroyed" in flames or the worker "[looking] forward to a comparatively easy spring & summer [but] now wincing [at the thought] of the labor and confusion ahead," St. Paulites weathered the situation with a surprising amount of good humor. For example, when Auerbach's store went up in flames in the spring of 1880—as eastern buyers flocked to the city "at the vending of damaged goods" and the general population stopped by the company's temporary "Wigwam" to gawk at the rubble—Boyle cheered for the team: "Hurrah! for the pluck and energy of [Auerbach] & Co., truly Phoenix like we have risen!" Other owners of leveled stores set up signs "among the grimy cellars," declaring "Pluck & Co. Will re-occupy this Site in 60 Days, with an entirely new Stock of Selected Goods, finer than ever. Temporary Address, next block." Spring floods prompted similar responses. To one Philadelphian traveling into the muck, a local statistician, "waving his arms like a preacher at a revival meeting," exclaimed, "That's what makes the North-west such a big success! You can't wipe us out by fire or flood."[37]

During the 1880s, Maurice Auerbach had emerged as one of St. Paul's most successful wholesalers. But as jobbing dominance passed from Galena to St. Louis, north to Chicago, then west to St. Paul, opportunities flourished for anyone cunning enough to compete with Auerbach and his mercantile peers. Success in wholesaling, like any other business, required attention to costs, for fires and floods and fluctuating demand reminded many a content entrepreneur that a "reversal of fortunes" could happen at any moment, "no matter how careful [he sought] to avoid it."[38]

Like railroad surveying work, wholesaling demands arrived in waves. In nineteenth-century St. Paul, wholesalers sought additional help during peak seasons but often needed to retrench for winter slowdowns. During the summer months, for example, Auerbach's dry goods "competition promise[d] to be active, [with other firms] offering goods low down in order to catch customers." During good times, employees like Boyle remarked, "the Firm have made a great deal of money during the past year and I hope they will evince a disposition to divide some of it with the boys." The key lay in knowing how "low down" one could go and how much money one could "divide with the boys" and still maintain profitability yet avoid large-scale cutbacks during lulls. Those who failed to prepare for these market realities soon found sheriffs presiding over their foreclosure proceedings.[39]

Auerbach succeeded where others failed principally because he managed risk by minimizing his purchasing, marketing, and distribution costs throughout the year. He also sold some of his interest in the firm as its operations expanded, partnering with other established entrepreneurs who understood the business or the intricacies of running larger-scale firms. This enabled him to "cash out" some of his equity and reduce his own exposure, all the while maintaining control. By acquiring new partners when sales surpassed the existing staff's management abilities or when partners left to pursue other opportunities, he escaped the rigidity that caused many firms to break under the strain of business vicissitudes. For example, when one of his partners withdrew to start a banking business, Auerbach reorganized the firm with new associates. In George Finch he found a managing partner capable of minimizing costs. In William Van Slyke he acquired an absentee partner with a purchasing department in New York, thereby allowing the firm to by-pass Chicago middlemen. By the time he married Henry Rice's daughter in 1880, cementing an alliance between two generations of Minnesota go-getters, Auerbach had acquired important business friends throughout the city. One of those connections, Norman Kittson, in failing health and wishing to stay closer to home, sold his shares in the Manitoba Road to the remaining Associates and their new partner, Richard Angus, in 1881. Auerbach retained the regional veteran as a partner to help the firm make the transition into increasingly specialized functions in purchasing, marketing, sales, and manufacturing divisions. Once again, overlapping generations of entrepreneurs collaborated to ensure each other's profits.[40]

By 1883, the Auerbach concern employed several hundred people, a hundred of whom sewed clothes in the manufacturing department of the firm's gingham and print division. Auerbach avoided some manufacturing expenses by contracting with local milliners and tailors during peak seasons. Similar arrangements by other firms provided not only opportunities for small business owners (both male and female) but also the context for the new "experts" and muckrakers who would soon step in to deal with a plethora of industrial conditions. In the meantime, Auerbach and other large firms continued to impose cost-cutting measures, "sweating" some newcomers while searching for ways to retain the loyalty of long-term employees. Purchasing managers shaved costs by sending drummers to buy goods at liquidation sales. The sales department negotiated exclusive relationships with retailers in places with sustained demand. In exchange for customer loyalty, Auerbach priced liquidation products just above cost. Ongoing competition from Chicago dictated such tactics. During the summer of 1880, for example, the Auerbach concern had "to sell some stuff very cheap[ly] in order to meet Chicago prices," and young Boyle reported, "more merchants go to that City of Wickedness this fall to buy goods than ever before." Wicked or not, when the larger center offered better rates, many "gave [Auerbach] the slip & went to Chicago" for their goods.[41]

Of course, none of these cost-cutting and marketing measures guaranteed success, but Auerbach and other successful entrepreneurs knew that inattention to such details assured failure, evidenced by the liquidation sales that kept pace with business start-ups in the city. Moreover, the firm never forewent insurance, an expenditure that saved Auerbach several times when fires swept over the wholesaling district.[42]

Sustaining employee loyalty during peaks and valleys posed additional challenges to Auerbach and other businesses as St. Paul developed into the region's commercial center. When Auerbach reached new retail and wholesale highs, his New York partner's son, Charlie Van Slyke, left Merchants National Bank to join the firm. In this particular case, since Auerbach presided over both firms, Van Slyke's employment shift imperiled neither; however, many went to work for competitors, taking valuable information and business with them.[43]

To maintain loyalty and continuity, firms offered incentives ranging from sufficiently high salaries to loans for reliable and hard-working employees and profit-sharing deals. For example, during early August 1879, after climbing from an annual income of $180 as a feather picker to one of $600 as head of the flannel stock, Boyle declared, "the Firm will never regret giving me so handsome a raise." Two weeks later, after the firm hired several experienced salesmen from Chicago, Boyle announced, "a certain number of boys from each Department have entered into an alliance, offensive & defensive, to secure trade for ourselves and keep as much as possible from the new men, in order to show the Firm that it is to their interest to promote their old employees rather than place new ones over them." Auerbach and his partners paid attention to these threats, elevating some workers and at the same time hiring outsiders who promised to increase the company's sales. Some of "the boys" quit the firm when more lucrative opportunities arose, taking jobs as bank tellers, moving laterally into other wholesaling companies, advancing into salesman positions, joining the railroad, or starting businesses of their own. But many remained, including Boyle. Loyalty had its rewards, and Boyle's self-proclaimed "Cheek" netted him loans to settle some of his father's debts. Loyalty also had its price: those loans bound Boyle to the firm.[44]

By 1880, after several windfalls and retrenchments at the Auerbach concern, Boyle's fidelity earned him a raise in salary, to $1,200 per annum. Despite inflation, high rents, and his growing desire for a Prince Albert coat and vest, "for which, in course of time I will pay $56.00," Boyle made sizeable gains in his real wage status during these years. As a result, he sought greater entrance into society, attending events "to meet some of the people [he] want[ed] to know" and joining social clubs despite fees "too steep for [his] purse." He indulged in a daily newspaper and opened his first savings account. On prospects of becoming, first, head of the gingham and prints stock and then a general salesman, Boyle reported, "things look promising for me at the store, and consequently I feel encouraged to stop at no exertion to advance the interests of the concern." The next year, Boyle earned $1,800 (1,000 percent over 1877) as a drummer, boasting, "I have climbed several rungs on the figurative ladder; my present position is one of the best in the house." His loyalty wavered from time to time, but Boyle shared a trait common among late-nineteenth-century white-collar climbers: his growing social ambitions (and indebtedness to the firm) outweighed his desire to leave his job (and the security it offered). He lamented, "I do not like to see so many older & more experienced men coming into the firm," but their arrival strengthened his resolve to pay close attention to business. Given the opportunity to "drum" for the firm, Boyle further declared that competition "nerves me to greater exertions upon the matter of selling goods." Each of these resolves—some kept, some broken—benefited Auerbach as well, for in Boyle's efforts to better himself and the firm he worked many extra hours as a badge of professional dedication.[45]

Alas for Boyle, he lacked Auerbach's investment acuity. When the recession of 1882–83 forced the firm to make some changes, the upwardly mobile young drummer ignored the very market realities that his employer had parlayed into success. In the NPR celebration's wake, despite problems on Wall Street and Auerbach's advice, Boyle made his first "investment," in quickly depreciating NPR stock. Thereafter, he principally invested in the New Orleans lottery and other long shots. Periodic hard times induced the firm to make Boyle several propositions, including a percentage of its net profits instead of a raise. Boyle, however, consistently reached for a higher salary, until circumstances forced him to accept significantly diminished offers from the company. Inevitably, despite "airing" his "plans and hopes for the future" with "the boys," Boyle missed his opportunity, remaining a paid employee for the rest of his life. Worse, his later salaries reflected a decline in demand for his skills as catalogues and advertising increasingly replaced the drumming trade.[46]

Beyond wholesaling, the prestige of St. Paul's financial institutions increased during these years. Unfortunately, so did the temptation to embezzle funds, soon proving the fallibility of even the largest concerns, including Horace Thompson's First National Bank. Banking remained a risky business, not only in terms of investment choices but also in new hire selection as firms expanded beyond directors' abilities to place trusted—and appropriately skilled—friends and family members in key positions. By 1883, the First National had emerged as St. Paul's most esteemed bank. However, with his nose in the books of various undertakings, Horace Thompson no longer oversaw the firm's daily operations. Right alongside Auerbach, whose "latest sensation" in April 1883 came not from record sales but rather from "the defalcation" of its receiving clerk, the First National lost a teller who made off with "an enormous sum." Thompson's unfortunate inattention caused an "embarrassment" few thought possible. He recovered from the loss, but his experience showed, once again, that some of St. Paul's firms had outgrown their founders' management abilities.[47]

Growing pains extended to St. Paul's railroads as well, and by 1883 the Manitoba Road's directors had endured a few embarrassments of their own. Even before Hill and his associates formed the Syndicate that won the bid to build the CPR west from Winnipeg, Canadian protectionists had campaigned to keep the railroad's management out of American hands. Calling for an all-Canadian route to the Pacific, they now hoped to control the young transcontinental's management despite foreign investment. Given Hill's new status as an American, the Manitoba Road's incursions into Winnipeg and the western prairie provinces caused increased concern throughout Canada. During 1882, at the height of the all-Canadian campaign, the CPR—despite the government's generosity—proved to have a ravening appetite for further capital infusions. With investments in both the Manitoba Road and the CPR, Hill sought to retain a capable manager for the latter. He found that man in William C. Van Horne. Born in Chelsea, Illinois, in 1834, Van Horne had raised himself up from poverty, eventually working as a consolidator for the troubled Chicago, Milwaukee and St. Paul Road, in which role he lured business away from Hill's enterprises. Another competitor was the last thing Hill needed, so in 1882 he spirited Van Horne away to act as general manager for the CPR in Winnipeg. Van Horne's management returned the CPR to a semblance of profitability, but the cost-cutting schemes he employed soon revealed Hill's tactical error, one James J. would never forget.[48]

Hill sent Van Horne to Winnipeg in 1882 for several reasons: to overcome a dangerous local competitor; to break the logjam at the Minnesota-Manitoba border, where Canadian customs held up the Manitoba Road's regular freight as well as shipments of rails and crossties for CPR construction; and to jump-start the CPR at Winnipeg, where corruption, incompetence, and malingering had brought the project to a near standstill. Once in place, however, Van Horne saw a matchless opportunity to garner fortune and fame through the CPR's sweetheart deal, especially its monopoly guarantees. Consequently, he turned on Hill, siding with the customs officials at the border, holding onto the Manitoba Road's freight cars, and, as Hill saw it, stabbing him in the back with the sharpened serpent's tooth of a protégé's ingratitude. Soon after his arrival in Manitoba, Van Horne delighted Canadians and outraged his sponsor by declaring, "Hill has no business in Winnipeg!"[49]

Van Horne's transformation from American-born enthusiast to Canadian booster infuriated some Associates, namely the Americans, Hill and Kennedy. But it delighted Canadians Stephen and Smith, who had found at last a man who promised to complete the CPR, to bring them wealth and glory, and, best of all, to make them peers of the British realm. With this tempting prospect at hand, Stephen stepped down from the Manitoba Road's presidency and Stephen, Smith, and Angus surreptitiously began unloading their Manitoba Road shares, investing the proceeds in the struggling CPR. By selling their shares, the Canadians drove down the Manitoba Road's value and diminished the personal wealth of its new president, Hill. As the situation further deteriorated with another recession at the end of 1882, Hill toiled to protect his investments. He induced Marshall Field, the prominent Chicago wholesaler and large-scale western investor, to join the Manitoba's board and entered into alliances with other eastern capitalists he had met through John Kennedy.[50]

Then, on May 3, 1883, the Canadian government announced the decision to move forward with the all-Canadian CPR route to the Pacific, "even though it would cost more and traverse a barren country." Worse yet, the decree banned non-Canadian residents from actively participating in the CPR's management. While Van Horne prospered as a Winnipeg resident, the decision effectively shut out Hill. Although he had a sizeable investment in the CPR, this blow, on top of his partners' treachery, was the last straw. Selling all his CPR shares and plowing the proceeds into the Manitoba Road and other American enterprises, Hill severed ties with Canada and, "however reluctantly, close[d] the official [CPR] connection." Kennedy retired from active participation in his banking house to devote more time to his investments in Hill's roads while Stephen and Angus resigned from the Manitoba's board. Thus, the Associates' relationship dissolved as quickly as it had appeared, even though Stephen and Smith later returned to the Manitoba's board. Everyone had displayed where his "self interest" resided, and the Associates had defended themselves against "all comers," including each other.[51]

Minnesota's most important railroad enterprise had managed to avoid disaster. Hill diverted some of his $585,000 in CPR shares into other regional investments, joining Charles Pillsbury and other local nabobs in organizing the Minneapolis Union Railway and the Minneapolis Elevator Company. But embarrassment over the CPR fiasco coupled with these new investments further inflamed competition between Americans and Canadians and between St. Paulites and Minneapolitans. Among those rivalries, the Hill-Pillsbury railroad presented a direct threat to William D. Washburn's own Minneapolis and St. Louis Railroad, the line that had played such a dominant role in Minneapolis's bid for regional supremacy.[52]

Minneapolitans' Manufacturing Explosion

Between 1878 and 1883, on the river of wheat and timber that flowed into the milling district, Minneapolis emerged as the center of regional manufacturing. This new status strengthened older rivalries with St. Paul, whose residents continued to call Minneapolis their "suburb." In 1883, aiming to give St. Paulites their comeuppance, the Washburn-owned *Minneapolis Tribune* boasted that, beyond local consumption, Minneapolis shipped 1.65 million barrels of flour annually, more than any other flour-manufacturing emporium in the nation. Booster statisticians reported, "if piled one above the other, end to end, [those barrels] would reach 780 miles. The flour would make about 495,225,000 loaves of bread [which] piled would make, roughly calculated, a square pyramid with a base 300 feet square and a height of nearly 1,000 feet." These numerous loaves would feed the nation, nay, the world, they declared. Additionally, the *1880 Census of Manufactures* testified that Minneapolis sent out nearly 12 million board feet of lumber every thirty days, making it one of the nation's top three lumber-manufacturing centers as well. Minneapolitans bragged that these numbers "would give enough boards to build a single-plank walk around the world, with four or five thousand miles left over."[53]

The waterfall city's residents endured a number of trials on their way to wealth and glory in manufacturing metaphoric 1,000-foot-high pyramids and single-plank global walks. Rather than the perils associated with large-scale commercial enterprises, however, these ordeals centered on the explosive hazards of flour manufacturing, the flooding of logging operations, and a number of technological challenges.[54]

Their first test came not during a lull but rather at the height of flour-manufacturing success. Grinding wheat into flour creates a large quantity of dust, which Minneapolis millers removed to make the best-quality flour in the world. By 1878, the daily deposit of that dust reached nearly three thousand pounds in the Washburn "A" Mill alone. The "A" employed a small army of men to remove the dust from where it wafted and settled throughout the plant. According to one reporter, "the atmosphere of the whole mill became surcharged with exceedingly minute and fuzzy particles, very inflammable, and when mixed in certain proportions with the air, highly explosive." On May 2, 1878, just as dusk descended upon Minneapolis, "fate supplied the torch" to the Washburn "A" when a piece of wire fell into some iron rollers, sparking a "lightning-express journey" through the mill's machinery. Within seconds, an explosion completely demolished the Washburn "A," destroyed several other nearby mills, consumed millions of dollars in property, and killed sixteen people. The blast reverberated throughout the city, and even St. Paulites felt "the terrific force of the detonation."[55]

C. C. Washburn suspended operations for two years while he built a new mill, the tragedy inspiring yet another shift in flour manufacturing, last in the long line of Minneapolis milling innovations. Washburn invented a device to catch flour dust in bins; quickly adopted by other mills, his design confirmed Minneapolis's place as a world-class flour manufacturing center. Then, in 1882, following the lead of Appleton, Wisconsin, whose entrepreneurs built the nation's first hydroelectric plant, Minneapolitans erected their own central station at the waterfall, increasing productive capacity on both sides of the river. As the mills shifted to electric-powered (and -illuminated) manufacturing techniques, Minneapolis finally emerged as the most important manufacturing center northwest of Chicago. Although many might question the booster who claimed "flour-milling has become such a clean process that a lady might walk through every floor dressed in black velvet and come out perfectly free from 'flour crock,'" no longer could anyone doubt the city's hold over the wheat-growing region.[56]

But improved manufacturing processes and banner wheat crops combined to threaten the very success of the Minneapolis millers. As farmers and millers flocked to the region, they glutted the markets for both wheat and flour. Bushels of wheat, commanding $1.05 each in 1875, plummeted to eighty-three cents in 1883. Flour prices followed, from a high of $7.95 per barrel in 1882 down to $6.75 in 1883, a trend that promised to continue. Here, manufacturing and commercial strategies met, as cost cutting seemed the only way to maintain profitability in the wake of declining revenues. Inevitably, those who already enjoyed the economies of scale inherent in extensive operations possessed the best chance to realize even more. C. C. Washburn had previously consolidated his interests with those of western-shore miller John Crosby, and before the absentee owner died in 1882, the Washburn-Crosby firm managed to consume most of the mills on that side of the river. On the eastern shoreline, the Pillsburys combined the largest mill in the world with three other mammoth structures to create an even larger empire. They also expanded into grain elevators, railroads, and direct orders from foreign dealers, thereby lowering their storage, distribution, and transaction costs substantially. By the end of 1883, all other mills survived only in the shadows of the Washburn-Crosby and Pillsbury concerns.[57]

By the time Rockefeller's Standard Oil Trust ushered in the American corporate merger movement on January 2, 1882, Minnesota's new industrialists had moved to establish their own syndicates and trusts. These developments reflected a trend in the competitive national economy, but they also revealed the Twin Cities' maturity within it. People throughout the region began to speak of Minneapolis's "wheat ring" and to decry St. Paul's "financial graspers," an indictment with which Minneapolitans agreed wholeheartedly. Hill, in particular, irked Washburn and others involved in the "wheat ring." Through Marshall Field, he had joined a Chicago trust, submitting $75,000 as the "man representing western interests." Now that Hill had emerged as Manitoba Road president and a Minneapolis investor, Washburn convinced Pillsbury that the time had arrived to erect some walls between themselves and the grasping St. Paulite. The Pillsbury brothers wanted to have it both ways, however, so Charles maintained his association with Hill in various enterprises, including the Minneapolis Union Railroad, the St. Anthony Falls Water Power Company, and assorted grain elevator operations. Meanwhile, John Sargeant joined William D. Washburn, Thomas Lowry, and other Minneapolis millers in a scheme to bypass the Manitoba Road as well as all Chicago-based lines, thereby allow-

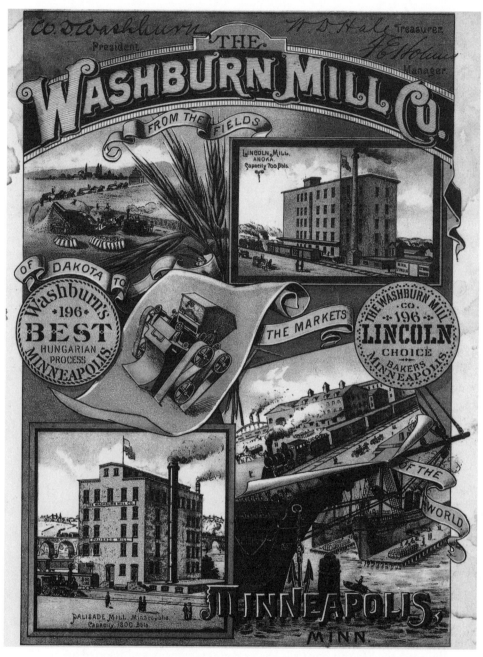

Advertising Minneapolis's international reach—"From the Fields of Dakota to the Markets of the World"—the Washburn Mill Company, led by the city's most ardent booster, W. D. Washburn, hoped to dethrone contenders closer to home, including James J. Hill, the Manitoba Road, and the city of St. Paul.

ing Minneapolis to take its rightful place as "the great emporium" of the American Northwest. Washburn's older brother, Israel Jr., had brought the idea to the Minneapolis Board of Trade in 1873, just before Cooke & Co. failed. W. D. now vigorously endorsed Israel's notion that Minneapolis millers needed their own railroad, one heading northward through Wisconsin to the CPR connection at Sault Ste. Marie, Ontario, then eastward to the Atlantic seaboard, making a beeline for European markets.[58]

To thwart Hill's expansionist plans, W. D. Washburn, John Pillsbury, Thomas Lowry, and other Minneapolis champions organized the Minneapolis, Sault Ste. Marie, and Atlantic Railway (Soo) under Wisconsin's general incorporation laws. With the recession in full swing, the new organization required a sizeable capital infusion to get it off the ground, and several years passed before the Soo directors found investors—namely Steven, Smith, and Angus—willing to venture in yet another western railroad enterprise. In launching the Soo, however, they set the stage for an all-out war between St. Paul and Minneapolis in the years that followed the NPR celebration of 1883.[59]

The Northern Pacific Celebration and Escalating Rivalries

On September 3, 1883, a Northern Pacific delegation roared into the Cities to celebrate the transcontinental connection between St. Paul–Minneapolis and the Pacific Ocean at Tacoma, Washington, and Portland, Oregon. The NPR's golden-spike moment, considered passé by the majority of Americans, nevertheless cast an enormous spell over the "New Northwest" and highlighted the metropolitan rivalries the three-year boom had engendered. In St. Paul, residents took "prompt action" to ready themselves for the arrival of NPR president Henry Villard and his entourage of five hundred guests. They spared nothing on the celebration's reception programs, decorations, invitations, banquet preparations, and building projects, constructing "magnificent" arches that declared such things as "N.P.R., the Connecting Link Between China and St. Paul." Residents boasted that "at every point appeared those little fluttering pennons bearing the magic characters, 'N.P.R.'—[with] over one hundred thousand displayed" throughout the city. By the time its citizens had lavished hundreds of thousands of dollars on the day's event, St. Paul ranked fourth in Bradstreet's annual tally of America's growth cities. Consequently, St. Paulites proclaimed their city "the metropolis of the Northwest," counting among its attributes the following: head of Mississippi River navigation, center of regional railways and politics, "gateway to the Pacific[,] and the depot and entrepot of a commerce continental in its proportions."[60]

Much evidence supported St. Paulites' claims to victory in the race for regional wealth and glory. By 1880, Americans had built 93,671 miles of railroad covering all of the country's then-settled regions. Within two years, railroaders added another 11,000 miles, 2,400 of those credited to St. Paul–based firms. During 1883, St. Paul's railroads reached west and north to Portland, Tacoma, and Winnipeg and connected south and east to the West's more mammoth eastern terminus at Chicago. "Like the spokes of an enormous wheel," 8,000 miles of Minnesota's 10,000-mile rail network radiated outward from the city. St. Paul–based railroads employed more than 64,000 men, some 13,000 of whom lived in the capital city, working in a hierarchy of positions ranging from executives to professionals, salesmen, clerks, skilled craftsmen, and day laborers.[61]

Wholesaling and financial institutions popped up alongside this expansion. The number of wholesale houses swelled from 223 employing 3,180 men and women on $46.5 million in sales in 1881 to 325 with 5,815 employees and sales reaching more than $72 million in 1883. St. Paul's total bank capital climbed from $900,000 in 1870 to $5.55 million, the business of its national banks alone increasing from $16.6 million in 1870 to nearly $104 million. Indeed, capital in St. Paul's national banks surpassed that in all of Wisconsin's national banks combined. By 1883, St. Paul stood at number nine on the nation's list of financial centers, just under St. Louis and just above New Orleans. Residents could boast that St. Paul, though still dwarfed by Chicago, had successfully joined the ranks of the nation's ten most important transportation and commercial centers. Joining a bevy of workers, small business operators, and families who arrived to participate in St. Paul's wealth creation, new railroad, wholesale, and banking employees increased the city's population from 41,498 in 1880 to an estimated 100,000 in 1883 (confirmed at 111,397 by the 1885 census).[62]

In a very real sense, the NPR celebration also belonged to James J. Hill, for through competitive posturing, local support, and business consolidations, the Associates' junior partner had forced the NPR to declare St. Paul (rather than Duluth or Minneapolis) the eastern terminus of its transcontinental road. With the NPR's lines promising to pull more settlers into the sparsely populated but resource-rich region, Hill reasoned he could build his own private, parallel, and profitable road to Washington on the strength of NPR-induced developments between Dakota Territory and the Pacific Northwest and the Manitoba Road's revenues in land-grant Minnesota. Hill received roaring applause at the NPR celebration's closing banquet, not only for his response to the tenth in a plethora of toasts but also because he had hosted one thousand delegates at the Manitoba Road's new luxury hotel, the Lafayette on Lake Minnetonka, Minnesota's million-dollar retreat for wealthy visitors and the Twin Cities' nouveau riche. Hill had risen through the ranks and had lavished money on the Cities' businesses and charity organizations—and regional residents admired him for both. Now that he had taken his place in the vanguard of Minnesota's urban-industrial elite, residents acknowledged that Mr. Hill had finally arrived.[63]

Minneapolitans celebrated St. Paul's success during the NPR festivities, but residents of the capital's so-called suburb put up a few banners of their own, including "statistics of the City of Minneapolis—commercial and manufacturing metropolis of the Northwest." These banners advertised the waterfall city's status as the state's largest population center, home to several important state officials (including U.S. representative W. D. Washburn and former governor J. S. Pillsbury); the world's flour-milling capital; a nationally ranked manufacturing hub; the "true gateway" into the trans-Mississippi West; and contender in all things commercial and financial. By the time its residents had spent their own hundreds of thousands of dollars on the NPR event, Minneapolis ranked fifth nationally on Bradstreet's city-growth list and claimed the number-one spot in the *1880 Census of Manufactures'* inventory of the nation's food suppliers. Minneapolitans bragged that their city's population had reached 46,867 during 1880, more than 5,000 over that of St. Paul. By 1883, statisticians claimed that Minneapolis housed 100,000 residents and—based on ratios used in city directory calculations—that St. Paul's population could boast no more than 78,000 souls. The 1885 census takers seemed to verify these disputed numbers, reporting Minneapolis's population of 129,200 that year, 19,000 more residents than St. Paul. At the same time, Minneapolis boosters claimed that their own jobbing trade employed $26.7 million in capital and 4,864 men—figures "nip and tuck" with St. Paul's totals—on sales that had reached $115.6 million, $40 million more than that of the capital city's "wholesale houses."[64]

By the time Minneapolitans incorporated the Soo in 1883, business rivalries had created a metropolitan complex capable of sustaining both emporiums despite the recession of 1882–83. Meanwhile, innovations in other areas combined to transform the social hierarchy and the psychology of work and leisure in both cities.

The New Metropolitan Complex

Along with railroad expansion, spectacular wheat harvests, and rapid immigration, the introduction of telephones and electric lights and the improvement of plumbing systems completely transformed everyday life in St. Paul–Minneapolis. Taken together, these enhancements made the Cities more attractive destinations for young professionals seeking oppor-

Completion of the Northern Pacific Railroad symbolized the triumph of St. Paul-Minneapolis "over all comers." Moreover, the NPR transcontinental celebration—one aspect of it, St. Paul's "Triumphal Arch," depicted here in an engraving by Charles Graham—fulfilled the dreams of Minnesota's territorial founders, namely, the transformation of these former wilderness outposts into the urban center of the New Northwest.

tunities in the booming Northwest. No longer twenty years behind the technological curve, Twin Cities businesses adopted and adapted these innovations during the late 1870s and early 1880s. In many ways, new competition from other established and aspiring cities forced them to do so.[65]

National and regional competition also prompted Minnesota's urban entrepreneurs to adopt cost-saving technologies such as the telephone, which provided instant, private communication. As early as 1877, W. D. Washburn experimented with Alexander Graham Bell's invention, introduced just the year before, and in 1880 Washburn contracted for "a long range machine" connecting his headquarters in Minneapolis with one of his lumberyards twenty miles distant. Through 1878, "the experience of carrying on a conversation with one ten miles away [remained] novel," and as late as June 2, 1879, Minneapolis postal clerk Dora Louise Jewett claimed she had "talked through the telephone the other day for the first time, but [found it] no trouble at all, [and] quite fun." Government offices lagged behind businesses, however; by the time of Jewett's telephone conversation, many Twin Cities companies had already put "the new invention into practical operation." St. Paul wholesalers in particular found the telephone "very useful at the store" as they "[received] orders verbally from Minneapolis every day." Indeed, by the end of 1880, although most business transactions still occurred via telegraph, Auerbach's Boyle reported that "telephone communication with Minneapolis and Stillwater [eighteen miles away] is becoming such a common occurrence that we have ceased to marvel at it."[66]

By the time New York and Chicago established long-distance telephone service during 1883, the gadget's novelty had subsided. Twin Cities businesses instituted 75-mile service that same year, and telephone chatters "hear[d] each other without the slightest difficulty." Several wealthy residents even had telephones in their homes, altering former visiting habits such as leaving cards and receiving strolling summer guests on the porch. Following the speed of adoption elsewhere, these numerous telephone installations signaled the Cities' ongoing efforts to remain competitive in the nation's rapidly changing environment.[67]

Electrical lighting—first perfected in 1878 at Thomas Edison's Electric Light Company of New York—continued the trend, ushering in the possibility of twenty-four-hour days. On March 11, 1882, St. Paul residents stopped at a new sash and blind factory near downtown "to see their exhibition of the electric light." According to Boyle, "this is the first time [we] have seen electricity successfully used [in either St. Paul or Minneapolis,] and the perfection of the lights surpassed my expectations." On April 17, the Auerbach emporium unveiled electric lights in the wholesaling district, and during the summer other large-scale firms followed. By the close of

1883—just two years after Edison introduced the world's first electric-light power plant, at Pearl Street, New York—both St. Paul and Minneapolis had passed ordinances for municipal electric lighting plants to run the cities day and night.[68]

Along with innovations in communication and power, the nation also introduced major improvements in plumbing during the 1880s. In the wake of better facilities, Minnesota's government officials were among the first to adopt inspection codes for health and safety standards. Consequently, people in St. Paul–Minneapolis boasted that their cities had all the "modern conveniences" near their downtown cores and that "suburban" improvements promised to follow shortly. As Boyle exclaimed in 1883, "Verily! We live in an age of wonders." Not everyone benefited from these wonders, but many young men and women believed technological advances would improve long-term prospects, particularly for those who could secure inflated salaries to operate cutting-edge equipment.[69]

At the same time, national innovations in large-scale firms and the growing prestige of business and engineering as academic subjects transformed life in St. Paul–Minneapolis tremendously. Entrepreneurial elites donated funds to the university as well as to other small business and technical colleges, inspiring young professional hopefuls to flock to the Cities. As one visitor during the NPR celebrations observed, both cities' "business communities consist of young, active men, who have mostly been schooled in mercantile pursuits in the Eastern states, but who find here opportunities for expansion and development not offered in their old homes." Joining their number, the aspiring attorney Henry Wenzell claimed that, despite lacking opportunities for young men in older, more established cities, "so much more is required in these younger communities at the West, that there is ample scope for young men of education," particularly those who "desire to identify [themselves] with the community, & to take interest in other matters not strictly within the professional pale."[70]

With optimistic entrepreneurs, new professionals, and white-collar climbers joining Minnesota's race for wealth creation, established businessmen like Hill and Washburn attained wealth and influence beyond their most extravagant flights of fancy. But importuning subjects soon appeared at the gates of the industrialists' newly built palaces, some seeking employment, others asking for return favors, patronage, money, protection, or, most importantly, the influential support of charitable and community-minded statesmen. With great wealth came greater obligations to the larger communities that had nurtured entrepreneurial ambitions. Successful businessmen who opened their wallets to educational, religious, social, and political causes soon prospered socially, gaining acceptance as Minnesota's exemplary citizens. Conversely, those who hoarded their amassed wealth lost the one thing many fame-seeking entrepreneurs craved most—veneration for their role in their city's triumphs over other aspiring urban centers.[71]

Emulating the largesse of urban industrialists elsewhere, Minnesota's new elites showered gratitude upon their respective cities during this period—building businesses, bridges, homes, and churches and donating funds for schools, social clubs, and additional community institutions. Their generosity increased the attractions of the Cities, and local residents boasted "how pleasantly things [had] changed [with their] own citizens making money [and] erecting magnificent and costly buildings." Some among them also remarked, "fortunately the management of the Manitoba Railroad has passed into the hands of St. Paul men, who live among us, and with large capital and great energy, St. Paul grows with their growth and strengthens with their strength." Hill and other elites also created a basis of comparison within the urban centers' increasingly stratified social hierarchies. Gazing up at the established entrepreneurs, a growing army of lower-middle-class clerks, tellers, sales personnel, telegraphers, and small business owners hoped to ascend the ranks just as they had.[72]

Perhaps few Irish waitresses believed they had a chance to rise from rags to riches alongside an entrepreneurial dockhand the way Mary Mehegan Hill had, but many shared young Boyle's general enthusiasm for expansion as he saw himself rising each "step on the figurative ladder of success" inside St. Paul's premier wholesaling establishment. Ascending in six years from day laborer to salesman, Boyle celebrated his ten-fold salary increase by trumpeting, "I don't think it is possible for any one who works on a salary to lead an easier, pleasanter, or more independent life than I do." That sense of liberation prompted some rather "sharp competition" as Boyle and others jockeyed for position during Minnesota's third boom, but it also confirmed the Cities' place in the region. As but one example, railroad rates decreased to such an extent that passengers could purchase tickets from St. Paul to Chicago for fifty cents, a pittance compared to previous years.[73]

The ample scope available to Wenzell, Boyle, and others transformed earlier roles as well, replacing those "laying up stock for the winter months" with a hierarchy of urban professionals and office workers seeking to profit from more expansion. Greater numbers of women joined the workforce, opening small businesses of their own—a veritable explosion of millinery shops, employment agencies, private schools, laundries, groceries, dress shops, and other retail stores. The Cities' business colleges welcomed both men and women for training in telegraphy, stenography, accounting, and other courses required for urban-industrial life. After all, St. Paul's business college exclaimed, "no young man or woman of the present, enlightened and progressive age is fully qualified for a responsible position in life without a thorough knowledge of bookkeeping and business training." By the end of the period, white- and pink-collar jobs proliferated throughout the Cities. Although men garnered the best salaries and dominated railroads and manufacturing plants, entrepreneurial impulses had transformed many women's public and private roles, not to mention patterns of work and leisure throughout the Twin Cities and their suburban hinterlands. With competition increasing and profits declining, many businessmen, searching for ways to lower labor costs, looked to female employees. As a result, in St. Paul–Minneapolis, like elsewhere in the United States, women began to replace men as clerical workers, and many women considered their new positions steppingstones to economic independence.[74]

As people from all walks of life celebrated the NPR transcontinental triumph in September 1883, urban enthusiasts knew they had fulfilled the dreams of Minnesota's territorial founders. The NPR's capitalization had reached $100 million, and the railroad's international shareholder roster numbered eight thousand. By comparison, in St. Paul–Minneapolis people claimed to know who owned their railroads, or at least most of the major stockholders—men the cities' residents had nurtured in their formative years. James J. Hill, an adopted Canadian turned American empire builder, had grown up among them. So had the Soo's William D. Washburn, the Maine lumberman-attorney turned Minneapolis Mill booster and resident political luminary. From 1878 to 1883, this local ownership, read local control, inspired confidence despite hard times attended by troubled railroad alliances, wholesaling retrenchment, banking embarrassments, shrinking flour profits, and a multitude of other modern concerns. In fewer than thirty-five years, residents of St. Paul–Minneapolis had constructed the metropolitan focus for the region's future.[75]

Conclusion

BY 1883, Minnesota's entrepreneurial boosters, hustlers, and speculators had created a metropolitan landscape considerably removed from the early collection of huts and shanties and far beyond anything Amelia Ullman's "community of interested members" had envisioned during the 1850s. Traveling from her new home in Chicago to St. Paul–Minneapolis during the 1880s, Ullman "sought something that might stand as a reminder of the past," but although "the land remained," she found "the character and contours" changed. "The Mississippi rolled on deep and regular towards the South," she mused, "and as I watched its surface sparkling in the light of the setting sun I thought of the days before when, as a young mother, my first babe in my arms, how the future spread out hopefully before me as I had come slowly up the current to the early landing place." As her reverie passed, she remembered that this time she had traveled quickly by train, and, looking around again, Ullman "found the brick and granite blocks, schools, churches, and public buildings of great and modern [cities] reaching out" toward new dreams.[1]

As other urban enthusiasts surveyed their "great and modern cities," they too saw change—outposts grown up into a business magnet for the New Northwest, along with political and social structures for further expansion. In many ways, their emporiums resembled those of the East. They had all the modern conveniences, especially railroads linking them to the larger world. They had built upon comparative advantages in timber and wheat just as eastern cities had built upon their own resources. They had ousted regional rivals for the spoils of the western prairies. But they could claim some unique features as well. Proximity to the Canadian border defined their struggle for supremacy over a region encompassing two nations. And both cities had managed to survive—and then prosper— in the competitive world of western developments, a showing all the more impressive considering their expanding mutual rivalry. Most important of all, they had accomplished their territorial founders' dreams, transforming wilderness outposts on the margins of the American empire into the most prosperous and influential metropolitan complex northwest of Chicago, complete with plentiful people, railroads, banks, wholesale houses, elegant homes, and flour and sawmills; with well-attended schools, churches, and social clubs; and with generously funded charity networks and city governments.

They had achieved these numerous feats on the strengths of nature's bounty, demand for wheat and timber products, internal and external capitalists, entrepreneurial talents, competitive posturing, production and consumption by more than two million people lured into their domain, and legal and financial support from federal, state, and local governments. Indeed, competition for the spoils of the Atlantic world economy had nurtured urban rivalries that prompted residents in St. Paul and Minneapolis to challenge other aspiring town builders as well as each other for regional supremacy. As American go-getters and expansionists, they instinctively adhered to the imperative that "If one puts up a fifty thousand dollar church, the other sees it and goes twenty-five thousand better, besides sending to Brooklyn for a preacher."[2]

Finding themselves in precisely the right place at precisely the right time, Minnesota's urban entrepreneurs profited by learning how to manipulate American political entities to best effect: by utilizing the government's legal and financial support to remove the Indians who stood in the way of hoped-for expansion; by acquiring lucrative government contracts to extract resources and to build trade; and by receiving government subsidies and land grants for infrastructural improvements, railroad construction, and agricultural development. Minnesotans approached 1849 optimistically but with relatively little experience in urban building schemes. Thirty-five years later they sat atop an agricultural empire extending west to the Pacific Ocean, north into Canada, south into Iowa and parts of Nebraska, and east into western Wisconsin.

In the classic work *Out of Our Past*, Carl Degler argued that growth-oriented "capitalism" arrived in North America onboard the first ships. Perhaps Degler overstated his case; at the very least, however, the European political economy crossed the Atlantic, carrying with it law, order, and a framework for mercantile empire building, along with the conviction that Europeans had the right to conquer and claim territories, to extract resources for the empire, and to remove whatever barriers stood between imperial dream and reality.[3]

As the thirteen colonies crafted their own nation after 1776, American politicians well understood, and moved to exploit, the imperialistic thrust, promising all the riches of the new empire to business enthusiasts who mobilized for expansion. Congress set up a legal framework to conquer Indian lands and wrote laws to protect and reward white migrants willing to undertake the risks associated with settlement west of established population centers. When wheat supplanted corn as the nation's food staple, many Americans migrated north and west, into the Ohio River Valley and beyond, where the soil promised great bounty. Eventually, as demands for building materials, food, and clothing increased throughout the Atlantic world market, some expansionists gazed toward the Upper Northwest, perceiving opportunities for wealth and self-aggrandizement in furs, timber, and the products of the fertile Red River Valley.

Optimism pervaded the United States during its high tide of territorial expansion, ushering in a period of competition for the riches of the trans-Mississippi West. People in St. Paul–Minneapolis merely enacted one in a series of conquests underwritten by the federal government to increase the wealth of the larger American empire-in-the-making. Some, such as James J. Hill, succeeded beyond their most "sanguine expectations" precisely because they emerged in and benefited from a society whose members not only supported but also demanded their entrepreneurial efforts. Socialized for competition, Hill and other Minnesotans thus sought to dominate their region using the same techniques as had their counterparts in Cincinnati, St. Louis, Chicago, and other cities. On the West Coast, San Franciscans followed a similar path. And, in the years that followed, entrepreneurs in Dallas, Denver, Los Angeles, Seattle, and other western cities moved to exploit their hinterlands in corresponding ways. In each case, urban boosters and builders understood that their labors must center on the larger nation's ambitions to free its citizenry from the rhythms of agricultural society and to adopt instead the time and work disciplines of urban-industrial life, whether in cities and towns or on commercial farms.[4]

By the time Minnesota became an American territory in 1849, the region's entrepreneurs had the assured backing of a strong federal government, complete with a system for Indian land acquisition, a Constitution to protect and promote their private property rights, and a Supreme Court that consistently ruled in favor of entrepreneurial start-ups against more established and, hence, monopoly-seeking corporations. Additionally, federal and state governments had moved to forgive failures and to shield risk takers, enacting bankruptcy laws and incorporation statutes with clauses to limit liability and to protect personal property against business failure. As the market revolution swept over the Atlantic during the nineteenth century, the federal government sheltered infant manufacturers through tariffs, encouraged technological espionage in Europe, protected inventors through patent law, and fostered innovations in transportation and communication to lower the transaction costs of transcontinental expansion. It encouraged European immigrants to people its new territories and its own citizens to settle west of established centers, promising economic opportunities, participation in an expanding political democracy, and social mobility in exchange for risks undertaken to accomplish the nation's larger goals. Ultimately, as successive generations accumulated experience through this process, commercial cities overtook agricultural communities as the focus for American life.

Although the federal government perfected the legal foundations for American continental expansion during the first half of the nineteenth century, as entrepreneurs wended their way toward the twentieth century they had to pass through several stages in the market economy's evolution. As developing urban centers, industries, transportation networks, and other innovations spread west, they carried regions from dependence on overland roads and waterways and specialized goods production through early railroad and industrial expansion and into large-scale agricultural and industrial production for mass distribution and consumption.

With each leap into larger networks—and as economic booms collapsed into financial panics and busts—entrepreneurs had to negotiate their place in the nation. While not all succeeded in realizing their bourgeois dreams, by working to improve their material net worth they participated in the creation of St. Paul–Minneapolis and other urban-industrial enclaves in the West. Developments between 1849 and 1883 brought wealth to the region and secured for St. Paulites and Minneapolitans the status they had coveted: for St. Paul, identification as the center of transportation, wholesale distribution, and finance for the northwestern borderlands; for Minneapolis, increasing recognition of its prominence as the flour-milling headquarters for the nation as well as the manufacturing hub for the northwestern interior's agricultural products.

Minnesota's connection—and occasional collision—with the larger market reveals the ways in which American entrepreneurs moved to exploit their principal assets. In Minnesota, hinterland wheat emerged as the best "chance to realize," and entrepreneurs mobilized their communities to transport it east via the most cost-effective means at their disposal, whether river, road, or rail. They also established banking, wholesaling, manufacturing, and immigration networks to profit from its cultivation and the consumers who produced it. Entrepreneurs in other places exploited different assets at different times, just as Minnesotans had made use of resources including furs and timber in response to consumer demand. The most successful among them took up positions in the transportation systems that promised to link them with government handouts, with other profitable businesses, and with regional assets.

The desire for modernity drove Americans to engage in rivalries for local and then regional and national control. But St. Paul–Minneapolis's experience shows that personal relationships and individuals as well as market forces guided the ebb and flow of life in the Twin Cities and their hinterland, reaffirming a truth seen before and after in other locations. Once-admired entrepreneurs faded into oblivion when their enterprises collapsed. Others died in disgrace for having quit their regions during hard times. Nobodies ascended on abilities, determination, connections, and deceptions. Workers admired their bosses one day and despised them the next, using job performance to reflect both sentiments. People built empires never totally free from financial embarrassment. Upstart entrepreneurs beat established ones at their own game. Some ascended the ranks as promoters and politicians rather than on business acumen. Others departed not in failure but rather as a consequence of success. And nature's revenge—communicated through fires, floods, and other phenomena—reminded everyone of the moment-to-moment potential for a "reversal of fortunes."

Although few Minnesotans perceived it during 1883, the NPR celebration represented another shift in the nation's—and the state's—history. The next year, the New York Stock Exchange crashed, signaling a prolonged recession and prompting the merger movement that resulted in national business consolidations among industrial elites anxious to avoid the vagaries of competition in an increasingly complex—and thus financially precarious—global economy. As smaller centers in the chain of American urban expansion, St. Paul and Minneapolis at first remained free from the most glaring problems associated with urban-industrial life. Before another decade passed, however, Minnesota's urban dwellers would face new challenges and conflicts as the U.S. connection with the market economy continued to evolve. Regardless, just as they had commemorated their triumphs during the 1850s and the post–Civil War boom, Twin Cities residents found cause for celebration during 1883. The NPR festivities confirmed their supremacy in the New Northwest. On the slim means and big dreams of boosters, hustlers, and speculators, they had built something. For the moment, that something constituted success enough.

Notes

NOTES TO THE INTRODUCTION

1. This study derives from the increasing recognition, among various scholars over the past three decades, that previous treatments of nineteenth-century industrialization have neglected the reciprocal influence of business, government, and society on the developments that shaped life in the United States and elsewhere. For a wider discussion of the historiographical debates germane to this book, see Wills, "Respectable Mediocrity" and "Tangled Webs"; Nobles, *American Frontiers;* John, "Elaborations, Revisions, Dissents."

2. Gaps, particularly geographical ones, remain in the literature on American industrialization. Walter Licht's recent synthesis, *Industrializing America,* rarely reaches beyond Chicago. Most monographs focus on the economic and labor history of textiles in New England; railroading, steel making, and milling in New York, Pennsylvania, and the South; the importance of Chicago and its hinterland; and mining in the far West. Several recent attempts to connect the less-than-laissez-faire role of the American government to the processes of urban-industrial change, particularly in the Old Northwest and California, have emerged. See, for example, Deverell, *Railroad Crossing;* Mould, *Dividing Lines;* Igler, *Industrial Cowboys;* and Gruenwald, *River of Enterprise.*

In his *Wealth of the Nation,* Stuart Bruchey placed American economic change within its legal and constitutional settings. Over the past decade, scholars have debated and revised this theme, producing an expanding literature devoted to the government's role in the economy as both investor in the market as well as regulator of it. See, for example, Hovenkamp, *Enterprise and American Law;* Taylor, *William Cooper's Town;* John, *Spreading the News;* Vance, *North American Railroad;* Monkkonen, *Local State;* Pursell, *Machine in America;* Reinhard, ed., *Power Elites and State Building;* McCraw, ed., *Creating Modern Capitalism;* Alexander, *Commodity and Propriety;* Bigham, *Towns and Villages;* Dobak, *Fort Riley;* and Andersson-Skog and Krantz, eds., *Institutions in the Transport and Communications Industries.*

3. A voluminous literature exists on the processes of British and European industrialization. See, for example, endnotes and bibliographies in Richards and MacKenzie, *The Railway Station;* Koditschek, *Class Formation;* Kemp, *Industrialization in Nineteenth-Century Europe* and *Historical Patterns of Industrialization;* and Teich and Porter, eds., *Industrial Revolution in National Context.*

Many immigrants had destinations in mind when they left their homes, and when they arrived in North America they shaped the environment as much as the North American experience influenced their outlook. See Erickson, *Leaving England,* and Erickson, ed., *Emigration From Europe;* Conzen, *Immigrant Milwaukee,* and Conzen, et al., "The Invention of Ethnicity"; Vecoli, "Resurgence of American Immigration History," and Vecoli and Sinke, eds., *Century of European Migrations;* Malchow, *Population Pressures;*

Holmquist, ed., *They Chose Minnesota;* Gjerde, *From Peasants to Farmers;* Kamphoefner, *Westfalians;* Ostergren, *A Community Transplanted;* and Debouzy, ed., *Shadow of the Statue of Liberty.* For an example of chain-migration in Minnesota, see Schoone-Jongen, "Cheap Land and Community."

4. For comparative purposes, see Johnson, *Shopkeeper's Millennium;* Mahoney, *River Towns in the Great West;* Cronon, *Nature's Metropolis;* Ayers, et al., *All Over the Map;* Dunaway, *First American Frontier;* Sheriff, *Artificial River;* and Miller, *City of the Century.*

5. In his classic *The Urban Frontier,* Richard Wade argued that urban and rural interests remained largely separate as Cincinnati, Lexington, Louisville, Pittsburgh, and St. Louis struggled for primacy, power, and "occasionally survival" in the urban West (336–41). Although St. Paul–Minneapolis confirms many of his findings, business and other sources for the period reveal that Minnesota's urban boosters and builders recognized the important synergy between (and interdependence of) urban and rural developments in the trans-Mississippi West. As urban enthusiasts sought to develop Minnesota and other regions in the trans-Mississippi West, many had to convince immigrants to settle in rural rather than urban regions. As rural dwellers fanned out into these sparsely populated regions, most hoped to profit from market expansion as well, either building smaller towns or engaging in large-scale, commercial production tied to urban-based networks. At times urban and rural residents cooperated; at times they competed. But when their interests diverged, most debates centered on who would (and should) profit from market participation. An extensive literature is devoted to city- and regional-systems, gateway cities, and urban rivalries. See, in particular, Cronon, *Nature's Metropolis,* as well as Bourne and Sim-

mons, eds. *Systems of Cities;* Meyer, "A Dynamic Model"; Pred, *Urban Growth and City-Systems;* Artibise, ed., *Town and City;* Harvey, *Urbanization of Capital;* Careless, *Frontier and Metropolis;* Cayton and Onuf, *Midwest and the Nation;* Hamer, *New Towns in the New World;* Mahoney, *River Towns in the Great West* and *Provincial Lives;* Adler, *Yankee Merchants;* Abbott, "Regional City and Network City"; Moehring, "Comstock Urban Network"; and Conzen, "Maturing Urban System."

6. For differences between the American and Canadian experience, see Cooke, "Imagining a North American Garden"; Bliss, *Northern Enterprise;* MacDonald, *Distant Neighbors;* Egnal, *Divergent Paths;* den Otter, *Philosophy of Railways;* and Wills, "Divided Loyalties."

7. See, in particular, Matthew Josephson's classic, *The Robber Barons,* as well as Martin, *James J. Hill;* Ingham, *Iron Barons;* Malone, *James J. Hill;* and Folsom, *Urban Capitalists* and *Myth of the Robber Barons.*

Our current understanding of railroads in American economic life rests largely on the works of two business history scholars—Alfred Chandler and Thomas Cochran—and their critics, exemplified by Robert Fogel and Albert Fishlow. See, in particular Chandler, *Railroads;* Cochran, *Railroad Leaders;* Fogel, *Railroads and American Economic Growth;* and Fishlow, *American Railroads.* From these initial debates, Chandler refined his earlier works; see his *Strategy and Structure, Visible Hand,* and *Scale and Scope.* Other important works include George Rogers Taylor's classic *The Transportation Revolution;* Taylor and Neu, *The American Railroad Network;* North, *Economic Growth of the United States;* Stilgoe, *Metropolitan Corridor;* Dunlavy, *Politics and Industrialization;* Heilbroner, *Economic Transformation of America;* and Veenendaal, *Slow Train to Paradise.* For an in-depth discussion of the Chandlerian debate, see "Comments on the Sources" in Martin, *Railroads Triumphant.* For an introduction to American entrepreneurship, see Livesay, ed., *Entrepreneurship and the Growth of Firms,* as well as Kirkland, *Dream and Thought;* Atherton, *Frontier Merchant in Mid-America;* Livesay, *American Made;* Abbott, *Boosters and Businessmen;* and Hughes, *The Vital Few.*

8. For early descriptions of the bluffs containing St. Paul–Minneapolis, see Pike, *Expeditions;* Wheelock, *Minnesota,* 5–72, 147; *Minnesota Pioneer* [hereafter *Pioneer*], 28 April 1849 and 28 November 1850; *Business Directory for the City of Saint Paul* (1856) [hereafter *1856 St. Paul Directory*], 3–11, St. Paul, Minnesota, City Directory Collection; Lewis, *Valley of the Mississippi,* 82–90; and Andreas, *Illustrated Historical Atlas,* 211, 218–23, 225.

9. Borchert, *America's Northern Heartland,* 31–51, convincingly argues that transportation played a key role in Minnesota's American settlement; however, by placing railroad developments in the 1870s at the center of "dissolving the wilderness," he tends to discount the central role that local residents played during the 1850s and early 1860s. See, for example, Wills, "Business Enterprise." John O'Sullivan qtd. in David Goldfield, et al., *American Journey,* 368. For contemporary accounts on city builders who influenced North American regional developments during the nineteenth century, see, for example, Ratzel, *Sketches of Urban and Cultural Life.* For the long arm of mythmaking in railroad developments in general and St. Paul's James J. Hill in particular, see "Immigrant Trains: Railroads Built This Town." In addition, see Kelley, *Origin and Progress;* Aiken, *The Grange;* Piott, *Anti-Monopoly Persuasion;* and Freyer, *Producers Versus Capitalists.*

10. Hill, *Highways of Progress,* 140–55; Gras, "Significance of the Twin Cities."

11. Hill, *Highways of Progress,* 140–55; Gras, "Significance of the Twin Cities."

NOTES TO CHAPTER 1

1. *An Act to Establish the Territorial Government of Minnesota,* U.S. House Files reprint, *Minnesota Republican,* 7 April 1849; *Bills from the House Files of the Minnesota Territorial Legislature* and *Bills from the Council File of the Minnesota Territorial Legislature, September 26, 1849,* Alexis Bailly Papers [hereafter Bailly Papers]; Wheelock, *Minnesota,* 70–72, 147; John Phillips Owens, Book Draft, Vol. 1, "Political History of Minnesota, from 1847–62" [ca. 1875], 37–98, John Phillips Owens Papers [hereafter Owens Papers]; Andreas, *Illustrated Historical Atlas,* 211, 218–23, 225; Williams, *History of the City,* 208; Mrs. Jacob Bass, *Reminiscences* [ca. 1900], Jacob Wales Bass and Family Papers [hereafter Bass Papers]; Burnquist, ed., *Minnesota and Its People,* 1:99–121, 225–26, 533–51; Folwell, *History of Minnesota,* 1:213–65.

2. Edward Duffield Neill qtd. in *1856 St. Paul Directory,* 4; Lanman, "Summer in the Wilderness," 75.

3. *1856 St. Paul Directory,* 1–6.

4. Williams, *History of the City,* 49. See also Lea, *Notes on Wisconsin Territory;* Peck, *A New Guide for Emigrants;* Colton, *Western Tourist and Emigrant's Guide;* Hurst, *Law and the Conditions of Freedom;* Kutler, ed., *Supreme Court and the Constitution;* Cochran, *Frontiers of Change;* Henretta, *Origins of American Capitalism;* Elkins and McKitrick, *Age of Federalism.*

5. U.S. Continental Congress, *Ordinance;* Jefferson, *Message.* For recent discussions on the American political economy during the early national period, including excellent bibliographies devoted to the subject, see Nelson, *Liberty and Property,* and Heilbroner, *Economic Transformation of America,* 1–115.

6. Colton, *Western Tourist and Emigrant's Guide,* 51. See also Leslie, "Trip from St. Anthony," 400; Williams, *History of the City,* 171; and endnotes in Rasmussen, *Absentee Landowning.*

7. Williams, *History of the City*, 177. See also Onuf, *Statehood and Union*; Larkin, *Reshaping of Everyday Life*; Williams, ed., *Northwest Ordinance*.

8. Lewis, *History of the Expedition*; Pike, *Expeditions*; Potter, *People of Plenty*; DeConde, *Affair of Louisiana*; Horwitz, *Transformation of American Law*; Cavan, *Lewis and Clark*.

9. Williams, *History of the City*, 49; Erickson, ed., *Emigration from Europe*; Cunningham, *Process of Government*; Horsman, *Diplomacy of the New Republic*; Risjord, *Jefferson's America*; Vecoli and Sinke, eds., *Century of European Migrations*; Sellers, *Market Revolution*; Robbins, *Colony and Empire*.

10. Colton, *Western Tourist and Emigrant's Guide*, 51; Lanman, "Summer in the Wilderness," 78. For discussions on Native American land cessions during the nineteenth century, see U.S. Department of the Interior, *Treaties*, and Prucha, *American Indian Treaties*.

11. Curtiss, *Western Portraiture, and Emigrants' Guide*. For comparative interpretations, see Hansen, *Old Fort Snelling*, and Dobak, *Fort Riley*. For discussions of the fur trade in the Upper Northwest, see, for example, Chittenden, *American Fur Trade*; Clayton, "Growth and Economic Significance"; Gilman, "Fur Trade"; Bailyn and Morgan, eds., *Strangers Within the Realm*; Haeger, *John Jacob Astor*; Ruggles, *A Country So Interesting*; and Whelan, "Dakota Indian Economics."

12. In recent years, increasing numbers of historians and historical geographers have drawn on immigrant guidebooks, travel literature, newspapers, diaries, and local histories to enhance our understanding of the cultural landscapes that developed during these nineteenth-century migrations. For contemporary accounts on population movements during the period, see St. John de Crèvecoeur, *Letters from an American Farmer*, 39–40; Tocqueville, *Democracy in America*; Trollope,

Domestic Manners; Mrs. Joseph [Amelia] Ullman, *St. Paul Forty Years Ago* [1896], Mrs. Joseph Ullman Papers [hereafter Ullman Papers]; Hall, *A Lady's Life*. See also Commager, ed., *America in Perspective*; Handlin, ed., *This Was America*; Pratt, *Imperial Eyes*; and Dunlop, *Sixty Miles from Contentment*.

13. Curtiss, *Western Portraiture, and Emigrants' Guide*, 54. Indeed, as George Rogers Taylor argued, "indications seem clear that this entrepreneurial group [involved in planning, organizing, financing, and managing new ventures in the transportation of manufactured goods, especially in the West] at least retained its proportionate share, and probably more, of the increase in wealth and income. It must not be forgotten, however, that risks were great and that there were many failures, especially during the recurrent financial crises." *Transportation Revolution*, 194. Minnesota's early entrepreneurs understood these realities and undertook the risks associated with creating transportation networks precisely because the potential rewards loomed large. See also Cochran, *Frontiers of Change*; Haites, Mak, and Walton, *Western River Transportation*; Horwitz, *Transformation of American Law*; Shaw, *Canals for a Nation*; Licht, *Industrializing America*; Sheriff, *Artificial River*; Glazer, *Cincinnati in 1840*.

14. See Mahoney, *River Towns in the Great West*, and Bigham, *Towns and Villages*.

15. Williams, *History of the City*, 43, 44, 106, 173; Bond, *Minnesota and Its Resources*; Colton, *Western Tourist and Emigrant's Guide*, 49–54; Andreas, *Illustrated Historical Atlas*, 210–12, 256; Ingersol, "Home of Hiawatha." See also North American Fur Trade Conference, *Fur Trade Revisited*.

16. Andreas, *Illustrated Historical Atlas*, 211–12, 256–69; Leslie, "Trip from St. Anthony," 400–402.

17. Blegen, ed., *Unfinished Autobiogra-*

phy, 13, 24; Williams, *History of the City*, 49.

18. Blegen, ed., *Unfinished Autobiography*, 9.

19. Blegen, ed., *Unfinished Autobiography*, 11, 15–16.

20. Andreas, *Illustrated Historical Atlas*, 211–23, 256; Book Draft, Vol. 1, Owens Papers. For an overview of the Indian Removal Act, see Wallace, *Long, Bitter Trail*.

21. Blegen, ed., *Unfinished Autobiography*, 33–36.

22. "Memorial," qtd. in Williams, *History of the City*, 59.

23. Henry Sibley to Ramsay Crooks, President, American Fur Company, New York, 29 September 1837, in Blegen, ed., *Unfinished Autobiography*, 66; Williams, *History of the City*, 48. Prior to 1849, American Indians possessed all but 24 square miles (out of a total 81,259 square miles) of Minnesota's land.

24. Williams, *History of the City*, 160; Andreas, *Illustrated Historical Atlas*, 211–12, 259. See also Gilman, Gilman, and Stultz, *Red River Trails*.

25. "Arrival of Our Delegate," *Pioneer*, 28 April 1849. Social profiles based upon quantitative analyses of U.S. Census Office, *Population Schedules of the Seventh Census of the United States, 1850: Minnesota Territory* [hereafter *1850 Population Schedules*]; *1856 St. Paul Directory; Saint Paul City Directory for 1856–57* [hereafter *1857 St. Paul Directory*], St. Paul, Minnesota, City Directory Collection; U.S. Bureau of the Census, *Schedules of the Minnesota Census of 1857* [hereafter *1857 Population Schedules*]; *Commercial Advertiser Directory for the City of Saint Paul, 1858–59* [hereafter *1858 St. Paul Advertiser*], St. Paul, Minnesota, City Directory Collection; *Commercial Advertiser Directory for Saint Anthony and Minneapolis* (1859) [hereafter *1859 Minneapolis Advertiser*], Minneapolis, Minnesota, City Directory Collection; Wheelock, *Minnesota*; and U.S. Census Office, *Eighth Census of the United States,*

1860: Minnesota Population Schedules [hereafter *1860 Population Schedules*]. Occupational categories based upon industry codes used in Philadelphia Project, *Occupation Dictionary Codebook*, 78–98.

26. Williams, *History of the City*, 64.

27. *Saint Anthony Express* [hereafter *Express*], 27 October 1855; Wheelock, *Minnesota*, 41–83; Williams, ed., *Guide to Minnesota*; Lewis, *Valley of the Mississippi*, 64–83; Andreas, *Illustrated Historical Atlas*, 227–29, 256.

28. Folwell, *History of Minnesota*, 1:454.

29. Kane, *Falls of St. Anthony*, discusses early milling ventures at St. Anthony Falls.

30. Wales, *Sketch of St. Anthony and Minneapolis*.

31. William Forbes 1849–59 correspondence, Cory-Forbes Family Papers [hereafter Cory-Forbes Papers]; February 1856 Invitation to an Anniversary Ball, 28 May 1858 letter of agreement between Forbes, Kittson, and Bailly, and shares in Minnesota State Mutual Fire & Marine Insurance Company, Bailly Papers; analysis of *1850 Population Schedules*, including 9-page preface; *1856 St. Paul Directory; 1858 St. Paul Advertiser; 1860 Population Schedules; Pioneer*, 25 March 1852; James M. Winslow, letter to his brother, 1 June 1851, James M. Winslow and Family Papers [hereafter Winslow Papers]; Flandrau, *Recollections*, 1–102; Assessor's Returns of Taxable Property, St. Paul, Wards 3 & 4, 1868, Ramsey County Records; Andreas, *Illustrated Historical Atlas*, 225, 256, 259, 365–66; Farnsworth, *Early History of St. Paul*; Burnquist, ed., *Minnesota and Its People*, 1:205–30, 291–302.

32. Schumpeter, *Theory of Economic Development*, 296–97. See also Porter and Livesay, *Merchants and Manufacturers*; Atherton, *Frontier Merchant*; Cochran, *Business in American Life* and *Frontiers of Change*; Livesay, *American Made* and "Entrepreneurial Dominance"; and Livesay, ed., *Entrepreneurship*.

33. *1850 Population Schedules.*

34. Flandrau, *Recollections,* 98.

35. Andreas, *Illustrated Historical Atlas,* 211–28, 256, 259; *1850 Population Schedules.*

36. Andreas, *Illustrated Historical Atlas,* 211–28, 256, 259; *1850 Population Schedules.*

37. Williams, *History of the City,* 172.

38. William Hartshorn and Co., St. Paul, 1847–48 General Merchandise and Fur Trade Ledger [hereafter Hartshorn Ledger]; Miscellaneous deeds, Hersey, Staples and Company Papers; 1850–55 Journal, especially accounts with A. L. Larpenteur and Borup & Oakes, William Branch Company, St. Paul; Parker, *Minnesota Handbook,* 22–28; Andreas, *Illustrated Historical Atlas,* 211, 225; Burnquist, ed., *Minnesota and Its People,* 1:216–26; 1849–55 Correspondence, Cory-Forbes Papers; Andreas, *Illustrated Historical Atlas,* 264; *1850 Population Schedules.*

39. Qtd. in Williams, *History of the City,* 178.

40. *1850 Population Schedules.*

41. Qtd. in Williams, *History of the City,* 132.

42. Williams, *History of the City,* 132.

43. Williams, *History of the City,* 149.

44. *1850 Population Schedules,* including narrative.

45. Cobb, comp., *American Railway Guide.*

46. Andreas, *Illustrated Historical Atlas,* 211–23, 256; Book Draft, Vol. 1, 37–98, Owens Papers; "Arrival of Our Delegate," *Pioneer,* 28 April 1849; *1850 Population Schedules.*

47. Qtd. in Williams, *History of the City,* 52, 181. See also *1850 Population Schedules,* including preface, 1–9.

48. *1850 Population Schedules;* Wheelock, *Minnesota;* Williams, ed., *Guide to Minnesota;* Andreas, *Illustrated Historical Atlas,* 227–29, 256.

49. Williams, *History of the City,* 207.

50. Douglas qtd. in *1850 Population Schedules,* preface, vii; Burnquist, ed., *Minnesota and Its People,* 1:225.

51. "Arrival of Our Delegate," *Pioneer,* 28 April 1849.

52. For comparative purposes, see Abbott, *Boosters and Businessmen.*

53. Williams, *History of the City,* 186, 188.

54. Andreas, *Illustrated Historical Atlas,* 210–18. By 1850, U.S. census takers estimated (no doubt liberally) that the whole number of acres under cultivation in Minnesota had reached 1,900. In 1860 those numbers climbed to 556,000, and during 1872 they reached 2.2 million. For a survey of rapid American migrations, see Wiebe, *Opening of American Society.*

55. Williams, *History of the City,* 201; *1850 Population Schedules;* 1849 correspondence, Cory-Forbes Papers.

NOTES TO CHAPTER 2

1. Statistics on population, wealth, and social distributions for the period based on quantitative analyses of *1850 Population Schedules; 1857 Population Schedules; 1857 St. Paul Directory; 1858 St. Paul Advertiser; 1859 Minneapolis Advertiser; 1860 Population Schedules.* See also 1849–54 Receipts, 1855 Bills of Lading, and *Reminiscence,* Fred A. Bill and Family Papers [hereafter Bill Papers]; Wheelock, *Minnesota.*

2. *Bills from the House Files of the Minnesota Territorial Legislature,* 22 October 1849, and *Bills from the Council File of the Minnesota Territorial Legislature,* 26 September 1849, Bailly Papers.

3. Wheelock, *Minnesota,* 147; Book Draft, Vol. 1, Owens Papers.

4. *Pioneer,* 6 June 1850; Parker, *Minnesota Handbook,* 63.

5. Lewis, *Valley of the Mississippi;* Colton, *Western Tourist and Emigrant's Guide,* 49–54; Farnsworth, *Early History of St. Paul,* 1–15; Andreas, *Illustrated Historical Atlas;* Bill, *Navigation Above St. Anthony Falls* [1870], Bill Papers; *St. Paul Forty Years Ago,* Ullman Papers; Peterson, "Early History of Steamboating"; Kunz, *St. Paul,* 10–13.

6. Amelia qtd. in Ullman Papers, 5. See also Bill Papers; *1856 St. Paul Directory*, 1–6.

7. Amelia qtd. in Ullman Papers, 2, 3; Edward Duffield Neill qtd. in *1856 St. Paul Directory*, 4–5; 1850s Correspondence, Bill Papers. During 1847, the Presbyterian Church had posted Neill in Galena, IL, a much more developed and "sophisticated" western river town.

8. Goodhue editorial, *Pioneer*, 28 April 1849; Neill qtd. in *1856 St. Paul Directory*, 5.

9. Amelia qtd. in Ullman Papers, 10, 28; *1856 St. Paul Directory*, narrative.

10. Amelia qtd. in Ullman Papers, 10, 28; *1856 St. Paul Directory*, 4; *Express*, 6 March 1852.

11. Bishop, *Floral Home*, 125; Andrews, *History of St. Paul*.

12. Goodhue qtd. in *Pioneer*, 28 April 1849.

13. Advertisements, *Pioneer*, 1849, MHS Newspaper Collections.

14. *1850 Population Schedules; Express*, 30 August 1851; "Claim Making and Pre-emption," *Republican*, 26 July 1855; Mc-Master, *60 Years on the Upper Mississippi*, 185–92; Bill Papers.

15. Stevens qtd. in *Express*, 27 October 1855; Lewis, *Valley of the Mississippi*, 64–72; *1858 Minneapolis Advertiser*, 2–11; Kane, *Falls of St. Anthony*, 1–11, 30–41.

16. Adam Smith qtd. in U.S. Census Office, *Manufactures of the United States in 1860; Compiled from the Original Returns of the Eighth Census* [hereafter *1860 Census of Manufactures*], iv. See also Smith, *Inquiry Into Nature and Causes*, 1:31–36, 376–427; Franklin Steele correspondence, 1849–51, Franklin Steele Papers [hereafter F. Steele Papers]; McMaster, *60 Years on the Upper Mississippi*, 57–60; *1859 Minneapolis Advertiser*, 2–23; Flandrau, *Recollections*.

17. St. Anthony's population profile analyzed in *1850 Population Schedules*. See also Franklin Steele correspondence, 1849–51, F. Steele Papers; McMaster, *60*

Years on the Upper Mississippi, 57–60; *Minnesotian*, 2 April 1853; *1859 Minneapolis Advertiser*, 2–23; Flandrau, *Recollections*.

18. *Pioneer*, 26 May 1849; *Minnesotian*, 2 April 1853; Smith, *Inquiry Into Nature and Causes*, 1:26–27; *Act To Establish the Territorial Government of Minnesota*, 3 March 1849, Minnesota Territorial Papers; *A Bill to Incorporate the Town of St. Paul in the County of Ramsey*, Bailly Papers; *1850 Population Schedules*.

19. *Pioneer*, 26 July and 16 August 1849 and 25 March 1852; 1849–55 correspondence, Cory-Forbes Papers; list of original directors for insurance company, Bailly Papers; 1868 Assessor's Returns of Taxable Property, MSA; *1850 Population Schedules; 1857 St. Paul Directory; 1858 St. Paul Advertiser; 1860 Population Schedules*; James M. Winslow to his brother, 1 June 1851, Winslow Papers; Flandrau, *Recollections*, 1–102; John B. Gillman to Nelly, 3 February 1856, John B. Gillman Papers [hereafter Gillman Papers]; Andreas, *Illustrated Historical Atlas*, 225, 256, 259, 365–66; Farnsworth, *Early History of St. Paul*.

20. William Forbes business papers, 1849–55, Cory-Forbes Papers; 1849–55 Bills Receivable, Hercules L. Dousman Papers [hereafter Dousman Papers]; *1850 Population Schedules*; newspaper advertisements in *Minnesota Register*, 7 April 1849, and in *Pioneer*, 26 July 1849, 6 June 1850, 3 July 1851, and 25 March and 1 July 1852; Frank B. Cressey, *Reminiscences of His Father*, Frank B. Cressey Family Papers.

21. *Minnesotian*, 2 April 1853; William Forbes business papers, 1849–55, Cory-Forbes Papers; 1849–55 Bills Receivable, Dousman Papers; *1850 Population Schedules*; newspaper advertisements in *Minnesota Register*, 7 April 1849, and in *Pioneer*, 26 July 1849, 6 June 1850, 3 July 1851, and 25 March and 1 July 1852; Flandrau, *Recollections*.

22. *1850 Population Schedules; 1857 St. Paul Directory; 1858 St. Paul Advertiser;*

1860 Census Schedules; Pioneer, 6 June 1850; Wheelock, *Minnesota,* 23–35.

23. William Forbes business papers, 1849–55, Cory-Forbes Papers; *1850 Population Schedules; 1857 St. Paul Directory; 1858 St. Paul Advertiser; 1860 Census Schedules.* See also *Pioneer,* 16 August 1849, 20 February 1850, 20 November 1851; Wheelock, *Minnesota,* 23–35.

24. *1850 Population Schedules; Pioneer,* 28 November 1850; *Express,* 30 August 1851; *1859 Minneapolis Advertiser,* appendix; Ely, "Minnesota: Its Extent"; Wheelock, *Minnesota,* 117–21, 130–45; Andreas, *Illustrated Historical Atlas,* 226–28, 366–69.

25. *Express,* 29 November 1851; *Republican,* 26 July 1855. See also Franklin Steele correspondence, 1849–51, F. Steele Papers; McMaster, *60 Years on the Upper Mississippi,* 57–60; *1859 Minneapolis Advertiser,* 2–23; Certificates for the Dakota Land Company (ten shares @ $100/), Traverse des Sioux Land Co. lot purchases (58 lots), *Recollections,* Legal Register, Charles E. Flandrau Papers [hereafter Flandrau Papers]; White, et al., comp., *Minnesota Votes,* 1–7, 11, 65–67, 153–54.

26. *Pioneer,* 28 April 1849.

27. *Express,* 28 February 1852; Financial Papers, Isaac Crowe Papers [hereafter Crowe Papers]. See also Smith, *Inquiry Into Nature and Causes,* 2:758–88.

28. 1849–55 correspondence, Cory-Forbes Papers. For comparative purposes, see, for example, Johnson, *Shopkeeper's Millennium.*

29. Goodhue editorial, *Pioneer,* 3 July 1851. See also 1849–55 correspondence, Cory-Forbes Papers; *Pioneer,* 25 March 1852; James Winslow to his brother, 1 June 1851, Winslow Papers; Flandrau, *Recollections,* 1–102; Farnsworth, *Early History of St. Paul;* John B. to Nelly, 3 February 1856, Gillman Papers.

30. *Pioneer,* 3 July and 4 September 1851 and 29 July 1852. See also Flandrau, *Recollections.*

31. *Pioneer,* 6 March and 1 July 1852.

32. *1850 Population Schedules; 1857 St. Paul Directory; 1857 Population Schedules; 1858 St. Paul Advertiser;* 1868 Property Assessment Returns, MSA; Farnsworth, *Early History of St. Paul.*

33. *1850 Population Schedules;* "Mr. Rice and the Land Sales," *Minnesotian,* 7 September 1855; Richard Chute to John S. Lovejoy, 15 November 1856, F. Steele Papers; *Reminiscences,* Bill Papers; Andreas, *Illustrated Historical Atlas,* 224–28, 268, 366–69; *1859 Minneapolis Advertiser.*

34. *Express,* 6 March 1852; *Pioneer,* 3 April 1852; *1857 St. Paul Directory.*

35. *Express,* 6 March 1852; *Pioneer,* 3 April 1852; *1857 St. Paul Directory.*

36. Sedgewick, "Great Excursion"; Babcock, "Rails West"; *1860 Census of Manufactures; Pioneer,* 6 June 1850 and 6 March 1852.

37. Sedgewick, "Great Excursion"; Babcock, "Rails West"; *1860 Census of Manufactures; Pioneer,* 6 June 1850 and 6 March 1852.

38. Cobb, comp., *American Railway Guide;* Ely, "Minnesota: Its Extent"; *Pioneer,* 13 January 1853; "Where People Come From and Where They Are Going," *Minnesotian,* 23 November 1855; *Express,* 22 March 1856; 1850s correspondence, Bill Papers; Book Draft, Vols. 1 and 2, Owens Papers; 1855–59 correspondence, *Early Minnesota History,* 21–28, William Pitt Murray Papers [hereafter Murray Papers]; Henry Rice from Washington, 8 July 1857, Henry Mower Rice Papers [hereafter Rice Papers]; analyses of *1858 St. Paul Advertiser, 1859 Minneapolis Advertiser, 1860 Population Schedules;* Wheelock, *Minnesota.*

39. Cobb, comp., *American Railway Guide.*

40. The *Pioneer,* 6 March 1852, changed and emphasized the wording, "*come away from the city—come to the West—come to Minnesota!*" See also *Pioneer,* 16 July 1852, and Register of Catholic Baptisms, Cathedral of St. Paul Papers [hereafter Cathedral Papers].

41. *1857 Population Schedules;* Holmquist, ed., *They Chose Minnesota,* 1–14.
42. *Minnesotian,* 26 July and 2 September 1855; Williams, ed., *Guide to Minnesota;* Wheelock, *Minnesota,* 106–7.
43. Bishop, *Floral Home,* 125.
44. Amelia qtd. in Ullman Papers, 4.
45. Ullman Papers, 1–10 (Amelia qtd., 2–3); 1850s Receipts and General Accounts, Rose Brothers Fur Company Records [hereafter Rose Records].
46. Amelia qtd. in Ullman Papers, 1, 2–3, 10–11; Abby Fuller to her niece, 1854, Abby Fuller Abbe Papers [hereafter Abbe Papers].
47. Amelia qtd. in Ullman Papers, 3; "Pioneer" qtd. in Williams, *History of the City,* 201. See also 1854–57 Miscellaneous Deeds, Mortgages, and Contracts, 1854–55 Accounts, William Fuson Davidson Papers [hereafter Davidson Papers]; 1850s correspondence and *Reminiscence,* Bill Papers.
48. Amelia qtd. in Ullman Papers, 16; Sarah to Lizzie, 2 September 1855, Abbe Papers; John A. McAuley Day Book, March-August 1855, John A. McAuley Account Books [hereafter McAuley Papers].
49. Amelia qtd. in Ullman Papers, 29, 16; 1850s correspondence, Bill Papers; 1854–57 Steamboat Passes and Tickets, Deeds, Mortgages and Contracts, and Cargo and Passenger Accounts, Davidson Papers; *Early Minnesota History,* 5–28, Murray Papers; "A Trip to Minnesota," *Boston Post,* 25 October 1856, *Boston Post* extracts, MHS Newspaper Collections; McMaster, *60 Years on the Upper Mississippi,* 185–92; Andreas, *Illustrated Historical Atlas,* 226.
50. Amelia qtd. in Ullman Papers, 24–25; Sarah to Lizzie, 2 September 1855, Abbe Papers; 1855 Account Book, McAuley Papers; *Reminiscences,* Bass Papers; 1853–57 Tax Receipts, Harriet B. Corbett and Family Papers; Rebecca Cathcart to Alexander Cathcart while he attends to business in the East during

1855–56, Alexander Henry Cathcart and Family Papers [hereafter Cathcart Papers]; Gillman, St. Paul, to wife Helen (Nelly) in Dansville, NY, 28 October 1855, 11 May 1856, Gillman Papers; Sister in Bangor, ME, to Harriet Godfrey, 20 March 1854, Ard Godfrey and Family Papers [hereafter Godfrey Papers].
51. 1849–55 correspondence, Cory-Forbes Papers; Flandrau, *Recollections;* advertisements in *Pioneer,* 1849–51, and in *Express,* 1851, MHS Newspapers Collections; Wheelock, *Minnesota,* 23–35.
52. *1850 Population Schedules; 1857 Population Schedules; 1856 St. Paul Directory; 1857 St. Paul Directory; 1858 St. Paul Advertiser; 1860 Population Schedules.* See also Carrie Thompson Memo Book [ca. 1827–87], Horace Thompson and Family Papers; J. E. Thompson obituary, 28 May 1876, Francis Byron Clark and Family Papers; Andreas, *Illustrated Historical Atlas,* 215–16, 266; *Minnesotian,* 2 April 1853.
53. Henry M. Dodge to Honorable P. B. Barbeau, 9 February 1856, Henry M. Dodge Papers [hereafter Dodge Papers]; *1856 St. Paul Directory; 1858 St. Paul Advertiser; 1860 Population Schedules;* Wheelock, *Minnesota.*
54. *1850 Population Schedules;* 1850s Correspondence, Bill Papers; David D. Merrill to "All Whom It May Concern," 3 May 1853, St. Paul First Baptist Church Papers [hereafter First Baptist Papers]; Day Book, March-August 1855, and 1855 Account Book, McAuley Papers; *1856 St. Paul Directory; 1860 Population Schedules;* Wheelock, *Minnesota;* Baldwin School, *Catalogues* [1854]; *Macalester College* [ca. 1870], F. Steele Papers; Benjamin Drew Private School Journal, 4–5, 12, 14, 22–24, Benjamin Drew Papers [hereafter Drew Papers]; *Minnesotian,* 2 April 1853 and 7 September 1855; *Pioneer,* 6 June 1854; Burnquist, ed., *Minnesota and Its People,* 1:86–89; Andreas, *Illustrated Historical Atlas,* 225, 256, 258ff; Andrews, *History of St. Paul;* 1854 correspondence and *Account of a*

Trip West, Abbe Papers; Ullman Papers; 1855–56 business papers and correspondence, Cathcart Papers; McMaster, *60 Years on the Upper Mississippi;* Receipts of I. & E. Rose, 1856 Day Book, 1855 General Accounts, Rose Records; 1853–55 American Fur Company correspondence and 1852–65 Bills Receivable, Dousman Papers; 1849–55 correspondence with Henry Rice, Henry H. Sibley, Josiah Snelling, Norman Kittson, and Franklin Steele, Bailly Papers; *History of the City of St. Paul,* James C. Burbank Papers [hereafter J. C. Burbank Papers]; List of the Pioneer Guard elected officers and stockholders of the St. Paul Fire & Marine Insurance Company, Henry Clay Burbank Papers [hereafter H. C. Burbank Papers]; Bills of Lading and Receipts, Bill Papers; Inventory of Personal and Real Estate, dated 1 February 1871, John Steele and Family Papers [hereafter J. Steele Papers]; *Acts of Incorporation and Standing Rules of the Common Council* [St. Paul, 1856], Ramsey County Records, MSA; *1857 Population Schedules; 1857 St. Paul Directory; 1858 St. Paul Advertiser.*

55. Amelia qtd. in Ullman Papers, 10–11.

56. 1849–55 Correspondence and Records for the Northwestern Express Company and J. C. & H. C. Burbank, Commission Merchants, J. C. Burbank Papers; 1849–55 William Forbes business papers and correspondence, Cory-Forbes Papers.

57. *Pioneer,* 6 and 9 June 1854; Parker, *Minnesota Handbook.*

58. 1849–55 Correspondence and Records for the Northwestern Express Company and J. C. & H. C. Burbank, Commission Merchants, J. C. Burbank Papers; lease agreement between Franklin Steele and others and J. C. Burbank, for wharf boat at St. Paul's upper landing, 22 March 1854, General Government Roads in Minnesota and Wisconsin, September 1855, F. Steele Papers.

59. 1852 Correspondence with S. H. Sargent, H. M. Rice, Alexander Wilkin, and David Olmstead, Hollingshead & Becker, St. Paul, Isaac Atwater, St. Anthony Mill Company, and A. Godfrey & Co., St. Anthony, and Hercules Dousman, Prairie du Chien, WI, F. Steele Papers; *1850 Population Schedules* and newspaper advertisements in *Express,* 29 November 1851 and 28 February 1852; Wales, *Sketch of St. Anthony and Minneapolis,* 1–6; *1859 Minneapolis Advertiser,* 15–21; Hartshorn Ledger; McMaster, *60 Years on the Upper Mississippi;* Andreas, *Illustrated Historical Atlas,* 216–18, 227–29; Folwell, *History of Minnesota,* 1:224–29, 251. For a detailed account of Franklin Steele's attempts to build up the falls and the problems he and others encountered during the 1850s, see Kane, *Falls of St. Anthony,* 1–29, and "Papers of John Harrington Stevens." See also Burnquist, ed., *Minnesota and Its People,* 1:454–58; Clayton, "Growth and Economic Significance."

60. 1849–55 Bills Receivable, Dousman Papers; *Express,* 30 August 1851; *Minnesotian,* 26 July 1855; *1850 Population Schedules; 1859 Minneapolis Advertiser,* appendix; Ely, "Minnesota: Its Extent"; Wheelock, *Minnesota,* 117–21, 130–45; Parker, *Minnesota Handbook,* 62–63; "Macalester College" subscription lists, Mississippi Bridge articles of incorporation, 22 December 1854, Henry Hastings Sibley to Franklin Steele, 18 February 1855, Saint Anthony Falls Water Power Company articles of incorporation, 26 February 1856, and County and City (Scrip) Tax Receipts for 1857, F. Steele Papers.

The Fort Snelling Military Reserve land sale provides an excellent example of the important role political friends played in early days. See H. M. Rice, Confidential to Steele, 6 April 1857, about the impending sale of Fort Snelling reserve; the 8 September 1857 agreement between Franklin and Annie Steele and Richard

Chute, St. Anthony, and John Prince, St. Paul, with the Steeles lending both Chute and Prince $50,000 for property in the Fort Snelling reserve; 1851 Fort Snelling correspondence and business papers between Franklin Steele and Ard Godfrey and other investors in Wisconsin, Missouri, and Iowa, including Hercules Dousman; and Henry Sibley to Steele, 18 February 1855, F. Steele Papers. In addition, see H. G. Emery, Bangor, ME, to Ard Godfrey, 7 January 1850, Godfrey Papers; Mail Book of Croffit & Clark, St. Anthony, C. H. Clark and Family Papers [hereafter C. H. Clark Papers]; Wilson, *Minneapolis and St. Anthony*, 5-6; Andreas, *Illustrated Historical Atlas*, 256; *1850 Population Schedules; 1859 Minneapolis Advertiser*, narrative and 15-18.

61. Henry Hastings Sibley to Franklin Steele, 18 February 1855, Confidential from William Hollingshead, St. Paul, to Franklin Steele, 24 May 1855, Mississippi Bridge articles of incorporation, 22 December 1854, Agreement between Franklin Steele, St. Anthony, and J. C. Burbank and C. J. Whitney, St. Paul, 22 December 1854, County and City (Scrip) Tax Receipts for 1857, Promissory notes from Franklin Steele to Henry Rice, 8 and 25 August 1857, and J. H. Stevens, St. Paul, to Franklin Steele, 10 January 1860, F. Steele Papers; J. B. Cunningham, New York, to Ard Godfrey, 29 March 1855, Godfrey Papers; *Express*, 24 January 1855; *Minnesotian*, 26 July 1855; Andreas, *Illustrated Historical Atlas*, 224-26, 256, 269; 1857 Financial Papers, Crowe Papers; Book Draft, Vol. 1, 44-61, Owens Papers.

62. Henry Hastings Sibley to Franklin Steele, 18 February 1855, Confidential from William Hollingshead, St. Paul, to Franklin Steele, 24 May 1855, Mississippi Bridge articles of incorporation, 22 December 1854, Agreement between Franklin Steele, St. Anthony, and J. C. Burbank and C. J. Whitney, St. Paul, 22 December 1854, County and City (Scrip)

Tax Receipts for 1857, Promissory notes from Franklin Steele to Henry Rice, 8 and 25 August 1857, and J. H. Stevens, St. Paul, to Franklin Steele, 10 January 1860, F. Steele Papers; J. B. Cunningham, New York, to Ard Godfrey, 29 March 1855, Godfrey Papers; *Express*, 24 January 1855; *Minnesotian*, 26 July 1855; Andreas, *Illustrated Historical Atlas*, 224-26, 256, 269; 1857 Financial Papers, Crowe Papers; Book Draft, Vol. 1, 44-61, Owens Papers.

63. Wheelock, *Minnesota*, 107-8; McMaster, *60 Years on the Upper Mississippi*, 185-92.

64. Henry Whipple, *Autobiography*, 13. See also Henry B. Whipple to North Western Express Company, 17 November 1859, and Whipple to North Western Express, 23 April 1860, Henry B. Whipple and Family Papers [hereafter Whipple Papers]; Ullman Papers; Bill Papers; Colton, *Western Tourist and Emigrant's Guide*, 49-54; Territorial papers, Murray Papers; 1855 St. Paul City tax receipts, for the home missionary, St. Paul Central Presbyterian Church, John G. Riheldaffer and Family Papers [hereafter Riheldaffer Papers]; David D. Merrill to his congregation, 3 May 1853, First Baptist Papers; Register of Catholic Baptisms, 1854-56, Cathedral Papers; John D. Pope, *Autobiography*, n.d., 27-29, John D. Pope Papers [hereafter Pope Papers]; Wheelock, *Minnesota*, 1-111, 122-33; Andreas, *Illustrated Historical Atlas*, 256; Farnsworth, *Early History of St. Paul*, 1-15; Cobb, comp., *American Railway Guide*; Ely, "Minnesota: Its Extent"; "Where People Come From and Where They Are Going," *Minnesotian*, 23 November 1855 (see also 30 June 1855); *Express*, 22 March 1856.

65. *1850 Population Schedules; 1857 Population Schedules;* Parker, *Minnesota Handbook*.

66. Bishop, *Floral Home*, 125; *Pioneer*, 21 June 1856; *Minnesotian*, 15 November 1856; *Saint Paul Financial, Real Estate, and Railroad Advertiser* [hereafter *Railroad*

Advertiser], 29 November 1856 and 21 February 1857; Andrews, *History of St. Paul.*
67. Wheelock, *Minnesota*, 122–34, 147.
68. Babcock, "Rails West," 141; Cobb, comp., *American Railway Guide;* Book Draft, Vols. 1 and 2, Owens Papers; 1855 Correspondence and *Early Minnesota History*, 21–28, Murray Papers; Parker, *Minnesota Handbook;* Henry Rice from Washington, 8 July 1857, Rice Papers.

NOTES TO CHAPTER 3
1. Babcock, "Rails West," 141; Cobb, comp., *American Railway Guide;* Minnesota Constitutional Convention, *Debates and Proceedings;* Book Draft, Vols. 1 and 2, Owens Papers; 1855 Correspondence and *Early Minnesota History*, 21–28, Murray Papers; Parker, *Minnesota Handbook;* Henry Rice from Washington, 8 July 1857, Rice Papers.
2. *Minnesota Gazetteer and Business Directory* (1865) [hereafter *1865 Business Directory*]; Pates and Shrief, *International Hotel Guide Book.*
3. *1857 St. Paul Directory*, 2–5 and advertisements; "What Strangers Say of St. Paul," signed by Invisible, and "Where the People Come From and Where They Are Going," *Minnesotian*, 30 June and 23 November 1855; "Loans" advertised from Boston, New York, Philadelphia, Chicago, Milwaukee, St. Louis, and elsewhere in *Pioneer, Minnesotian,* and *Express*, 1853–57, MHS Newspaper Collections; Western Emigration Agency, Chicago, to Henry H. Sibley, Governor of the State of Minnesota, 2 May 1859, Henry Hastings Sibley Papers [hereafter Sibley Papers]; Holmquist, ed., *They Chose Minnesota*, 1–14.
4. *1850 Population Schedules; 1857 Population Schedules;* Ely, "Minnesota: Its Extent"; Wilson, *Minneapolis and St. Anthony;* Pates and Shrief, *International Hotel Guide Book.*
5. Amelia qtd. in Ullman Papers, 29. See also Lewis, *Valley of the Mississippi;*

Railroad Advertiser, 29 November 1856; *Express*, 22 March and 21 June 1856; *Minnesotian*, 15 November 1856; Parker, *Minnesota Handbook;* Wheelock, *Minnesota*, 106–7; *1850 Population Schedules; 1857 Population Schedules; 1858 St. Paul Advertiser; 1859 Minneapolis Advertiser; 1860 Population Schedules.*
6. Qtd. in "Chicago and St. Louis: Which Shall Secure the Trade of Minnesota?" *Express*, 22 March 1856; excerpts from "A Trip to Galena," *Express*, 21 June 1856; "Correspondence of the Journal, Letters from Out West No. 3," *Boston Daily Journal* extracts, MHS Newspaper Collections.
7. Chandler, *Visible Hand*, 81–121.
8. *1857 St. Paul Directory; 1858 St. Paul Advertiser; 1859 Minneapolis Advertiser;* Wheelock, *Minnesota*, 154–58; Chandler, *Visible Hand*, 81–121.
9. *Railroad Advertiser*, 29 November 1856; *Express*, 22 March and 21 June 1856; *Minnesotian*, 15 November 1856; Wheelock, *Minnesota*, 106–7.
10. 1855–61 Bills of Lading, Receipts, and *Reminiscence*, Bill Papers; McMaster, *60 Years on the Upper Mississippi.*
11. 1854–56 Miscellaneous Deeds, Mortgages, and Contracts, 1861 Ledger and 1857–72 Minute Book, LaCrosse and Minnesota Steam Packet Co., 1859–61 Minute Book, Marine Bank of St. Paul, and Accounts (promissory notes signed for property, etc.), Davidson Papers; *Navigation Above St. Anthony Falls* and Miscellaneous Articles, Bill Papers; Correspondence and Receipts with J. C. & H. C. Burbank & Co., Flandrau Papers; Pates and Shrief, *International Hotel Guide Book;* McMaster, *60 Years on the Upper Mississippi.*
12. "The North-Western Express Company," *Minnesotian*, 21 March 1857. See also 1858 Correspondence and Receipts, J. C. & H. C. Burbank & Co., Flandrau Papers; *Red River of the North*, Bill Papers; 1849–62 Papers, J. C. Burbank Papers.

13. Papers and Business Correspondence, J. C. Burbank Papers; 1858 Correspondence and Receipts, J. C. & H. C. Burbank & Co., Flandrau Papers; *Red River of the North*, Bill Papers.

14. *Minnesotian*, 7 February and 5 May 1857; *Express*, 12 March 1856; *Republican*, 28 June and 26 July 1855; *1856 St. Paul Directory*; *1859 Minneapolis Advertiser*; Wheelock, *Minnesota*, 105-8; Wales, *Sketch of St. Anthony and Minneapolis*; David Merritt to son Benjamin, 26 March 1857, Benjamin Merritt Papers [hereafter Merritt Papers]; Sarah Cavender's February 1857 journal, Elisha D. K. Randall Papers [hereafter Randall Papers]; Ullman Papers, 3; Babcock, "Rails West."

15. *Minnesotian*, 7 February and 5 May 1857; *Express*, 12 March 1856; *Republican*, 28 June and 26 July 1855; *1856 St. Paul Directory*; *1859 Minneapolis Advertiser*; Wheelock, *Minnesota*, 105-8; Wales, *Sketch of St. Anthony and Minneapolis*; David Merritt to son Benjamin, 26 March 1857, Merritt Papers; Sarah Cavender's February 1857 journal, Randall Papers; Ullman Papers, 3; Babcock, "Rails West."

16. *1856 St. Paul Directory*, 21. See also *1857 Population Schedules; 1858 St. Paul Advertiser*; Pates and Shrief, *International Hotel Guide Book*; Parker, *Minnesota Handbook*; and Wheelock, *Minnesota*, 106-7. One Bostonian snob offered a slightly different version of St. Paul's boom: "Folks in the Eastern States run the idea generally that to get rid of [their own] hard times, all they have to do is to come *out West*, and somebody will meet them on the levee as soon as they have crossed the *Mississippi*, take them by the hand, and *lead them on to fortune and fame*." However, he sneered, "People meet them at the levee, but getting rich is quite another affair, for of all the men with whom I am acquainted at the West, not one has made a fortune . . . aside from

speculation in lands." 17 September 1857, *Boston Daily Post*.

17. Farnsworth, *Early History of St. Paul*, 1-15. See also Lewis, *Valley of the Mississippi*; Colton, *Western Tourist and Emigrant's Guide; 7th Anniversary History*, Pope Papers; Ullman Papers, 18-25; Wheelock, *Minnesota*, 23-25.

18. 1854-56 Miscellaneous Deeds, Mortgages, and Contracts, 1861 Ledger and 1857-72 Minute Book, LaCrosse and Minnesota Steam Packet Co., 1859-61 Minute Book, Marine Bank of St. Paul, and Accounts (promissory notes signed for property, etc.), Davidson Papers; *Red River of the North*, Bill Papers; *1857 St. Paul Directory*; *1858 St. Paul Advertiser*; *1860 Population Schedules*; Pates and Shrief, *International Hotel Guide Book*; McMaster, *60 Years on the Upper Mississippi*; Holmquist, ed., *They Chose Minnesota*, 153-84.

19. *1857 Population Schedules; 1860 Population Schedules*; Holmquist, ed., *They Chose Minnesota*, 130-52.

20. *7th Anniversary History*, Pope Papers; *1860 Population Schedules*; *1857 St. Paul Directory*; *1858 St. Paul Advertiser*; *1859 Minneapolis Advertiser*; Wheelock, *Minnesota*; Ullman Papers, 18-25.

21. 1856-61 Correspondence and Miscellaneous Papers, James J. Hill Papers, General Correspondence [hereafter JJH GC]; comparisons between *1857 Population Schedules*, *1857 St. Paul Directory*, *1858 St. Paul Advertiser*, *1860 Population Schedules*, and *1865 Business Directory*.

22. 1856-61 Correspondence and Miscellaneous Papers, JJH GC; comparisons between *1857 Population Schedules*, *1857 St. Paul Directory*, *1858 St. Paul Advertiser*, *1860 Population Schedules*, and *1865 Business Directory*.

23. *1857 St. Paul Directory* narratives; *1857 Population Schedules; 1858 St. Paul Advertiser; 1860 Population Schedules*.

24. Minnesota and Pacific Railroad Company shares, 31 July 1858, Andrew

Ryan McGill and Family Papers; William Pitt Murray 1855–65 correspondence, *Early Minnesota History,* 21–28, 1854–67 Letterbook, Murray Papers; Henry M. Rice 1856–57 Letterpress Book, Rice Papers; *1857 Population Schedules; 1857 St. Paul Directory; 1858 St. Paul Advertiser; 1859 Minneapolis Advertiser; 1860 Population Schedules;* White, et al., comp., *Minnesota Votes,* 1–7, 11, 65–67, 153–54.

25. *1857 St. Paul Directory,* narrative; George G. to Lizzie Davis, 24 July 1869, George Aaron Chapin and Family Papers [hereafter Chapin Papers]. See also data on Young Men's Christian Association, William F. Mason and Family Papers [hereafter Mason Papers]; St. Paul Turners Papers; and 1859–61 St. Anthony and Minneapolis Typographical Union Records, 1859 Printers Union President's Journal, Josiah Blodgett Chaney and Family Papers. For business influences on religious life in St. Paul–Minneapolis during the period, see also James F. Heyward deed, 1858, and mortgage deed to the German Lutheran Trinity Church, 7 April 1860, Trinity Lutheran Church, St. Paul, Records; Edward Eggleston, St. Paul, to his wife, 11 April 1858 and from St. Anthony, 6 May 1862, Edward Eggleston Papers; St. Paul City tax receipts, 1855–60, for the home missionary, St. Paul Central Presbyterian Church, Riheldaffer Papers; 1852–59 Certificates of Transfer, 1857 Annual Meeting, church history by John D. Pope, n.d., 3–6, 1858 Board of Trustees Minute Book, and letter from David D. Merrill to his congregation, 3 May 1853, First Baptist Papers; Register of Catholic Baptisms, 1854–56, Cathedral Papers; Lewis, *History of House of Hope,* 1–7; George Street Biscoe letters to his daughter Ellen, 25 August 1860 and 22 April 1862, George Street Biscoe and Family Papers; 1857 Mount Zion incorporation, Mount Zion Hebrew Congregation, St. Paul, Papers; Henry B. Whipple to Banking House of Dana and White, St. Paul,

22 October 1859, to North Western Express Company, 17 November 1859, 23 April 1860, 23 February, 12 April, and 13 August 1861, Whipple Papers; *Autobiography,* 27–29, Pope Papers.

26. Amelia qtd. in Ullman Papers, 5, emphasis added; *1857 St. Paul Directory,* banking and loan advertisements.

27. *Financial and Real Estate Advertiser,* 16 February 1855; Parker, *Minnesota Handbook,* 1–28, 62–63; *1856 Business Directory; 1857 St. Paul Directory.*

28. Amelia qtd. in Ullman Papers, 23. See also 1854–58 Plat Maps, John D. Ludden Papers [hereafter Ludden Papers]; Brother in Keesville, NY, to Ebenezer Brewer Mattocks, 5 November 1857, 15 June 1858, 11 April 1859, and from his mother, 6 February 1861, Ebenezer Brewer Mattocks and Family Papers [hereafter Mattocks Papers]; John N. Treadwell, hardware store bookkeeper, to friend Bush, 30 July 1858, John N. Treadwell Papers [hereafter Treadwell Papers]; Chandler B. Adams 1857 Diary entries, Chandler B. Adams Papers; "A Brief Story of Saint Paul's NEW-Old Store, Field-Schlick," Field-Schlick Records; *1857 St. Paul Directory; 1858 St. Paul Advertiser; 1859 Minneapolis Advertiser;* Wheelock, *Minnesota; 1860 Population Schedules.*

29. Rice to Franklin Steele, 27 May 1861, F. Steele Papers. See also Ullman Papers, 22; comparison of *1850 Population Schedules* and *1860 Population Schedules;* and J. K. Mellin, Minneapolis, to Charles Clark, St. Paul, 31 March 1858, C. H. Clark Papers.

30. St. Paul, City of, *Acts of Incorporation;* St. Paul Common Council, *Charters and Ordinances.*

31. *Macalester College* [ca. 1870], F. Steele Papers; St. Paul Board of Education, *Public School System;* Baldwin School, *Catalogues* [1854]; Benjamin Drew Private School Journal, 4–5, 12, 14, 22–24, Drew Papers.

32. 1854–58 Plat Maps, Ludden Papers;

Wheelock, *Minnesota*, 81–83; *1857 St. Paul Directory*.

33. Wales, *Sketch of St. Anthony and Minneapolis; 1860 Population Schedules* (mean real and personal property values aggregated at $565 per person in St. Anthony, $537 in Minneapolis, and $1,213 in St. Paul).

34. Wales, *Sketch of St. Anthony and Minneapolis;* 1852–65 Bills Receivable, Dousman Papers; *Act of the Legislative Assembly of the Territory of Minnesota, Establishing Saint Anthony Falls Water Power Company*, 26 February 1856, and Rice to Steele, 27 May 1861, F. Steele Papers; *1850 Population Schedules; 1860 Population Schedules*.

35. Andreas, *Illustrated Historical Atlas*, 228, 268; *Biographical Dictionary*, 172–73, 816–18, 864–70, 910–13, 1018–23; Kane, *Falls of St. Anthony*, 30–61.

36. Wales, *Sketch of St. Anthony and Minneapolis;* St. Anthony Falls Water Power Company correspondence, F. Steele Papers.

37. Richard Chute to John S. Lovejoy, 15 November 1856, F. Steele Papers; 1852–65 Bills Receivable, Dousman Papers; Ramsey County Auditor, *Delinquent Tax Sale Record, 1859*, MSA; Andreas, *Illustrated Historical Atlas*, 268; "The Growth of St. Anthony," *Express*, 29 November 1851; "Minnesota As It Is—No. 11, Expense of Living," 7 July 1855 and "Minnesota As It Is—No. 13," 26 July 1855, *Republican;* Wales, *Sketch of St. Anthony and Minneapolis;* 1858–61 St. Paul City Bond Record, St. Paul Comptroller and Miscellaneous Records, MSA; Holmquist, ed., *They Chose Minnesota*, 55–72, 130–84; *1857 Population Schedules; 1859 Minneapolis Advertiser; 1860 Population Schedules*.

38. Richard Chute to John S. Lovejoy, 15 November 1856, F. Steele Papers; 1852–65 Bills Receivable, Dousman Papers; Ramsey County Auditor, *Delinquent Tax Sale Record, 1859*, MSA; Andreas, *Illustrated Historical Atlas*, 268; "The Growth

of St. Anthony," *Express*, 29 November 1851; "Minnesota As It Is—No. 11, Expense of Living," 7 July 1855 and "Minnesota As It Is—No. 13," 26 July 1855, *Republican;* Wales, *Sketch of St. Anthony and Minneapolis;* 1858–61 St. Paul City Bond Record, St. Paul Comptroller and Miscellaneous Records, MSA; Holmquist, ed., *They Chose Minnesota*, 55–72, 130–84; *1857 Population Schedules; 1859 Minneapolis Advertiser; 1860 Population Schedules*.

39. *1865 Business Directory;* Wales, *Sketch of St. Anthony and Minneapolis;* Confidential from Henry M. Rice to Franklin Steele, 28 August 1865, Richard Chute to Steele, 27 September 1865, F. Steele Papers; Lucian Putnam, Minneapolis lumber merchant, to George Moore, 27 March 1866, George Nelson Moore Papers [hereafter Moore Papers]; Andreas, *Illustrated Historical Atlas*, 228, 268; State of Minnesota, County of Hennepin, District Court, Fourth Judicial District, *The St. Anthony Falls Water Power Company, plaintiff, vs. The City of Minneapolis, defendant* [1882], James J. Hill Papers [hereafter JJHP]; *Biographical Dictionary*, 172–73, 816–18, 864–70, 910–13, 1018–23. For a detailed account of the varying business strategies employed by the Minneapolis and St. Anthony interests, as well as the ways in which each company transformed the waterfall, see Kane, *Falls of St. Anthony*.

40. *1859 Minneapolis Advertiser; 1860 Population Schedules*. See also 1856 Letter introducing William Dean, to John S. Pillsbury, William Blake Dean and Family Papers; *1865 Business Directory; Biographical Dictionary*, 172–73, 816–18, 864–70, 910–13, 1018–23; *Reminiscences*, Simeon Pearl Folsom Papers [hereafter Folsom Papers]; Kane, *Falls of St. Anthony*, 30–61.

41. *1859 Minneapolis Advertiser; 1860 Population Schedules*. See also 1856 Letter introducing William Dean, to John S. Pillsbury, William Blake Dean and Fam-

ily Papers; *1865 Business Directory; Biographical Dictionary,* 172–73, 816–18, 864–70, 910–13, 1018–23; *Reminiscences,* Folsom Papers; Kane, *Falls of St. Anthony,* 30–61.

42. *Railroad Advertiser,* 16 February 1855; *1857 Population Schedules; 1858 St. Paul Advertiser; 1859 Minneapolis Advertiser; 1860 Population Schedules;* Wheelock, *Minnesota; Minnesotian,* 14 January 1854; *Real Estate Advertiser,* 16 and 23 February 1855; Letters to Charles Clark from J. K. Mellin, Minneapolis, 31 March 1858, from Charles Schaffler of Le Sueur, 14 January 1859, from Rob Robinson, Portland, OR, 10 July 1859, and from Fred P. Moseley, New York, November 1860, C. H. Clark Papers; Henry M. Dodge to the Honorable P. B. Barbeau, 9 February 1856, Dodge Papers; Mark A. Hoyt Diary, 19 May 1862, John Franklin Hoyt and Family Papers [hereafter Hoyt Papers]; "Memorandum of Doubtful Accounts," in 1859–64 Cash Book, Mason Papers; Sarah Cavender's School Manuscript, December 1857, Randall Papers; 1850–65 letters, Merritt Papers; Letters from his brother in Keesville, NY, 15 November 1857–7 May 1861, Mattocks Papers; Wescott Wilkin to his Brother Alex, 24 January 1858, Alexander Wilkin and Family Papers [hereafter Wilkin Papers]; Letter, 30 July 1858, Treadwell Papers; Editions of literary society of St. Paul paper readings, 22 October, 5 and 19 November, and 31 December 1857, 14 January 1858, Philecclesian Society Papers [hereafter Philecclesian Papers]; Richard Chute to Franklin Steele, St. Anthony Falls Water Power Company, 15 November 1856, William A. Croffitt to Steele, 30 September 1857, Hercules Dousman to Steele, 18 July 1858, F. Steele Papers; Parker, *Minnesota Handbook.*

43. Lewis, *Valley of the Mississippi; 1857 St. Paul Directory; 1858 St. Paul Advertiser; 1859 Minneapolis Advertiser; Railroad Advertiser,* 29 November 1856; *Express,* 22

March, 21 June, and 15 November 1856; William Haywood "Circular," *Minnesotian,* 7 February 1857; "Railroads" and "The Railroad Grant," *Minnesotian,* 5 May 1857.

44. Lewis, *Valley of the Mississippi; 1857 St. Paul Directory; 1858 St. Paul Advertiser; 1859 Minneapolis Advertiser; Railroad Advertiser,* 29 November 1856; *Express,* 22 March, 21 June, and 15 November 1856; William Haywood "Circular," *Minnesotian,* 7 February 1857; "Railroads" and "The Railroad Grant," *Minnesotian,* 5 May 1857.

45. Donnelly, *Emigrant Aid Journal,* 4 July 1857.

46. *Winona Republican,* 5 May 1857; "Railroad Meeting—Great Enthusiasm" and "Rail Road Grants—How Preemptions Along the Line of Roads are Affected," *Pioneer,* 27 and 28 March 1857.

47. David M. Merritt to Benjamin Merritt, 26 March 1857, Merritt Papers; Gillman to Nellie, 28 October 1855, Gillman Papers.

48. David M. Merritt to Benjamin Merritt, 26 March 1857, to son Benjamin and sister Sarah, 26 October and 14 December 1857, Merritt Papers; "Railroads," "Railroad Land Grants—A Minnesota Policy," and "Railroad Companies," *Railroad Advertiser,* 26 November 1856, 25 April and 2 May 1857; Lizzie Fuller to sister Abby, 9 June and 5 July 1856, Abbe Papers; Truman White to Sister Helen, 10 June 1856, Truman S. White Papers [hereafter White Papers]; James Mumford to his wife in Brooklyn, NY, 10 December 1855, 7 April, 28 July, and 14 September 1856, 16 and 25 May 1857, James Mumford Papers; *Reminiscences,* Bass Papers; Bettee Hockley Russell Palmer to her mother in Burlington, VT, 9 February 1858, Palmer Letters; Ullman Papers, 6–11.

49. 1857 Annual Meeting, Ladies Benevolent Society, First Baptist Papers; Sarah Cavender, December 1857 School Manuscript, Randall Papers.

50. "Banking," and "Industry vs. Banks and Railroads," *Pioneer,* 20 and 27 No-

vember 1851; *Real Estate Advertiser*, 16 February 1855; Taylor, *Railroad System;* Theodore French to his father in New Hampshire, 12 July 1858, and 1861–76 Foreclosure sales, Charles C. Lund Papers [hereafter Lund Papers]. For a narrative on the events leading up to the 1857 panic, see Gibbons, *Banks of New-York*. On ante-bellum failures and the new challenges and opportunities they engendered, see Balleisen, *Navigating Failure*.

51. "Past, Present and Prospective Population of the Western Cities—Chicago, Toledo and St. Paul," *Minnesotian*, 15 November 1856; "Railroad Land Grants—A Minnesota Policy," *Railroad Advertiser*, 25 April 1857.

52. Minnesota Constitutional Convention, *Debates and Proceedings*, 343–98.

53. Minnesota State Auditor, *Report of Investigation Committee of Finance on County Indebtedness, 1858*, Miscellaneous Records, Ramsey County, MSA; "The Minnesota & Pacific Railroad Company is Bankrupt—without means or credit—cannot even pay their employees," *Railroad Advertiser*, 27 March 1858; Gibbons, *Banks of New-York*. See also O. T. Maxon's letter to the editor, discussing Minnesotans' fears of Wisconsin-based railroads, *Minnesotian*, 3 March 1857.

54. *$1000 Bond of the Territory of Minnesota, Bound Unto William H. English*, Territorial Papers, MSA; Book Draft, Vol. 1, 471, Owens Papers; "A Safe Currency" and "The Financial Conditions of Our Territory—Proposed Means of Relief," *Railroad Advertiser*, 3 and 24 October 1857.

55. *Act Proposing a Loan of State Credit; Trust Deed of the Southern Minnesota Railroad Company*, 14 July 1858, Sibley Papers; Wheelock, *Minnesota*, 113–15; *Minnesotian*, 10 April 1857; *Pioneer*, 15 November 1857, 19 January, 7 February, 15 March, and 9, 11, and 16 April 1858; *Winona Republican*, 28 April and 5 May 1857 and 10 March 1858; "The Loan Question Briefly and Fully Discussed," *Pioneer*, 28 March 1858;

Chicago Tribune excerpt on Minnesota's $5 million loan, *Railroad Advertiser*, 24 April 1858; *In Testimony Whereof,* the Governor of said Territory has hereunto annexed his name and caused the great seal of said Territory to be affixed this 26th day of May A.D. 1857 [in this instance,] S. Medary, Governor of Minnesota Territory, MSA; *$1000 Bond of the Territory of Minnesota, Bound Unto William H. English*, 5 May 1857, Territorial Papers, MSA; "Memorandum of Doubtful Accounts," in 1859–64 Cash Book, Mason Papers.

56. On the $5 million railroad loan, see *Act Proposing a Loan of State Credit* and *Trust Deed of the Southern Minnesota Railroad Company*, Sibley Papers. See also Minnesota and Pacific Railroad, *First Report; Minnesotian*, 18 April 1858; *Pioneer*, 19 January, 7 February, 15 March, and 9, 11, and 16 April 1858; Book Draft, Vol. 2, 700–855, plus 35-page Appendix, Owens Papers. See also *Railroad Advertiser*, 27 March 1858; Schuckers, *Finances;* and Fridley, "Public Policy and Minnesota's Economy."

57. Letters to Charles Clark from J. K. Mellin, Minneapolis, 31 March 1858, from Charles Schaffler of Le Sueur, 14 January 1859, from Rob Robinson, Portland, OR, 10 July 1859, from Fred P. Moseley, New York, November 1860, C. H. Clark Papers; Mark A. Hoyt Diary, 19 May 1862, Hoyt Papers; "Memorandum of Doubtful Accounts," in 1859–64 Cash Book, Mason Papers; Sarah Cavender's School Manuscript, December 1857, Randall Papers; 1850–65 letters received, Merritt Papers; Letters from his brother in Keesville, NY, 15 November 1857–7 May 1861, Mattocks Papers; Letter from Wescott Wilkin to his Brother Alex, 24 January 1858, Wilkin Papers; Letter, 30 July 1858, Treadwell Papers; *Chronicle*, 22 October, 5 and 19 November, and 31 December 1857 and 14 January 1858, Philecclesian Papers; *Minnesotian*, 21 July 1857; Minnesota Constitutional Convention, *Debates and Proceedings*.

58. *Proceedings of the Board of County Commissioners of Ramsey County and Common Council, of the City of St. Paul, for the abatement of Delinquent Taxes, under Act of the Minnesota Legislature, Approved March 11, 1862,* St. Paul Post Office Records, 1846–61, and Justice Dockets, 1857–62, Ramsey County, MSA; *Act Proposing A Loan of State Credit;* "The Financial Conditions of Our Territory—Proposed Means of Relief" and "The Minnesota & Pacific Railroad Company is Bankrupt—Without Means or Credit—Cannot Even Pay Their Employees," *Railroad Advertiser,* 24 October 1857, 27 March and 19 June 1858; *Railroad Bond Currency Meeting in Minneapolis,* 2 July 1859, and *Governor's Message,* 7 December 1859, Minnesota Governors, Sibley, MSA; Petty Accounts, Ludden Papers; Brother in New York to Ebenezer Brewer Mattocks, 15 November 1857–7 May 1861, Mattocks Papers; Auditor's Office to William Lochren, 14 November 1860, N. H. Heniup to Lochren, 17 October 1862, Complaint of John Martin, John Pillsbury, Asa B. Barton, Thomas F. Andrews, Sumner W. Farnham, David A. Secombe, John B. Gilfillan, John Dudley, Ashley C. Morrill, Jacob K. Sidle, Henry G. Sidle, and Henry F. Brown against Richard Chute, Franklin Steele, John S. Prince, and the St. Anthony Falls Water Power Company, 1857–64, William Lochren Papers [hereafter Lochren Papers]; Edmund Rice to Henry H. Sibley, 14 December 1859, Sibley Papers; Notice of discontinued service, *Railroad Advertiser,* 19 June 1858; condition of cities discussed, *Pioneer,* 1 June 1859 and 8 September 1860; *Express,* 22 December 1860.

59. Lizzie to Abby, 20 October 1857, Lizzie's 1857 House Accounts, Abbe Papers; Maria Madison and Miss Moseley in *Chronicle,* 19 November 1857, Philecclesian Papers; Minnesota State Auditor, *Report of Investigation Committee, 1858,* MSA; 1858–62 Annual Meetings, Ladies Benevolent Society, First Baptist Papers; David

Merritt to Benjamin, 12 October and 3 December 1858, 25 July, 10 and 27 August, and 2 October 1859, 23 January, 27 August, and 24 November 1861, and 6 October 1862, Merritt Papers; "LATE NEWS: Financial Affairs" and "The Sober-Second Thought" *Pioneer,* 7 October and 15 November 1857; "Another Slander Refuted" and "The Situation of the St. Paul Merchants, Their Resources, and Liabilities," *Railroad Advertiser,* 14 and 21 November 1857; Taylor, *Railroad System;* Theodore French to his father in New Hampshire, 12 July 1858, 1861–76 Foreclosure sales, Lund Papers; *Early Minnesota History,* Murray Papers.

60. Minnesota and Pacific Railroad, *First Report of the Chief Engineer;* James J. Hill to William, 11 February 1858, Hill, from the office of Borup & Champlin, wholesale grocers, forwarding and commission merchants, 30 January 1860, JJH GC; Bishop, *Floral Home;* Minnesota Constitutional Convention, *Debates and Proceedings;* James Madison Bowler, St. Anthony, to Lizzie, Nininger, 20 April 1860 and 27 April 1861, James Madison Bowler Papers [hereafter Bowler Papers]; Julia (Forbes) Bailly to brother William Forbes, 24 June 1861, 1861–66 Cash Book, Journal kept by Louis Blum, clerk, Cory-Forbes Papers; Income Tax for 1862, F. Steele Papers; 1849–74 Bills Receivable, Dousman Papers; Charles Borup obituary, stating he died suddenly in 1859, Rice Papers; St. Paul, Subscription List, 1861–65, MHS; Wheelock, *Minnesota,* 135–47; 1858–63 Railroad Matters File, Minnesota Governors, Sibley, MSA; James W. Taylor, office of the Minnesota and Pacific Railroad Company, St. Paul, to Franklin Steele, 17 January 1859, Henry Rice, Washington, DC, to Steele, 18 February 1859, Richard Chute, in New York, to Steele, throughout 1859, H. L. Dousman, Prairie du Chien, to Steele, 18 July 1858, F. Steele Papers; Wescott Wilkin to brother Alex, 24 January 1858, Wilkin Pa-

pers; E. S. Edgerton, banking house, St. Paul, to Isaac Crowe, attorney, St. Anthony, 25 October 1859, Crowe Papers; Correspondence, Notary Public for the State of Minnesota, Murray Papers.

61. Truman White to Cousin Mollie, 10 April 1860, White Papers; Charles Borup obituary, Rice Papers; Gibbons, *Banks of New-York*, 370; *1860 Population Schedules.*

62. "A Trip To Minnesota," *Boston Post*, 10 December 1856, *Boston Post* extracts, MHS Newspaper Collections; "Origin of the Panic," *Railroad Advertiser*, 3 October 1857.

63. Wheelock, *Minnesota*, 135.

64. Ramsey County Auditor, *Delinquent Tax Sale Record, 1859*, MSA; *Railroad Bond Currency Meeting in Minneapolis*, 2 July 1859, Sibley Papers. See also "Memorandum of Doubtful Accounts," Mason Papers; Brother in New York to Ebenezer Brewer Mattocks, 15 November 1857–7 May 1861, Mattocks Papers; Auditor's Office to William Lochren, 14 November 1860, N. H. Heniup to Lochren in St. Anthony, 17 October 1862, Complaint of John Martin, et al., against Richard Chute, Franklin Steele, John S. Prince, and the St. Anthony Falls Water Power Company, 1857–64, Lochren Papers; Edmund Rice to Henry H. Sibley, 14 December 1859, Sibley Papers; *Pioneer*, 8 September 1860; *Express*, 22 December 1860; James. W. Taylor, office of the Minnesota and Pacific Railroad Company, St. Paul, to Steele, 17 January 1859, H. L. Dousman, Prairie du Chien, to Steele, 18 July 1858, Henry Rice, Washington, DC, to Steele, 18 February 1859, and Chute, in New York, to Steele, throughout 1859, F. Steele Papers; Wescott Wilkin to brother Alex, 24 January 1858, Wilkin Papers; E. S. Edgerton to Isaac Crowe, 25 October 1859, Crowe Papers; Correspondence, Notary Public for the State of Minnesota, Murray Papers; Book Draft, Vol. 1, Owens Papers; Wheelock, *Minnesota*, 135–47.

65. Richard Chute to Steele, 28 October 1858, F. Steele Papers.

66. Ramsey County Auditor, *Delinquent Tax Sale Record, 1859*, MSA; Henry H. Sibley, *Message of Governor Sibley, June 3, 1858*, John Wilson, Chicago, to Alexander Ramsey, Governor Elect of the State of Minnesota, 21 November 1859, Sibley Papers; Wheelock, *Minnesota*, 83–100.

67. Henry Rice, Washington, DC, to Steele, 27 May 1861, F. Steele Papers.

68. "Visit of William H. Seward, and His Party," *Saturday Evening Post*, extracts from Charles Francis Adams Jr. journals, 25 November 1922, Charles Francis Adams and Family Papers. See also Charles Schaffler to Clark, 14 January 1859, Fred P. Moseley to Clark, November 1860, C. H. Clark Papers; Diary, 19 May 1862, Hoyt Papers; 1859–64 "Memorandum of Doubtful Accounts," Mason Papers; 1858 Correspondence and Receipts, J. C. & H. C. Burbank & Co., Flandrau Papers; *Red River of the North*, Bill Papers; Pates and Shrief, *International Hotel Guide Book; 1860 Population Schedules; 1858 St. Paul Advertiser; 1859 Minneapolis Advertiser; Express*, 22 December 1860.

69. 1858 Correspondence and Receipts, Flandrau Papers; 1852–65 Bills Receivable, Dousman Papers; *Red River of the North*, Bill Papers; *1860 Population Schedules; 1865 Business Directory.*

70. 1858 Correspondence and Receipts, Flandrau Papers; 1852–65 Bills Receivable, Dousman Papers; *Red River of the North*, Bill Papers; *1860 Population Schedules; 1865 Business Directory.*

71. *Red River of the North*, Bill Papers; 1854–61 Miscellaneous Deeds, Mortgages, and Contracts, 1861 Ledger and 1857–72 Minute Book, LaCrosse and Minnesota Steam Packet Co., 1859–61 Minute Book, Marine Bank of St. Paul, and Accounts, Davidson Papers; *1850 Population Schedules; 1857 Population Schedules; 1858 St. Paul Advertiser; 1859 Minneapolis Advertiser; 1860 Population Schedules;* samples of ad-

vertisements and weekly summaries of business progress, particularly connections and gains made by J. C. Burbank & Co., in *Express, Minnesotian,* and *Pioneer,* 1855–60, MHS Newspaper Collections.

72. Ramsey County Auditor, *Delinquent Tax Sale Record, 1859,* MSA; 1861–66 Journal, kept by dry-goods clerk Louis Blum, Cory-Forbes Papers.

73. *1860 Population Schedules; 1865 Business Directory.*

NOTES TO CHAPTER 4

1. Borrett, *Letters,* 63–64, 126–27.

2. Hans Mattson qtd. in *New London (CT) Chronicle,* 6 July 1867, Hans Mattson and Family Papers [hereafter Mattson Papers].

3. James Madison Bowler to Lizzie, 27 April 1861, Bowler Papers; Julia (Forbes) Bailly to brother William Forbes, 24 June 1861, Louis Blum 1862 journal entries, Cory-Forbes Papers; Richard Chute to Franklin Steele, 15 January 1864, F. Steele Papers; *1865 Business Directory;* Williams, ed., *Guide to Minnesota,* 26–35; Taylor, *Through to St. Paul and Minneapolis,* 35–37; Land, *Historical and Descriptive Review,* 10–59.

4. Comparisons of agricultural, manufacturing, and employment statistics for 1850, 1860, and 1870 based on *1860 Census of Manufactures,* clxxxiii–iv, 24, 277–84, and Walker, *Ninth Census* [hereafter *1870 Census of Manufactures*], 7, 81–91, 310–11, 392–93, 588–89, 592–99, 826–30. See also *1858 St. Paul Advertiser; 1859 Minneapolis Advertiser;* and *1860 Population Schedules.*

5. Mattson qtd. in *New London (CT) Chronicle,* 6 July 1867, Mattson Papers; *1860 Population Schedules; 1865 Population Schedules; 1865 Business Directory;* U.S. Bureau of the Census, *Census of the State of Minnesota* [hereafter *1870 Population Schedules*]; McMaster, *60 Years on the Upper Mississippi,* 185–92, 245–47.

6. *1865 Business Directory;* 1868 Assessor's Returns, MSA; *1870 Population Sched-*

ules; *1870 Census of Manufactures;* Chandler, *Scale and Scope,* 47–233.

7. 1854–65 Deeds, Mortgages, and Contracts, LaCrosse and Minnesota Steam Packet Company 1862 Journal entries, 1862–65 Ledger entries, and 1857–65 Minute Book, Marine Bank of St. Paul 1859–65 Minute Book, Cargo, and 1860–65 Passenger Accounts, and 1861–65 Accounts, Davidson Papers; McMaster, *60 Years on the Upper Mississippi,* 185–92.

8. Pates and Shrief, *International Hotel Guide Book; 1859 Minneapolis Advertiser* narrative; Heaton, *Summary Statement;* St. Paul and Pacific Railroad [hereafter SP&P], *Revenue, Resources* [1862], JJH GC; *1865 Business Directory* narrative; McClung's *St. Paul Directory for 1866* [hereafter *1866 St. Paul Directory*], narrative, St. Paul, Minnesota, City Directory Collection. See Twain, *Life on the Mississippi,* and McMaster, *60 Years on the Upper Mississippi,* for examples of the sentimental viewpoint.

9. *An Open Letter to the Hon. W. D. Washburn* [ca. 1888]. See also *1859 Minneapolis Advertiser,* 1–21; *1860 Population Schedules; 1860 Census of Manufactures; 1865 Population Schedules.*

10. *1859 Minneapolis Advertiser,* 1–21; *1860 Population Schedules; 1860 Census of Manufactures; 1865 Business Directory;* Andreas, *Illustrated Historical Atlas,* 228, 268; *Biographical Dictionary,* 172–73, 816–18, 864–70, 910–13, 1018–23.

11. *1865 Business Directory; Biographical Dictionary,* 172–73, 816–18, 864–70, 910–13, 1018–23.

12. *1865 Business Directory;* Confidential from Henry M. Rice to Franklin Steele, 28 August 1865, Richard Chute to Steele, 27 September 1865, F. Steele Papers; Lucian Putnam, Minneapolis lumber merchant, to George Moore, 27 March 1866, Moore Papers; Andreas, *Illustrated Historical Atlas,* 228; *St. Anthony Falls Water Power Company, plaintiff, vs. The City of Minneapolis, defendant,* [1882], JJHP.

13. *Record of the Board of Directors,* 10 and 11 March, 2 June, and 18 July 1862, SP&P Minutes, Great Northern Railway Records [hereafter GNR Records].
14. *Record of the Board of Directors,* March–July 1862, and 1862–70 Indentures, Miscellaneous Financial Records, Foreclosure Proceedings, W. K. Mendenhall to Hon. Willis Drummond, 4 June 1873, including *The Northern Pacific Rail-Road Company vs. The St. Paul and Pacific Rail-Road Company, Brief of W. T. Steiger Attorney of the St. P. & P. R. R. Co.,* New York Office Files, and SP&P Histories, SP&P, GNR Records; Claims of DeGraff & Others, SP&P [1871–88], Minnesota Governors, Horace Austin, MSA; *Original Agreement for Reorganization of the First Division St. Paul & Pacific Railroad Co., & Resolution of Directors Authorizing Same,* 17 December 1875, Office of Trustees of the First Division of the SP&P, "To Whom It May Concern," 9 October 1876, *Net Earnings of the St. Paul and Pacific Railroad Company, through 1876,* JJH GC; *Classified Business Directory and Guide Book* (1880–81) [hereafter *1881 Business Directory*], 5–12.
15. Borrett, *Letters,* 153; *Record of the Board of Directors,* 10 March, 29 June, and 18 July 1862, SP&P, GNR Records.
16. "Opening of the Railroad to St. Anthony," *Pioneer,* 29 June 1862; *A Picture of St. Paul,* Amherst H. Wilder Foundation Records [hereafter Wilder Records]; SP&P, *Revenue, Resources,* JJH GC; *1865 Business Directory,* narrative sections.
17. James W. Taylor to Franklin Steele, 17 January 1859, H. L. Dousman to Steele, 18 July 1858, Henry Rice to Steele, 18 February 1859, F. Steele Papers; E. S. Edgerton to Isaac Crowe, 25 October 1859, Crowe Papers; 1859–61 Correspondence, Notary Public for the State of Minnesota, Murray Papers; Wheelock, *Minnesota,* 135–47; *Pioneer,* 29 June 1862; *A Picture of St. Paul,* Wilder Records; SP&P, *Revenue, Resources,* JJH GC.

18. *Reminiscences,* Folsom Papers; John Prince to Franklin Steele, 23 February 1864, Extracts from Half-Breed Dacotah or Sioux Scrip Act of July 17, 1864, F. Steele Papers; *Pioneer,* 14 October 1862; Anderson, *Little Crow,* 123–65ff.
19. Qtd. in *1866 St. Paul Directory,* 197; J. C. Burbank Papers; Wescott Wilkin to Goshen, NY, 19 April 1863, S. W. to Sarah, 27 June 1863, Wilkin Papers; Anderson, *Little Crow,* 123–65.
20. J. C. Burbank Papers; H. C. Burbank Papers.
21. *1860 Population Schedules; 1865 Business Directory.*
22. J. C. Burbank Papers; H. C. Burbank Papers.
23. *1865 Population Schedules; 1865 Business Directory;* J. C. Burbank Papers; H. C. Burbank Papers; North-Western Express Company Papers.
24. *1860 Census of Manufactures* compared to *1870 Census of Manufactures; 1865 Business Directory* narratives; Borrett, *Letters,* 150–66.
25. "Remarks of Mr. C. C. Andrews in the Senate of Minnesota, January 11, 1860, in Favor of the Homestead Law," *Homestead Resolutions,* C. C. Andrews Miscellaneous Pamphlets [hereafter Andrews Pamphlets]; St. Paul, Subscription List, 1861–65, MHS; Borrett, *Letters,* 92–93; 145–47; Disturnell, *Great Lakes,* 181–92.
26. Disturnell, *Tourist's Guide;* Hayden, *Great West; 1881 Business Directory.*
27. *1865 Business Directory.*
28. Donnelly qtd. in a speech given on 27 February 1864 in support of a federal bureau of immigration, *Congressional Globe,* 38th Cong., 1st sess., part 1, 858; Wescott to Alexander Wilkin, 30 June 1864, Wilkin Papers; Milton Buswell to Oliver, 17 September 1865, Milton Buswell and Family Papers [hereafter Buswell Papers]; Sarah H. D. Chapin Family Expenses, 1865–66, Chapin Papers; Governor Marshall, Letters Received, Land and Railroads, 1866–67, MSA; Ramsey County,

1864–67 Assessor's Reports, 1865 assessed property by ward, St. Paul City Council, Miscellaneous Records, MSA; *1865 Business Directory*, narrative; *Tribune's Directory for Minneapolis and St. Anthony, 1871–72* [hereafter *1871 Minneapolis Directory*], narrative, Minneapolis, Minnesota, City Directory Collection; *1865 Population Schedules; 1866 St. Paul Directory*, narrative.

29. Borrett, *Letters*, 70; *1865 Population Schedules;* Milton Buswell to Oliver, 17 September 1865, Buswell Papers; Sarah H. D. Chapin Family Expenses, 1865–66, Chapin Papers; Ramsey County 1864–67 Assessor's Reports, 1865 assessed property by ward, St. Paul City Council, Miscellaneous Records, MSA; *1865 Business Directory;* Williams, ed., *Guide to Minnesota*, 26–35.

30. 1862–66 Bills Receivable, Dousman Papers; *1866 St. Paul Directory;* 1862–65 Journal and 1861–65 Ledger, LaCrosse and Minnesota Steam Packet Company, 1866 Wheat Account, Davidson Papers; James J. Hill to William Davidson, 27 January 1864, JJH GC.

31. *First Report of the Railroad Commissioner* [1871].

32. *Agreement between the St. Paul and Pacific Railroad Company and E.B. Litchfield*, in SP&P Histories and Related Papers, and SP&P Voucher Records, SP&P, GNR Records; *First Report of the Railroad Commissioner* [1871].

33. 1862–65 *Record of the Board of Directors*, 1–59, SP&P, GNR Records.

34. Henry Hastings Sibley to Hercules Dousman, 11 July and 18 December 1866, E. F. Drake to Dousman, 1 December 1866, *1867 Report to the Stockholders of the Minnesota Valley Railroad*, Dousman Papers; *1865 Business Directory; 1866 St. Paul Directory.*

35. Washburn, *From the North-West to the Sea; Life of Thomas Hawley Canfield*, 20–29; Northern Pacific Railroad [hereafter NPR], *Sketch of Its History*, 3–4; Smalley, *History of the Northern Pacific*, 97–105.

36. Minnesota State Board of Immigration, *Minnesota as a Home; 1865 Business Directory; Minneapolis Directory* (1865) [hereafter *1865 Minneapolis Directory*], Minneapolis, Minnesota, City Directory Collection; *1865 Population Schedules; 1866 St. Paul Directory;* Disturnell, *Tourist's Guide*, 41–64; Minnesota State Board of Immigration, *Annual Report.*

37. Minnesota State Board of Immigration, *Annual Report;* McMaster, *60 Years on the Upper Mississippi.*

38. Borrett, *Letters*, 70, 154.

39. *1865 Business Directory; 1865 Minneapolis Directory; 1865 Population Schedules; 1866 St. Paul Directory.*

40. 1862–66 Bills Receivable, Dousman Papers; *1866 St. Paul Directory*, 211–15; 1862–65 LaCrosse and Minnesota Steam Packet Company Journal, 1866 Wheat Account, Davidson Papers; James J. Hill to William Davidson, 27 January 1864, William E. Wellington, superintendent for the North Western Packet Company, Dubuque, to James J. Hill, 26 March 1866, JJH GC.

41. On land grants, see, for example, Martin, *Railroads Triumphant*, 168–74.

42. *Annual Report of the Railroad Commissioner of Minnesota* [1877]; Andreas, *Illustrated Historical Atlas*, 212; Atwater, ed., *History of the City*, 671.

43. Andreas, *Illustrated Historical Atlas*, 212; Atwater, ed., *History of the City*, 671; Borrett, *Letters*, 67. See also St. Paul, Minneapolis and Manitoba Railway Company [hereafter SPM&M], *Records and Indentures*, 92–94, and *Undated Laws*, 37–38; *History*, SP&P, GNR Records; *First Report of the Railroad Commissioner* [1871], 20–25; *Annual Report of the Railroad Commissioner of Minnesota* [1877], 23–25, 99–109.

44. Borrett, *Letters*, 67. See also SPM&M, *Records and Indentures*, 92–94, and *Undated Laws*, 37–38; *History*, SP&P, GNR Records; *First Report of the Railroad Commissioner* [1871], 20–25; *Annual Report*

of the Railroad Commissioner of Minnesota
[1877], 23–25, 99–109.

45. *Special Meeting of the Stockholders of the St. Paul and Pacific Railroad Company,* 19 March 1867, SP&P, GNR Records.

46. 1866–68 *Record of the Board of Directors,* SP&P, GNR Records; SPM&M, *Records and Indentures,* 92–94, and *Undated Laws,* 37–38; *First Report of the Railroad Commissioner* [1871], 20–25.

47. Sixth Mortgage, First Division, St. Paul and Pacific Railroad Company, 1 July 1868, to George Becker, Horace Thompson, and Samuel Tilden, trustees, to secure bonds for $6 million covering its railroad from St. Anthony and Breckenridge, 216 miles, and all of its land grant between St. Anthony and Breckenridge, also covering Mortgage Four, and the bonds thereby secured for $1.5 million, for the First Division's line on 60 miles, as well as on all land grants pertaining to the Division, in SPM&M, *Records and Indentures;* George Becker, president First Division, SP&P, to Governor William R. Marshall, 25 August 1868, Edmund Rice, president of the Saint Paul and Chicago Railway, to Marshall, 8 September 1868, Minnesota Governors, Marshall, MSA.

48. Minnesota Irish Immigration Bureau, *Address.* For other immigration guides and promotions, see Disturnell, *Tourist's Guide,* 64; Minnesota State Board of Immigration, *Minnesota as a Home* and *Annual Report;* Charles Pasavant to Governor William R. Marshall, 30 May 1866, B. A. Froiseth to Marshall, 25 February 1867, N. E. Nelson to Marshall, 16 March 1867, Hans Mattson to Marshall, 4 April 1867, George Becker to Marshall, 27 March 1866, Henry T. Johns to Marshall, 21 March 1867, George Becker to Marshall, 28 August 1868, Minnesota Governors, Marshall, MSA; Hans Mattson, special correspondence to the *New London (CT) Chronicle,* 6 July 1867, Dillon O'Brien, St. Paul, to Mattson, 7 July 1867, Scrapbook entry, creating the Minnesota

Board of Emigration, 13 March 1867, Mattson Papers; Mattson, *Reminiscences,* 97–116; H. C. Fahnestock, London, to Jay Cooke, 13 October 1868, Frank H. Clark to Cooke, 19 October 1868, W. L. Banning, St. Paul, to Cooke, 30 December 1868, Jay Cooke Papers [hereafter Cooke Papers].

49. William Banning to Jay Cooke, 30 December 1868, Cooke Papers; *First Report of the Railroad Commissioner* [1871], 1–40; *Annual Report of the Railroad Commissioner of Minnesota* [1877], 14–78.

50. 1868 Assessor's Returns, MSA; Governor William R. Marshall's 1868 Message and *Minnesota As It Is In 1869,* Minnesota Governors, Marshall, MSA; Minnesota State Board of Immigration, *Annual Report;* Williams, ed., *Guide to Minnesota;* Goddard, *Where to Emigrate; 1870 Census of Manufactures,* 7, 81–91, 310–11, 392–93, 588–89, 592–99, 826–30; Young, *Information for Immigrants,* 78–83, 213–19, and *Labor in Europe and America; First Report of the Railroad Commissioner* [1871]; Fishlow, *American Railroads,* 99–160; *1860 Population Schedules; 1865 Business Directory; 1870 Population Schedules.*

NOTES TO CHAPTER 5

1. *1866 St. Paul Directory,* 278.

2. For various linkages created between Minnesota's emerging elites and more established capital, railroad, and business networks in La Crosse, Milwaukee, Chicago, and New York during the Civil War period, see business advertisements and directors/executives listed in *1865 Business Directory* narratives, particularly those on pages 102–5, 140–42, 150–52, 229–322. See also statistical tables and narratives in *1870 Census of Manufactures,* 10–11, 39–40, 388–89, 588–633, 683–84, 760–78, 802–3, 808–9, comparing Minnesota's wealth, manufacturing, and influence between 1860 and 1870. For an introduction to the voluminous literature on American entrepreneurship and the problems associated with failure in the wake of

rapid technological change, economic expansion, and success, see Livesay, ed., *Entrepreneurship*, and for a discussion about the longevity of entrepreneurs as historical actors during booms and busts, see Livesay, "Entrepreneurial Dominance."

3. Statistics for the period based upon *1865 Population Schedules; 1870 Population Schedules; 1870 Census of Manufactures*, 10–11, 39–40, 388–89, 588–633, 685–84, 760–78, 802–3, 808–9; *First Report of the Railroad Commissioner* [1871]; *Annual Report of the Railroad Commissioner of Minnesota* [1877], particularly the railroad mileage table contained on page 23. In addition, see Brennan, *St. Paul & Sioux City* (1873) [hereafter *1873 Sioux City Directory*]; *Report of the Main Line, First Division, St. Paul and Pacific Railroad Company to the Railroad Commissioner of the State of Minnesota* [1875], 2, 13–18, GNR Records; Mattson, *Reminiscences*, 97–111; Young, *Information for Immigrants*, 78–73, 213–19; Minneapolis Board of Trade, *Annual Exhibit*. For other cost-of-living comparisons between Minnesota and the rest of the United States, Canada, and Europe, see Young, *Labor in Europe and America*, particularly 242–33, 353, 360, 370–76, 379, 381, 420, 436–85, 492–552, 555–64, 626–32, 652, 672–73, 681, 712–14, 745, and on Minnesota compared to the American East and South, 805 and 827–41. Comparisons of real wages, that is, daily wages of agricultural and mechanical laborers, and cost of living in towns of the states and territories (including provisions—groceries, dry goods, fuel—monthly housing rents, and weekly board) contained in Young, *Labor in Europe and America*, 78–73, 213–19, show that, as demands for wheat increased throughout the United States during the period 1866–72, St. Paul–Minneapolis's real wages increased relative to the rest of the country's principal cities.

4. *1865 Business Directory; 1866 St. Paul Directory; 1870 Population Schedules*; Ullman Papers, 75–78.

5. "Local Affairs," *Pioneer*, 2 January 1866. See also *1865 Population Schedules*; Minnesota Board of Immigration, *Minnesota as a Home*; 1868 Assessor's Returns, Ramsey County Records, MSA.

6. Henry Hastings Sibley qtd. in Tallmadge, *Facts*, 1–3; *1866 St. Paul Directory*; 1868 Assessor's Returns, MSA; *Story of Amherst H. Wilder*, Wilder Records; Goddard, *Where to Emigrate*, 14–21, 229; James J. Hill to J. E. Brett, 2 March 1867, James J. Hill Papers, Letterpress Books [hereafter JJH LB], 543–45; Hill to Will, 5 March 1867, JJH LB, 547; *1870 Census of Manufactures*, 7; Minute Books, Northwestern Union Packet Company, 1867–70 Ledger, LaCrosse and Minnesota Steam Packet Company, Davidson Papers; *Annual Report of the Railroad Commissioner of Minnesota* [1877].

7. George Chapin to Cousin Lizzie Davis in Boston, 25 June 1869, Sarah Chapin to George Sr., 27 April 1867, Chapin Papers.

8. 1868–72 "Society Pages," MHS Newspaper Collections; Brother Albert, St. Paul, to Sister Carrie in Ohio, about opening a grocery store in St. Paul after graduating from college in Ohio, 28 March 1866, Father in Minneapolis to Daughter, about chained migrations from Ohio, 13 July 1872, and Emma, Minneapolis, to Sister, discussing the changes in household management and accounts since arrival, 8 December 1873, Edwin Hacker Brown Papers; "Picturesque Views," 415; *Illustrated St. Paul*, 33, 36–39.

9. Horatio Alger Jr.'s stories sold by the millions during the last quarter of the nineteenth century. See, for example, Carl Bode's introduction in Alger, *Ragged Dick and Struggling Upward*, ix–xxi; Twain and Warner, *Gilded Age*; Hill, *Highways of Progress*; Gardner, *Horatio Alger*; Weiss, *American Myth*; Hoyt, *Horatio's Boys*; Gutman, *Work, Culture, and Society*; Beauchamp, "Ragged Dick"; Nackenoff, *Fictional Republic*; and Calhoun, *Gilded*

Age. See also Livesay, *Andrew Carnegie* and *American Made*, and Martin, *James J. Hill*.

10. Judge M. B. Koon qtd. in Publicity Club of Minneapolis, *Story of the Testimonial Dinner*, 44; James J. Hill to William, 11 February 1858, Hill, from office of Borup & Champlin, wholesale grocers, forwarding and commission merchants, 30 January 1860, JJH GC; Channing Seabury to his uncle in Brooklyn, NY, 9 August 1864, Channing Seabury and Family Papers [hereafter Seabury Papers]; SP&P, Record of the Proceedings of the Board of Directors, 1866–68, SP&P, GNR Records; R. R. Nelson, SP&P, to Governor Marshall, 23 June 1866, George Becker, First Division, SP&P, to Marshall, 17 August 1866, E. F. Drake, MVR, to Marshall, 22 November 1866, W. L. Banning, Lake Superior & Mississippi Railway Company, to Marshall, 11 December 1866, Minnesota Governors, Marshall, MSA; *1865 Business Directory; 1866 St. Paul Directory*.

11. James J. Hill to Captain William Fuson Davidson, declining offer, 27 January 1864, JJH GC; 1866–68 Journal, LaCrosse and Minnesota Steam Packet Company, 1866–68 Wheat Account, Davidson Papers; Street Assessments, owners in the Rice and Irvine Addition of St. Paul, St. Paul Bridge Company stockholders lists [1866], St. Paul City Council, Miscellaneous Records, MSA; *Story of Amherst H. Wilder*, Wilder Records; 1863–68 Letterpress Books, List of Directors of the First National Bank of St. Paul [1873], Dousman Papers; List of Offices and Directors of the St. Paul Iron Works and St. Paul Fire & Marine Insurance Company, Moses P. Hayes Papers [hereafter Hayes Papers]; *1865 Business Directory*; 1868–1870 papers, North-Western Express Company Papers; J. C. Burbank Papers; H. C. Burbank Papers; 1868 Assessor's Returns, MSA; Hill, *Highways of Progress*, 156–208.

12. *Articles of Agreement* between the First Division of the SP&P and James J. Hill, for rental of a freight house between the railroad track and Mississippi River, 6 February 1866, JJH GC; Hill, *Highways of Progress*, 140–55.

13. William E. Wellington, North Western Packet Company, Dubuque, IA, "Confidential" to James J. Hill, 22 and 30 March 1866, and "Personal" to Hill, 26 March 1866, *Articles of Agreement* between James J. Hill and Blanchard & Wellington of Dubuque, IA, for a copartnership in transportation, storage, and commission business at St. Paul, under the name "James J. Hill & Co.," 1 April 1866 (Hill's cash capital amounting to $2,500; Blanchard & Wellington agreeing to act as invisible partners in the firm, with Hill devoting 100 percent of his time to management and operation, working closely with the First Division, SP&P), Wellington "Personal" to Hill, 29 August 1866, SP&P Invoices, April-December 1866, Blanchard & Wellington, Railroad and Steamboat Transportation Agents, to Hill, 18 December 1866, JJH GC.

14. Hill to H. B. Wilkin, Milwaukee, 11 January and 6 April 1867, to "Friend Coyner," 12 January 1867, to H. W. Carr, Chicago, 27 January, "Confidential" to Culver & Co., Chicago, 8 February 1867, to "Friend Will," 8 February and 15 March 1867, to C. Ross, 21 February 1867, to J. E. Brett, 2 March 1867, to H. B. William, 5 March 1867, to H. E. Sargent, 21 June 1867, to W. P. Wellington, Dubuque, 17 July 1867, to Newson, St. Louis, 17 July 1867, JJH LB. See also *Memorandum of Agreement* between James J. Hill and the SP&P, for handling freight, 15 January 1867, and Confidential from Wellington to Hill, 22 January 1867, JJH GC.

15. Marriage Certificate, 17 August 1867, JJH GC; Tax and Assessment Receipts, 1851–70, Personal Finance Files, JJHRL; Real Estate Deeds and Abstracts, 1864–73, JJHRL; Lindley, *James J. and Mary T. Hill*.

16. *Articles of Agreement* between James J. Hill, Egbert S. Litchfield, and the SP&P, 16 September 1867, JJH GC; Hill to J. R. Tupper, New York, about lowering costs on shipments from New York to the Red River Valley with Kittson, 19 May and 5 June 1868, Hill to P. D. Armour, Milwaukee, discussing HBC shipments of pork to St. Paul, 17 June 1868, Hill to Captain A. M. Hutchinson, St. Louis, about Red River Valley government business, 6 July 1868, Hill to John Freeman, Chicago, about English goods traveling into the British Possessions, 31 August 1868, JJH LB; *1873 Sioux City Directory.*

17. *1865 Business Directory; 1866 St. Paul Directory;* Land, *Historical and Descriptive Review,* 20, 37, 72–160.

18. "Local Affairs," *Pioneer,* 2 January 1866; *1865 Business Directory.*

19. *1871 Minneapolis Directory;* Society Pages, *Minneapolis Tribune* [hereafter *Tribune*], through 1872, particularly "Happy New Year Minneapolis" open-house announcements, MHS Newspaper Collections; Andreas, *Illustrated Historical Atlas,* 228, 268; Washburn, *From the North-West to the Sea; Biographical Dictionary,* 172–73, 816–18, 864–70, 910–13, 1018–23; Atwater, ed., *History of the City,* 372, 527, 535, 544–68, 587–90, 600–608, 616, 675, 865–1019.

20. *1860 Census of Manufactures;* Minnesota Board of Immigration, *Minnesota as a Home; 1865 Population Schedules; 1865 Business Directory; 1870 Census of Manufactures;* Hanson, comp., *Grand Opening,* 71–87; Atwater, ed., *History of the City,* 578.

21. "The Tunnel Company: A Full Statement from Mr. Eastman, History and Explanation of All That has Transpired," *St. Anthony Falls Democrat* supplement, 15 April 1870; Atwater, ed., *History of the City,* 577–79.

22. *Memorandum of Agreement* between William W. Eastman and John L. Merriam, and Hercules Dousman, for the purchase of Nicollet Island, at the Falls of St. Anthony, Hennepin County, 1 August

1865, Wilder Records. See also *1865 Business Directory,* 103–6; "The Tunnel Company," *St. Anthony Falls Democrat* supplement, 15 April 1870; *1871 Minneapolis Directory;* Richard Chute to Franklin Steele, 27 September 1865, 4 and 12 April 1866, 3 and 10 January 1870, and 24 February 1871, F. Steele Papers; Quit-Claim deed and perpetual leases, John Sargeant Pillsbury and Family Papers [hereafter Pillsbury Papers]; Wilder, Burbank & Co. 1870 Government Shipping Ledger, H. C. Burbank Papers; Channing Seabury to his uncle, 28 March, 27 May, and 23 September 1866, and 15 and 22 May 1867, Seabury Papers; 1868 Assessor's Returns, MSA; Williams, ed., *Guide to Minnesota,* 26–39; 1868–72 Account Book, Noyes Bros. & Cutler Records [hereafter Noyes Records]; Land, *Historical and Descriptive Review,* 38–55, 63, 75, 87, 95, 116, 137–55, 161; "St. Paul! Buildings! Erected this Year, Total Expenditures $1,735,761! Growth of the City," *Pioneer,* 31 December 1871; Andreas, *Illustrated Historical Atlas,* 228; Hanson, comp., *Grand Opening,* 70–87; *Biographical Dictionary,* 1019; Atwater, ed., *History of the City,* 526–35, 577–84, 654.

23. Henry Sibley to Hercules L. Dousman, 1 July 1866, E. F. Drake to Dousman, 1 December 1866, Dousman Papers; Channing Seabury to his uncle, 28 March, 27 May, 23 September 1866 and 15 and 22 May 1867, Seabury Papers.

24. *St. Anthony Water Falls Water Power Company vs. The City of Minneapolis* [1882], 1–7, JJHP; Atwater, ed., *History of the City,* 527–44.

25. *1871 Minneapolis Directory;* Andreas, *Illustrated Historical Atlas,* 228, 268; Washburn, *From the North-West to the Sea,* 1–11; Fuller, *Manufacturing Interests;* Special File #1, JJHRL; *Biographical Dictionary,* 172–73, 807–14, 816–18, 826–70, 889–90, 910–17, 1018–23; Burnquist, ed., *Minnesota and Its People,* 1:317–25; Atwater, ed., *History of the City,* 87–95, 337–52, 527–609, 620–53; Kane, *Falls of St. Anthony,* 42–80.

26. Gates A. Johnson to William Lochren, 4 June 1870, Lochren Papers; *1871 Minneapolis Directory;* Andreas, *Illustrated Historical Atlas,* 228, 268; Washburn, *From the North-West to the Sea*; *Biographical Dictionary,* 172–73, 816–18, 864–70, 910–13, 1018–23; Atwater, ed., *History of the City,* 372, 527, 535, 544–68, 587–90, 600–608, 616, 675, 865–1019.

27. *1871 Minneapolis Directory;* Washburn, *From the North-West to the Sea*; Fuller, *Manufacturing Interests;* Special File #1, JJHRL; *Biographical Dictionary,* 172–73, 807–14, 816–18, 826–70, 889–90, 910–17, 1018–23; Burnquist, ed., *Minnesota and Its People,* 1:317–25; Atwater, ed., *History of the City,* 87–95, 337–52, 527–609, 620–53; Kane, *Falls of St. Anthony,* 62–80.

28. *Annual Report of the Railroad Commissioner of Minnesota* [1877], 23–25, 108; St. Paul, Minneapolis & Manitoba Railway Company, *Records and Indentures,* JJHRL.

29. *History of the St. Paul & Sioux City Railroad, 1864–1881,* J. C. Burbank to W. F. Davidson, 28 April 1871, J. C. Burbank Papers; 1866–73 Cash Books, Northwestern Union Packet Company, 1866–72 Wheat Ledgers, Minute Books and Payroll accounts, St. Paul Elevator Company, 1866–72 Northwestern Union Packet Company records, 1866–72 Minute Books, People's Line, Minute Books, Sauk Rapids Water Power Company, 1867 stock ledgers, Minute Books, Merchants Southern Packet Company, 1866 incorporation, St. Paul Printing Press Company records, 1868–72 St. Louis and St. Paul Packet Company records, Davidson Papers; *First Report of the Railroad Commissioner* [1871], 12–13.

30. *Annual Report of the Railroad Commissioner of Minnesota* [1877], 23–25; Goddard, *Where to Emigrate,* 14–21, 229; *1870 Census of Manufactures,* 7; *History of the St. Paul & Sioux City Railroad,* Burbank to Davidson, 28 April 1871, J. C. Burbank Papers; Minute Books, Northwestern Union

Packet, 1867–70 Ledger, LaCrosse and Minnesota Steam Packet Company, Davidson Papers.

31. *First Report of the Railroad Commissioner* [1871], 9–40; Kloos, *Report;* Chicago, Milwaukee and St. Paul Railway [hereafter CM&SP], *Guide for Tourists;* NPR, *Guide;* 1871–73 Net Earnings, First Division, SP&P, JJH GC; *Report of the Northern Pacific Railroad Company to the Board of Railroad Commissioners of the State of Minnesota* [1874], Northern Pacific Railway Company Records [hereafter NPR Records]; *Annual Report of the Railroad Commissioner of Minnesota* [1877], 23–25; NPR, *Sketch of Its History,* 1–4.

32. H. C. Fahnestock, London, to Jay Cooke, 13 October 1868, W. L. Banning, St. Paul, to Cooke, 30 December 1868, J. W. Taylor, St. Paul, to Cooke, 21 October 1869, A. B. Nettleton, Duluth, to Cooke, 11 August 1871, Jay Cooke to Harry Cooke, 28 November 1871, Cooke Papers; *First Report of the Railroad Commissioner* [1871], 23; NPR, *Guide,* 1–7; C. C. Andrews, *How Jay Cooke Came to Finance the Northern Pacific,* and *Chicago Republican,* 5 January 1868, 1–4, Andrews Pamphlets; P. W. Holmes, J. Cooke & Co., to W. Cooke, 6 September 1871, Northern Pacific Land Department Records [hereafter NPR Land Records]; *Annual Report of the Railroad Commissioner of Minnesota* [1877], 23–25, 108; House of Representatives of the Minnesota State Legislature, *Remarks of Mr. Delano, Relative to a Bill, declaring all the lands, property, privileges, rights and franchises pertaining to the uncompleted parts of the lines of the St. Paul and Pacific Railroad Company forfeited to the State of Minnesota,* 22 February 1875, 1–6, Special File, Early Railroad Data, JJHRL; NPR, *Sketch of Its History,* 1–5; *Life of Thomas Hawley Canfield,* 20–29; Mattson, *Reminiscences,* 114–19.

33. A. B. Nettleton, Duluth, to Cooke, 11 August 1871, Jay Cooke to Harry Cooke, 28 November 1871, Cooke Papers;

First Report of the Railroad Commissioner [1871], 23.

34. Kloos, *Report*, 3–30; *Report of the Northern Pacific* [1874], 19, NPR Records; NPR, *Guide*, 37, and *Red River Country*, 1–3; *Remarks of Delano*, 1–6, *Memorial of DeGraff & Co., to the Legislature of Minnesota* [1878], 1–4, Early Railroad Data, JJHRL.

35. 1871 Net Earnings, First Division, SP&P, JJH GC; SP&P First Mortgage Bond, 1 April 1871, Monthly Construction Estimates, and Meeting, 1 February 1871, Record of the Board of Directors, SP&P, GNR Records; Kloos, *Report*, 3–30; *Remarks of Delano*, 3–7, Early Railroad Data, JJHRL; A. B. Nettleton to Jay Cooke, 11 August 1871, Frank H. Clark, then president of the Lake Superior and Mississippi Railroad, St. Paul, to Cooke, 14 October 1871, Cooke to Governor Smith, 31 January 1872, Cooke Papers; French Society of St. Paul to Horace Austin, 11 February 1871, Minnesota Governors, Horace Austin, MSA.

36. *First Report of the Railroad Commissioner* [1871], 9–40; *Annual Report of the Railroad Commissioner of Minnesota* [1877], 23–25, 101–2; Scandinavian Emigrant Agency to J. Gregory Smith, president, NPR, St. Albans, NY, 25 January 1870, "Report of the National Immigration Convention," Chicago, 23 November 1870, A. B. Nettleton to Jay Cooke, 31 January 1871, John S. Loomis to Frederick Billings, 20 February 1871, A German Immigrant to Cooke, April 1871, Nettleton to Cooke, 19 May 1871, John Loomis, "Northern Pacific Report," 30 May 1871, George Sheppard, London, to Billings, New York, 24 June 1871, NPR Land Records; Banking House of Jay Cooke & Co., New York, to W. Cooke, 6 September 1871, Loomis to Billings, 13 September 1871, Loomis to Cooke, 24 November 1871, NPR Records; Industrial Exhibition Company, New York, to Governor Horace Austin, 22 July 1870, E. Page Davis, Com-

missioner of Immigration for Minnesota, New York, to Austin, 24 August 1870, Minnesota State Agent, Milwaukee, to Austin, 1 September 1870, Claims of De Graff and others, St. Paul and Pacific, to Austin, John Schroeder, Clerk, Minnesota State Board of Immigration, 1871 Report to Austin, Minnesota Governors, Horace Austin, MSA; 25 October 1871 diary entry, Abraham McCormick Fridley and Family Papers; NPR, *Guide*, 35–37; Young, *Information for Immigrants*, 78–83, 213–15, 224–29; Lake Superior and Mississippi Railroad Company, *Lands for Emigrants*, 1–10; *Statement*, SP&P, December 1873, JJH GC; SP&P, *Records and Indentures*, 93–96; St. Paul and Duluth Railroad, *Homes for the Million*, 1–31, 50; *Report of the Northern Pacific* [1874], NPR Records; Land, *Historical and Descriptive Review*, 15; SPM&M, *Facts About Minnesota*, 48; Mattson, *Reminiscences*, 98–119; *Report of the Main Line, First Division, St. Paul and Pacific Railroad Company to the Railroad Commissioner of the State of Minnesota* [1875], 2, 13–18, GNR Records. See also Veenendaal, *Slow Train to Paradise*.

37. *History of the St. Paul & Sioux City Railroad*, J. C. Burbank to W. F. Davidson, 28 April 1871, J. C. Burbank Papers; Jay Cooke to Harry Cooke, 28 November 1871, Cooke to Governor Smith, 31 January 1872, Cooke Papers; CM&SP, *Guide for Tourists*. See also Twain and Warner, *Gilded Age*, and Josephson, *Robber Barons*.

38. J. W. Taylor, U.S. Consulate, Winnipeg, to Jay Cooke, 5 January 1871, Cooke Papers; Washburn, *From the North-West to the Sea*; Argyll, *Canadian North-West*, 17–20.

39. Robert Bell, "On the Commercial Importance"; Haldane, *3800 Miles Across Canada*. On Canadian nationalism, see Cooke, "Imagining a North American Garden."

40. J. W. Taylor to Jay Cooke, 5 January 1871, Cooke to Governor Smith, 25 November 1871 and 31 January 1872, Cooke

Papers; Haldane, *3800 Miles Across Canada;* Hill, *Highways of Progress;* Lipset, *Continental Divide.* On the history of the Canadian Pacific Railroad [hereafter CPR], see Cruise and Griffiths, *Lords of the Line.*

41. Qtd. in Washburn, *From the North-West to the Sea,* 6.

42. Jay Cooke to Harry Cooke, 28 November 1871, Cooke Papers.

43. *First Report of the Railroad Commissioner* [1871], 1.

44. *1873 Sioux City Directory,* 58–60; Jay Cooke to Henry Whipple, 23 February 1872, Cooke Papers; *Statement* re: SP&P, December 1873, JJH GC.

45. *First Report of the Railroad Commissioner* [1871], 4, 17, 20; *1865 Population Schedules; 1870 Population Schedules; 1870 Census of Manufactures.*

46. "Only Through Route Between St. Paul and Chicago," *Pioneer,* 19 February 1872; Becker qtd. in St. Paul Common Council, *Proceedings,* 11; Andreas, *Illustrated Historical Atlas; Annual Report of the Railroad Commissioner of Minnesota* [1877].

47. *Annual Report of the Railroad Commissioner of Minnesota* [1877]; 1871–73 Net Earnings, First Division, SP&P, JJH GC; *Report of the Northern Pacific* [1874], NPR Records.

48. *1870 Census of Manufactures; 1870 Population Schedules; First Report of the Railroad Commissioner* [1871].

49. Hill, *Highways of Progress,* 85–100.

50. Correspondence of Hill, Griggs, & Co., especially agreements and exhibits attached to *Articles of Co-Partnership* between James J. Hill, Chauncy Griggs, and George S. Acker, 1 January 1872, partnership agreement with Norman Kittson, 19 January 1872, and financial arrangements made with the SP&P, Sioux City, and NPR, JJH GC.

51. *1865 Business Directory; 1866 St. Paul Directory;* Biographical data and correspondence, Maurice Auerbach and Family Papers [hereafter Auerbach Papers]; Hanson, comp., *Grand Opening,* 70–71.

52. Hanson, comp., *Grand Opening,* 70–71.

53. George Chapin to Lizzie Davis, 29 September 1872, Chapin Papers; J. W. Castle to William Lochren, 3 June 1870, Gates A. Johnson to Lochren, 4 June 1870, Lochren Papers; 1863–70 Real Estate Book, for holdings in the Twin Cities, and 1873–82 Cash Book, St. Paul Elevator, balance carry-overs, Davidson Papers; *Story of Amherst H. Wilder,* Wilder Records; *1873 Sioux City Directory;* Hanson, comp., *Grand Opening,* 71–87; *Land, Historical and Descriptive Review,* 72–160.

54. George Chapin to Lizzie Davis, 29 September 1872, Chapin Papers; J. W. Castle to William Lochren, 3 June 1870, Gates A. Johnson to Lochren, 4 June 1870, Lochren Papers; 1863–70 Real Estate Book, for holdings in the Twin Cities, and 1873–82 Cash Book, St. Paul Elevator, balance carry-overs, Davidson Papers; *Story of Amherst H. Wilder,* Wilder Records; *1873 Sioux City Directory;* Hanson, comp., *Grand Opening,* 71–87; *Land, Historical and Descriptive Review,* 72–160.

55. *First Report of the Railroad Commissioner* [1871]; *1865 Population Schedules; 1870 Population Schedules;* 1868 Assessors Returns, MSA; Williams, ed., *Guide to Minnesota,* 26; Railroad Commissioner, 1872–73 Annual Reports, GNR Records; "Commercial Market" summaries for St. Paul, Minneapolis, Milwaukee, Chicago, and New York, 1866–72, *Pioneer,* MHS Newspaper Collections; *Land, Historical and Descriptive Review,* 90–91.

56. George Chapin to Lizzie Davis, 22 August 1869, Chapin Papers.

57. See Cronon, *Nature's Metropolis.*

58. George Chapin to his father in Boston, 14 April 1870, Chapin Papers; Andreas, *Illustrated Historical Atlas,* 228; *Biographical Dictionary,* 172–73, 807–14, 816–18, 826–28, 864–70, 889–90, 910–17, 1002–7, 1018–23; Atwater, ed., *History of the City,*

87, 95, 372, 527–84, 587–92, 600–16, 631–75; Ingersol, "Home of Hiawatha."

59. Quit-Claim deed and perpetual leases, Pillsbury Papers; State of Minnesota, *St. Anthony Water Falls*, 1–7; *Ordinance* for the Minnesota Central Rail Road to construct machine and engine shops in Minneapolis [1870], Lochren Papers; Taylor, *Through to St. Paul and Minneapolis;* Treasurer's Office, Hennepin County, Minneapolis, to Franklin Steele, 15 March 1869, Richard Chute to Steele, on authorization to close Steele's business connections with the St. Anthony Falls Water Power Company by selling his bonds, 3 January 1870, and Chute to Steele, 24 February 1871, F. Steele Papers. On 3 January 1870, Frederick Butterfield of New York, Richard and Samuel Chute, John S. Pillsbury, John Farnham, and S. W. Martin reorganized the St. Anthony Falls Water Power Company to consolidate the business expenses and damages caused by the former directors' mismanagement, the tunnel's collapse, and the fires that destroyed so many mills on the St. Anthony side. By February 1871, Butterfield and his associates had disbursed the funds necessary for consolidating the company's efforts to end the St. Anthony Falls Water Power Company's unending troubles. See also Indenture made from the St. Anthony Water Power Company to Levi Butler, O. C. Merriam, and James S. Lane, Pillsbury Papers.

60. *1870 Census of Manufactures; 1870 Population Schedules;* Minnesota Secretary of State, *Census of the State of Minnesota* (1875) [hereafter *1875 Population Schedules*]; U.S. Census Office, *Report on the Manufactures of the United States at the Tenth Census, June 1, 1880* [hereafter *1880 Census of Manufactures*].

61. *Annual Report of the Railroad Commissioner of Minnesota* [1877]; 1871–73 Net Earnings, First Division, SP&P, JJH GC; *Report of the Northern Pacific* [1874], 19, NPR Records.

62. For general developments between 1866 and 1868, see, Disturnell, *Tourist's Guide;* Williams, ed., *Guide to Minnesota;* and Andreas, *Illustrated Historical Atlas.* For discussions on Minneapolis's canal and dam-building projects that threatened the stability of the waterfall, see St. Anthony Falls Water Company to Eastman, Judd, Merriam and Wilder, showing the reorganization of the water company under the direction of Richard Chute (also president), John S. Pillsbury (secretary and treasurer), Frederick Butterfield (New York), Samuel H. Chute (who originally conceived the plan to save the waterfall by building the timbered apron), John Martin, and S. W. Farnham, 23 November 1869, Wilder Records; Edward T. Abbott, *Old Time Reccolections [sic] Minneapolis St. Paul* [1871–73], Edward T. Abbott Papers [hereafter Abbott Papers].

63. *First Report of the Railroad Commissioner* [1871], 9–40; Kloos, *Report;* CM&SP, *Guide for Tourists;* NPR, *Guide.*

64. Minnesota Office of the Railroad Commissioner, *Annual Reports;* C. R. Chisholm & Co. [headquartered in Montreal], *Chisholm's All-Round Route,* 220–21; Butterworth, *Zigzag Journeys,* 161–233.

65. *1871 Minneapolis Directory,* narratives.

NOTES TO CHAPTER 6

1. Washburn, *From the North-West to the Sea.*

2. Proclamation of Governor Pillsbury, 30 August 1876, Minnesota Governors, J. S. Pillsbury, MSA. Rølvaag, *Giants in the Earth,* 340–41, provides an excellent fictional account of this phenomenon. See also Atkins, *Harvest of Grief.*

3. *Remarks of Delano,* Early Railroad Data, JJHRL; SP&P, *Agreement of 1874;* Original agreement for the reorganization of the First Division, SP&P, and Resolution of Directors authorizing same, 17 December 1875, JJH GC. See also J. Botsford, treasurer of the First Division, SP&P, to

"Henry," 5 September 1876, and To Whom it May Concern from the Office of the Trustees of the First Division, SP&P, regarding the company's default on the payment of interest under certain mortgages, totaling $15 million, 9 October 1876, JJH GC. On 9 October 1876, Edmund Rice, Horace Thompson, and John S. Kennedy constituted the company's trustees. Hill's correspondence, dealing largely with his warehousing, steamboating, coal, and wood trade during the late 1860s and 1870s, shows that he had a long-standing interest in Manitoba and the Red River Valley's development, and that established entrepreneurs throughout St. Paul introduced him into the region. See in particular, 1866–68 letters to Egbert S. Litchfield and the Northwestern Fuel Company (organized in 1877) and its predecessors, including Hill's partners Chauncy Griggs and George Acker, JJH LB. In addition, correspondence throughout Box 03, Folders 21–23, JJH GC, touches on the fuel supply business and the introductions Hill received into the larger business community.

4. Washburn, *From the North-West to the Sea*, 2–3. See also *1873 Sioux City Directory*.

5. CM&SP, *Summer Resorts; St. Paul City Directory for 1875* [hereafter *1875 St. Paul Directory*], St. Paul, Minnesota, City Directory Collection; 1870–77 Correspondence & Miscellaneous Papers, Protestant Home of St. Paul, *Pioneer* clipping, 25 January 1877, "Home for the Friendless: Interesting History of This Useful Charity—Reports of Officers and Managers for the Ensuring Year," and 1871–99 Stock and Bond Register, Wilder Records; City of St. Paul, *Financial Reports of the City Comptroller* [1873–74], "Act to Establish Summit Avenue, March 6, 1871," 260, St. Paul, Ramsey County, MSA; Father to Sarah, noting that Summit Avenue lots started to sell at $300 and $600 per lot in 1871, 9 August 1871, and George

Chapin to Lizzie Davis, 29 September 1872, Chapin Papers; 1863–74 Real Estate Book, for holdings in the Twin Cities, Davidson Papers; *1873 Sioux City Directory*, 226; *Photographs of Early St. Paul*, from the collection of Edward A. Bromley, Reserve Album 113; comparison of *1870 Census of Manufactures* and *1880 Census of Manufactures;* American Society of Civil Engineers [hereafter ASCE], *Fifteenth Annual Convention*.

6. *1873 Sioux City Directory*, 226. See also 1869–1914 Indentures, Quit-Claim Deeds, & Memorandums, Nicollet Island, Wilder Records; W. A. Gorman, comp., *The Charter and Ordinances of the City of St. Paul* [1875], Ramsey County, MSA; 1873–82 Cash Book, St. Paul Elevator, balance carry-overs, Davidson Papers; 1871–73 Net Earnings, First Division, SP&P, JJH GC; *Report of the Northern Pacific* [1874], 2, 19, NPR Records; Andreas, *Illustrated Historical Atlas*, 224–46.

7. Greeley in Atwater, ed., *History of the City*, 576 (see also 335, 545–55, 568, 572, 576–89, 677–78); Washburn, *From the North-West to the Sea*, 9–10; *Biographical Dictionary*, 868–72; ASCE, *Fifteenth Annual Convention; 1870 Census of Manufactures* compared with *1880 Census of Manufactures*.

8. Washburn, *From the North-West to the Sea*, 3–6, 9–11.

9. Private from Lippman, Rosenthal, & Co., Amsterdam, to John S. Kennedy, 2 May 1876, SP&P, GNR Records; NPR, *Annual Report to the Railroad and Warehouse Commission* [1876], NPR Records. Net Earnings statements, 30 June 1871–31 December 1876, JJH GC. See also 1876 List of Rolling Stock, First Division SP&P, n.d., and J. P. Farley to J. S. Kennedy & Company, 7 August 1877, SP&P, GNR Records; "Jay Cooke & Co.'s Affairs, A Poor Prospect for Creditors," *Pioneer*, 31 January 1874.

10. *Annual Report of the Railroad Commissioner of Minnesota* [1881], 9.

11. Waite qtd. in Hurst, *Law and the Conditions of Freedom*, 88 (see also 6–8, 51, 89). In addition, see Kelley, *Origin and Progress;* Aiken, *The Grange;* Woods, *Knights of the Plow.*

12. *Annual Report of the Railroad Commissioner of Minnesota* [1881], 9.

13. 1858–1902 St. Paul City Bond Record, St. Paul Comptroller and Miscellaneous Records, MSA; Syndicate of St. Paul Banks to the Mayor and Common Council of the City of Saint Paul, 19 January 1875, Finance Committee Files, St. Paul City Council, Gorman, *Charter and Ordinances,* 252, 255–58, 361, St. Paul, Ramsey County, MSA; 1870s Proposals/Bids, 1870–82 St. Paul Bridge Committee, 1870–79 Gas, St. Paul Common Council, Miscellaneous Records, MSA; 1871–99 Stock and Bond Register, 1870–77 business records, Wilder Records; *1875 St. Paul Directory; 1881 Business Directory;* ASCE, *Fifteenth Annual Convention.*

14. Petitioners to Committee on Police, 3 May and 1 September 1874, Board of Public Works, 1874 Annual Report, and Miscellaneous Records, St. Paul Common Council, MSA; W. A. Gorman to St. Paul City Council, 3 March 1874, St. Paul City Council, Ramsey County, MSA; *Charter and Ordinances of the City of Minneapolis* [1872], Minneapolis City Council, *Minneapolis City Charter and Ordinances* [1905], Minneapolis Charter and Ordinances, Department of Health, MSA; *Reccolections,* Abbott Papers.

15. City of St. Paul, *Financial Reports, 1872–1882,* MSA; 1870s Proposals/Bids, 1870–82 St. Paul Bridge Committee, 1870–79 Gas, St. Paul Common Council, Miscellaneous Records, MSA; 1871–99 Stock and Bond Register, Wilder Records.

16. City of St. Paul, *Financial Reports, 1872–1882,* MSA; 1870s Proposals/Bids, 1870–82 St. Paul Bridge Committee, 1870–79 Gas, St. Paul Common Council, Miscellaneous Records, MSA; 1871–99 Stock and Bond Register, Wilder Records.

17. J. H. Stewart, April 1872 address, Alderman Johnson, 21 May 1872, qtd. in St. Paul Common Council, *Proceedings* [1874], 2; *Charter and Ordinances of the City of Minneapolis,* Minneapolis City Council, *Minneapolis City Charter and Ordinances,* Minneapolis Charter and Ordinances, Department of Health, MSA; Board of Public Works, *Annual Report* [1874], Miscellaneous Records, St. Paul City Council, Ramsey County, MSA; Secretary of the State Board of Health, *The Relations of Scholastic Methods to the Health of Pupils in the Public Schools,* Health Department Publications, MSA; *First Annual Report of the Public Examiner of the State of Minnesota* [1879], Public Examiner, Biennial Reports, MSA; *Reccolections,* Abbott Papers.

18. City of St. Paul, *Financial Reports* [1882]; Board of Public Works, *Annual Report* [1874], MSA; 1870–83 Ways & Means, 1855–80 Wood Inspector, 1871–80 Property Owners in Dayton addition, St. Paul City Council, Miscellaneous Records, Ramsey County, MSA; *First Annual Report of the Public Examiner of the State of Minnesota* [1879], Public Examiner, Biennial Reports, MSA; Minneapolis City Council, *Minneapolis City Charter and Ordinances* [1905], Department of Health, MSA; *1881 Business Directory.*

19. Arvid Person to his parents in Sweden, 16 April 1874, 13 July and 5 August 1875, 26 April 1877, OI, Arvid Person Papers [hereafter Person Papers]. See also Young, *Labor in Europe and America;* Catholic Colonization Bureau, *An Invitation to the Land.* On price comparisons between the 1870s and 1880s, see Noyes Bros. & Cutler, *Illustrated Catalogue.*

20. 28 April and 29 and 30 May 1877 diary entries, Michael J. Boyle Papers [hereafter Boyle Papers] (see also pre-1877 diaries); *1870 Population Schedules; 1875 Population Schedules;* U.S. Bureau of the Census, *Census of the State of Minnesota* (1880) [hereafter *1880 Population Sched-*

ules]; *1875 St. Paul Directory;* Minneapolis Board of Trade, *History and Growth of Minneapolis.* See also Wills, "Respectable Mediocrity."

21. 19 July 1881 diary entry, Boyle Papers.

22. *1875 St. Paul Directory,* 21–27; *1880 Population Schedules; 1881 Business Directory;* 1866–73 Journal, Musical Hall Association, Davidson Papers; State of Minnesota, *Record of Poor Relief,* MSA; ASCE, *Fifteenth Annual Convention; Illustrated St. Paul,* 16–129.

23. *1875 St. Paul Directory,* 21–27; *1880 Population Schedules; 1881 Business Directory;* 1866–73 Journal, Musical Hall Association, Davidson Papers; State of Minnesota, *Record of Poor Relief,* MSA; ASCE, *Fifteenth Annual Convention; Illustrated St. Paul,* 16–129. For a discussion of the "managerial revolution," see Chandler, *Visible Hand.*

24. *1875 St. Paul Directory.*

25. National Protection and Collection Bureau, *Monthly Report for Members Only* [1873], reveals that, in St. Paul in particular, many of the people who subscribed were bankers and wholesaling elites, including Horace Thompson, Maurice Auerbach and his dry goods associates, Charles E. Mayo's wholesaling hardware concern, Nicols and Dean's wholesale iron and heavy hardware emporium, Noyes Bros & Cutler, St. Paul's preeminent wholesale druggists, and those associated with St. Paul's harvester works and lumber companies. See also *1875 St. Paul Directory; Illustrated St. Paul,* 84–90; 1871–99 Stock and Bond Register, Wilder Records.

26. Twain and Warner, *Gilded Age,* 193; *1880 Population Schedules; 1881 Business Directory.*

27. *1875 St. Paul Directory; 1880 Population Schedules; 1881 Business Directory;* Amherst Wilder Obituary, *Pioneer,* 13 November 1894.

28. 1876–77 diary entries, Boyle Papers;

Auerbach Papers; *1875 St. Paul Directory;* 1869–77 correspondence, ledgers, advertising, brochures, and newspaper clippings, Noyes Records; Arvid Person to parents, 16 April 1874, 13 July and 5 August 1875, and 26 April 1877, Person Papers; SP&P Payroll notations [April 1878], SP&P, GNR Records; *1870 Census of Manufactures; 1880 Census of Manufactures; 1873 Sioux City Directory,* 7–9, 226; ASCE, *Fifteenth Annual Convention; Illustrated St. Paul,* 6, 48; Burnquist, ed., *Minnesota and Its People,* 1:239–44.

29. James H. Woolsey's bankruptcy statement of creditors, his failed Twin City business concern owing money to people not only in the Twin Cities, but also in New York, St. Louis, Cincinnati, Philadelphia, Baltimore, Chicago, Rochester, NY, New Haven, CT, and Boston and Springfield, MA, 24 December 1877, Noyes Records. In addition, see 1855–76 Accounts Receivable, J. Steele Papers; requests for extension of credit from A. Martin, Pelican Saw and Planing Mills, New Orleans, 7 October 1875, Confidential Notification Sheet of the Mercantile Agency of R. G. Dun & Co., St. Paul, no. 21, Tuesday, 2 November 1875, judgements, etc., McCaine Bros & Barteau, 4 September 1877, Munger, Markell & Co., Duluth, 13 September 1877, Averill Russell & Co., Minneapolis, 10 December 1877, James H. Woolsey, 12 December 1877, Clarke & McClure manufactures and dealers in lumber, St. Cloud, 2 December 1874, H. B. Morrison, Clearwater, 7 January 1875, Peleg, Burdicks, Brooksville, 8 January 1875, E. G. Hill & Brox., Little Falls, 30 January 1875, North Western Saw Mills, Stillwater, 3 February 1875, Ball, Bryan & Dickinson, manufactures of flour barrel staves and handling, 6 February 1875, North Western Saw Mills, 9 April 1875, Confidential Notification Sheet of the Mercantile Agency of R. G. Dun & Co., St. Paul, no. 15, Tuesday, 21 September 1874, J. H. Taylor

& Co., manufacturers and dealers in lumber, St. Paul, 8 January 1874, R. L Frazee, Hobart, 9 June 1874, Pine City Lumber Co., 3 March 1874, Muskegon Iron Works, May 1874, Pine City Lumber Company, 8 September 1874, Jewitt Mills, WI, 21 September 1874, Alexander Rodgers, Muskegon Iron Works, 12 September 1874, Indenture between St. Anthony Iron Works and St. Anthony Falls Water Power Company, 3 July 1873, Notes & Bills Receivable, Hayes Papers; Claims, Folders 05-07, Lochren Papers; Henry T. Welles to Franklin Steele, 10 May 1877, Nicollet Island lease, 1 November 1877, F. Steele Papers; 1875 correspondence, JJH GC; *Pioneer,* 14 November 1876.

30. *1870 Population Schedules; 1880 Population Schedules; 1875 St. Paul Directory;* "Picturesque Views," 415; Williams, ed., *Guide to Minnesota,* 27-39; Hayden, *Great West,* 251-56; Harry H. Young, "The Great West," extracted from *Chicago Times,* 3 July 1880; Taylor, *Through to St. Paul and Minneapolis,* 35-37; City of St. Paul, *Financial Reports, 1872-1882;* Minnesota Department of Public Instruction, *Circular; Illustrated St. Paul,* 16-129.

31. *1875 St. Paul Directory; 1881 Business Directory.*

32. *First Annual Report of the Public Examiner of the State of Minnesota* [1879], 1-47, Public Examiner, Biennial Reports, MSA; ASCE, *Fifteenth Annual Convention;* Fairchild and Davidson Real Estate Agents to James J. Hill, 17 June 1884, overleaf containing St. Paul Chamber of Commerce condensed *Annual Report* [1883], JJH GC; *Illustrated St. Paul,* 84-93; "Special Extra Number, Descriptive of and Illustrating St. Paul, Minnesota," 16-18.

33. Minneapolis Board of Trade, *Annual Exhibit;* ASCE, *Fifteenth Annual Convention; Biographical Dictionary,* 868-70; Atwater, ed., *History of the City,* 587-92, 608-9, 631-32; Washburn qtd. in Kane, *Falls of St. Anthony,* 88.

34. 1876-77 Minute Book entries, including membership rolls, 12-16, and Clipping File, Minnesota Millers State Association Records [hereafter Minnesota Millers Records]; Atwater, ed., *History of the City,* 590, 619.

35. Atwater, ed., *History of the City,* 587-90.

36. ASCE, *Fifteenth Annual Convention; Biographical Dictionary,* 868-70; Atwater, ed., *History of the City,* 587-92, 608-9, 631-32.

37. ASCE, *Fifteenth Annual Convention; 1881 Business Directory.*

38. *Biographical Dictionary,* 816-18, 889-90, 910-17; Atwater, ed., *History of the City,* 603-7.

39. Atwater, ed., *History of the City,* 584-87, 590-92, 602-7.

40. *Biographical Dictionary,* 1002-3; Atwater, ed., *History of the City,* 603, 610-11.

41. 1876-77 Minute Book, and Clipping File, Minnesota Millers Records; *Biographical Dictionary,* 1002-3; Atwater, ed., *History of the City,* 590, 603, 610-19.

42. *1875 St. Paul Directory; 1881 Business Directory.*

43. Lumber Sales Register, 30 June 1877-1 December 1881, Cole and Weeks, Minneapolis, Records; ASCE, *Fifteenth Annual Convention;* Atwater, ed., *History of the City,* 543-44, 566-75; *Biographical Dictionary,* 807-14ff.

44. Atwater, ed., *History of the City,* 337-41, 351-52, 654, 657; *Reccolections,* Abbott Papers.

45. Lease agreement between St. Anthony Falls Water Power Company and Harmon M. Martin and Moses P. Hayes, 30 December 1865, C. R. Bushnell & Co., St. Anthony, manufacturing license from the U.S. Internal Revenue office, 1 May 1867, Hayes Papers; *Minneapolis Business Souvenir,* 4, 7-15, 24-33; Atwater, ed., *History of the City,* 632, 657-71.

46. *1881 Business Directory;* Atwater, ed., *History of the City,* 580, 629-30. For

tours of the business elites' residential dwellings and business houses, see Franklin Steele obituary, F. Steele Papers; and *Minneapolis: Central Park Region.*

47. SP&P, *Agreement of 1874,* giving the Minneapolis and St. Louis Railway the right to construct, maintain, and operate its railroad upon the First Division's main line in Hennepin County; *Illustrated St. Paul,* 45; "Train Schedules," *Pioneer,* 31 December 1873–77, MHS Newspaper Collections; Atwater, ed., *History of the City,* 33, 361.

48. St. Paul & Pacific #59, George Stephen & Associates, purchase of St. Paul & Pacific Bonds [1876–80], SP&P, GNR Records.

49. "Purchase of the St. Paul & Pacific by Canada and Minnesota Parties," *Pioneer,* 26 October 1877; Hanson, comp., *Grand Opening.*

50. "Purchase of the St. Paul & Pacific by Canada and Minnesota Parties," *Pioneer,* 26 October 1877; Hanson, comp., *Grand Opening.*

51. Operating Reports, Main Line, January 1872–February 1876, Branch Line, January 1872–February 1876, SP&P, Desk Files, Norman Kittson Estate and Dutch Bondholders Committee, Record of the Board of Directors, SP&P and St. Paul, Minneapolis, and Manitoba Railroads [1862–80], GNR Records; 1876–77 Correspondence between Hill, Stephen, Smith, Kittson, and Kennedy, JJH GC; Hill to Smith, Kittson, and Stephen, 11 June–23 August 1877, Hill to Stephen, Kennedy, Smith, and Kittson, 24 February–6 October 1878, JJH LB.

52. Hill, *Highways of Progress,* 140–55; Cruise and Griffiths, *Lords of the Line,* 9–17, 25–29.

53. Articles of Incorporation of the North-Western Fuel Company, 1 May 1877, and other business correspondence with Kittson and others [1875–77], JJH GC.

54. Kittson and Hill to Johan Carp, Utrecht, Holland, 26 May 1877, Carp to

Hill and Kittson, 11 and 30 July 1877, JJH GC; Hill to the Honorable Donald A. Smith, M. P., Montreal, 11 June and 4 and 23 August 1877, to Carp, 10 July 1877, to S. E. Merrill, General Manager, Milwaukee, 21 July 1877, to My Dear Captain, 10 July 1877, to Kittson, 14 August 1877, to George Stephen, Montreal, 23 August 1877, to E. V. Holcombe, Fishers Landing, 28 August 1877, JJH LB.

55. "Address of James J. Hill" in Hanson, comp., *Grand Opening,* 57–58; Cruise and Griffiths, *Lords of the Line,* 1–27.

56. Minnesota Office of the Railroad Commissioner, *Sixth Annual Report* [1877], 1–25, 105–9, and *Communication* [1879]; Cruise and Griffiths, *Lords of the Line,* 1–92.

57. SP&P #59, George Stephen & Associates, purchase of St. Paul & Pacific Bonds [1876–80], SP&P, GNR Records; C. Horetzky, *Some Startling Facts;* Bell, "On the Commercial Importance." See also Martin, *James J. Hill,* 114–236; Cruise and Griffiths, *Lords of the Line,* 1–92; Veenendaal, *Slow Train to Paradise;* Wills, "Divided Loyalties," 8–16.

58. J. P. Farley, general manager and receiver for the SP&P roads, to J. S. Kennedy & Co., 7 August 1877, SP&P #61–#63, 1875–77 Trustees files, SP&P #59, George Stephen & Associates, purchase of St. Paul & Pacific Bonds [1876–80], SP&P #60, Treasurer for 1876–79 Trustee's reports, SP&P #67, 1868–77 Miscellaneous Documents, SP&P Capital Stock Certificates #1–88, First Division Branch Line 1876–79 Common Stock Certificates #97–136, SP&P, GNR Records.

59. Farley to J. S. Kennedy & Co, 7 August 1877, Hill to Kennedy, personal, 12 June 1878, SP&P, GNR Records; C. H. Bigelow and Horace Thompson to Hill, 11 August 1876, Office of Trustees of the First Division of the SP&P "To Whom It May Concern," regarding default on payment of interest, 9 October 1876, Thompson to Kittson, 3 June 1878, Stephen to

Hill, 17 August 1878, JJH GC; Hill to Kittson, 14 August 1877, Hill to Stephen, 14 August 1877, JJH LB.

60. SP&P #59, George Stephen & Associates, purchase of St. Paul & Pacific Bonds [1876–80], SP&P, GNR Records.

61. E. V. Holcombe to James J. Hill, 28 October 1877, congratulating Hill on the secret arrangements that had placed the railroad in his hands, JJH GC.

NOTES TO CHAPTER 7

1. Hanson, comp., *Grand Opening;* ASCE, *Fifteenth Annual Convention;* 1883–84 Cash Book, McAuley Papers; Ingersol, "Home of Hiawatha," 80; Land, *Historical and Descriptive Review; 1881 Business Directory;* 27 August and 1, 2, and 4 September 1883 diary entries, Boyle Papers; Chamber of Commerce of Minneapolis and Minneapolis Board of Trade, *Joint Annual Report; Minneapolis: Central Park Region;* 1880–83 Subscriptions and Donations, James J. Hill Donation Book, JJHRL; CM&SP, *Land of Promise;* NPR, *Northern Pacific Railway Business Directory* (1883) [hereafter *1883 Business Directory*].

2. Hill, Personal and Confidential, to Stephen, 19 October 1878, JJH LB; SP&P, *Annual Reports to the Railroad Commissioner of Minnesota* [1875–79], Hill to Kennedy, 12 June 1878, SP&P, GNR Records; Hill, *Highways of Progress,* 93–94, 98–99.

3. Hanson, comp., *Grand Opening,* 57–58; 3–11 September 1883 diary entries, Boyle Papers; *Pioneer,* 4 September 1883.

4. Taylor, *Through to St. Paul and Minneapolis,* 37.

5. Hill to Stephen, 8 March 1878, Hill to J. S. Kennedy & Co., 11 April 1878, JJH LB; Agreement between Committee of Dutch Bondholders and George Stephen, Donald A. Smith, N. W. Kittson, and James J. Hill, 5 January 1878, "Associates" agreement, 21 January 1878, Hill to Stephen, 7 June 1878, Memorandum, 28 June 1878, JJH GC.

6. Stephen to Hill, 8 April 1878, Hill

to Kittson, St. Paul, Western Union telegram, 25 May 1878, Thompson to Kennedy, 12 July 1878, JJH GC. See also J. P. Farley to J. S. Kennedy & Co., 7 August 1877, Edmund Rice to Kennedy, 21 April 1879, Telegram from H. R. Bigelow to Kennedy, 27 December 1879, George L. Otis to Rice, 19 April 1879, Kennedy to Rice, 21 April 1879, and SP&P #56, 1878–79 George Stephen & Associates negotiations with Litchfield, New York Office Files, April 1878 SP&P Payroll, Hill to Kennedy, 23 February 1878, Stephen to Kennedy, 28 November 1878, SP&P, GNR Records; Hill to E. A. Coming, Sioux City, IA, 22 February 1878, Hill to J. S. Kennedy & Co., 25 February and 11 April 1878, Hill to Stephen, 8 March 1878, JJH LB; 11 February 1881 diary entry, Boyle Papers.

7. Thompson to Kennedy, 12 July 1878, JJH GC. Trouble with the Milwaukee Road and other Chicago-based lines working with the NPR persisted throughout the period. See, for example, Angus to S. S. Merrill, General Manager, CM&SP, Milwaukee, 4 May 1880, JJH LB.

8. Hill to Kennedy, 12 June 1878, Hill and Kittson to Stephen, 16 June 1878, Stephen to Kennedy, 29 October 1878, SP&P, GNR Records; Kittson to Stephen, 13 June 1878, Hill to Stephen, 10, 18, and 29 June and 1 and 26 August 1878, JJH LB; Tentative Agreement between the NPR and the Associates, July 1878, Stephen to Hill, about Kittson managing steamboat matters between St. Paul and Winnipeg, 23 August 1878, private from Ignatius Donnelly to Hill, inside information on building near Little Falls, 19 November 1879, JJH GC.

9. Stephen to Kennedy, 29 October 1878, Billings to Stephen, 31 October 1878, SP&P #57, 1877–79 George Stephen and Associates negotiations with the Northern Pacific, Hill to J. S. Kennedy & Co., 15 July 1879, SP&P, GNR Records; Hill to Stephen, 31 October and 4 November

1878, JJH LB; Thompson to Kennedy, 12 July 1878, Kennedy to Thompson, 16 July 1878, Hill to Stephen, 22 July 1878, Stephen to Hill, 21 August 1878, Stephen to Hill, 7, 10, and 17 January 1879, JJH GC; Hanson, comp., *Grand Opening*, 3–4.

10. *Articles of Incorporation*, 23 May 1879, confirmed by Act of the Legislature of the State of Minnesota, 7 March 1881, George Stephen & Associates, costs associated with acquiring the St. Paul and Pacific [1878], SP&P #58, 1876–80 Purchase of the St. Paul and Pacific Bonds, GNR Records; SPM&M, *By-Laws; Annual Report of the Railroad Commissioner of Minnesota* [1881]; Hanson, comp., *Grand Opening*, 4. For various letters of congratulations, see President's Office Files, GNR Records.

11. Hill to Stephen, 28 October 1878 and January 1879 correspondence, to Kennedy, 30 October 1878, 20 and 28 January, 17 and 23 February, 15 and 23 April, and 29 May 1879, to W. F. Luxton, Winnipeg, 12 April 1879, to C. L. Grant, 19 April 1879, to Charles Pillsbury, 8 June 1879, JJH LB; Hill to J. S. Kennedy & Co., 15 July and 11 August 1879, Comptroller's Office Files, GNR Records; Henry Rice to Kittson and Hill, 24 August 1878, Stephen to Hill, 26 August 1878, Kennedy to Stephen, 28 August 1878, Hill to Kennedy, 8 September 1878, Stephen to Hill, 3 and 4 October 1878, Thompson to Stephen, 7 October 1878, Stephen to Edwin C. Litchfield, 8 October 1878, Stephen to Hill, 9 October 1878, Year-end statement for the SP&P and First Line Division, 31 December 1878, JJH GC. In the 9 October 1878 letter, Stephen declares that "a settlement with Litchfield and our N. P. friends would bring us close up to the object we have in view, namely *reorganization*."

12. J. W. Taylor, U.S. Consulate, Winnipeg, to Hill, 19 January and 22 March 1879, Stephen to Hill, 19 and 24 March 1879, JJH GC; Angus to Stephen, 27 October 1880, to Honorable Howard, Secretary, discussing the Syndicates' proposal to build the CPR and its consummation, 19 November 1880, JJH LB.

13. 1878–83 correspondence from Hill to Stephen, JJH LB.

14. Stephen to Hill, 18 April 1879, JJH GC.

15. Hill's 1878–83 correspondence, JJH GC and JJH LB.

16. 11 February and 8 and 9 April 1879 diary entries, Boyle Papers; *Reccolections*, Abbott Papers; Francis S. Hinkley, Minneapolis Elevator Company, 2 December 1879, JJH GC.

17. *Grip* qtd. in Brown, ed., *Illustrated History of Canada*, 340.

18. Currie, *Letters of Rusticus*, 45–46.

19. Marquis of Lorne qtd. in Argyll, *Canadian North-West*, 17, 20; Washburn, *From the North-West to the Sea*, 6.

20. Hill, *Highways of Progress*, 93–94, 98–99, 148. See also Cruise and Griffiths, *Lords of the Line*, 93–126, on some of Stephen's Canadian deal making during the period.

21. Hill to J. S. Kennedy & Co., 11 August 1879, Comptroller's Office, GNR Records; Hall, *A Lady's Life*, 98. See also Hill to J. J. Hargrove, Winnipeg, 10 January 1880, Personal to Angus, 8 July 1880, E. V. Holcombe, Winnipeg and Western Transportation Company Limited, to Hill, 13 July and 1 August 1880, Private Angus to Hill, 11 January 1881, JJH GC; Hill to William C. Van Horne, General Superintendent, Milwaukee Road, 23 June 1880, attempting to hire him away from the rival railroad and into the Manitoba Road–Canadian Pacific Railroad project, 23 June 1880, JJH LB; *Reccolections*, Abbott Papers, 4.

22. Operating ratio, the standard calculation of railroad efficiency, measures the ratio of operating expenses to operating income. See tabulation of Financial Operating Results of the First Division, SP&P, 1871–76 and first six months of 1877,

JJH GC. See also SPM&M, *Report of the Directors* and *Red River Valley.*

23. Hill to C. C. Wheeler, Chicago, 23 November 1880, Volume P-5, offering to pay a general superintendent $10,000 per annum if Wheeler can find a suitable candidate, JJH LB. See also Hill to Stephen, 28 January 1879, to Messrs. Beedo & Bray, Minneapolis, 7 April 1880, to John Porteau, General Attorney, Montreal, 26 April 1880, to E. R. Holden, New York, 7 May 1880, to John D. Hinde, St. Louis, 9 September 1880, to George Stephen and John S. Kennedy, 13 September 1880, to A. L. Melzer, Berlin, 13 September 1880, JJH LB; Confidential from Captain Morris, St. Anthony Falls Water Power Company, East Minneapolis, to Hill, 25 June 1881, *Articles of Incorporation of the St. Paul Union Depot Company,* 25 January 1879, and Executive Office of the State of Minnesota, line completed from St. Vincent to the international boundary, approved by John S. Pillsbury, 10 January 1879, JJH GC; *Annual Report of the Railroad Commissioner of Minnesota* [1881]; Farley to Kennedy, 18 March 1879, Hill to Kennedy, 12 August 1879, Comptroller's Office, and D. C. Bell, Minnesota Linseed Oil Company, Minneapolis, to Hill, 23 January 1879, L. R. Bently, Winnipeg, to Hill, 1 August 1879, President's Office, Chapter 318, special laws of Minnesota, "Act Relating to the St. Paul Union Depot Company, June 1, 1879," Comptroller's Office, and St. Anthony Water Power Company, Comptroller's Office, GNR Records.

24. *Annual Report of the Railroad Commissioner of Minnesota* [1881], in particular Exhibits "A" and "B"; Hill to R. B. Bloomfield, Agent at Willmar, about an "interview with General Washburn," 14 October 1880, to Hamilton Browne, IA, discussing Washburn's proposal to venture together in coal companies, 5 August 1880, JJH LB; Private from Washburn to Hill, declaring that he hoped he had heard false rumors about Hill building lines compet-

itive to his own, 2 April 1881, Washburn to Hill, 17 September 1882, Washburn to Hill, confidential, 29 January and 15 February 1882, Kennedy to Hill, 16 February 1882, George M. Rissing to Hill, 28 September 1882, JJH GC; Inventory of the estate of Franklin Steele and Annie Steele, as of August 1881, F. Steele Papers; 5 November 1878 diary entry, Boyle Papers.

25. Of course, Minnesotans endured many trials during their conversion from isolation to increasingly interdependent urban-rural systems, including reduced profits in grain and flour as a result of over-production in wheat between 1880 and 1883, and the latter year's recession that illustrated some of Henry George's 1879 judgments about the problems associated with increased want in the midst of plenty. Farmers and laborers revived old concerns; regardless, general enthusiasm for Minnesota's wealth-creators persisted. See George, *Progress and Poverty;* Hanson, comp., *Grand Opening;* Richard B. Angus to John S. Kennedy, about grain markets, 22 April 1880, Comptroller's Office, and A. A. Ackerly, St. Paul Station, to Hill, about a short-lived walkout protesting night work, 21 August 1880, and confirming authorization to give passes to employees so they could attend the state fair, 7 September 1880, President's Office, GNR Records; ASCE, *Fifteenth Annual Convention;* Minnesota Office of the State Railroad Commissioner, *Communication,* qtd. in *Annual Report of the Railroad Commissioner of Minnesota* [1881], 5–6. See also Johnson, *A Tale of Two Cities.*

26. 14 June 1880 diary entry, Boyle Papers.

27. Land, *Historical and Descriptive Review,* 13. See also 1879 Payrolls, General Office, SP&P and Manitoba Road, GNR Records; "Picturesque Views," 415; Sweetman, *Recent Experiences;* St. Louis and St. Paul Packet Company, *Our Last Season's Log Book,* 22–24; Butterworth, *Zigzag Journeys,* 182–97.

28. *American Traveller's Journal,* 7–8; Land, *Historical and Descriptive Review,* 9, 14; Hill to Stephen, 18 July 1878, Hill to Stephen, 23 April 1879, JJH LB; Hill to J. S. Kennedy & Co., 15 July and 11 August 1879, Comptroller's Office, Edward T. Nichols Files, GNR Records.

29. *1880 Population Schedules; 1880 Census of Manufactures,* xxxiii, 5–8, 44–50, 137–40, 273–77, 379–80; U.S. Bureau of Statistics, Treasury Department, *Tables Showing Arrivals;* Minnesota Secretary of State, *Census of the State of Minnesota* (1885) [hereafter *1885 Population Schedules*]; SPM&M, *Red River Valley;* Hill to Kennedy, reporting "we are getting more settlers than ever before and of a better class than I can send going into a new country," 13 April 1881, JJH LB; Van Horne to C. Drinkwater, CPR Secretary, stating that the CPR had reached Calgary, Alberta, 18 March 1882, JJH GC. See also Tassé, *North-West.* A Canadian booster, Tassé compares Minnesota and Manitoba.

30. St. Paul and Duluth Railroad, *Homes for the Million,* 50.

31. St. Paul and Sioux City Railroad Company, *Facts, Fancies, and Conclusions* and *Southwestern Minnesota;* CM&SP, *Tourists' Manual;* SPM&M, *Annual Report* [1881]; State of Minnesota, *Report of the Board of Immigration of the State of Minnesota* [1881]; Catholic Colonization Bureau, *An Invitation to the Land.*

32. *1881 Business Directory; Annual Report of the Railroad Commissioner of Minnesota* [1881]; *1875 Population Schedules; 1880 Population Schedules; 1885 Population Schedules;* 23 June 1880 diary entry, Boyle Papers; comparison of food prices, McAuley Papers.

33. Land, *Historical and Descriptive Review,* 28. See also 1873–82 Cash Book, St. Paul Elevator, 1873–83 Journal, Box 117, Volume 42, 1872–86 Ledger, Northwestern Union Packet Company, 1866–82 Wheat Ledger, Stock Ledger, St. Louis and St. Paul Packet Company, 1866–88 Ledger,

People's Line, Davidson Papers; St. Louis and St. Paul Packet Company, *The Mississippi;* ASCE, *Fifteenth Annual Convention.*

34. John Ireland to Hill, on Irish Colonization project, 7 and 8 January 1880, Molyneux St. John to Richard B. Angus, 3 February, 5 and 26 March, 22 April, 4 May, and 7 June 1880, on competition for British-Isle immigrants from Canada and the necessity to move into the German and Scandinavian regions for settlers (additional letters from St. John laced throughout Box 12 folders and Volume R-26, JJH LB, particularly to Angus, 4 December 1880), W. D. Ingus, London, to Hill, 21 April 1881, JJH GC; Hill to Angus, 27 March 1882, Hill to Stephen, 6 April 1882, JJH LB; Johnson, *A Tale of Two Cities.*

35. Land, *Historical and Descriptive Review,* 28. See also "Picturesque Views"; ASCE, *Fifteenth Annual Convention.* On rising social expectations, see, in particular, Longstreet's American best-seller, *Social Etiquette,* the first elaboration of modern social aspirations that launched similar books throughout the nation, including Minnesota publications such as *The Manners That Win.*

36. Land, *Historical and Descriptive Review,* 11, 27–28.

37. 7, 13, 23, 29, and 31 March 1880 diary entries, Boyle Papers. See also Taylor, *Through to St. Paul and Minneapolis.*

38. 13 March 1880 diary entry, Boyle Papers. See also liquidation notices, *Pioneer* and *Tribune,* 1878–83, MHS Newspaper Collections; ASCE, *Fifteenth Annual Convention.*

39. 7 January 1880 (see also 2 December 1878, 1 December 1880, and 2 September 1882) diary entries, Boyle Papers; James H. Woolsey's bankruptcy statement of creditors, 24 December 1877, Noyes Records.

40. Kittson sold out to the other associates on 24 May 1881 and joined Auerbach, Finch, and Van Slyke on 31 December 1881. See Comptroller's Office, GNR

Records; 18 October 1880 and 10 January 1883 diary entries, Boyle Papers. On Auerbach, see Bankers' Association of Minnesota to Hill, 15 June 1882, President's Office, GNR Records; ASCE, *Fifteenth Annual Convention.*

41. 5 January 1878, 11 September 1880, and 25 January 1881 diary entries, Boyle Papers (in addition, see 1881–83 diary entries in general for the growth of the firm); ASCE, *Fifteenth Annual Convention; 1881 Business Directory.*

42. Liquidation Sale notices, *Pioneer* and *Tribune*, 1878–83, MHS Newspaper Collections.

43. 30 September 1880 diary entry, Boyle Papers.

44. Year-end memoranda, 1878, and 5 and 14 August 1879 diary entries (see also summer of 1879 and 1880, on job-hopping), Boyle Papers.

45. 28 March and 20 August 1881, 16 May and 3 October 1882, and 17 September 1883 diary entries, with the dawning realization that he had a "design of going into society to a moderate extent," Boyle Papers (Volume 8, 1883, elaborates on his desires of "going into society," on both a moderate and immoderate scale). See also *American Traveller's Journal*, 7–8; Henry Wenzell, Metropolitan Hotel, St. Paul, 24 October 1882, Henry B. Wenzell and Family Papers [hereafter Wenzell Papers]; Hilkey, *Character Is Capital.*

46. 26 September 1883 and 18 December 1887 diary entries, Boyle Papers.

47. 27 April 1883 diary entry, Boyle Papers.

48. Horetzky, *Some Startling Facts;* Hill to W. H. Lyons, Winnipeg, 21 January 1881, Hill to Charles Tuttle, Winnipeg, 21 January 1881, Angus to C. Drinkwater, 13 and 20 July 1881, Stephen to Kennedy, 8 August 1881, Angus to J. H. McTavish, 18 August 1881, Hill to Angus, 23 January 1882, Hill to Van Horne, 27 April 1882, Stephen to Van Horne, 7 July 1882, Stephen to Sir John A. McDonald, 19

August 1882, Hill to Stephen, 8 September 1882 and 25 July 1883, Hill to Stephen, personal, 30 June 1882, JJH LB; Cruise and Griffiths, *Lords of the Line*, 22–32.

49. Angus to Hill, 2 December 1881, Van Horne to Hill, 18 and 22 March 1882, Van Horne to the Associates, 20 May 1882, Hill to Angus, private and confidential, 19 June 1882, Stephen to Hill, private, 26 June 1882, Van Horne to Hill, 19 and 26 June 1882, Van Horne to Hill, 30 June and 3 and 4 July 1882, Van Horne to Hill, 12 and 13 July 1882, JJH GC; Hill to Stephen, personal, 20 August 1883, JJH LB.

50. J. S. Kennedy Tod to Hill, 18 March 1882, Stephen to Hill, 10 September 1882, Kennedy to Hill, 3 October 1882, private, 30 October 1882, private, 1, 4, and 9 November 1882, 16 November 1882, confidential, 20 and 30 December 1882, 4 January 1883, private, 9 January 1883, personal, 18 January and 7 and 16 February 1883, Donald Smith to Hill, private, 26 April 1883, Kennedy to Hill, private, 30 April 1883, 7 May 1883, extract from the 9 May meeting of the CPR board of directors, Statement of Account, 23 May 1883, Kennedy to Hill, confirming the Canadian associates the responsible short-selling parties, 28 May 1883, JJH GC.

51. Kennedy to Hill, 13 February and 27 April 1883, Tod to Hill, 9 July 1883, Angus and Stephen (letter of resignation) to Hill, 12 July 1883, J. Kennedy Tod to Hill, 16 and 19 July 1883, D. Willus James to Hill, 25 July 1883, Shearman & Sterling, law offices, New York, to Hill, 26 July 1883, Angus to Hill, private, pooling agreements between Smith, Hill, Stephen, Kennedy, and others, 27 July and 18 and 19 October 1883, Kennedy to Hill, private, 30 October 1883, J. S. Kennedy and Co. to Hill, announcing Kennedy's retirement, 2 November 1883, Kennedy to Hill, strictly confidential, about the proceeds of Hill's CPR stock and the stock in the Manitoba pool, 5 November 1883, Kennedy to Hill, 15 and 17 November 1883,

JJH GC; Hill to Kennedy, 3 January 1883, Hill to Angus, 3 May 1883, JJH LB. For one of Hill's new notions of self-interest, see St. Paul and Northern Pacific Railway Company, *Articles of Incorporation* and *By-Laws*.

52. Hill to Kennedy, including Minneapolis Union Railway Articles of Incorporation, 4 February 1882, Comptroller's Office, GNR Records; Hill to Angus, 19 February 1882, to L. S. Buffington, Architect, Minneapolis, 17 March 1882, to C. H. Pettit, Treasurer, Minneapolis Elevator, 5 September 1882, JJH LB; Hill Ledger 2, Accounts, Financial Records, 1882–85, Personal Finance, JJHRL; Agreement to assist St. Paul Harvester Works, 27 January 1883, JJH GC.

53. Ingersol, "Home of Hiawatha," 78–79; Hayden, *Great West,* 254–56; *1881 Business Directory*.

54. Chamber of Commerce of Minneapolis, *Joint Annual Report*. On Minneapolis as a manufacturing center and its inability to compete with St. Paul's dry goods wholesalers, see 8, 10, and 17 November and 15 and 16 December 1880 diary entries, Boyle Papers (on 16 December, Boyle argued, "I do not entertain the popular St. Paul prejudice against Minneapolis. It is a fine town and I like its people."); W. D. Lynn, 5 December 1881, F. Steele Papers.

55. Ingersol, "Home of Hiawatha"; *1881 Business Directory;* Chamber of Commerce of Minneapolis, *Joint Annual Report*. On the rebuilt Washburn mill, see 19 June 1880 diary entry, Boyle Papers; Taylor, *Through to St. Paul and Minneapolis,* 37; *American Traveller's Journal,* 7.

56. Taylor, *Through to St. Paul and Minneapolis,* 35–37; *1881 Business Directory;* Hanson, comp., *Grand Opening*.

57. *Minneapolis: Central Park Region;* Ingersol, "Home of Hiawatha," 75; Hanson, comp., *Grand Opening,* 57; Early Railroad Data, JJHRL; 10 July 1883 diary entry, Boyle Papers; *1881 Business Direc-*

tory; Chamber of Commerce of Minneapolis, *Joint Annual Report,* 97–98.

58. Taylor, *Through to St. Paul and Minneapolis,* 37; Hill to Kennedy, 4 February 1882, Comptroller's Office, GNR Records; Marshall Field to Hill, 29 June 1882, JJH GC.

59. *Report of the Minneapolis, Sault Ste. Marie and Atlantic Railway Company, to the Board of Railroad and Warehouse Commissioners of Minnesota, for the Year Ending June 30, 1888,* Soo Line Railroad Company Records.

60. Hanson, comp., *Grand Opening,* 16, 27; ASCE, *Fifteenth Annual Convention*.

61. St. Paul Chamber of Commerce, *Annual Report* [1883], Fairchild & Davidson to Hill, 17 June 1884, JJH GC; *1880 Census of Manufactures;* Land, *Historical and Descriptive Review,* 66–68; *1885 Population Schedules; 1883 Business Directory;* Johnson, *A Tale of Two Cities*.

62. St. Paul Chamber of Commerce, *Annual Report* [1883], Fairchild & Davidson to Hill, 17 June 1884, JJH GC; *1880 Census of Manufactures;* Land, *Historical and Descriptive Review,* 66–68; *1885 Population Schedules; 1883 Business Directory;* Johnson, *A Tale of Two Cities*.

63. Lake Minnetonka Guest Register. Minneapolitans tended to frequent the "Highland Club" at Lake Minnetonka while St. Paulites generally patronized White Bear Lake; that is, until the Hotel Lafayette made Lake Minnetonka an exclusive resort. Thereafter, Twin City masses tended to visit Lakes Calhoun and Harriet in Minneapolis and White Bear Lake and Lake Como in St. Paul, particularly after urban elites donated funds to build them up as amusement parks on the model of New York's Coney Island. See, for example, St. Paul and Sioux City Railroad Company, *Picturesque Minnesota;* 17 July and 23 August 1883 diary entries, Boyle Papers; *Minneapolis: Central Park Region;* Hanson, comp., *Grand Opening,* 57–58; ASCE, *Fifteenth Annual Convention;*

Hill Donation Book, JJHRL; Hill to Hotel Proprietor in Tiffin, OH, October 1882, JJH LB.

64. Minneapolis, *1884 Annual Report; Tribune Handbook of Minneapolis; 1880 Census of Manufactures*, xxxiii, 5–8, 44–50, 137–40, 273–77, 379–80; *1885 Population Schedules*, 26; Johnson, *A Tale of Two Cities*.

65. Land, *Historical and Descriptive Review*; ASCE, *Fifteenth Annual Convention*; Hanson, comp., *Grand Opening*. See also, Kwolek-Folland, *Engendering Business*.

66. Dora to her mother, 2 June 1877, Edward Sidney Pattee and Family Papers [hereafter Pattee Papers]; 4 June 1879 and 18 December 1880 diary entries, Boyle Papers.

67. 30 October 1883 diary entry, Boyle Papers.

68. Department of Health, Miscellaneous Records, and Water Analysis Reports, MSA; 11 March and 17 April 1882 and 8 September and 28 November 1883 diary entries, Boyle Papers.

69. Department of Health, Miscellaneous Records, and Water Analysis Reports, MSA; 11 March and 17 April 1882 and 8 September and 28 November 1883 diary entries, Boyle Papers.

70. Henry Wenzell, 24 October 1882, Wenzell Papers; Hill Donation Book, JJHRL; ASCE, *Fifteenth Annual Convention*; Hanson, comp., *Grand Opening*, 90; 4 September 1883 diary entry, stating that "the celebrations of yesterday have intensified the spirit of rivalry between St. Paul and Minneapolis," Boyle Papers. See also St. Louis and St. Paul Packet Company, *Our Last Season's Log Book*, 22–24.

71. *1881 Business Directory*; Hanson, comp., *Grand Opening*; ASCE, *Fifteenth Annual Convention*; "Begging Letter" files and Hill Donation Book, JJHRL; C. McReeve, City Bank, Minneapolis, to Hill, 7 June 1883, North Star Real Estate Exchange, Minneapolis, to Hill, 7 June 1883, E. M. Runyan to Hill, overleaf, list-

ing the people's choice for the most prominent men in St. Paul, 7 June 1883, E. T. Nichols, assistant secretary, to A. H. Bode, comptroller, 12 July 1883, JJH GC. See also Kirkland, *Dream and Thought*.

72. St. Paul Common Council, *Proceedings* [1882], 131; *1880 Population Schedules; 1881 Business Directory*; Land, *Historical and Descriptive Review*, 66–69; Hanson, comp., *Grand Opening; 1885 Population Schedules*; St. Paul Chamber of Commerce to Hill, private, 11 October 1883, Minnesota Magdalen Society request for funds, JJH GC; "Happy New Year, 1879," list of entertainers and hostesses, *Tribune*, 1878, MHS Newspaper Collections; "Picturesque Views"; Boyle, on elites donating funds at the orphan's fair and to Irish famine victims, 12 November and 18 December 1879 and 4 January and 26 February 1880, Boyle Papers; Metropolitan Opera House Records, Louis N. Scott and Family Papers.

73. 23 November 1882 and 24 May 1883 diary entries, Boyle Papers; Manvel to J. S. Kennedy, 21 November 1882, Comptroller's Office, GNR Records.

74. Land, *Historical and Descriptive Review*, 114–43; Henry Wenzell, 24 October 1882, Wenzell Papers; Hanson, comp., *Grand Opening*; Dora Jewett to her mother, 27 January 1878, Pattee Papers.

75. *Report of the Northern Pacific Railroad Company to the Railroad Commissioner of the State of Minnesota* [1882], NPR Records; Land, *Historical and Descriptive Review*, 82.

NOTES TO THE CONCLUSION

1. Amelia qtd. in Ullman Papers, 82, 12.

2. Taylor, *Through to St. Paul and Minneapolis*, 37.

3. Degler, *Out of Our Past*.

4. Hill to J. S. Kennedy & Co., 15 July 1879, SP&P, GNR Records. See Igler, *Industrial Cowboys*, as well as this volume's Introduction for comparative studies.

Bibliography

ARCHIVES

JJHRL   James J. Hill Reference Library, St. Paul, Minnesota

MHS   Minnesota Historical Society, St. Paul, Minnesota

MSA   Minnesota State Archives, MHS, St. Paul, Minnesota

PRIMARY SOURCES
Manuscript Collections

Abbe, Abby Fuller. Papers. MHS.

Abbott, Edward T. Papers. MHS.

Adams, Chandler B. Papers. MHS.

Adams, Charles Francis and Family. Papers. MHS.

Amherst H. Wilder Foundation. Records. MHS.

Andrews, C. C. Miscellaneous Pamphlets 1–17, 1865–1890s. MHS.

Auerbach, Maurice and Family. Papers, MHS.

Bailly, Alexis. Papers. MHS.

Bass, Jacob Wales and Family. Papers. MHS.

Bill, Fred A. and Family. Papers. MHS.

Biscoe, George Street and Family. Papers. MHS.

Bowler, James Madison. Papers. MHS.

Boyle, Michael J. Papers. MHS.

Bromley, Edward A. Early Photographs of St. Paul. MHS Sound and Visual Collection.

Brown, Edwin Hacker. Papers. MHS.

Burbank, Henry Clay. Papers. MHS.

Burbank, James C. Papers. MHS.

Buswell, Milton and Family. Papers. MHS.

Cathcart, Alexander Henry Family. Papers. MHS.

Cathedral of St. Paul. Papers. MHS.

Chaney, Josiah Blodgett and Family. Papers. MHS.

Chapin, George Aaron and Family. Papers. MHS.

Clark, Charles Henry and Family. Papers. MHS.

Clark, Francis Byron and Family. Papers. MHS.

Cole and Weeks, Minneapolis. Records. MHS.

Cooke, Jay. Papers. MHS.

Corbett, Mrs. Harriet B. and Family. Papers. MHS.

Cory-Forbes Family. Papers. MHS.

Cressey, Frank B. and Family. Papers. MHS.

Crowe, Isaac. Papers. MHS.

Davidson, William Fuson. Papers. MHS.

Dean, William Blake and Family. Papers. MHS.

Dodge, Henry M. Papers. MHS.

Dousman, Hercules L. Papers. MHS.

Drew, Benjamin. Papers. MHS.

Eggleston, Edward. Papers. MHS.

Farnsworth, John A. *The Early History of St. Paul.* 1868. MHS.

Field-Schlick, St. Paul. Records. MHS.

First Baptist Church, St. Paul. Papers. MHS.

Flandrau, Charles E. Papers. MHS.

Folsom, Simeon Pearl. Papers. MHS.

Fridley, Abraham McCormick and Family. Papers. MHS.

Gillman, John B. Papers. MHS.

Godfrey, Ard and Family. Papers. MHS.

Great Northern Railway Company. Records. Includes St. Paul and Pacific and St. Paul, Minneapolis and Manitoba Records. MHS.

Hayes, Moses P. Papers. MHS.

Hebrew Ladies Benevolent Society. Papers. MHS.

Hersey, Staples and Company, Stillwater. Papers. MHS.

Hill, James J. Papers, including addresses, begging letter files, donation book, early railroad data special file, general correspondence, letterpress books, personal finance files, real estate deeds and abstracts, and St. Anthony Falls Water Power Company special file #1. JJHRL.

House of Hope Presbyterian Church, St. Paul. Records. MHS.

Hoyt, John Franklin and Family. Papers. MHS.

Illingsworth, William H. Reserve Album 54. MHS Photograph Collection.

Lake Minnetonka Guest Register. MHS.

Lewis, G. Winthrop, compiler. *History of the House of Hope Church, 1856–1914, At the Request of F. G. Ingersoll, the Oldest Living Member of the House of Hope Church. St. Paul.* 1939. MHS.

Lochren, William. Papers. MHS.

Ludden, John D. Papers. MHS.

Lund, Charles C. Papers. MHS.

McAuley, John A. Account books. MHS.

McGill, Andrew Ryan and Family. Papers. MHS.

Mason, William F. and Family. Papers. MHS.

Mattocks, Ebenezer Brewer and Family. Papers. MHS.

Mattson, Hans and Family. Papers. MHS.

Merritt, Benjamin. Papers. MHS.

Minnesota. Department of Health. Records. MSA.

Minnesota. Governor. Files. MSA.

Minnesota. Hennepin County. Records. MSA.

Minnesota. Minneapolis. Records. MSA.

Minnesota. Public Examiner. Biennial Reports. MSA.

Minnesota. Ramsey County. Records. MSA.

Minnesota. Record of Poor Relief. MSA.

Minnesota. St. Paul. Records. MSA.

Minnesota Millers State Association. Records. MHS.

Minnesota Territorial Papers. MSA.

Moore, George Nelson. Papers. MHS.

Mount Zion Hebrew Congregation, St. Paul. Papers. MHS.

Mumford, James. Papers. MHS.

Murray, William Pitt. Papers. MHS.

Northern Pacific Railway. Land Department Records. Microfilm Collections. MHS.

Northern Pacific Railway Company. Records. MHS.

North-Western Express Company. Papers. MHS.

Noyes Bros. & Cutler. Records. MHS.

Owens, John Phillips. Papers. MHS.

Palmer, Bettie. Letter. MHS.

Pattee, Edward Sidney and Family. Papers. MHS.

Person, Arvid. Papers. MHS.

Philecclesian Society. Papers. MHS.

Pillsbury, John Sargeant and Family. Papers. MHS.

Pope, John. Papers. MHS.

Randall, Elisha D. K. Papers. MHS.

Rice, Henry Mower. Papers. MHS.

Riheldaffer, John G. and Family. Papers. MHS.

Rose Brothers Fur Company, St. Paul. Records. MHS.

St. Paul. Subscription List to Encourage Enlistment During the Rebellion, 1861–65. FF613.S4. MHS.

St. Paul Turners. Papers. MHS.

St. Paul Union Stockyards Company, South Saint Paul, MN. Records. MHS.

Scott, Louis N. and Family. Papers. MHS.

Seabury, Channing and Family. Papers. MHS.

Sibley, Henry Hastings. Papers. MHS.

Soo Line Railroad Company. Records. MHS.

Steele, Franklin. Papers. MHS.

Steele, John and Family. Papers. MHS.

Thompson, Horace and Family. Papers. MHS.

Treadwell, John N. Papers. MHS.

Trinity Lutheran Church, St. Paul. Records. MHS.

Ullman, Mrs. Joseph (Amelia). Papers. MHS.

Upton, Benjamin Franklin. Photographs. MHS Photograph Collection.

Wenzell, Henry B. and Family. Papers. MHS.

Whipple, Henry B. and Family. Papers. MHS.

White, Truman S. Papers. MHS.

Wilkin, Alexander and Family. Papers. MHS.

William Branch Company, St. Paul. Records. MHS.

William Hartshorn and Co., St. Paul. General Merchandise and Fur Trade Ledger, 1847–48. MHS.

Winslow, James M. and Family. Papers. MHS.

Government Documents

Jefferson, Thomas. *Message from the President of the United States, Supplementary to His Message of the Sixth Instant, Communicating Documents Respecting Louisiana.* Washington, DC, 1805. Ann Arbor, MI: University Microfilms, United States President (1801–1809: Jefferson), film B1549, Reel 16, No. 1034.

Lea, Albert Miller. *Notes on Wisconsin Territory, with a Map.* Philadelphia, PA: Henry S. Tanner, 1836. Ann Arbor, MI: University Microfilms, American Culture Series, Film B1512, Reel 79.2.

Lewis, Meriwether. *History of the Expedition Under the Command of Captains Lewis and Clark; to the Sources of the Missouri, Thence Across the Rocky Mountains and Down the River Columbia to the Pacific Ocean, Performed during the Years 1804–5–6.* Philadelphia, PA: Bradsford and Inskeep, 1814. Library of Congress Microfiche Card Q1352.

Minnesota, State of. *Territorial Census of 1857: Population Schedules.* Washington, DC. MHS Microfilm Collections.

Minnesota Secretary of State. *Census of the State of Minnesota, 1865.* St. Paul: Frederick Driscoll, 1866. In *Minnesota Executive Documents, 1865.* MHS.

———. *Census of the State of Minnesota by Counties, Towns, Cities, and Wards, May 1, 1875.* St. Paul: Pioneer Press Co., 1876. In *Minnesota Executive Documents,* 1875, vol. 1. MHS.

———. *Census of the State of Minnesota by Counties, Towns, Cities, and Wards, May 1, 1885.* St. Paul: Pioneer Press Co., 1886. In Minnesota Executive Documents, 1886, vol. 1. MHS.

U.S. Bureau of Statistics, Treasury Department. *Tables Showing Arrivals of Alien Passengers and Immigrants in the United States from 1820 to 1888.* Washington, DC: Government Printing Office, 1889.

U.S. Bureau of the Census. *Census of the State of Minnesota, by Counties, Towns, Cities, and Wards, as Enumerated by Authority of the United States Bureau of the Census, 9th Census, June 1, 1870.* St. Paul: Pioneer Press Company, 1871. MHS Microfilm Collections.

———. *Census of the State of Minnesota, by Counties, Towns, Cities, and Wards, as Enumerated by Authority of the United States Bureau of the Census, 10th Census, June 1, 1880.* Washington, DC: Government Printing Office. MHS Microfilm Collections.

U.S. Census Office. *Eighth Census of the United States, 1860: Minnesota Population Schedules.* Washington, DC: Government Printing Office. MHS Microfilm Collections.

———. *Manufactures of the United States in 1860; Compiled from the Original Returns of the Eighth Census.* Washington, DC: Government Printing Office, 1865. JJHRL.

———. *Population Schedules of the Seventh Census of the United States, 1850: Minnesota Territory.* 55. Washington, DC: Government Printing Office, 1963. MHS Microfilm Collections.

——. *Report on Manufacturing Industries in the United States at the Eleventh Census: 1890, Part II, Statistics of Cities.* Washington, DC: Government Printing Office, 1895. JJHRL.

——. *Report on the Manufactures of the United States at the Tenth Census, June 1, 1880.* Washington, DC: Government Printing Office, 1883. JJHRL.

——. *Twelfth Census of the United States, Taken in the Year 1900, Manufactures, Part II, States and Territories, Volume III.* Washington, DC: Government Printing Office, 1900. JJHRL.

U.S. Continental Congress. *An Ordinance for the Government of the Territory of the United States, North-west of the River Ohio. Philadelphia, 1787.* Ann Arbor, MI: University Microfilms. Early American Imprints 45181.

Walker, Francis Amasa, for the U.S. Secretary of the Interior. *Ninth Census of the United States, Volume III, The Statistics of the Wealth and Industry of the United States.* Washington, DC: Government Printing Office, 1872. JJHRL.

Wheelock, Joseph, for the Minnesota Bureau of Statistics. *Minnesota: Its Place Among the States, Being the First Annual Report of the Commissioner of Statistics, for the Year Ending Jan 1st, 1860.* St. Paul: W. R. Marshall, 1862. Library of Congress Microfiche Card A-96, 127.

Newspapers

All newspaper collections cited are at the MHS

Boston Daily Journal
Boston Post
Emigrant Aid Journal of Minnesota (Nininger)
Fergus Falls (MN) Journal
Minneapolis Tribune
Minnesota Pioneer
Minnesota Register
Minnesota Republican
Minnesotian
Saint Anthony Express

Saint Anthony Falls Democrat
Saint Paul Financial and Real Estate Advertiser
Saint Paul Financial, Real Estate and Railroad Advertiser
Winona (MN) Republican

**Published Works
and Printed Materials**

Act Proposing a Loan of State Credit to the Land Grant Railroad Companies with Arguments in Favor of Its Approval by the People. St. Paul: Pioneer and Democrat, 1858. MHS.

American Society of Civil Engineers. *Fifteenth Annual Convention of the American Society of Civil Engineers, held at St. Paul, Minn., June 19–22, 1883.* St. Paul: n.p., 1883. MHS.

American Traveller's Journal: Devoted to Travel, Descriptions, and Illustrations of American and Foreign Scenery. New York: The American Traveller's Publishing Co., 1881. MHS.

Andreas, A. T. *An Illustrated Historical Atlas of the State of Minnesota.* Chicago: A. T. Andreas, 1874. MHS.

Andrews, C. C. *History of St. Paul, Minn., with Illustrations and Biographical Sketches of Some of Its Prominent Men and Pioneers.* Syracuse, NY: D. Mason & Co., 1890. MHS.

Annual Report of the Railroad Commissioner of Minnesota, for the Year Ending June 30, 1880. Compiled by William R. Marshall. St. Peter, MN: J. K. Moore, 1881. MHS.

Annual Report of the Railroad Commissioner of Minnesota, for the Year Ending June 30, 1876. Compiled by William R. Marshall. St. Paul: Pioneer Press Co., 1877. MHS.

Argyll, John Douglas Sutherland Campbell. *The Canadian North-West: Speech Delivered at Winnipeg by his Excellency the Marquis of Lorne, Governor General of Canada, after his Tour Through Manitoba and the North-West, During the*

Summer of 1881. Ottawa: n.p., 1881. MHS.

Associated Charities of Minneapolis. *Annual Report of the Assorted Charities of Minneapolis*. Minneapolis: The Charities, 1889–1901. MHS.

Atwater, Isaac, ed. *History of the City of Minneapolis, Minnesota*. New York: Munsell, 1893. MHS.

Baldwin School. *Catalogues of the Baldwin School and the Academic Department of the College of Saint Paul, Minnesota*. St. Paul: Minnesotian offices, 1854. MHS.

Bell, Robert. "On the Commercial Importance of Hudson's Bay, with Remarks on Recent Surveys and Investigations." *Proceedings of the Royal Geographical Survey* 10 (October 1881): 577–86. MHS.

The Biographical Dictionary and Portrait Gallery of Representative Men of Chicago, Minnesota Cities and the World's Columbian Exposition, with Illustrations on Steel. Chicago: American Biographical Publishing Co., 1892. MHS.

Bishop, Harriet. *Floral Home; or, First Years in Minnesota: Early Sketches, Later Settlements, and Further Developments*. New York: Sheldon, Blakeman and Co., 1857. MHS.

Bond, John Wesley. *Minnesota and Its Resources: To Which Are Appended Campfire Sketches, or, Notes of a Trip from St. Paul to Pembina and Selkirk Settlement on the Red River of the North*. New York: Redfield, 1853. MHS.

Borrett, George Tuthill. *Letters from Canada and the United States*. London: J. E. Adlard and Bartholomew Close, printers, 1865. MHS.

Brennan, John. *St. Paul & Sioux City and Sioux City & St. Paul R.R. Directory and Business Guide*. Sioux City, IA: Sioux City Times Job Printing House, 1873. MHS.

Burnquist, Joseph A. A., ed. *Minnesota and Its People*. Vol. 1. Chicago: S. J. Clarke Publishing Co., 1924. MHS.

Butterworth, Hezekiah. *Zigzag Journeys in the Western States of America: The Atlantic to the Pacific. A Summer Trip of the Zigzag Club from Boston to the Golden Gate*. London: Dean and Son, 1883. MHS.

Canadian Pacific Railway. *Annual Report for the Year 1889, and Report of the Proceedings at the Ninth Annual Meeting of the Shareholders, Held at the General Offices of the Company, Montreal, on Wednesday, 14th May, 1890*. Montreal: The Company, 1890. MHS.

Catholic Colonization Bureau. *An Invitation to the Land: Reasons and Figures*. St. Paul: Pioneer Press, 1877. MHS.

Chamber of Commerce of Minneapolis and Minneapolis Board of Trade. *Joint Annual Report of the Chamber of Commerce and Board of Trade of the City of Minneapolis*. Minneapolis: Tribune Job Rooms Printing, 1884. MHS.

Chicago, Milwaukee and St. Paul Railway. *Dakota, the Land of Promise: How to Go & What to Do When You Get There*. Milwaukee, WI: Riverside Printing Co., 1883. MHS.

———. *Guide for Tourists, Business-Men, Emigrants, and Colonists*. Chicago: The Railway, 1871. MHS.

———. *Summer Resorts and Watering Places of the North-West Illustrated*. Chicago: Rand, McNally and Co., 1874. MHS.

———. *Tourists' Manual to the Health and Pleasure Resorts of the Golden Northwest*. Chicago: The Railway, 1880. MHS.

Chisholm, C. R. & Co. *Chisholm's All Round Route and Panoramic Guide of the St Lawrence . . . and Western Tourist's Guide to the Famous Summer Resorts of the Great Far West, Embracing Detroit, Chicago, Milwaukee, St. Paul, Minneapolis, &c*. Chicago: C. R. Chisholm, 1881. MHS.

Classified Business Directory and Guide Book of St. Paul and Minneapolis. St. Paul and Minneapolis: E. P. Shellenberg and Co., 1881. MHS.

Cobb, Charles, comp. *American Railway Guide: Pocket Companion for the United States.* New York: Curran Dinsmore, 1854. MHS.

Colton, Joseph Hutchinson. *The Western Tourist and Emigrant's Guide through the States of Ohio, Michigan, Indiana, Illinois, Missouri, Iowa and Wisconsin and the Territories of Minnesota, Missouri, and Nebraska: Being an Accurate and Concise Description of Each State and Territory, and Containing the Routes and Distances on the Great Lines of Travel.* New York: J. H. Colton, 1855. MHS.

Currie, David. *The Letters of Rusticus: Investigations in Manitoba and the North-West, for the Benefit of Intending Emigrants.* Montreal: J. Douglas and Son, 1880. MHS.

Curtiss, Daniel S. *Western Portraiture, and Emigrants' Guide: A Description of Wisconsin, Illinois, and Iowa; with Remarks on Minnesota, and Other Territories.* New York: J. H. Colton, 1852. MHS.

Disturnell, John. *The Great Lakes, or Inland Seas of America: Embracing a Full Description of Lakes Superior, Huron, Michigan, Erie, and Ontario; Rivers St. Mary, St. Clair, Detroit, Niagara, and St. Lawrence; Lake Winnipeg, Etc.: Together with the Commerce of the Lakes, and Trips Through the Lakes: Giving a Description of Cities, Towns, Etc., Forming Altogether a Complete Guide for the Pleasure Traveller and Emigrant.* New York: C. Scribner, 1865. MHS.

———. *Tourist's Guide to the Mississippi River: Giving All the Railroad and Steamboat Routes Diverging from Chicago, Milwaukee, and Dubuque, Toward St. Paul, and the Falls of St. Anthony; Also, Railroad and Steamboat Routes from Chicago and Milwaukee to Lake Superior; Together with an Account of Cities and Villages, and Objects of Interest, on the Route and in the Upper Valley of the Mississippi.* New York: American News Company, 1866. MHS.

Ely, Dr. ——— "Minnesota: Its Extent, Fertility, Agricultural Resources, Schools, Rapid Growth, St. Paul, St. Anthony, Population in 1854, &c., &c." *De Bow's Review of Industrial Resources, Statistics, Etc.* 17:4 (October 1854): 350–61. MHS.

First Report of the Railroad Commissioner with Reports of Railroad Corporations, for the Year Ending August 31, 1871. Compiled by A. J. Edgerton. St. Paul: D. Ramaley, 1871. MHS.

Flandrau, Charles E. *Recollections of the Past in Minnesota.* St. Paul: Pioneer Press Co., 1881. MHS.

Fuller, M. A. *Map of the Manufacturing Interests at the Falls of St. Anthony in the City of Minneapolis, Minn.* St. Paul: A. J. Reed, 1873. MHS.

Goddard, Frederick B. *Where to Emigrate and Why.* New York: F. B. Goddard, 1869. MHS.

Great Northern Railway. *First Annual Report of the Great Northern Railway Company, Fiscal Year Ending June 30th, 1890.* St. Paul: The Company, 1890. JJHRL.

Great Northern Railway Company. *Annual Reports.* St. Paul: The Company, 1891–95. MHS.

Haldane, J. W. C. *3800 Miles Across Canada.* London: Simpkin, Marshall, Hamilton, Kent and Co., 1900. MHS.

Hall, Mrs. Cecil. *A Lady's Life on a Farm in Manitoba.* London: W. H. Allen and Co., 1884. MHS.

Hanson, J. H., compiler. *Grand Opening of the Northern Pacific Railway: Celebration at St. Paul, Minnesota, The Eastern Terminus, September 3, 1883.* St. Paul: Brown and Treacy, 1883. MHS.

Hayden, F. V. *The Great West: Its Attractions and Resources. Containing a Popular Description of the Marvelous Scenery, Physical Geography, Fossils, and Glaciers of This Wonderful Region; and the Recent Explorations in the Yellowstone Park, "The Wonderland of America,"*

Also, Valuable Information to Travellers and Settlers Concerning Climate, Health, Mining, Husbandry, Education, the Indians, Mormonism, the Chinese; with the Homestead, Pre-emption, Land, and Mining Laws. Bloomington, IL: C. R. Brodix, 1880. MHS.

Heaton, David. *Summary Statement of the General Interests of Manufacture and Trade Connected with the Upper Mississippi; Together with T. M. Griffith and C. L. Anderson, The Hydrographical Survey and Geology of the Mississippi River from Ft. Snelling to St. Anthony Falls.* Minneapolis: State Atlas Book and Job Printers, 1862. MHS.

Hill, James J. *Highways of Progress.* New York: Doubleday, Page, 1910. Reprint, New York: Arno Press, 1973. Page references are to the 1910 edition. JJHRL.

Horetzky, C. *Some Startling Facts Relating to the Canadian Pacific Railway and the North-West Lands, Also a Brief Discussion Regarding the Route, the Western Terminus and the Lands Available for Settlement.* Ottawa: Free Press offices, 1880. MHS.

Illustrated St. Paul: A Souvenir of the St. Paul Dispatch. St. Paul: Dispatch, 1892. MHS.

Johnson, Charles W. *Another Tale of Two Cities: Minneapolis and St. Paul Compared, Being a Statement of the Facts and Issues Growing out of the Enumeration of the Cities of Minneapolis and St. Paul by Agents of the United States for the Eleventh Census.* Minneapolis: n.p., 1890. MHS.

———. *A Tale of Two Cities: Minneapolis and St. Paul Compared.* Minneapolis: Johnson, Smith and Harrison, 1885. MHS.

King, Charles. "The Twin Cities of the Northwest." In *Cosmopolitan* (October 1890). MHS.

Kloos, J. H. *Report Relative to the Resources, Population & Products of the Country Along the Brainerd and St. Vin-*cent Extensions of the St. Paul & Pacific Railroad, and to the Land Grant, Traffic and Prospects of These Railroad Lines.* St. Paul: Pioneer Printing Co., 1871. MHS.

Lake Superior and Mississippi Railroad Company. *Lands for Emigrants: Lake Superior and Mississippi Railroad, St. Paul to Duluth, Minnesota.* New York: Cushing Bardua and Co., 1871. MHS.

Land, John E. *Historical and Descriptive Review of the Industries of Saint Paul, 1882–83, Trade, Commerce and Manufactures: Manufacturing Advantages, Business and Transportation Facilities, Together with Sketches of the Principal Business Houses and Manufacturing Concerns in St. Paul.* St. Paul: J. E. Land, 1883. MHS.

Lanman, Charles. "A Summer in the Wilderness; Embracing a Canoe Voyage up the Mississippi and around Lake Superior." *The United States Democratic Review* 21:109 (July 1847). MHS.

Leslie, Frank. "A Trip from St. Anthony to Lake Minnetonka and Shakopee Lakes, Minnesota Territory." *Frank Leslie's Illustrated Newspaper* 3:77 (30 May 1857). MHS.

Life of Thomas Hawley Canfield: His Early Efforts to Open a Route for the Transportation of the Products of the West to New England, by Way of the Great Lakes, St. Lawrence River and Vermont Railroads, and His Connection with the Early History of the Northern Pacific Railroad, from the History of the Red River Valley, North Dakota and Park Region of Northwestern Minnesota. Burlington, VT: n.p., 1889. MHS.

Lindley, Clara Hill. *James J. and Mary T. Hill, an Unfinished Chronicle by Their Daughter.* New York: North River Press, 1948. JJHRL.

McMaster, S.W. *60 Years on the Upper Mississippi: My Life and Experiences.* Rock Island, IL: n.p., 1893. MHS.

The Manners that Win: Compiled from the Latest Authorities. Minneapolis: Buckeye Publishing Co., 1882. MHS.

Mattson, Hans. *Reminiscences: The Story of an Emigrant.* St. Paul: D. D. Merrill Co., 1891. MHS.

Minneapolis, City of. *1884 Annual Report.* Minneapolis: n.p., 1885. MHS.

Minneapolis, Minnesota. City Directory Collection. 1859–. MHS.

Minneapolis Board of Trade. *Annual Exhibit of the Manufacturing and Commercial Industry of the City of Minneapolis for 1872: Its Resources, Progress, Beauty of Location, Healthfulness, Attractions, and Advantages as a Place of Settlement for all Seeking a Home or a Location for a Business.* Minneapolis: Board of Trade, 1873. MHS.

———. *History and Growth of Minneapolis, Minnesota.* Minneapolis: Johnson, Smith and Harrison, 1884. MHS.

Minneapolis Business Souvenir. Minneapolis: Bacheller and Furbush, 1885. MHS.

Minneapolis: The Central Park Region of the Northwest. Minneapolis: Johnson, Smith and Harrison, 1883. MHS.

Minnesota, State of. *Annual Report of the Secretary of State to the Legislature of Minnesota for the Fiscal Year Ending July 31, 1886.* St. Paul: Pioneer Press Co., 1886. MSA.

Minnesota and Pacific Railroad. *First Report of the Officers of the Minnesota and Pacific Railraod Company, Presented January 12, 1858.* St. Paul: Goodrich, Somers and Co, 1858. MHS.

Minnesota Constitutional Convention. *Debates and Proceedings of the Constitutional Convention for the Territory of Minnesota, to Form a State Constitution Preparatory to Its Admission into the Union as a State.* St. Paul: G. W. Moore, 1858. MHS.

Minnesota Department of Public Instruction. *Circular Issued by the Superintendent of Public Instruction for the State of Minnesota.* St. Paul, March 24, 1878. MSA.

Minnesota Gazetteer and Business Directory, for 1865, Containing a List of Cities, Villages, and Post Offices in the State; a List of Business Firms; State and County Organizations; a Classified Business Directory, Arranged Alphabetically in Towns; Also Advertisements of Leading Business Houses Throughout the State; with Much Other Useful Information. St. Paul: Groff and Bailey, 1865. MHS.

Minnesota Irish Immigration Convention. *Address of the Minnesota Irish Emigration Convention, Held in the City of St. Paul, Minnesota, January 28, 1869, to the People of Ireland.* St. Paul: Northwestern Chronicle Printing, 1869. MHS.

Minnesota Office of the Railroad Commissioner. *Annual Reports of the Railroad Commissioner, for the Years Ending June 30, 1872–1877.* St. Paul: various printers, 1872–77. MSA.

———. *Communication of the Minnesota Railroad Commissioner.* Minneapolis: Johnson, Smith and Harrison, 1879. MHS.

———. *Communication of the Minnesota Railroad Commissioner* [with reports of railroad corporations included], *1879–1883.* St. Paul: various printers, 1880–84. MSA.

———. *Railroad Map of Minnesota.* St. Paul: A. J. Reed, 1873. MHS.

Minnesota State Board of Immigration. *Annual Report of the Board of Immigration to the Legislature of Minnesota for the Year Ending November, 1867.* St. Paul: The Board, 1868. MHS.

———. *Minnesota as a Home for Immigrants, Being the First and Second Prize Essays Awarded by the Board of Examiners.* St. Paul: n.p., 1865. MHS.

———. *Report of the Board of Immigration of the State of Minnesota.* St. Paul: The Board, 1881. MHS.

Minnesota State Business Directory. Minneapolis: Warner and Foote, 1881. MHS.

National Protection and Collection Bureau, St. Paul Branch, Rogers & Rogers Attorneys. *Monthly Report for Members Only.* St. Paul: Ramaley and Cunningham, 1873. MHS.

Northern Pacific Railroad. *Sketch of Its History: Delineations of the Divisions of Its Transcontinental Line; Its Features as a Great Through Route from the Great Lakes to the Pacific Ocean; Its Relations to the Chief Water Ways of the Continent.* Chicago: Rand, McNally, 1882. MHS.

Northern Pacific Railway. *The Northern Pacific Railway Business Directory, 1883–84, Containing a Classified List of All Business and Professional Men on the Line of the Northern Pacific Railway, from Bozeman, Montana, to St. Paul and Duluth Inclusive, Also Sketches of all Important Towns and Illustrations of Points of Interest.* Minneapolis: Mowry and Fairbank, 1883. MHS.

———. *The Red River Country and Northwestern Minnesota, Letters to the* New York Tribune, Chicago Tribune, *and* Springfield Republican, *from Distinguished Journalists, Descriptive of the Climate, Soil, Resources and Prospects of the Country Traversed by the Northern Pacific Railroad, the Real Estate Security of the Company's 7–30 Land Grant Gold Bonds.* Philadelphia, PA: J. Cooke, 1871. MHS.

Northern Pacific Railway Company. *Guide to the Northern Pacific Railroad Lands of Minnesota.* Boston: Rand, Avery & Co., 1872. JJHRL.

Noyes Bros. & Cutler. *Illustrated Catalogue.* New York: Charles M. Cornwell, 1878. MHS.

Open Letter to the "Hon." W. D. Washburn. St. Paul: n.p., 1888. MHS.

Parker, Nathan H. *The Minnesota Handbook for 1856–57: With a New and Accurate Map.* Boston: J. P. Jewett and Co., 1856. MHS.

Pates, David, and Charles Shrief. *International Hotel Guide Book to St. Paul and Vicinity, and Minnesota Generally.* St. Paul: Pioneer Printing Co., 1860. MHS.

"Picturesque Views in St. Paul and Vicinity." *New York Daily Graphic: An Illustrated Evening Newspaper* 17:1698 (30 August 1878): 415. MHS.

Publicity Club of Minneapolis. *The Story of the Testimonial Dinner to Mr. George A. Brackett.* Minneapolis: The Club, 1910. MHS.

Sabin, Dwight M. *Sabin's Reply to the Washburn Slanders: Washburn Explodes His Immoral Dynamite Bomb and is Hoisted by His Own Petard.* St. Paul: n.p., 1889. MHS.

St. Louis and St. Paul Packet Company. *The Mississippi.* St. Louis, MO: The Company, 1880. MHS.

———. *Our Last Seasons Log Book: Notes Here and There Upon the Upper Mississippi.* New York: Leve and Alden's Publication Department, 1883. MHS.

St. Paul, City of. *Acts of Incorporation and Standing Rules of the Common Council, and Ordinances of the City of Saint Paul, Minnesota Territory, 1855–56.* St. Paul: Minnesotian office, 1856. MHS.

St. Paul, Minneapolis and Manitoba Railway Company. *Annual Reports.* St. Paul: Pioneer Press Company, 1878–91. JJHRL.

———. *By-Laws of the Saint Paul, Minneapolis & Manitoba Railway Company,* May 23, 1879. St. Paul: The Company, 1879. JJHRL.

———. *Facts About Minnesota: Condensed and Compiled from Official Records; Reliable, Practical Information for Immigrants, with a Valuable Map.* St. Paul: Pioneer Press, 1879. MHS.

———. *Records and Indentures,* April 1, 1886. St. Paul: Pioneer Press Company, 1886. JJHRL.

——. *Red River Valley: The Land of Golden Grain.* St. Paul: The Company, 1882. MHS.

——. *Report of the Directors for the Year Ending 30th June 1880.* St. Paul: Pioneer Press Co., 1880. MHS.

——. *Undated Laws.* St. Paul: The Company, n.d. MHS.

St. Paul, Minnesota. City Directory Collection. 1856–79. MHS.

St. Paul and Duluth Railroad Company. *Homes for the Million on the Line of the St. Paul and Duluth Railroad: The Best Location in the West for Small Farmers; and the Advantages to Settlers of the Country between St. Paul and Lake Superior; the Best Country for Grain, Grass, Stock-Raising, and the Dairy Business.* St. Paul: The Company, 1880. MHS.

St. Paul and Northern Pacific Railway Company. *Articles of Incorporation, Formerly the Western Railroad Co. of Minnesota, May 8, 1883.* Boston: J. A. Lowell and Co., 1883. MHS.

——. *By-Laws of the Saint Paul and Northern Pacific Railway Company, May 29, 1883.* Boston: J. A. Lowell and Co., 1883. MHS.

——. *Revenue, Resources and Commercial Importance of the Work: First Report of the Chief Engineer to the President of the Minnesota and Pacific Railroad Co. (now St. Paul, Minneapolis, and Manitoba Railway Co.), Presented January 12, 1858.* St. Paul: Goodrich, Somers and Co., 1858. Reprint, St. Paul: Pioneer Press Co., 1901. MHS.

St. Paul and Pacific Railroad Company. First Division. *Agreement of 1874: First Division of St. Paul and Pacific Railroad Co. with Minneapolis and St. Louis Railway Co.* Minnesota: n.p., 1874. MHS.

St. Paul and Sioux City Railroad Company. *Facts, Fancies, and Conclusions: Read and Reflect.* St. Paul: The Company, 1880. MHS.

——. *Picturesque Minnesota: A Guide for Tourists, Sportsmen, and Invalids Who Contemplate Visiting the Beautiful Summer Resorts of the Northwest.* Minneapolis: Wilcox and Diamond, 1879. MHS.

——. *Southwestern Minnesota, Embracing the Counties . . . ; the Wheat Garden, Indian Corn Region, and Grazing Country of the Northwest.* St. Paul: The Company, 1880. MHS.

St. Paul Board of Education. *Public School System; with Rules and Regulations of the Board of Education of the City of St. Paul, as Revised and Amended May 5, 1862, and the Act Relative to Free Schools, as Amended by Acts of February 10, 1860, February 26, 1860, and February 15, 1862.* St. Paul: Pioneer Printing Co., 1862. MHS.

St. Paul City Clerk. *City Government of St. Paul, Minn., 1885–86.* St. Paul: St. Paul Herald Printers, 1886. MHS.

St. Paul Common Council. *The Charter and Ordinances of the City of Saint Paul (to August 1st, 1863, Inclusive) Together with Legislative Acts Relating to the City.* St. Paul: Daily Pioneer Official Printing, 1863. MHS.

——. *Proceedings of the Common Council of the City of St. Paul for the Year Ending April 9th, 1882.* St. Paul: Press Printing Co., 1882. MSA.

St. Paul Society for the Relief of the Poor. *Fourteenth Annual Report, for the Year Ending Tuesday, January 14, 1890, With a Brief History of the Organization.* St. Paul: William E. Banning, 1890. MHS.

Salient Facts About St. Paul: Some of Her Scenic Attractions. St. Paul: Dispatch Job Printing, 1896. MHS.

Sedgewick, C. M. "The Great Excursion to the Falls of St. Anthony." *Putnam's Monthly* 4 (1854): 325. MHS.

Sixth Annual Report of the Trade and Commerce of Minneapolis for the Year Ending December 31, 1888. Compiled for the Chamber of Commerce by C. C. Sturtevant. Minneapolis: Tribune Job Printing Co., 1889. MHS.

"Special Extra Number, Descriptive of and Illustrating St. Paul, Minnesota." *The American Journal of Progress, an Illustrated Review of American Advancement in Manufactures, Commerce, Architecture, Science, and Finance.* New York, 1899. MHS.

Sweetman, John. *Recent Experiences in the Emigration of Irish Families.* Dublin: M. H. Gill and Son, 1883. MHS.

Tallmadge, Alfred S. *Facts: Abridged from the Report of the St. Paul Chamber of Commerce.* St. Paul: Brown, Treacy, 1890. MHS.

Tassé, Elie. *The North-West: The Province of Manitoba and North-West Territories—The Extent—Salubrity of the Climate—Fertility of the Soil—Products—Regulations Concerning Lands—Prices of Cereals and Farm Implements—Salaries and Wages—Travelling Routes by Land and Water, etc., etc.* Ottawa: Le Canada Offices, 1880. MHS.

Taylor, Frank H. *Through to St. Paul and Minneapolis in 1881, Including the Experiences of Our Triumvirate in Wisconsin and Along the Upper Mississippi.* Philadelphia, PA: Craig, Finley and Co., 1881. MHS.

Taylor, James W. *Railroad System of the State of Minnesota, with Its Railroad, Telegraphic and Postal Connections, Reported to the Common Council of the City of St. Paul, March 31, 1859, in Pursuance of a Resolution of the Council, and Ordered to be Printed.* St. Paul: Pioneer Printing Co., 1859. MHS.

Tribune Hand-Book of Minneapolis: With Map and Illustrations. Minneapolis: Tribune Co., 1884. MHS.

Wales, William W. *Sketch of St. Anthony and Minneapolis, Minnesota Territory.* St. Anthony: W. W. Wales, 1857. MHS.

Washburn, Israel Jr. *From the North-West to the Sea: Remarks of Israel Washburn Jr. Before the Board of Trade of the City of Minneapolis, April 7, 1873.* Portland, ME: Portland Board of Trade, 1873. MHS.

Washburn, William Drew. *The Octopus: Shall the People Rule?* Minneapolis: n.p., 1901. MHS.

Watson & Co.'s Classified Business Directory of Minneapolis, St. Paul, and Other Enterprising Cities of Minnesota and Wisconsin, 1899–1900. New York: The Company, 1900. MHS.

Williams, J. Fletcher, ed. *The Guide to Minnesota, Containing Full Information for the Traveler, Pleasure Seeker and Immigrant, Concerning All Routes of Travel to and in the State; Sketches of Towns and Cities on the Same, etc., etc.* St. Paul: Burritt, 1868. MHS.

———. *A History of the City of St. Paul to 1875.* 1876. Reprint, St. Paul: Minnesota Historical Society Press, 1983. Page references are to the 1876 edition. MHS.

Wilson, Joseph M. *Minneapolis and St. Anthony Falls: With a Description of the Country Above the Falls, from Authentic Sources.* Philadelphia, PA: The Author, 1857. MHS.

Young, Edward, U.S. Treasury Department, Bureau of Statistics. *Information for Immigrants, Relative to the Prices and Rentals of Land, the Staple Products, Facilities of Access to Market, Cost of Farm Stock, Kind of Labor in Demand in the Western and South States, etc., etc.* Philadelphia, PA: Samuel D. Burlock, 1871. MHS.

———. *Labor in Europe and America: A Special Report on the Rates of Wages, the Cost of Subsistence, and the Condition of the Working Classes in Great Britain, France, Belgium, Germany, and Other Countries of Europe, Also in the United States and British America.* Philadelphia, PA: S. A. George, 1875. MHS.

SECONDARY AND OTHER PUBLISHED SOURCES

Abbott, Carl. *Boosters and Businessmen: Popular Economic Thought and Urban*

Growth in the Antebellum Middle West. Westport, CT: Greenwood Press, 1981.

———. "Regional City and Network City: Portland and Seattle in the Twentieth Century." *Western Historical Quarterly* 23 (August 1992): 293–322.

Adler, Jeffrey S. *Yankee Merchants and the Making of the Urban West: The Rise and Fall of Antebellum St. Louis.* New York: Cambridge University Press, 1991.

Aiken, David Wyatt. *The Grange: Its Origin, Progress, and Educational Purposes.* Philadelphia, PA: J. A. Wagenseller, 1884.

Alexander, Gregory S. *Commodity and Propriety: Competing Visions of Property in American Legal Thought, 1776–1970.* Chicago: University of Chicago Press, 1997.

Alger, Horatio Jr. *Ragged Dick and Struggling Upward.* 1868 and 1890. Reprinted together, New York: Viking, 1985.

Anderson, Gary Clayton. *Little Crow, Spokesman for the Sioux.* St. Paul: Minnesota Historical Society Press, 1986.

Andersson-Skog, Lena, and Olle Krantz, eds. *Institutions in the Transport and Communications Industries: State and Private Actors in the Making of Institutional Patterns, 1850–1990.* Canton, MA: Science History Publications, 1999.

Appleby, Joyce. *Capitalism and a New Social Order: The Republican Vision of the 1790s.* New York: New York University Press, 1984.

Artibise, Alan F. J., ed. *Town and City: Aspects of Western Canadian Urban Development.* Regina, SK: Canadian Plains Research Center, 1981.

Atherton, Lewis E. *The Frontier Merchant in Mid-America.* Columbia: University of Missouri Press, 1971.

Atkins, Annette. *Harvest of Grief: Grasshopper Plagues and Public Assistance in Minnesota, 1873–78.* St. Paul: Minnesota Historical Society Press, 1984.

Ayers, Edward L., et al. *All Over the Map: Rethinking American Regions.* Baltimore, MD: Johns Hopkins University Press, 1996.

Babcock, Charles F. "Rails West: The Rock Island Excursion of 1854." *New Haven (CT) Palladium,* June 1–15, 1854. Reprinted in *Minnesota History* 34 (Winter 1954): 133–43.

Bailyn, Bernard, and Philip D. Morgan, eds. *Strangers Within the Realm: Cultural Margins of the First British Empire.* Chapel Hill: University of North Carolina Press, 1991.

Balleisen, Edward J. *Navigating Failure: Bankruptcy and Commercial Society in Antebellum America.* Chapel Hill: University of North Carolina Press, 2001.

Beauchamp, Gorman. "Ragged Dick and the Fate of Respectability." *Michigan Quarterly Review* 31 (Summer 1992): 324–45.

Bigham, Darrel E. *Towns and Villages of the Lower Ohio.* Lexington: University Press of Kentucky, 1998.

Blackford, Mansel G., and K. Austin Kerr. *Business Enterprise in American History,* 2nd ed. Boston: Houghton Mifflin, 1990.

Blaszczyk, Regina Lee. *Imagining Consumers: Design and Innovation from Wedgwood to Corning.* Baltimore, MD: Johns Hopkins University Press, 2000.

Blegen, Theodore C., ed. *The Unfinished Autobiography of Henry Hastings Sibley, Together with a Selection of Hitherto Unpublished Letters from the Thirties.* Minneapolis: Voyageur Press, F. T. Phelps, 1932.

Bliss, Michael. *Northern Enterprise: Five Centuries of Canadian Business.* Toronto: McClelland and Stewart, 1987.

Borchert, John R. *America's Northern Heartland.* Minneapolis: University of Minnesota Press, 1987.

Bourne, L. S., and J. W. Simmons, eds. *Systems of Cities: Readings on Structure,*

Growth, and Policy. New York: Oxford University Press, 1985.

Brooks, Charles E. *Frontier Settlement and Market Revolution: The Holland Land Purchase.* Ithaca, NY: Cornell University Press, 1996.

Brown, Craig, ed. *The Illustrated History of Canada.* 4th ed. Toronto: Key Porter Books, 2003.

Bruchey, Stuart. *The Wealth of the Nation: An Economic History of the United States.* New York: Harper and Row, 1988.

Calhoun, Charles W. *The Gilded Age: Essays on the Origins of Modern America.* Wilmington, DE: Scholarly Resources, 1996.

Careless, J. M. S. *Frontier and Metropolis: Regions, Cities, and Identities in Canada Before 1914.* Toronto: University of Toronto Press, 1989.

Cavan, Seamus. *Lewis and Clark and the Route to the Pacific.* New York: Chelsea House Publishers, 1991.

Cayton, Andrew R. L., and Peter S. Onuf. *The Midwest and the Nation: Rethinking the History of an American Region.* Bloomington: Indiana University Press, 1990.

Chandler, Alfred D. Jr., comp. and ed. *The Railroads: The Nation's First Big Business; Sources and Readings.* New York: Harcourt, Brace and World, 1965.

——. *The Railroads: Pioneers in Modern Management.* New York: Ayer Company Publishers, 1980.

——. *Scale and Scope: The Dynamics of Industrial Enterprise, a History, 1880s–1940s.* Cambridge, MA: Belknap Press, 1994.

——. *Strategy and Structure: Chapters in the History of the Industrial Enterprise.* Cambridge, MA: MIT Press, 1962.

——. *The Visible Hand: The Managerial Revolution in American Business.* Cambridge, MA: Belknap Press, 1977.

Chittenden, Hiram Martin. *The American Fur Trade of the Far West: A History of the Pioneer Trading Posts and Early Fur Companies of the Missouri Valley and the Rocky Mountains and of the Overland Commerce with Santa Fe.* 1902. Stanford, CA: Academic Reprints, 1954.

Clayton, James L. "The Growth and Economic Significance of the American Fur Trade, 1790–1890." *Minnesota History* 40 (Winter 1966): 210–20.

Cochran, Thomas C. *Business in American Life: A History.* New York: McGraw-Hill, 1972.

——. *Challenges to American Values: Society, Business, and Religion.* New York: Oxford University Press, 1985.

——. *Frontiers of Change: Early Industrialism in America.* New York: Oxford University Press, 1981.

——. *Railroad Leaders, 1845–1890: The Business Mind in Action.* Cambridge, MA: Harvard University Press, 1953.

Commager, Henry Steel, ed. *America in Perspective: The United States Through Foreign Eyes.* New York: Random House, 1947.

Conzen, Kathleen Neils. *Immigrant Milwaukee, 1836–1860: Accommodation and Community in a Frontier City.* Cambridge, MA: Harvard University Press, 1976.

Conzen, Kathleen Neils, David A. Gerber, and Ewa Morawska. "The Invention of Ethnicity: A Perspective from the U.S.A." *Journal of American Ethnic History* 12 (1992): 3–63.

Conzen, Michael P. "The Maturing Urban System in the United States." *Annals of the Association of American Geographers* 67 (March 1997): 88–108.

Cooke, Ramsay. "Imagining a North American Garden: Some Parallels and Differences in Canadian and American Culture." *Canadian Literature* 103 (1984): 10–26.

Cronon, William. *Nature's Metropolis: Chicago and the Great West.* New York: W. W. Norton, 1992.

Cruise, David, and Allison Griffiths. *Lords of the Line: The Men Who Built the* CPR. Markham, ON: Viking Press, 1988.

Cummings, Scott, ed. *Business Elites and Urban Development: Case Studies and Critical Perspectives.* Albany: State University of New York Press, 1988.

Cunningham, Noble E. Jr. *The Process of Government Under Jefferson.* Princeton, NJ: Princeton University Press, 1979.

Debouzy, Marianne, ed. *In the Shadow of the Statue of Liberty: Immigrants, Workers, and Citizens in the American Republic, 1880–1920.* Urbana: University of Illinois Press, 1992.

DeConde, Alexander. *This Affair of Louisiana.* New York: Scribner, 1976.

Degler, Carl N. *Out of Our Past: The Forces that Shaped Modern America.* New York: Harper, 1959. Reprint, New York: Harper and Row, 1984.

den Otter, A. A. *The Philosophy of Railways: The Transcontinental Railway Idea in British North America.* Toronto: University of Toronto Press, 1997.

Deverell, William. *Railroad Crossing: Californians and the Railroad, 1850–1910.* Berkeley: University of California Press, 1994.

Dobak, William A. *Fort Riley and Its Neighbors: Military Money and Economic Growth, 1853–1895.* Norman: University of Oklahoma Press, 1998.

Dowd, Gregory Evans. *A Spirited Resistance: The North American Indian Struggle for Unity, 1745–1815.* Baltimore, MD: Johns Hopkins University Press, 1992.

Dublin, Thomas. *Transforming Women's Work: New England Lives in the Industrial Revolution.* Ithaca, NY: Cornell University Press, 1994.

Dunaway, Wilma A. *The First American Frontier: Transition to Capitalism in Southern Appalachia, 1700–1860.* Chapel Hill: University of North Carolina Press, 1996.

Dunlavy, Colleen A. *Politics and Industrialization: Early Railroads in the United States and Prussia.* Princeton, NJ: Princeton University Press, 1994.

Dunlop, M. H. *Sixty Miles from Contentment: Traveling the Nineteenth-Century American Interior.* Boulder, CO: Westview Press, 1998.

Eggert, Gerald G. *Harrisburg Industrializes: The Coming of Factories to an American Community.* University Park: Pennsylvania State University Press, 1993.

Egnal, Marc. *Divergent Paths: How Culture and Institutions Have Shaped North American Growth.* New York: Oxford University Press, 1996.

Elkins, Stanley, and Eric McKitrick. *The Age of Federalism: The Early American Republic, 1788–1800.* New York: Oxford University Press, 1993.

Erickson, Charlotte. *Leaving England: Essays on British Emigration in the Nineteenth Century.* Ithaca, NY: Cornell University Press, 1994.

———, ed. *Emigration From Europe, 1815–1914: Select Documents.* Cambridge, UK: A. and C. Black, 1976.

Erickson, Erling A. *Banking in Frontier Iowa, 1836–1865.* Ames: Iowa State University Press, 1971.

Fishlow, Albert. *American Railroads and the Transformation of the Antebellum Economy.* Cambridge, MA: Harvard University Press, 1965.

Fogel, Robert. *Railroads and American Economic Growth: Essays in Econometric History.* Baltimore, MD: Johns Hopkins University Press, 1964.

Folsom, Burton W. Jr. *The Myth of the Robber Barons.* 3rd ed. Herndon, VA: Young America's Foundation, 1996.

———. *Urban Capitalists: Entrepreneurs and City Growth in Pennsylvania's Lackawanna and Lehigh Regions, 1800–1920.* Baltimore, MD: Johns Hopkins University Press, 1981.

Folwell, William Watts. *A History of Minnesota.* Vol. 1. St. Paul: Minnesota Historical Society Press, 1956.

Freyer, Tony A. *Producers Versus Capitalists: Constitutional Conflict in Antebellum America.* Charlottesville: University Press of Virginia, 1994.

Fridley, Russell W. "Public Policy and Minnesota's Economy—A Historical View." *Minnesota History* 46 (Spring 1975): 175–84.

Gamber, Wendy. *The Female Economy: The Millinery and Dressmaking Trades, 1860–1930.* Urbana: University of Illinois Press, 1997.

Gardner, Ralph D. *Horatio Alger, or The American Hero Era.* Mendota, IL: Wayside Press, 1964.

Garner, John S., ed. *The Company Town: Architecture and Society in the Early Industrial Age.* New York: Oxford University Press, 1992.

George, Henry. *Progress and Poverty: An Inquiry into the Cause of Industrial Depressions, and of Increase of Want with Increase of Wealth, The Remedy.* New York: Robert Schalkenbach Foundation, 1879. Reprint, 1979.

Gibbons, J. S. *The Banks of New-York, Their Dealers, the Clearing House, and the Panic of 1857.* New York: D. Appleton, 1858.

Gilman, Rhoda R. "The Fur Trade in the Upper Mississippi Valley, 1630–1850." *Wisconsin Magazine of History* 58 (Autumn 1974): 8–13.

Gilman, Rhoda R., Carolyn Gilman, and Deborah M. Stultz. *The Red River Trails: Oxcart Routes Between St. Paul and the Selkirk Settlement, 1820–1870.* St. Paul: Minnesota Historical Society Press, 1979.

Gjerde, Jon. *From Peasants to Farmers: The Migration from Balestrand, Norway, to the Upper Middle West.* New York: Cambridge University Press, 1985.

Glazer, Walter. *Cincinnati in 1840: The Social and Functional Organization of an Urban Community During the Pre–Civil War Period.* Columbus: Ohio State University Press, 1999.

Glickman, Lawrence B., ed. *Consumer Society in American History: A Reader.* Ithaca, NY: Cornell University Press, 1999.

Goldfield, David, et al. *The American Journey: A History of the United States,* Vol. I. Upper Saddle River, NJ: Prentice Hall, 1998.

Goodrich, Carter. *Government Promotion of American Canals and Railroads, 1800–1890.* New York: Columbia University Press, 1960.

Gras, Norman S. B. "The Significance of the Twin Cities for Minnesota History." *Minnesota History* 7 (March 1926): 3–17.

Greenberg, Brian. *Worker and Community: Response to Industrialization in a Nineteenth-Century American City, Albany, New York, 1850–1884.* Albany: State University Press of New York, 1985.

Greene, Jack P. *The Intellectual Construction of America: Exceptionalism and Identity from 1492 to 1800.* Chapel Hill: University of North Carolina Press, 1993.

Gruenwald, Kim M. *River of Enterprise: The Commercial Origins of Regional Identity in the Ohio Valley, 1790–1850.* Bloomington: Indiana University Press, 2002.

Gutman, Herbert G. *Work, Culture, and Society in Industrializing America: Essays in American Working-Class and Social History.* New York: Knopf, 1977.

Haeger, John D. *John Jacob Astor: Business and Finance in the Early Republic.* Detroit, MI: Wayne State University Press, 1991.

Haites, Erik F., James Mak, and Gary M. Walton. *Western River Transportation: The Era of Early Internal Development, 1800–1860.* Baltimore, MD: Johns Hopkins University Press, 1975.

Hamer, David. *New Towns in the New World: Images and Perceptions of the Nineteenth-Century Urban Frontier.*

New York: Columbia University Press, 1990.

Handlin, Oscar, ed. *This Was America: True Accounts of People and Places, Manners and Customs, as Recorded by European Travelers to the Western Shore in the Eighteenth, Nineteenth, and Twentieth Centuries.* Cambridge, MA: Harvard University Press, 1949. Reprint, 1969.

Hansen, Marcus Lee. *Old Fort Snelling, 1819–1858.* Iowa City: State Historical Society of Iowa, 1918. Reprint, Minneapolis: Ross and Haines, 1958.

Harvey, David. *The Urbanization of Capital: Studies in the History and Theory of Capitalist Urbanization.* Baltimore, MD: Johns Hopkins University Press, 1985.

Heilbroner, Robert L. *The Economic Transformation of America, 1600 to the Present.* 3rd ed. Fort Worth, TX: International Thompson Publishing, 1994.

Henretta, James A. *The Origins of American Capitalism: Collected Essays.* Boston: Northeastern University Press, 1991.

Hidy, Ralph W., Muriel E. Hidy, Roy V. Scott, and Don L. Hofsommer. *The Great Northern Railway: A History.* Boston: Harvard Business School Press, 1986. Reprint, Minneapolis: University of Minnesota Press, 2004.

Hilkey, Judy. *Character Is Capital: Success Manuals and Manhood in Gilded Age America.* Chapel Hill: University of North Carolina Press, 1997.

Holmquist, June Drenning, ed. *They Chose Minnesota: A Survey of the State's Ethnic Groups.* St. Paul: Minnesota Historical Society Press, 1981.

Horsman, Reginald. *The Diplomacy of the New Republic, 1776–1815.* Arlington Heights, IL: H. Davidson, 1985.

Horwitz, Morton J. *The Transformation of American Law, 1780–1860.* Cambridge, MA: Harvard University Press, 1977.

Hovenkamp, Herbert. *Enterprise and American Law, 1836–1937.* Cambridge, MA: Harvard University Press, 1991.

Hoyt, Edwin Palmer. *Horatio's Boys: The Life and Works of Horatio Alger, Jr.* Radnor, PA: Chilton Book Company, 1974.

Hughes, Jonathan. *The Vital Few: The Entrepreneur and American Economic Progress.* 2nd ed. New York: Oxford University Press, 1986.

Hurst, James Willard. *Law and the Conditions of Freedom in the Nineteenth-Century United States.* Madison: University of Wisconsin Press, 1956.

Huston, James L. *Securing the Fruits of Labor: The American Concept of Wealth Distribution, 1765–1900.* Baton Rouge: Louisiana State University Press, 1998.

Igler, David. *Industrial Cowboys: Miller & Lux and the Transformation of the Far West, 1850–1920.* Berkeley: University of California Press, 2001.

"The Immigrant Trains: Railroads Built This Town." *(Minneapolis–St. Paul) City Pages* 17:815 (17 July 1996): 3.

Ingersol, Ernest. "The Home of Hiawatha." *Harper's New Monthly Magazine* (October 1883): 68–80.

Ingham, John N. *The Iron Barons: A Social Analysis of an American Urban Elite, 1874–1965.* Westport, CT: Greenwood Press, 1978.

John, Richard R. "Elaborations, Revisions, Dissents: Alfred D. Chandler Jr.'s *The Visible Hand* after Twenty Years." *Business History Review* 71 (Summer 1997): 151–200.

———. *Spreading the News: The American Postal System from Franklin to Morse.* Cambridge, MA: Harvard University Press, 1995.

Johnson, Paul E. *A Shopkeeper's Millennium: Society and Revivals in Rochester, New York, 1815–1837.* New York: Hill and Wang, 1978.

Josephson, Matthew. *The Robber Barons: The Great American Capitalists, 1861–1901.* New York: Harcourt, Brace and Company, 1934. Reprint, 1962.

Kamphoefner, Walter. *The Westfalians: From Germany to Missouri.* Princeton, NJ: Princeton University Press, 1987.

Kane, Lucile. *The Falls of St. Anthony: The Waterfall that Built Minneapolis.* St. Paul: Minnesota Historical Society Press, 1987.

———. "The Papers of John Harrington Stevens." *Minnesota History* 34 (Winter 1954): 144–48.

Kelley, Oliver H. *Origin and Progress of the Order of the Patrons of Husbandry in the United States, a History from 1866 to 1873.* Philadelphia, PA: J. A. Wagenseller, 1875. Reprint, Westport, CT: Hyperion Press, 1975.

Kemp, Tom. *Historical Patterns of Industrialization.* 2nd ed. New York: Longman, 1993.

———. *Industrialization in Nineteenth-Century Europe.* 2nd ed. New York: Longman, 1985.

Kirkland, Edward C. *Dream and Thought in the Business Community, 1860–1900.* Ithaca, NY: Cornell University Press, 1956.

Koditschek, Theodore. *Class Formation and Urban-Industrial Society: Bradford, 1750–1850.* New York: Cambridge University Press, 1990.

Kunz, Virginia Brainard. *St. Paul: Saga of an American City, An Illustrated History.* Woodland Hills, CA: Windsor, 1977.

Kutler, Stanley I., ed. *The Supreme Court and the Constitution: Readings in American Constitutional History.* Boston: Houghton Mifflin, 1969. 3rd. ed., New York: Norton, 1984.

Kwolek-Folland, Angel. *Engendering Business: Men and Women in the Corporate Office, 1870–1930.* Baltimore, MD: Johns Hopkins University Press, 1994.

Larkin, Jack. *The Reshaping of Everyday Life, 1790–1840.* New York: Harper and Row, 1988.

Leach, William. *Land of Desire: Merchants, Power, and the Rise of a New American Culture.* New York: Pantheon Books, 1993.

Lewis, Henry. *The Valley of the Mississippi Illustrated.* Translated from the original 1854 German by A. Hermina Poatgieter. Edited with an introduction and notes by Bertha L. Heilbron. St. Paul: Minnesota Historical Society Press, 1967.

Licht, Walter. *Industrializing America: The Nineteenth Century.* Baltimore, MD: Johns Hopkins University Press, 1995.

Lipset, Seymour Martin. *Continental Divide: The Values and Institutions of the United States and Canada.* New York: Routledge, 1990.

Livesay, Harold C. *American Made: Men Who Shaped the American Economy.* Boston: Little, Brown, 1979.

———. *Andrew Carnegie and the Rise of Big Business.* Boston: Little, Brown, 1975. Reprint, New York: Longman, 2000.

———. "Entrepreneurial Dominance in Businesses Large and Small, Past and Present." *Business History Review* 63 (Spring 1989): 1–15.

———, ed. *Entrepreneurship and the Growth of Firms.* Vol. 1 and 2. Brookfield, VT: Edward Elgar Publishers, 1995.

Longstreet, Abby Buchanan. *Social Etiquette of New York.* New York: D. Appleton and Co., 1887.

McCormick, Richard P. "The 'Ordinance' of 1784?" *William and Mary Quarterly* 50:1 (January 1993): 112–22.

McCraw, Thomas K., ed. *Creating Modern Capitalism: How Entrepreneurs, Companies, and Countries Triumphed in Three Industrial Revolutions.* Cambridge, MA: Harvard University Press, 1997.

MacDonald, Norbert. *Distant Neighbors: A Comparative History of Seattle and Vancouver.* Lincoln: University of Nebraska Press, 1987.

Mahoney, Timothy. *Provincial Lives: Middle-Class Experience in the Antebel-*

lum Middle West. New York: Cambridge University Press, 1999.

——. *River Towns in the Great West: The Structure of Provincial Urbanization in the American Midwest, 1820–1870.* New York: Cambridge University Press, 1990.

Malchow, Howard L. *Population Pressures: Emigration and Government in Late Nineteenth-Century Britain.* Palo Alto, CA: Society for the Promotion of Science and Scholarship, 1979.

Malone, Michael P. *James J. Hill: Empire Builder of the Northwest.* Norman: University of Oklahoma Press, 1996.

Martin, Albro. *James J. Hill and the Opening of the Northwest.* New York: Oxford University Press, 1976. Reprint, St. Paul: Minnesota Historical Society Press, 1991.

——. *Railroads Triumphant: The Growth, Rejection, and Rebirth of a Vital American Force.* New York: Oxford University Press, 1992.

Marx, Leo. *The Machine in the Garden: Technology and the Pastoral Ideal in America.* New York: Oxford University Press, 1964. Reprint, 2000.

Meyer, David R. "A Dynamic Model of the Integration of Frontier Urban Places into the United States System of Cities." *Economic Geography* 56 (1980): 120–40.

Miller, Donald L. *City of the Century: The Epic of Chicago and the Making of America.* New York: Simon and Schuster, 1996.

Moehring, Eugene. "The Comstock Urban Network." *Pacific Historical Review* 66 (August 1997): 337–62.

Monkkonen, Eric H. *The Local State: Public Money and American Cities.* Stanford, CA: Stanford University Press, 1995.

Mould, David H. *Dividing Lines: Canals, Railroads, and Urban Rivalry in Ohio's Hocking Valley, 1825–1875.* Dayton, OH: Wright State University Press, 1994.

Nackenoff, Carol. *The Fictional Republic: Horatio Alger and American Political Discourse.* New York: Oxford University Press, 1994.

Nelson, John R. Jr. *Liberty and Property: Political Economy and Policymaking in the New Nation, 1789–1812.* Baltimore, MD: Johns Hopkins University Press, 1987.

Nobles, Gregory. *American Frontiers: Cultural Encounters and Continental Conquest.* New York: Hill and Wang, 1997.

North, Douglass. *The Economic Growth of the United States, 1790–1860.* New York: Norton, 1961.

North American Fur Trade Conference. *The Fur Trade Revisited: Selected Papers of the Sixth North American Fur Trade Conference, Mackinac Island, Michigan, 1991.* Edited by Jennifer S. H. Brown, W. J. Eccles, and Donald P. Heldman. East Lansing: Michigan State University Press, 1994.

Novak, William J. *The People's Welfare: Law and Regulation in Nineteenth-Century America.* Chapel Hill: University of North Carolina Press, 1996.

Olson, Sherry. "Occupations and Residential Spaces in Nineteenth-Century Montreal." *Historical Methods* (Summer 1989): 81–96.

Onuf, Peter S. *Statehood and Union: A History of the Northwest Ordinance.* Bloomington: Indiana University Press, 1987.

Ostergren, Robert. *A Community Transplanted: The Trans-Atlantic Experience of a Swedish Immigrant Settlement in the Upper Middle West, 1835–1915.* Madison: University of Wisconsin Press, 1988.

Peck, John Mason. *A New Guide for Emigrants to the West: Containing Sketches of Michigan, Ohio, Indiana, Illinois, Missouri, Arkansas, with the Territory of Wisconsin and the Adjacent Parts.* 2nd ed. Boston, 1837. University Microfiche C2143.

Peterson, William J. "The Early History of Steamboating on the Minnesota River." *Minnesota History* 11:2 (June 1930): 123–27.

Philadelphia Project. *Occupation Dictionary Codebook.* Philadelphia, PA: n.p., 1989.

Pike, Zebulon Montgomery. *The Expeditions of Zebulon Montgomery Pike, to Headwaters of the Mississippi River, through Louisiana Territory, and in New Spain, during the Years 1805–6–7.* New York: F. P. Harper, 1895. Reprint, Minneapolis: Ross and Haines, 1965.

Piott, Steven L. *The Anti-Monopoly Persuasion: Popular Resistance to the Rise of Big Business in the Midwest.* Westport, CT: Greenwood Press, 1985.

Porter, Glenn, and Harold C. Livesay. *Merchants and Manufacturers: Studies in the Changing Structure of Nineteenth-Century Marketing.* Baltimore, MD: Johns Hopkins University Press, 1971.

Potter, David M. *People of Plenty: Economic Abundance and the American Character.* Chicago: University of Chicago Press, 1954.

Pratt, Mary Louise. *Imperial Eyes: Travel Writing and Transculturation.* New York: Routledge, 1992.

Pred, Allan R. *Urban Growth and City Systems in the United States, 1840–1860.* Cambridge, MA: Harvard University Press, 1980.

Prucha, Francis Paul. *American Indian Treaties: The History of a Political Anomaly.* Berkeley: University of California Press, 1994.

Pursell, Carroll. *The Machine in America: A Social History of Technology.* Baltimore, MD: Johns Hopkins University Press, 1995.

Rasmussen, Barbara. *Absentee Landowning and Exploitation in West Virginia, 1760–1920.* Lexington: University Press of Kentucky, 1994.

Ratzel, Friedrich. *Sketches of Urban and Cultural Life in North America.* Trans.

and ed. by Stewart A. Stehlin. New Brunswick, NJ: Rutgers University Press, 1988.

Reinhard, Wolfgang, ed. *Power Elites and State Building.* New York: Oxford University Press, 1996.

Richards, Jeffrey, and John M. MacKenzie. *The Railway Station: A Social History.* New York: Oxford University Press, 1986.

Risjord, Norman K. *Jefferson's America, 1760–1815.* Madison, WI: Madison House, 1991. Reprint, Lanhan, MD: Rowman and Littlefield, 2002.

Robbins, William G. *Colony and Empire: The Capitalist Transformation in the American West.* Lawrence: University Press of Kansas, 1994.

Rølvaag, O. E. *Giants in the Earth: A Saga of the Prairie.* New York: Harper and Brothers, 1927.

Ruggles, Richard I. *A Country So Interesting: The Hudson's Bay Company and Two Centuries of Mapping, 1670–1870.* Montreal: McGill-Queen's University Press, 1991.

St. John de Crèvecoeur, J. Hector. *Letters from an American Farmer.* 1782. Reprint, with an introduction by Warren Barton Blake. New York: Oxford University Press, 1997.

Schoone-Jongen, Robert. "Cheap Land and Community: Theodore F. Koch, Dutch Colonizer." *Minnesota History* 53 (Summer 1993): 214–24.

Schuckers, J. W. *The Finances: Panics and Specie Payments.* Philadelphia, PA: Henry Carey Baird, 1877.

Schumpeter, Joseph. *The Theory of Economic Development: An Inquiry into Profits, Capital, Credit, Interest, and the Business Cycle.* Cambridge, MA: Harvard University Press, 1934. Reprint, New Brunswick, NJ: Transaction Books, 1983.

Schuyler, David. *The New Urban Landscape: The Redefinition of City Form in Nineteenth-Century America.* Baltimore, MD: Johns Hopkins University Press, 1986.

Sellers, Charles G. *The Market Revolution: Jacksonian America, 1815–1846.* New York: Oxford University Press, 1991.

Shaw, Ronald E. *Canals for a Nation: The Canal Era in the United States, 1790–1860.* Lexington: University Press of Kentucky, 1990.

Sheriff, Carol. *The Artificial River: The Erie Canal and the Paradox of Progress, 1817–1862.* New York: Hill and Wang, 1996.

Smalley, Eugene Virgil. *History of the Northern Pacific Railroad.* New York: Arno Press, 1975.

Smith, Adam. *An Inquiry Into the Nature and Causes of the Wealth of Nations.* Vol. 1 and 2. 1776. Chicago: University of Chicago Press, 1976.

Spears, Timothy B. *100 Years on the Road: The Traveling Salesman in American Culture.* New Haven, CT: Yale University Press, 1995.

Stilgoe, John R. *Metropolitan Corridor: Railroads and the American Scene.* New Haven, CT: Yale University Press, 1983.

Taylor, Alan. *William Cooper's Town: Power and Persuasion on the Frontier of the Early American Republic.* New York: Alfred A. Knopf, 1995.

Taylor, George Rogers. *The Transportation Revolution, 1815–1860.* New York: Rinehart, 1951. Reprint, New York: Harper and Row, 1968. Page references are to the 1951 edition.

Taylor, George Rogers, and Irene D. Neu. *The American Railroad Network, 1861–1890.* Cambridge, MA: Harvard University Press, 1956.

Teich, Mikuláš, and Roy Porter, eds. *The Industrial Revolution in National Context: Europe and the U.S.A.* New York: Cambridge University Press, 1996.

Thompson, E. P. *The Making of the English Working Class.* New York: Vintage Books, 1966. Reprint, New York: Penguin, 1980.

Tocqueville, Alexis de. *Democracy in America.* 1862. Chicago: University of Chicago Press, 2000.

Trachtenberg, Alan. *The Incorporation of America: Culture and Society in the Gilded Age.* New York: Hill and Wang, 1982.

Trollope, Frances. *Domestic Manners of the Americans.* London: Whittaker, Treacher and Co., 1832.

Twain, Mark. *Life on the Mississippi.* 1896. New York: Penguin Books, 1984.

Twain, Mark, and Charles Dudley Warner. *The Gilded Age: A Tale of Today.* 1873. New York: Oxford University Press, 1996.

U.S. Department of the Interior. *Treaties, and Land Cessions, Between the Bands of the Sioux and the United States of America, 1805–1906.* Greeley: Museum of Anthropology, University of Northern Colorado, 1972.

Vance, James E. Jr. *The North American Railroad: Its Origin, Evolution, and Geography.* Baltimore, MD: Johns Hopkins University Press, 1995.

Vecoli, Rudolph. "The Resurgence of American Immigration History." *American Studies International* 17 (1979): 44–66.

Vecoli, Rudolph, and Suzanne Sinke, eds. *A Century of European Migrations, 1830–1930.* Urbana: University of Illinois Press, 1991.

Veenendaal, Augustus J. Jr. *Slow Train to Paradise: How Dutch Investment Helped Build American Railroads.* Stanford, CA: Stanford University Press, 1996.

Wade, Richard C. *The Urban Frontier: The Rise of Western Cities, 1790–1830.* Cambridge, MA: Harvard University Press, 1959. Reprint, Urbana: University of Illinois Press, 1996. Page references are to the 1959 edition.

Wallace, Anthony F. C. *The Long, Bitter Trail: Andrew Jackson and the Indians.* New York: Hill and Wang, 1993.

———. *Rockdale: The Growth of an American*

Village in the Early Industrial Revolution. New York: Knopf, 1978.

——. *St. Clair: A Nineteenth-Century Coal Town's Experience with a Disaster-Prone Industry.* New York: Knopf, 1987.

Weiss, Richard. *The American Myth of Success: From Horatio Alger to Norman Vincent Peale.* New York: Basic Books, 1969.

Whelan, Mary K. "Dakota Indian Economics and the Nineteenth-Century Fur Trade." *Ethnohistory* 40 (Spring 1993): 246–76.

White, Bruce, et al., comp. *Minnesota Votes: Election Returns by County for Presidents, Senators, Congressmen, and Governors, 1857–1977.* St. Paul: Minnesota Historical Society Press, 1977.

White, W. Thomas. "Race, Ethnicity, and Gender in the Railroad Work Force: The Case of the Far West, 1883–1918." *Western Historical Quarterly* 26:3 (July 1983): 265–83.

Wiebe, Robert H. *The Opening of American Society: From the Adoption of the Constitution to the Eve of Disunion.* New York: Knopf, 1984.

Williams, Frederick D., ed. *The Northwest Ordinance: Essays on Its Formulation, Provisions, and Legacy.* East Lansing: Michigan State University Press, 1989.

Wills, Jocelyn A. "Business Enterprise and the Construction of American Community Life in the Northwest: St.

Paul, Minnesota, 1849–1862." *Essays in Economic and Business History* 15 (1997): 135–53.

——. "Divided Loyalties: Private Ambition, Nation-Building, and the Railroad Racket along the Northwestern Borderlands, 1877–1883." *Journal of the West* 39:2 (Spring 2000): 8–16.

——. "Respectable Mediocrity: The Everyday Life of an Ordinary American Striver, 1876–1890." *Journal of Social History* 37.2 (Winter 2003): 323–49.

——. "Tangled Webs: Entrepreneurial Dreams, Imperial Designs, and the Evolution of Nineteenth-Century Urban Elites, St. Paul–Minneapolis, Minnesota, 1849–1883." PhD diss., Texas A&M University, 1998.

Wise, S. F., A. B. McKillop, and Paul Romeny, eds. *God's Peculiar Peoples: Essays on Political Culture in Nineteenth Century Canada.* Ottawa, ON: Carleton University Press, 1993.

Woods, Thomas A. *Knights of the Plow: Oliver H. Kelley and the Origins of the Grange in Republican Ideology.* Ames: Iowa State University Press, 1991.

Wrigley, E. A. *Continuity, Chance and Change: The Character of the Industrial Revolution in England.* New York: Cambridge University Press, 1988.

Zunz, Olivier. *Making America Corporate, 1870–1920.* Chicago: University of Chicago Press, 1990.

Index

Page numbers in *italic* refer to illustrations.

Acker, George S., coal: 141–42
agriculture: commercial, 108–11, 113–14.
See also Land; Resource Extraction;
Wheat
American-Canadian: borderlands, and
The Associates, 171–87, 198–99;
competition, 135–39, 191; cultural
comparisons, 5–6, 99, 218n6; relations/free trade, 67. See also Competition; Rivalries
American Fur Company: 16
Angus, Richard B., "Syndicate" and CPR:
182–83; and Manitoba Road, 198–99
Associates, The: 172–83, 186–87,
198–99. See also Angus, Richard B.;
Hill, James J.; Kennedy, John S.; Kittson, Norman W.; Smith, Donald;
Stephen, George
Atlantic world: migrations, 55–60, 78,
109, 188–91, 217n3
Auerbach, Maurice, dry goods: 157; and
St. Paul's commercial/wholesaling expansion, 142, 159–60, 193–97
Auerbach, Finch, & Van Slyke: 159–60,
193–97; and Canada's tariff, 183–84

bankruptcy and business failure: 94–96,
160–61; and lessons from/about, 62,
125, 154, 194–96; panics and, 152–53,
156–58; railroads, 91–93
banks: and Minnesota's free banking bill,
91. See also Capital; Capitalists; Investments; Networks; individual banks
Banning, William, banking: and Lake Superior Railroad, 118
Becker, George, lawyer, railroads: and
SP&P and First Division, 135, 139

Bishop, Harriet, Protestant education: 44,
56
boardinghouse hotels: 58–59, 76, 77, 80
boosters: immigration, 109, 113; Minneapolis, 41, 70–71, 127–28, 199–200,
205; railroad and townsite, 86–90; regional, 48–49, 189–93; St. Paul,
75–76, 106, 122–23, 143; Twin Cities,
38–39, 52, 150–52. See also Competition; Rivalries
Borup, Charles, banking: 60, 94
Borup & Oakes, banking: 60–61
Boyle, Charles, surveying: 77, 156–57,
188
Boyle, Michael J., laborer: 156–57, 188,
193–97, 207–8
Brackett, George, milling: and Minneapolis Mill, 130–31; and NPR,
134–35
Bradstreet's Mercantile Agency: city
rankings, 203, 205
bridges: built by St. Paul-based railroads,
115, 133; Minneapolis, 170; St. Anthony, 64–68
Burbank, Henry, groceries: 74, 107
Burbank, James C., overland express: 97,
106–8, 111, 150; and MVR, 115; and
North-Western Express Company,
62–63, 74; and St. Paul banking syndicate, 158; and St. Paul City Railway,
143; and SP&P, 116–17
business: cash-only policy, 62–63, 74, 97;
consolidation, 168–69; and cost control, 195; and floating costs, 71–72;
government collaboration, 50–54, 83,
90–96, 100–102, 106–8, 111, 116–17,
217n1, 218n5; and industrialization,
119–27, 147–48, 217n2; investment
vs. speculation, 158–61; and territorial

281

Boosters, Hustlers, and Speculators was designed by Will Powers at the Minnesota Historical Society Press and set in Adobe Caslon by Judy Gilats at Peregrine Graphics Services, St. Paul. Printed by Maple Press, York, Pennsylvania.